# SPORT IN SOCIAL DEVELOPMENT

## TRADITIONS, TRANSITIONS, AND TRANSFORMATIONS

**Alan G. Ingham, PhD**
Miami University

**John W. Loy, PhD**
University of Otago

Editors

**Human Kinetics Publishers**

**Library of Congress Cataloging-in-Publication Data**

Sport in social development : traditions, transitions, and
  transformations / Alan G. Ingham, John W. Loy, editor.
    p.    cm.
  Includes bibliographical references and index.
  ISBN 0-87322-467-1
  1. Sports--Sociological aspects.  I. Ingham, Alan G.  II. Loy,
John W.
  GV706.5.S7337     1993                          92-38866
  306.4'83--dc20                                   CIP

ISBN: 0-87322-467-1

**Acquisitions Editor**: Richard D. Frey, PhD; **Developmental Editor**: Marni Basic: **Assistant
Editors**: Valerie Hall, Dawn Roselund, Lisa Sotirelis, Julie Swadener, and John Wentworth;
**Copyeditor**: Chris DeVito; **Proofreader**: Tom Rice; **Indexer**: Theresa J. Schaefer; **Produc-
tion Director**: Ernie Noa; **Typesetter and Text Layout**: Julie Overholt; **Text Design**: Jody
Boles; **Cover Design**: C.J. Petlick; **Printer**: Braun-Brumfield

Printed in the United States of America

10  9  8  7  6  5  4  3  2  1

**Human Kinetics Publishers**
Box 5076, Champaign, IL 61825-5076
1-800-747-4457

*Canada*: Human Kinetics Publishers, P.O. Box 2503,
Windsor, ON N8Y 4S2
1-800-465-7301 (in Canada only)

*Europe*: Human Kinetics Publishers (Europe) Ltd.,
P.O. Box IW14, Leeds LS16 6TR, England
0532-781708

*Australia*: Human Kinetics Publishers, P.O. Box 80,
Kingswood 5062, South Australia
618-374-0433

*New Zealand*: Human Kinetics Publishers,
P.O. Box 105-231, Auckland 1
(09) 309-2259

In Memory Of
Robert S. Hutton, Sr., 1939-1991
our colleague and friend
at UCLA and the University of Washington

Bob was an instructor in the Department of Physical Education at UCLA when I joined the faculty as an assistant professor in 1967. Being the youngest members of the department, we soon became close colleagues and remained lasting friends. I respected Bob's hard-nosed critiques of my work and his willingness to master ideas and materials outside his immediate area of expertise. I also admired Bob's effort to mentor junior faculty when he became the chair of the Department of Kinesiology at the University of Washington. Those benefitting from his mentorship included Jack Berryman, Alan Ingham, and Steve Hardy, three individuals whom I had the pleasure of teaching at the University of Massachusetts.

*John Loy*

We had the privilege of working under Bob's leadership while we were assistant professors in the Department of Kinesiology at UW. Our responsibilities were in sport studies. As is typical in such departments, our program was dwarfed by exercise science. What made our experience rare, however, was a chairman from among the "scientists" who valued our work as much as the work being done in the labs. There was never any question with Bob Hutton that our work was as vital to the department as his or anyone else's. Indeed, Bob took great pains to understand the different research traditions in sport studies.

Bob was a neurophysiologist whose own research tradition followed the canons of positivism. The reader will find little of that in this volume. And yet, more than any "scientist" we know, Bob Hutton grew to appreciate deeply the critical perspectives exemplified in these essays.

Bob's fairness was put to the test when the recession began in 1981 and the University faced severe budget reductions. Sport studies was suddenly in a precarious position. Bob fought to keep the sport studies unit open, because he believed that what we called kinesiology demanded perspectives from the social sciences and the humanities.

During a 3-year struggle that ended with the closing of the entire department, Bob discovered the value of critical perspectives that challenge commonplace assumptions about the "natural order" in a university or anywhere else. It is this perspective that we celebrate in this volume.

We learned a great deal from Bob about courage, fairness, and sacrifice. A Fellow in the American Academy of Physical Education, he was a productive and successful scholar. This continued during his years as a chair. Indeed, his admonition to any colleagues contemplating administration was to quit whenever they found scholarship impossible. Somehow, Bob was able to balance his obligations. As a chair he saw his job to consist largely in creating an environment in which faculty could work with vigor and excitement.

*Alan Ingham & Stephen Hardy*

We dedicate this volume to Bob Hutton, to his scholarship and, above all, to his interest in and admiration for alternative approaches to knowledge. We hope that these essays challenge the "commonplace" in ways that Bob Hutton would have enjoyed.

# Contents

# Preface

This book offers a challenge to the conventional, statistical, neo-positivistic paradigm that has been dominant within North American sport studies. *Sport in Social Development: Traditions, Transitions, and Transformations* seeks to advance the cause of a new agenda for sport studies based on a cultural studies perspective that offers an attractive alternative to orthodox, mainstream sociology. Cultural studies is eclectic in terms of both theory and method and has at times drawn from such diverse academic discourses as communication studies, film theory, history, literary criticism, philosophy, politics, semiotics, and sociology. Thus cultural studies is cross-disciplinary in nature and challenges the disciplinary and subdisciplinary loyalties of legitimacy in sport studies.

Because it is eclectic and continually evolving, cultural studies doesn't represent a single, dominant theoretical or methodological position. However, it does offer an antireductionist, materialist, nonessentialist strategy for analyzing relationships between culture and power. The dynamism of cultural studies is particularly relevant for the critical analysis of the production and influence of different and changing sporting practices.

This book examines the interpenetration of sport and social process. Rather than focus on sport in particular, it emphasizes physical culture in general. It directs attention to social practices in the context of physical activities, showing how they constitute core elements of social development in specific cultures in particular historical periods. The authors who have contributed to this book do not see themselves as anthropologists, historians, kinesiologists, or sociologists per se, but as scholarly explorers bringing to bear whatever disciplinary tools are needed to analyze the text of sport in the sociopolitical context of social development.

This book is designed for use as a supplementary text in sociology of sport, as well as in related areas such as American Studies, Cultural Studies, Gender Studies, Leisure Studies, and courses in comparative physical education. The selections are directed at upper level undergraduate and graduate students specializing in the sociology of sport in departments of kinesiology, physical education, sociology, sport studies, and leisure studies. They are also aimed to appeal to selected members of a more general professional audience interested in the dynamics of sport and social change.

Our goal in choosing selections for *Sport in Social Development* was to highlight the work of authors who examine significant sport-related issues from unique cultural studies perspectives. Each chapter is to be read as an individual contribution to the critical evaluation of sport and games as a cultural expression of responses to social development.

Although the selections are necessarily eclectic in terms of topics, we have brought an epistemological coherence to them by asking authors to anchor their essays around Raymond Williams's (1977) theme of dominant, residual, and emergent cultural practices. We chose this theme for two reasons. First, it highlights the cultural studies perspective that underlies this book. Second, it recognizes the complexity of social development and provides insights into the currently fashionable theory of hegemony.

The concept of hegemony is admittedly a very difficult notion to comprehend. Accordingly, chapter 1, by Ingham and Hardy, "Introduction: Sports Studies Through the Lens of Raymond Williams," acquaints the reader with the problematic of hegemony and explicates the concepts of dominant, residual, and emergent cultural practices. Drawing on Williams's theoretical understanding of cultural production and transformation, the remaining chapters examine a wide range of sporting practices situated in contrasting cultures, diverse historical periods, and a variety of geographical regions.

Chapters 2 through 5 are the most historically oriented contributions to this book. Chapter 2, "Ancient Athletic Motifs and the Modern Olympic Games," by Slowikowski and Loy, shows how in the course of centuries athletic motifs such as agon, fire, gift-giving, pilgrimage, and vegetation have survived and have been revived in the present in unique ways to guide the traditions and practices of the modern Olympic Games. Chapter 3, "Sport and the Victorian Gentleman," by Morford and McIntosh, examines how sport emerged as a unique English institution in the late 19th century and illustrates the latent effects of the Victorian legacy of sport development in our contemporary concerns about amateurism, racism, and sexism in sport. Chapter 4, "Transforming into a Tradition: Rugby and the Making of Imperial Wales, 1890-1914," by Andrews and Howell, focuses on a given sport, in a specific national context, within a particular time period. This chapter highlights the reciprocal relationship between the development of a sport and the development of a nation in terms of specific sociocultural relations and processes. Chapter 5, "Sport and Social Change in Latin America," by Arbena, gives a historical account of the development of sport in Latin America in terms of conquest, domination, cultural adaptation, and diffusion from 1492 to 1930, analyzes the popularization of sport from 1930 to the present, and discusses 20th-century revolutionary alternatives of sporting practices.

The conflictual nature of the development and adaptation of sport shown at the societal level by Arbena is highlighted at the subcultural level of analysis by Donnelly in chapter 6, titled "Subcultures in Sport: Resilience and Transformation." He demonstrates how selected sport subcultures serve as resilient and conservative maintainers of past traditions, provide mechanisms of resistance to present traditions, and at rare times act as agencies of transformation in changing the dominant sport culture.

Reflective of the historical periods and sports that they cover, chapters 2 through 6 clearly detail the masculine hegemony in dominant sporting practices. In contrast, chapter 7, "Sexual Oppression in Sport: Past, Present, and Future Alternatives," by Dewar, and chapter 8, "Gender on the Sports Agenda," by Hargreaves, center attention on women in sport. Both chapters explicate the concept of gender, discuss gender discrimination in sport, emphasize the need to study gender relations rather than sex differences, and offer significant suggestions for future research and social change in sport.

The last three chapters of this book direct attention to the political economy of sports, with particular reference to Canada, America, and England, respectively. Chapter 9, "Labor Relations in Sport: Central Issues in Their Emergence and Structure in High-Performance Sport," by Beamish, examines in depth the changing relationship between Canada's elite athletes and the National Sport Organizations and Sport Canada. This chapter highlights the exploitative employee-employer relationship in the labor process underlying high-performance sport in the western world. Chapter 10, "Professional Team Sport and the American City: Urban Politics and Franchise Relocations," by Schimmel, Ingham, and Howell, addresses the relationship between sport and community with respect to the logic of capitalist relations. This chapter deals with this relationship in terms of the microeconomy of the professional sport industry on one hand, and in terms of the broader context of urban politics on the other hand. Chapter 11, "Civic Ideology in the Public Domain: Victorian Ideology in the 'Lifestyle Crisis' of the 1990s," by Clarke, argues that sport is not just a form of popular culture but an important form of participative culture, involving many members of the public in its active production. This chapter offers a thoughtful account of the development of sports in terms of emergent and residual patterns of sporting culture, with special emphasis on organized sport, municipal provision, capitalization, and commercialization.

Although the chapters in combination cover a variety of topics, our overall emphasis is on depth rather than breadth of coverage. The cost of this emphasis is that certain important omissions have been made with respect to both the institutional and relational analyses of sport in society. For example, the reader will find in-depth analyses of the relationship between sport and the institutional spheres of economics, mass media, and politics, but little analysis of the relationships between sport and the institutional spheres of education, family, religion, or science. Similarly, the reader will find in-depth analyses of sport and selected power relationships such as class and gender relations, but little analysis of ethnic or race relations.

The benefit of our emphasis on depth rather than breadth of coverage is that the reader will achieve insight into how the work of Raymond Williams in particular, and cultural studies in general, provides theoretical and methodological perspectives that are useful for interpreting the whole realm of sport and physical culture within the dynamics of biography, history, and social structure.

We hope that the critical essays in this book challenge the "commonplace" and the many "taken-for-granted" notions about sport in modern society. We also hope that the reader will gain an appreciation that in addition to being an alternative theoretical perspective for the study of sport, cultural studies is a political, pedagogical, and personal project for every scholar who undertakes a cultural analysis of sport. In an effort to personalize the several projects constituting this book, we include individual pictures and profiles of each author. These photos and brief biographies will, we hope, make the authors seem less anonymous to the readers.

# About the Authors

## David L. Andrews

*Birthplace*—London, England

*Formal Education*—BEd (Honors), Physical Education and History, College of St. Mark and St. John, 1985
MS, Kinesiology, University of Illinois at Urbana-Champaign, 1991

*Present Position*—Doctoral candidate, Department of Kinesiology, University of Illinois at Urbana-Champaign

*Scholarly Interests*—Cultural studies, national popular culture, the affective economy, the body, sociology of sport

*Hobbies*—Following the fluctuating fortunes of Fulham F.C. and the Welsh International XV

*Sport Activities*—Association football, "fair weather" running with J.W. Loy and R.E. Rinehart

## Joseph L. Arbena

*Birthplace*—Philadelphia, Pennsylvania, USA

*Formal Education*—AB, Foreign Affairs, George Washington University, 1961
PhD, History, University of Virginia, 1970

*Present Position*—Professor, Department of History, Clemson University

*Scholarly Interests*—Sport and politics and sport and nationalism in Latin America; music as an expression of historical and cultural development in Latin America; the interaction among culture, ideas, and social structures

*Hobbies*—Photography, Latin music, travel, wines

*Sport Activities*—Watching many, playing few

# Rob Beamish

*Birthplace*—Ottawa, Ontario, Canada

*Formal Education*—BA/BPHE, Queen's University, 1972
BEd, Queen's University, 1973
MA, Sociology, Queen's University, 1977
PhD, Sociology, University of Toronto, 1985

*Present Position*—Associate Professor, Department of Sociology and School of Physical and Health Education, Queen's University, Kingston, Ontario

*Scholarly Interests*—The high-performance sport system from the perspective of the athlete, the labor process, the history of the publication of Marx's literary estate, the reconstruction of social and political theory

*Hobbies*—Reading, spending time with my family, drinking good coffee

*Sport Activities*—Skating quickly over thin ice, swimming against the tide, playing handball with my critics, running up bills at used book stores

# Alan Clarke

*Birthplace*—Sheffield, England

*Formal Education*—BSc 2.1 (Hons) Sociology and Politics, University of Salford, 1976
MA, Criminology, University of Sheffield, 1977
PhD, Sociology and Cultural Studies, Open University, 1986

*Present Position*—Academic Director, Centre for Leisure and Tourism Studies, University of North London

*Scholarly Interests*—Attitudes to leisure; history and development of sport, especially soccer; major event organization; policy analysis of leisure, including arts and cultural industries; sociology and social policy of leisure

*Sport Activities*—Supporting Sheffield Wednesday Football Club and joining in almost anything else going—soccer, cricket, and tennis especially

# Alison Dewar

*Birthplace*—Hong Kong

*Formal Education*—BEd (Honors), Physical Education, Dunfermline College of Physical Education, 1979
MPE, Physical Education, University of British Columbia, 1983
EdD, Curriculum Studies, University of British Columbia, 1986

*Present Position*—Assistant Professor, Department of Physical Education, University of British Columbia

*Scholarly Interests*—Women in sport and physical education—specifically the ways that sport and physical education are used to create and promote images of the body, skill, health, and well-being that support existing relations of power and privilege

*Hobbies*—Running, women's music, Feminist mysteries, cooking

*Sport Activities*—Running, cycling, and walking

# Peter Donnelly

*Birthplace*—Chester, England

*Formal Education*—Cert Ed, Physical Education and Geography, City of Birmingham College of Education, 1967
BA, Physical Education, Hunter College, City University of New York, 1973
MS, Sport Studies, University of Massachusetts, Amherst, 1976
PhD, Sport Studies, University of Massachusetts, Amherst, 1980

*Present Position*—Associate Professor, Department of Physical Education, McMaster University, Hamilton, Ontario

*Scholarly Interests*—Sport, culture, and subcultures; popular culture; the politics of representation in areas such as youth sports and recreational land use

*Sport Activities*—Rock climbing (increasingly proving the inverse relationship between age and risk-taking), soccer, racquetball (with more enthusiasm than skill)

# Stephen Hardy

*Birthplace*—Boston, Massachusetts, USA

*Formal Education*—AB, Latin, Bowdoin College, 1970
MA, History, University of Massachusetts at Amherst, 1976
MS, Physical Education, University of Massachusetts at Amherst, 1976
PhD, Sport Studies, University of Massachusetts at Amherst, 1980

*Present Position*—Associate Professor and Chair, Department of Physical Education, University of New Hampshire

*Scholarly Interests*—Historical continuities in sport, history of ice hockey, sport management and marketing, social theory

*Hobby*—Writing fiction that may never be published

*Sport Activities*—Coaching youth soccer and hockey, jogging and skiing, watching most spectator sports

# Jennifer A. Hargreaves

*Birthplace*—Rushey Green, London, England

*Formal Education*—Teachers Certificate of the University of London in Physical Education, Dartford College, 1958
Academic Diploma in Education, University of London, 1976
MA in the Sociology of Education, University of London, 1979

*Present Position*—Reader in the politics and sociology of sport at the Roehampton Institute (validated by the University of Surrey)

*Scholarly Interests*—Politics of sport, gender relations in sport, body culture, ethnographic studies of urban dance, representations of the female body in sport

*Sport Activities*—Nowadays mostly a spectator, but keen to swim whenever I have time

# Jeremy W. Howell

*Birthplace*—Kidwelly, Wales

*Formal Education*—BA, (Honors), Physical Education and Education, University of North Wales, 1978
MS, Kinesiology, University of Washington, 1984
PhD, Kinesiology, University of Illinois, 1990

*Present Position*—Fitness Director, San Francisco Bay Club; affiliated as a consultant with the University of California, Berkeley's extension program, Certificate in Health and Exercise: Fitness and Intervention

*Scholarly Interests*—Communication, postmodernism, media studies

*Sport Activities*—Play for Old Blues rugby club; represented Welsh Universities, Combined England and Wales Universities in rugby

# Alan G. Ingham

*Birthplace*—Manchester, England

*Formal Education*—City of Leeds College of Education and Carnegie College of Physical Education, 1967
BEd (Honors), University of Leeds, 1968
MS, Physical Education, Washington State University, 1969
PhD, Sociology, University of Massachusetts, 1978

*Present Position*—Associate Professor, Department of Physical Education, Health and Sport Studies, Miami University, Ohio

*Scholarly Interests*—Social inequality, professional sport and urban politics, sport heroes and heroines in the reproduction and transformation of social structure, social theory

*Hobbies*—Cooking, photography, reading spy novels, watching *Coach* and the PBS mystery programs

*Sport Activities*—Once an active participant in soccer and squash, but crippled by excess I turned to coaching: head coach, WSYSA Select Team Program (1980-1984) and assistant coach, Miami University Men's Varsity Soccer (1984-1991); USYSA Region 4 Coaching Staff, 1984. Walking with a headstrong dog.

# John W. Loy

*Birthplace*—Dodge City, Kansas, USA

*Formal Education*—BS, Lewis and Clark College, 1961
MA, University of Iowa, 1963
PhD, University of Wisconsin–Madison, 1967

*Present Position*—Established Chair, School of Physical Education, University of Otago, Dunedin, New Zealand

*Scholarly Interests*—Sociology of sport, the agon motif, physical culture in general and body culture in particular

*Hobbies*—Collecting rare sporting books, reading mysteries, attending parties with Brian Sutton-Smith

*Sport Activities*—Having beaten Max and Reet Howell in doubles and Barry McPherson in singles, I retired from tennis; I now spend my leisure time running with my graduate advisees, including an annual 7.4-mile cross-country race.

# Martha J. McIntosh

*Birthplace*—Windsor, Ontario, Canada

*Formal Education*—BPHE, University of Toronto, 1986

*Present Position*—MPE student, University of British Columbia

*Scholarly Interests*—The bidding process to host the Olympic Games

*Hobbies*—Photography, languages, travel

*Sport Activities*—Former runner and swimmer turned recreational hiker and alpine skier

# W. Robert Morford

*Birthplace*—Sungei Siput, Malaysia

*Formal Education*—BPE, University of British Columbia, 1956
MPE University of British Columbia, 1959
EdD, University of California (Berkeley), 1963

*Present Position*—Professor, School of Physical Education, University of British Columbia

*Scholarly Interests*—Theory of agonetic behavior, Victorian Athleticism

*Hobbies*—Birding, photography, collecting tribal art, wilderness travel

*Sport Activities*—Former rugby player, one-time aspiring handball player, now contented jogger

# Kimberly S. Schimmel

*Birthplace*—Cambridge, Ohio, USA

*Formal Education*—BA, Muskingum College, 1983
MA, Miami University, 1987
PhD candidate, University of North Carolina at Greensboro (degree expected, May 1993)

*Present Position*—Visiting Instructor, Miami University, Oxford, Ohio

*Scholarly Interests*—Sociopolitical issues of professional sport franchises and urban communities; class, race, and gender issues in the sport–society dialectic

*Hobbies*—Watching college basketball, reading about college basketball, music

*Sport Activities*—Former college basketball player relegated to the intramural leagues

# Synthia S. Slowikowski

*Birthplace*—Chester, Pennsylvania, USA

*Formal Education*—BS, Physical Education, University of Delaware, 1978

MS, Kinesiology, University of Washington, 1982

PhD, The Interdisciplinary Graduate Program in the Humanities (history, classics, and physical education), The Pennsylvania State University, 1988

*Present Position*—Assistant Professor, Department of Kinesiology, University of Illinois at Urbana-Champaign

*Scholarly Interests*—Ancient Greek history, cultural studies, postmodernity

*Hobbies*—Spending time with my husband and children

*Sport Activities*—An occasional jog, a rare field hockey match

# Acknowledgments

Several contributors to *Sport and Social Development* benefited from the collegiality, friendship, mentorship, or teaching of the late Charles Hunt Page (1909-1992). Those of us who had our lives touched by Charles, directly or indirectly, salute him, especially for his tolerance of our "arrogance of ignorance."

Throughout the endeavor of preparing this book, we have been fortunate to have the support of publisher Rainer Martens. Although he was well aware that our undertaking would not by itself build a new wing at Human Kinetics, he nevertheless pledged Human Kinetics' energy and resources to our project. His commitment demonstrates yet again his willingness to promote our field as a whole.

We also pay tribute and express our great gratitude to our developmental editor, Marni Basic. Her diligence, enthusiasm, expertise, and persistence have markedly improved this book and have made the author/publisher relationship a joyful one.

Finally, we are deeply indebted to Christine Ingham, who retyped several manuscripts published herein and suffered over a number of years through every stage of the production of this book—without divorcing Alan or removing John from her list of good friends.

# CHAPTER 1

# Introduction: Sport Studies Through the Lens of Raymond Williams

*Alan G. Ingham*
*Stephen Hardy*

We have chosen the theme of *dominant-residual-emergent* for these essays because we believe it highlights the complexity of social development and provides insights into the currently fashionable theory of hegemony. While Butsch (1990) provides a useful overview of hegemony theory as used in scholarship on leisure, it is clear that hegemony is a very difficult concept to apprehend. What Williams (1977) helps us to see is that the control or influence implied in hegemony—the ''dominant''—is never total or complete. Rather, it always exists in relation to alternative or oppositional practices or ideas, some of which may themselves become dominant, some of which may become incorporated into the dominant culture. Practices that tie the present to the past may be termed *residual*; those that tie the present to the future may be termed *emergent*. Thus Williams's theme requires scholars to analyze the connections/disconnections between the past, present, and future that arise within the context of the present. As Williams argues (1977, pp. 121-122), one can hardly appreciate a dominant culture in isolation.

Through their own interpretations of Williams (1977), the authors of the essays in this book continue to transform our understanding of domination and hegemony. This corresponds with other changes that have occurred within Western Marxist thought as intellectuals and politicians of the left have tried to comprehend what

---

*Note.* All passages from Raymond Williams's work *Marxism and Literature*, 1977, are reprinted by permission of Oxford University Press.

Marx really meant and have reinterpreted his ideas under pressures of changing political circumstance. In brief, the concept of hegemony has become a far more inclusive concept than perhaps Marx or Engels intended because it now embraces issues (e.g., patriarchy, racism, inner colonialism, and imperialism) that go beyond purely class relations and class ideologies. Here, hegemony theory itself constitutes a critique of economic reductionism and functionalist Marxism. The contribution of hegemony theory alerts us to go beyond the economic determinants of transformations in sporting practices by asking how the economic determinants articulate with and may be influenced by politico-juridical and moral concerns about the use of time and space and power relations concerned with who gets what and why (see Gruneau, 1988; Hargreaves, in this book; Hargreaves, 1986; Ingham, 1982; Ingham and Hardy, 1984).[1]

## Hegemony and Ideology

The basic idea in the modern construction of the concept of hegemony—the dominant—is to be found in *The German Ideology* (Marx & Engels, 1970). There Marx and Engels posed a fundamental question: How can a given political-economic order be made to appear legitimate? In response, they turned to an analysis of ideology. They stated:

> The ideas of the ruling class are in every epoch the ruling ideas, i.e., the class which is the ruling material force of a society, is at the same time its ruling intellectual force. The class which has the material production at its disposal, has control at the same time over the means of mental production, so that thereby, generally speaking, the ideas of those who lack the means of mental production are subject to it. The ruling ideas are nothing more than the ideal expression of the dominant material relationships grasped as ideas; hence of the relationships which make one class the ruling one, therefore, the ideas of its dominance. (p. 64)

Here we find a lurking reductionism (i.e., economic determinism) which had to be readdressed. Gramsci (1971) took up the challenge. As Joll (1977) explains:

> Gramsci saw, in a way few other Marxists have done, that the rule of one class over another does not depend on economic or physical power alone but rather on persuading the ruled to accept the system of beliefs of the ruling class and to share their social, cultural and moral values. (p. 8)

In addition, as Hall, Lumley, and McLennan (1978) argue, Gramsci rarely used the term ideology itself,

> but rather a range of terms that serve, more or less, as equivalents— ''philosophies'', ''conceptions of the world'', ''systems of thought'' and forms of consciousness. He also [employed] notions such as ''common sense'', which though not equivalent to ideologies refer to their substrata. (pp. 47-49)

So hegemony is a much broader concept than ideology—it is more complete in its effects than ideology, if it is achieved, because it welds together not only the fundamental classes, but also the fractions within these classes into a sociohistorical bloc. Effective hegemony thus naturalizes a social order as *the* social order—an apparent reification of extant relations that leads us to discount the possibility of social transformation.

In other words, if we are to use the concept of hegemony, we must not think of its effects in terms of a crude form of domination of one class over others, for this would place too much emphasis on the coercive use of force or a modified, social control theory. Rather, we must think of hegemony more from a perspective of consensus that is produced when upper levels of ideology and lower levels of "ideology" (common sense) coincide (see Hall et al., 1978, p. 63; Hoffman, 1984). Under such circumstances, the dominant bloc, as we noted earlier, holds sway over the whole of institutionalized social relations. This point is important because it alerts us to the idea that a ruling class may or may not have hegemonic authorization. That is, while all relations of domination and subordination are power relations, the ways in which power is exercised at a given historical period can be coercive (nonhegemonic) or anchored in consent (hegemonic) and can lead to various levels of resistance and/or incorporation (accommodation) (see Anderson, 1980, chap. 2; Hall et al., 1978, p. 68; Williams, 1977, p. 112). Williams's contribution to Gramsci is to emphasize the continuous relationships of present to past and of present to future. With this in mind let us turn to his notion of the *residual*.

## The Residual in the Present

Williams (1977) distinguishes between the "residual" and the "archaic":

> By "residual" I mean something different from the "archaic", though in practice these are often very difficult to distinguish. Any culture includes available elements of its past, but their place in the contemporary cultural process is profoundly variable. I would call the "archaic" that which is wholly recognized as an element of the past, to be observed, to be examined, or even on occasion to be consciously "revived" in a deliberately specializing way. (pp. 121-122)

In the world of sport, we might point to the Olympic Games, for they illustrate both the archaic and the residual, particularly in the relationship between the ancient and the modern games. For example, the Nazis deliberately revived the ancient use of flame or fire for stylized use with the Berlin Games. This would be an example of the archaic (see Mandell, 1971). At the same time, we can demonstrate how certain historical motifs, including the flame, have become residual elements in the modern games.

To continue with Williams (1977):

> What I mean by the "residual" is very different [from the archaic]. The residual, by definition, has been effectively formed in the past, but it is still

active in the cultural process, not only and often not at all as an element of the past, but as an effective element of the present. Thus certain experiences, meanings, and values which cannot be expressed or substantially verified in terms of the dominant culture, are nevertheless lived and practiced on the basis of the residue—cultural as well as social—of some previous social and cultural institution or formation. It is crucial to distinguish this aspect of the residual, which may have an alternative or even oppositional relation to the dominant culture, from that active manifestation of the residual (this being its distinction from the archaic) which has been wholly or largely incorporated into the dominant culture. (p. 122)

As Williams notes, residual practices may lie outside the dominant, or they may be incorporated. Again the world of sport provides examples of each.

One is the concept of community. At times, notions of the way collective life "used to be" provide vehicles of opposition to dominant culture. Local advocates for 19th-century parks and playgrounds thus sometimes presented a residual bucolic vision in their struggle with urban industrial capitalism (Hardy & Ingham, 1983). At the same time, the concept of community has often been incorporated into urban politics; it has been used by civic leaders to mask reality in the interests of civic boosterism. Thus historical images of the bonds among citizens, players, and their "owners" have been used to sell public stadium debt for private profit (see Ingham, Howell, & Schilperoort, 1987; Schimmel, Ingham, & Howell, chapter 10 of this book).

Another example is the moral panic concerning law and order. We hear our parents say "It was never like this before the war" or "You used to be able to walk the streets at night" as a critique of what they perceive as a new crime wave involving mugging and hooliganism, or urban terrorism. At the same time, the moral panic is fully incorporated in law and order campaigns and what Hall (1978, p. 22) has called the bad news theory of good news (i.e., newsworthiness). This *real* fear on the part of the victimized and the fear as socially constructed by the media discourse is nowhere better exemplified than in the problem of soccer hooliganism (see the discourses on Hillsborough by Taylor, 1989, 1991). Soccer hooliganism is a worldwide phenomenon. Despite this, it is presented as if it were an English peculiarity, even by the English tabloid press, which is read by the very people who suffer from the human costs of social neglect—the absolute and relative deprivations of reformed, liberal, supply-side market policies. Real fear *is real* from the standpoint of the victimized; but media-constructed amplification spirals may be ideologically contoured to drive a wedge into working-class solidarity by making bourgeois distinctions between the respectable and unrespectable. We say bourgeois because the media "literati" or any literati generally do not come from the working class (see Hoggart, 1970). Those who do come from the working class merely remember their origins as a backcloth and a place you visit. Thus policing the crisis is generally endorsed even if the style of policing is class and race contoured—a community service orientation in the white suburbs, a military orientation in the impoverished black "neighborhoods" (see Lea & Young, 1984, pp. 167-184), and an ambiguous reaction to crowd control in English soccer (see Buford, 1991; Williams, Dunning, & Murphy, 1984; and Williams & Wagg, 1991).

The above examples emphasize what Williams (1977) stressed, namely that "it is in the incorporation of the actively residual—by reinterpretation, dilution, projection, discriminating inclusion and exclusion—that the work of selective tradition is especially evident" (p. 123). At the same time, one often can see the residual sometimes posing a risk to the dominant, that is, the reaching back into the past to reclaim and reassert actual meanings and values that "represent areas of human experience, aspiration, and achievement which the dominant culture neglects, undervalues, opposes, represses, or even cannot recognize" (Williams, 1977, pp. 123-124).

One example of such alternative or oppositional culture occurred in 19th-century American boxing. As Gorn (1986) has conveyed, bareknuckle boxing was a residual attraction to large segments of urban workers who were losing control of their traditional crafts. Between roughly 1820 and 1860, many of the old trades—with their established relations of apprentices, journeymen, and masters—had begun to dissolve and transform into more rationalized enterprises of employer and employee, with a related diminution of craft skills, mutuality of interests, and opportunities for mobility. Many workers looked to residual (although now urbanized) forms of leisure for the value and esteem they no longer found at work. In Gorn's words, "For many men, the realm of play more than work now held out the best chance for finding a sense of challenge and fulfillment" (p. 133).

Nowhere was this more clearly apparent than in boxing, where the rituals of challenges, contracts, training regimens, and ring routines turned pugilism into a "surrogate workplace." In boxing too, gambling and brute force retained links to traditional forms of male status that bourgeois critics could never understand. As Gorn (1986) summarized the "meanings of prize fighting":

Divided by neighborhood, ethnic, and workplace tensions, large segments of the lower classes were nonetheless united in opposition to key Victorian values, values on which an onerous new social system was built. Every bout inverted bourgeois and evangelical assumptions about such fundamental social phenomena as money, gender, and violence. More, the prize ring conveyed its own alternative outlook. Pugilism was an autonomous expressive form that symbolically opposed the drift of modern society. In crucial ways, then, boxing during the age of the heroes captured the values, the ethos, the distinct culture of countless working men who felt dispossessed amidst the Victorian era's heady optimism. (pp. 146-47)

In the end, as Gorn outlines, much of this oppositional element was eventually incorporated into the dominant culture via Queensbury rules and the "strenuous life" of Teddy Roosevelt and his ilk.[2]

Another example of the residual as oppositional occurred in the mid-1980s, when there was an attempt to create a superleague in English soccer.[3] Economics stood at the heart of the project: The stronger, more lucrative clubs colluded to create a scheme that would enhance their profits—a strategy that would probably have resulted and will result in the disenfranchisement of clubs excluded from the proposed cartel and the dissolving of the Football League. While we in North America view the cartelized production of professional team sport events as normal (e.g., the majors and the minors), and generally accept the monopoly and monopsony practices associated with the major league structures, such an arrangement in England will entail a radical restructuring of both the sport's production and the sport-community relation, for in England virtually every city and large town has *its* club, especially in the rust-belt North. Indeed, many of the largest cities are hosts to more than one club. One can only wonder about what the social and cultural consequences will be of the planned introduction under the auspices of the Football Association of a Premier League and of the concomitant reductions to second class status of those clubs that remain within the Football League. How will the actively incorporated residual respond to the emergent within the dominant?

## The Emergent in the Present

The above leads us to Williams's (1977) concept of the emergent. To continue with Williams:

> By "emergent" I mean, first, that new meanings and values, new practices, new relationships and kinds of relationship are continually being created. But it is exceptionally difficult to distinguish between those which are really elements of some new phase of the dominant culture . . . and those which are substantially alternative or oppositional to it: emergent in the strict sense, rather than merely novel. (p. 123)

Williams emphasizes class, the formation of a new class, the coming to consciousness of a new class, and within this the emergence of a new cultural formation as his example, noting that the latter will be uneven and incomplete while the new class is still subordinate within the old social stratification system. Like Thompson (1963), Williams focuses on the emergence and consolidation of the working class (although he and Thompson had a long debate concerning the old and new left and their respective orientations to materialist analysis). But we wish to focus on the bourgeoisie for our examples, because a case can be made that it was this class that wrought the major changes in sporting recreations sometimes called modernization, which we refer to as valorization, rationalization, and civilization. The changes we are referring to are captured in ideal-typical form in Table 1.1.

We start with the civilizing process. It was a long, drawn-out process (see Elias, 1978) that involved a decreasing tolerance for direct physical coercion and affectual violence. It, at times, involved clashes of class consciousness and of class cultures as the old middle class sought to replace the aristocracy and gentry as the dominant class and to assert its cultural conceptions as the incipient, hegemonic culture. Here the emergent was truly oppositional in several respects: It was fundamentally instrumental and utilitarian, thus challenging the aristocratic mode of existence on the grounds that the latter was more concerned with conspicuous consumption than

**Table 1.1   An Ideal-Typical Portrayal of "Organized" Sport in Two Historical Time-Frames**

| Premodern | Modern |
| --- | --- |
| 1. *Locales*—spas, resorts, social clubs, taverns, natural sites, and designated sites maintained by subscription fees (i.e., jockey club courses). | 1. *Locales*—principally "enclosed" arenas, stadia, pavilions, "athletic sport" clubs, and publicly sponsored "playing fields." |
| 2. *Organization*—local, regional, and, in some sports, intersectional; events often the result of challenges; tavern keeper sponsorship, fetes, and fairs. No administrative organs with supralocal metapower. Club organization with a collegial pattern of decision-making. No player associations or "organized" labor. | 2. *Organization*—centralized with local, regional, or geographic devolution of administrative routine central regulatory agencies, international committees and sport federations; representational or collegial policy-making with bureaucratic administration; central administrative organs have supralocal metapower. Events are "sanctioned" by respective sport federations. Players are organized into "associations." Key principle: the league and/or circuit. |
| 3. *Regulation*—rules quite complex and attuned to conventional standards of etiquette, fashion, and style. Local in scope and oftentimes based on the mutual consent of parties involved. Sometimes intentionally esoteric. | 3. *Regulation*—rules quite complex & attuned to manipulation-avoidance standardized & exoteric; systematized; manipulated and, hence, calculative and conditional; imperative control & enforcement; as much of the "spirit" converted into the "letter" as is possible so as to avoid ambiguity; extrainstitutional intervention (i.e., courts and congress now involved). |
| 4. *Recruitment*—based on interest, subscription, invitation, challenge, cultural and peer pressure; not generally tied to ability; for life. | 4. *Recruitment*—feeder-system apprenticeship; based on universalistic criteria; cultural, peer, community, and economic inducements; longevity tied to potential gate and performance values; key principle: career. |
| 5. *Action-orientations*—eustress seeking, conviviality, festivity, display, social approbation, exhibit skill and prowess, social solidarity; tradition, affectual, and when tied to the status order, value-rational. | 5. *Action-orientations*—profit and performance, professionalism, instrumentally rational or calculative, conditional means to an end, unitary value—meritocracy. |

*(continued)*

**Table 1.1** *(continued)*

| Premodern | Modern |
|---|---|
| 6. *Normative framework*—traditional conceptions of elite and popular culture; amateurism; when intellectualized, sport viewed as a means to health and fitness, to character development and, by a few religious leaders, as a means to spiritual fulfillment; some politicization; "organic" connection to collectivity. | 6. *Normative framework*—modern mass society conceptions of work, service, and entertainment; commercialism; sport sanctioned by rhetorical claims to fitness and health, character development, intellectual growth, responsibility training, self-discipline, etc., "politicized" estranged. |
| 7. *Technicization*—nonscientific; some instructional discourses; some "expert" opinions; use of communications media in the form of journals, magazines, newspapers; few technological props; mensuration primarily evidenced in "the turf"; few professional specialists in the "support" services. | 7. *Technicization*—"scientific"—rationality pervasive; major emphasis upon technique; much technological tinkering with both props and the human body; intellectualized strategically and intellectualization evident in the growth of the "sport sciences"; much use, indeed financial dependence on, the mass media; much mensuration re records and productivity/performance increments; paramedical and medical support services; business management orientation in administrative personnel; proliferation of experts, pseudoexperts/specialists. |

*Note.* From "Methodology in the Sociology of Sport: From Symptoms of Malaise to Weber For a Cure" by A. Ingham, 1979, *Quest, 31*(2), pp. 187-215. Copyright 1979 by the National Association for Physical Education in Higher Education. Reprinted by permission.

conspicuous industry and therefore was more wasteful than penurious (see Gouldner, 1970, chap. 3; Ossowska, 1970, chap. 4; Veblen, 1953).

Also, and more important for our purposes, the emergent contrasted the bourgeois ethos to that of the nobility ethos in ways that would have an impact on the contents, forms, and relations in leisure at large and sport in particular. That is, the bourgeoisification process would pit respectability against prodigality; temperance and prudence against profligacy; humility and dignity against vanity, honor, and distinction; merit against rank as rationales for deference (see Berger, Berger, & Kellner, 1973, pp. 83-96; Ossowska, 1970, pp. 124-182). While we tend to agree with Elias (1978) and others that the civilizing process was a long revolution, we would point to the period from 1840 to 1914 as the climacteric, both in England and the U.S.A. (see Ingham, 1978; Ingham & Beamish, 1993).

In general terms (see Table 1.1), most popular sporting recreations of the "prebourgeois" period can be characterized as follows: They were informally organized;

they reflected local social structure; they were governed by orally transmitted, customary rules rooted in provincial traditions. Except for the turf sport of horse racing, they required no special facilities and, hence, had few spatial or temporal restrictions; they were not structurally or relationally complex and, therefore, required little or no role specialization; there were few constraints placed on spontaneity and emotional impulsiveness; and finally, many sporting recreations were quite brutal.

Given the absence of spatial or temporal restrictions and emotional restraint, it is little wonder that the more boisterous and brutal forms became targets for suppression by the reform-minded, industrious, precise, and to use Arnold's (1969, p. 101) class nomenclature, "particularly stiff-necked" Philistines. The frequent attempts at suppression were initially only partly successful, however, because it was not possible to destroy the traditional and dominant ethos that condoned festivity and ritual, and that sanctioned the sporting activities of *both* the Barbarians and Populace alike. This is evident in the sputtering attempts of the bourgeoise to suppress boxing, blood sports, or Saint Monday on either side of the Atlantic (Gorn, 1986; Malcolmson, 1973, pp. 13-14; Reid, 1976).

Particularly in Britain, the alliance between some Barbarians (Aristocrats) and Populace—an alliance frequently evidenced in the paternalistic attitude that the former selectively held towards the latter's recreational pursuits—was exemplified in a shared passion for the blood sports. The blood sports of these Barbarians and Populace reflected a lusty eudaemonism[4] and a penchant for gambling that the rational utilitarians and the reform-minded had difficulty in understanding or accepting as fitting conduct for a progressive society. But the alliance between the Barbarians and Populace made the suppression of the blood sports a difficult task. How could the bourgeoisie condemn the blood sports of the Populace on grounds that, at the same time, would not impugn the moral standards of the aristocracy? How could they argue that cruel sports gave rise to cruel men or were the expressions of carnality and profligacy without offending their superiors? Caught on the horns of this dilemma, the bourgeoisie were forced to derive subtle distinctions between the genteel and the coarse, the refined and the reprobate, the humane and the inhumane, the temperaments of the wild and domestic animal, and the private and public execution of such activities.

Obviously, such distinctions were hypocritical and socially invidious, and could only result in insidious, class-biased legislation—the suppression of the pit and tether sports involving domestic animals (e.g., cock and dog fighting, bull baiting) and the toleration of the "free run for life" sports involving wild animals (e.g., fox hunting) (see Berryman, 1974). That the passing of such legislation occurred attests that, by the middle of the 19th century, the Barbarians were beginning to pay lip service to bourgeois morality and that the new mode of production (industrial capitalism) was making the aristocracy and gentry more dependent on the bourgeoisie for their base of political support (see Arnold, 1969, chap. 3).

During the first half of the 19th century in the U.K. and before the Civil War in the U.S.A., the bourgeoisie seemed more inclined to avoid (at least in public) and condemn rather than contribute to the Anglo sporting tradition. But we should note that a class is not a homogeneous category. The bourgeoisie was caught between incorporation (via emulation) and resistance. This cultural problematic is captured in the Victorian period and especially within the private schools of England.[5] The private schools began to be invaded by the wealthy bourgeoisie in the 1830s, when the success of the industrial capitalist order was reasonably assured and when the wealthier bourgeoisie had achieved a measure of self-confidence hitherto unknown.

Although the wealthier English bourgeoisie were anxious to have access to the prestige that attendance at the private schools conveyed and, thereby, to warren into the ascriptive privileges of the aristocracy and gentry concerning imperial, political, military, and civic office, they were critical of the extant educational system (especially its nonutilitarian, classical curriculum, the absence of adult authority, and the bullying and brutality involved in the "fagging" system) because it did not suit their needs or reflect their civilizing ideals (see Arnstein, 1973, 1975; Mallea, 1972; Mangan, 1981; Wilkinson, 1964). Thus, they pressed for reform. Initial reform, however, did not represent a victory for the bourgeoisie, for it was something of a compromise—a compromise designed to fuse the aristocracy, gentry, and wealthier elements of the bourgeoisie into a gentlemanly ruling class (see Mallea, 1972, p. 11) or as Wilkinson (1964) phrases it, the private schools were the instruments of a subliminal "extraordinary strategy" (p. ix) by which bourgeois talent was captured in the promotion of gentry class power. The compromise effected in the "reformed" schools thus did not result in the thoroughgoing bourgeoisification of gentry culture or a thoroughgoing gentrification of bourgeois culture.

Rather, it produced a peculiar interpretation of high culture: It was what the less affluent middle class and the proletariat lacked (see Birnbaum, 1969, p. 138). And, while the compromise produced some modification in the concept of the gentleman (see Morford & McIntosh, chapter 3 in this book), it preserved the invidious distinctions that inhered in the use of this label of social approbation. The *haute bourgeoisie* would initiate the modernizing transformation of sport in what has been termed the English Athletic Revival and would provide an ideology that justified their involvement in sporting practices: "Muscular Christianity."

Such an ideology would identify those qualities of character—manliness, vigor, self-restraint, courage—that were requisites of gentlemanly status. The Juvenalian aphorism, *mens sana in corpore sano*, was revitalized, albeit within the limits of amateurism as a form of social exclusion/closure and within the transmutations that occurred in sport as a result of the bourgeoisification process (i.e., formalization, codification, spatial and temporal limitation, impulse canalization)—a process of rationalization (see Dunning & Sheard, 1979). Thus, tradition and emergence, incorporation and qualified resistance, produced a horizontal class diffusion of organized sports and games which would later be followed by a vertical diffusion of sports and games as the *haute bourgeoisie* attempted to incorporate the working class into their hegemonic definition of character. This cultural complexity was reproduced in the U.S.A. (Goldstein, 1989, has outlined its resultant tensions in the early days of baseball.) As a result, the American athletic revival represented one more contradiction in the rhetoric of "nonegalitarian classlessness" (Ossowski, 1963, chap. 7) contained within the American Dream.

# The Oppositional Versus the Merely Novel

As Williams notes, it is really difficult to separate the truly oppositional from the merely novel. This problematic is exemplified in the valorization process—the commercialization and professionalization of sport. The valorization of sport and other forms of recreation was both merely novel *and* radically emergent—merely novel in that it represented the extension of the socialization of capitalism's production and consumption relations into the realm of sport; radically emergent in that it would superimpose exchange values onto use-values and thereby turn sporting practices into a capital/labor relation that was increasingly oriented to the market. In short, one fraction of the bourgeoisie became increasingly interested in the value-creating capacity of labor and less in its purely use-creating capacity.

Let us define use-value and exchange-value before discussing why the ascendance of the latter represented a radically emergent turn of events. Following Mandel (1970):

> Every product of human labor normally possesses utility; it must be able to satisfy a human need. We may therefore say that every product of human labor has a *use-value*. . . . Together with this use-value, a product of human labor can also have another value, an *exchange-value*. It may be produced for exchange on the market place, for the purpose of being sold, rather than for direct consumption by the producers or by wealthy classes. A mass of products which has been created for the purpose of being sold can no longer be considered as the production of simple use-values; it is now a production of *commodities*. The commodity, therefore, is a product created to be exchanged on the market, as opposed to one which has been made for direct consumption. *Every commodity must have both a use-value and an exchange-value.* It must have a use-value or else nobody would buy it. (pp. 9-10)

The valorization of sport labor and sport products was radically emergent then because it changed both the production and consumption of the sporting event. Clarke and Critcher (1985) express the consumption side as follows:

> We want to suggest that it is possible to think of three possible sorts of relationship between a citizen and a cultural institution: those of member, customer or consumer. The member has an active commitment to the institution, which is run on his or her behalf, and over which the membership exercises collective control. The *customer's* stake is that of habit. Mutual expectations arise, and a contract of sorts is evolved, which both sides are reluctant to abandon. The *consumer*, however, has neither the commitment of the member, nor the informal contract of the customer. His or her expectations are altogether more specific: the maximisation of immediate satisfaction. If goods or services are not provided in the manner or at the price required, then the consumer will go elsewhere. . . . the powers involved in consumer sovereignty are of a specific kind. The sanctions possessed by the consumer are entirely *negative* (we can choose not to buy). (pp. 95-97)

On the production side, voluntaristic participation in production (e.g., the early clubs in many sports) would be replaced by binding, contractual agreements, a process that would turn the "member" athlete into first a tradesperson, and later a professional—the distinctions between the latter and the former being merely a change in the way the athlete/laborer was socially viewed.

The valorization of certain sporting practices represented a struggle between fractions of the bourgeoisie, the ungentrified and the gentrified, and it eventually pushed the latter onto the sidelines. This is not to say that valorized sport and its concomitant form of social relations extirpated other forms of sporting relations— indeed it can be argued that recreational and representational sports retain a mixed mode of production (see Clarke, chapter 11 in this book)—but the valorization process when accompanied by the rationalization of sport's social organization and the commodification of sporting goods has produced a relatively new cultural institution that is dominant in contemporary society and hegemonic in its trickle-down effect into sporting relations at nonelite levels of participation. Sport emerged as the ultimate expression or *the* cultural formation derived from play. As Hardy (1986, 1990a, 1990b) has argued, this process resulted in the emergence of a new industry of providers who had inordinate influence in the marketplace:

> Control in the marketplace does make a difference. A relative handful of rules committees do control the game forms played by most Americans, and relatively few manufacturers do supply the goods used at all levels. For almost a hundred years this network of expert coaches, journalists, administrators, manufacturers, and dealers has largely shaped the boundaries of American sport. (1990a, pp. 93-94)

Beamish (see chapter 9) outlines the effects of this broad process on labor relations in Canadian sport (see also Dworkin, 1981; Staudohar, 1986, for the USA).

On both sides of the Atlantic (cf. Vamplew, 1988; Staudohar, 1986) the results included antagonisms between owners and players as the latter sought to strengthen their collective bargaining power by contesting such things as the fixed maximum wage, pension plans, and binding contracts that restricted player movement in the sport's labor market (i.e., the monopsony principle). While there were many agents in the valorization process, our choice for exemplars would include William Hulbert, the Spalding brothers, and James E. Sullivan. These men effectively fashioned the National League, the AAU, and Spalding & Bros. sporting goods into prominent and well-connected arms of an industry that at times approached cartel-like control of both raw materials, labor, and consumer markets for sport products (see Hardy, 1990b; Ingham et al., 1987; Levine, 1984; Schimmel, Ingham, & Howell, chapter 10 in this book). Here, it can be argued that the valorization process proceeded at a faster and more effective pace in the U.S. than in the U.K. (or, for that matter, the rest of the world). The same can be said for the rationalization process; the U.S. led the way in the creation of that pyramidal system of recruitment and allocation that we call the feeder system. It is a system on which the economic reproduction of elite-amateur and professional sport has become dependent. And as Smith (1988) has shown, the process had rendered American collegiate sport commercial and in many ways professional by 1900.

Although the distance of history permits us to recognize the emergence and ascendancy of a bourgeois capitalist order in the world of sport, we must emphasize the complexities of this process. Thus we must stress—as do the authors in this book—the importance of human agency. As Anderson (1980) emphasizes, agency is attuned to goals, and goals are produced both for us and by us. Further, how we set our goals is deeply rooted in "lived experience" and in the conditions of our existence. Thus, it behooves us to note that throughout this chapter we have attempted to assert the view that classes are not categorical, homogeneous entities (see Willis, 1990). To be sure, classes are positioned and ranked primarily by the mode (i.e., forces and relations) of production, but this does not necessarily lead to a "class in itself for itself" form of consciousness. Fractions do exist within classes and, as Parkin (1979) has observed, insufficient attention has been paid to issues of status as it relates to open and closed relations and hence to practices of exclusion and usurpation that are not attributable to class relations per se, but that may be derived from them (see Murphy, 1984; Turner, 1988).

Gender relations are a primary example; they reveal the complex intersections of class and status relations, and of the effective mobilization of counter or alternative hegemony within the enablements and constraints of the dominant (see Barrett, 1980; Carrigan, Connell, & Lee, 1985; Connell, 1987; Hargreaves, chapter 8 in this book; Vertinsky, 1990). Feminism in this regard has never been a coherent, systematized ideology; nor has it appealed to women as a category of the whole. It only appears relatively coherent in its critique of patriarchy and patriarchy's extreme form of hegemonic masculinity. As a critique of patriarchy's extreme form, it has attracted some men to a feminist, strategic position (see Carrigan et al., 1985; Connell, 1987; Hearn, 1987).

These points are illustrated by Anderson (1980, pp. 19-20), who identifies three "levels" of agency (see also Flacks, 1988). The first level of agency involves the making of everyday life. It involves day by day private decisions concerning the cultivation of a career, the choices concerning cohabitation, how to maintain a home, the purchase of short-term or durable goods, should the lawn be sprayed (appearance versus environmental pollutants), and so on. These decisions are inscribed within existing social relations and typically reproduce them. The second and third levels of agency are more public. Typically, fewer people are involved in a conflictual, public conflagration. Many public conflicts do not aim to transform social relations outside of the liberal democratic, capitalist umbrella. Rather, many public conflicts are aimed at producing equity within the extant political economy. They are strategies of incorporation that seek to include the excluded and most times are strategies that wave the banner of "equality of opportunity" or distributive justice.

But some do engage in the third level of agency, which goes beyond acts of mere resistance or redress. They engage in a quest for the remodeling of their collective mode of existence and the political-moral-juridical system. Instead of equity and equality of opportunity, they seek "equality of condition" and, therefore, seek to usurp traditional and dominant privileges in status and political-economic power.

To follow Anderson (1980), what we are suggesting is that feminism, for example, does represent a desire to change the imbalance of power that exists in social structures, but apart from this there is not an overwhelming consensus concerning how to win this war of strategic position, nor is there consensus concerning the level of agency to be employed in usurpationary actions aimed at redressing grievances and relative deprivations. Thus, and to focus on sport, we note that efforts aimed at redressing the gender inequalities in sport have focused moral attention on distributive issues rather than on the remodeling of whole social structures with which sport articulates (see Dewar, chapter 7, and Hargreaves, chapter 8, in this book). The latter would entail the collective will and the knowledge of how to radically transform, through strategic coalitions, gendered power relations in a way that could create new societies by mastering old ones—a transformation that could not be completed by a regendering of social relations per se, but would require the democratization of all power relations, especially those anchored in property and scarcity (see Murphy, 1984). Here, one must note the increasing feminization of poverty (see Goldberg & Kremen, 1990).

Hargreaves (chapter 8) addresses the fractions that exist in the feminist movement in terms similar to those outlined earlier in this chapter. She points to the strategies advocated by feminists as a way of identifying the fractions per se. The strategies aimed at achieving equality range from pragmatic to separatist to the more utopian (we use this in a nonpejorative sense) gender-cooperative. These strategies articulate with the emphases placed on the connections between gender and the situated experiences of genders vis-à-vis class, ethnicity, sexual preferences, religious preferences, and so on. Thus, among others there are liberal feminists, radical feminists, Marxist feminists, socialist feminists, lesbian feminists. Democratizing sport thus more or less (depending on strategic position) involves the deconstruction of endemic features of the dominant sporting forms and relations—to wit, sport's reproduction of aggressive competition, chauvinism, sexism, racism, xenophobia, physical and psychological abuse of athletes, violence, and commodification—forms and relations that oppress both women and men.

## Conclusion

We return to the problematic of hegemony and to Williams (1977). He, in a rather tortuous statement, asserts:

A lived hegemony is always a process. It is not, except analytically, a system or a structure. It is a realized complex of experiences, relationships, and activities, with specific and changing pressures and limits. In practice, that is, hegemony can never be singular. Its internal structures are highly complex, as can readily be seen in any concrete analysis. Moreover (and this is crucial, reminding us of the necessary thrust of the concept), it does not just passively exist as a form of dominance. It has continually to be renewed, recreated, defended, and modified. It is also continually resisted, limited, altered, challenged by pressures not at all its own. . . . That is to say, alternative political and cultural emphases, and the many forms of opposition and struggle, are important not only in themselves but as indicative features of what the hegemonic process has in practice had to control. (pp. 112-113)

In this regard, *periodicity* in historical analysis is terribly important in the analysis of sport's contents, forms, and relations, for in any given period there will always be a dialectic of incorporation and resistance. Social transformation is not an unfolding evolutionary process, but a process that takes place over contested terrain. Sometimes, we retrospectively see a *longue duree* (organic) and at other times precipitous human agency (conjunctural). Concrete analyses, rather than theoretical fixations, expose the essences of discontinuities within the appearances of continuity and the appearances of discontinuity within, relatively speaking, the essences of continuity.

It is important that readers attend to the theme underlying the essays in this anthology. We draw attention to the differences between orthodox (mainstream) and heterodox agendas in sport studies (see Beamish, 1990; Ingham, 1991). *Sport in Social Development* is not constrained by a subdisciplinary orientation that succumbs to the orthodox paradigm (structural-functionalist, positivism) in sociology. In the past 18 years, we have witnessed what Giddens has called the collapse of the orthodox consensus. Perhaps collapse is too strong a word: We have witnessed challenges to the mainstream. Equally important, the idea that a discipline can monopolize the right to the analysis of a topical field of inquiry has been deconstructed by cross-disciplined approaches and approaches that are agnostic when it comes to disciplinary boundary maintenance (see Baron, 1985). Together with the above changes, there have been changes in discourse. The new discourses are complex because social relations are complex. Few of us can accept lawlike, one way, cause and effect relationships that disregard human agency in social transformation and social continuity. Nor can we accept the axiomatic method in which explanations are deduced from a postulate that is regarded as a self-evident truth. We do accept that there are crucial determinations that influence the course of events, but we reject simplistic reductionism of any stripe. All of these challenges can be found in this anthology.

## Acknowledgment

We appreciate the comments of Peter Donnelly on the first draft of this essay.

## Notes

1. For a detailed overview of the concept of hegemony, we recommend a reading of Stuart Hall et al. (1978), "Politics and Ideology: Gramsci."
2. For 20th-century tensions within boxing, see Roberts (1983), Sammons (1988), and Sugden (1987).
3. The "super-league" is now a reality. In terms of political-economic historicity, the English are 75 years or so behind the U.S. They could benefit from a

reading of American materials concerning monopoly and monopsony, and the way they have affected the professional sport franchise/community relation. A primer is provided in Ingham, Howell, and Schilperoort (1987).

4. Bernard (1968, p. 8) states that eudaemonism or eustress-seeking is associated with excitement and adventure. It is fun, it enhances vital sensations, it "turns people on," it releases energy. Normally the label *eudaemonistic* is applied almost exclusively to the culture of the nobility. However, as Veblen (1953) observed, it might also describe tendencies of the delinquent working class. We do note that the various American notions of "republican" virtue seemed to reduce the prominence of American gentry—vis-à-vis their British counter-parts—in the defense of such traditional pastimes (see Gorn, 1986; Jable, 1973).

5. The private schools of Britain are referred to as The Public Schools. At the end of the 17th century, these schools were known as "grammar," "public," or "endowed" schools. Originally, they were nonprofit schools teaching grammar (specifically Latin grammar) that had received an endowment enabling the general public to make use of them. The income from the endowment would be used to pay a salary to the headmaster, and, if the endowment was of sufficient size, assistant masters also would be hired. By the end of the 17th century, many of these schools had started to take in fee-paying scholars to supplement their income, and so the model of the present-day private "public" school had started to develop. This oxymoron remains because all "public" schools are primarily fee-dependent, boarding schools that recruit their students from the more affluent sectors of society while providing scholarships to the brightest of those in need.

# References

Anderson, P. (1980). *Arguments within English Marxism*. London: Verso.

Arnold, M. (1969). *Culture and anarchy*. Cambridge: The University Press.

Arnstein, W. (1973). The survival of the Victorian aristocracy. In F. Jaher (Ed.), *The rich, the well-born, and the powerful* (pp. 203-257). Urbana, IL: University of Illinois Press.

Arnstein, W. (1975). The myth of the triumphant Victorian middle class. *The Historian, 37*, 205-221.

Baron, S. (1985). The study of culture: Cultural studies and British sociology compared. *Acta Sociologica, 28*, 71-85.

Barrett, M. (1980). *Women's oppression today: Problems in Marxist feminist analysis*. London: Verso.

Beamish, R. (1990). A review of McPherson, B., Curtis, J., & Loy, J. *The social significance of sport: An introduction to the sociology of sport*. Champaign, IL: Human Kinetics (1989). *International Review for the Sociology of Sport, 25*, 323-325.

Berger, P., Berger, B., & Kellner, H. (1973). *The homeless mind: Modernization and consciousness*. Garden City, NY: Doubleday & Co.

Bernard, J. (1968). The eudaemonists. In S. Klausner (Ed.), *Why man takes chances: Studies in stress-seeking* (pp. 6-47). Garden City, NY: Anchor Books.

Berryman, J. (1974). *Anglo-American blood sports*. Unpublished master's thesis, University of Massachusetts, Amherst.

Birnbaum, N. (1969). *The crisis of industrial society*. New York: Oxford University Press.

Buford, B. (1991). *Among the thugs.* New York: Norton.

Butsch, R., (Ed.) (1990). *For fun and profit: The transformation of leisure into consumption.* Philadelphia: Temple.

Carrigan, T., Connell, R., & Lee, J. (1985). Toward a new sociology of masculinity. *Theory and Society,* **14**, 551-604.

Clarke, J., & Critcher, C. (1985). *The devil makes work: Leisure in capitalist Britain.* Houndmills: Macmillan Press.

Connell, R. (1987). *Gender and power: Society, the person, and sexual politics.* Stanford: Stanford University Press.

Dunning, E., & Sheard, K. (1979). *Barbarians, gentlemen and players.* New York: New York University Press.

Dworkin, J. (1981). *Owners versus players: Baseball and collective bargaining.* Boston: Auburn House.

Elias, N. (1978). *The civilizing process* (E. Jephcott, Trans.). New York: Urizen Books.

Flacks, R. (1988). *Making history: The American left and the American mind.* New York: Columbia University Press.

Goldberg, G., & Kremen, E. (1990). *The feminization of poverty: Only in America?* Westport, CT: Greenwood Press.

Goldstein, W. (1989). *Playing for keeps: A history of early baseball.* Ithaca: Cornell University Press.

Gorn, E. (1986). *The manly art: Bare-knuckle prize fighting in America.* Ithaca: Cornell University Press.

Gouldner, A. (1970). *The coming crisis of western sociology.* New York: Basic Books.

Gramsci, A. (1971). *Selections from the prison notebooks.* (Q. Hoare & G. Smith, Eds. and Trans.). New York: International.

Gramsci, A. (1978). *Letters from prison.* L. Lawyer (Ed. and Trans.). New York: Harper and Row.

Gruneau, R. (1988). Modernization or hegemony: Two views on sport and social development. In J. Harvey & H. Cantelon (Eds.), *Not just a game* (pp. 9-32). Ottawa: University of Ottawa Press.

Hall, S. (1978). The treatment of "football hooliganism" in the press. In R. Ingham (Ed.), *Football hooliganism* (pp. 15-36). London: Inter-Action.

Hall, S., Lumley, B., & McLennan, G. (1978). Politics and ideology: Gramsci. In Centre for Contemporary Cultural Studies, *On ideology* (pp. 45-76). London: Hutchinson University Library.

Hardy, S. (1986). Entrepreneurs, organizations, and the sport marketplace: Subjects in search of historians. *Journal of Sport History,* **13**, 14-33.

Hardy, S. (1990a). Adopted by all the leading clubs: Sporting goods and the shaping of leisure, 1800-1900. In R. Butsch (Ed.), *For fun and profit: The transformation of leisure into consumption* (pp. 71-101). Philadelphia: Temple University Press.

Hardy, S. (1990b). Entrepreneurs, structures, and the sportgeist: old tensions in a modern industry. In D. Kyle & G. Stark (Eds.), *Essays on sport history and sport mythology* (pp. 45-82). College Station: Texas A & M Press.

Hardy, S., & Ingham, A. (1983). Games, structures, and agency: Historians on the American play movement. *Journal of Social History,* **17**, 285-301.

Hargreaves, J. (1986). *Sport, power and culture.* New York: St. Martin's Press.

Hearn, J. (1987). *The gender of oppression: Men, masculinity, and the critique of Marxism.* Brighton: Wheatsheaf Press.

Hoffman, J. (1984). *The Gramscian challenge: Coercion and consent in Marxist political theory.* Oxford: Basil Blackwell Ltd.

Hoggart, R. (1970). *The uses of literacy.* New York: Oxford University Press.

Ingham, A. (1978). *American sport in transition: The maturation of industrial capitalism and its impact upon sport.* Unpublished doctoral dissertation, University of Massachusetts, Amherst.

Ingham, A. (1979). Methodology in the sociology of sport: From symptoms of malaise to Weber for a cure. *Quest*, **31(2)**: 187-215.

Ingham, A. (1982). Sports, capital logic and hegemony: A rejoinder. In H. Cantelon & R. Gruneau (Eds.), *Sport, culture and the modern state* (pp. 198-208). Toronto: University of Toronto Press.

Ingham, A. (1991). Some not so new arguments in support of heterodox agendas in the study of sport. *International Review for the Sociology of Sport*, **26(1)**, 53-60.

Ingham, A., & Beamish, R. (1993). The industrialization of the United States and the "bourgeoisification" of sport. In E. Dunning, J. Maguire, & R. Pearton (Eds.), *The sports process*. Champaign, IL: Human Kinetics.

Ingham, A., & Hardy, S. (1984). Sport: Structuration, subjugation, and hegemony. *Theory, Culture, & Society*, **2(2)**, 85-103.

Ingham, A., Howell, J., & Schilperoort, T. (1987). Professional sports and community: A review and exegesis. In K. Pandolf (Ed.), *Exercise and Sport Sciences Reviews*, **15**, 427-465.

Jable, T. (1973). The Pennsylvania Sunday Blue Laws of 1779: A view of Pennsylvania society and politics during the American Revolution. *Pennsylvania History*, **40**, 413-26.

Joll, J. (1977). *Gramsci*. Glasgow: Fontana/Collins.

Lea, J., & Young, J. (1984). *What is to be done about law and order?* Harmondsworth: Penguin Books.

Levine, P. (1984). *A.G. Spalding and the rise of baseball: The promise of American sport.* New York: Oxford University Press.

Malcolmson, R. (1973). *Popular recreations in English society: 1700-1850.* Cambridge: Cambridge University Press.

Mallea, J. (1972). Class and sport: The Victorian legacy. Paper presented at the American Sociological Association's annual meetings, New Orleans, August.

Mandel, E. (1970). *An introduction to Marxist economic theory.* New York: Pathfinder Press.

Mandell, R. (1971). *The Nazi Olympics*. New York: Macmillan.

Mangan, J.A. (1981). *Athleticism and the Victorian and Edwardian public school.* Cambridge: Cambridge University Press.

Marx, K. (1963). *The eighteenth brumaire of Louis Bonaparte.* New York: International.

Marx, K., & Engels, F. (1970). *The German ideology.* New York: International.

Murphy, R. (1984). The structure of closure. *British Journal of Sociology*, **35**, 547-567.

Ossowska, M. (1970). *Social determinants of moral ideas.* Philadelphia: University of Pennsylvania Press.

Ossowski, S. (1963). *Class structure in the social consciousness.* London: Routledge & Kegan Paul.

Parkin, F. (1979). *Marxism and class theory: A bourgeois critique.* New York: Columbia University Press.

Reid, D. (1976). The decline of Saint Monday, 1766-1876. *Past and Present*, **71**, 76-101.

Roberts, R. (1983). *Papa Jack: Jack Johnson and the era of white hopes.* New York: Free Press.

Sammons, J. (1988). *Beyond the ring: The role of boxing in American society.* Urbana, University of Illinois Press.

Smith, R. (1988). *Sports and freedom: The rise of big-time college athletics.* New York: Oxford University Press.

Staudohar, P.D. (1986). *The sports industry and collective bargaining.* New York: Cornell University Press.

Sugden, J. (1987). The exploitation of disadvantage: The occupational sub-culture of the boxer. In J. Horne et al. (Eds.), *Sport, leisure and social relations* (pp. 187-209). London: Routledge & Kegan Paul.

Taylor, I. (1989). Hillsborough, 15 April 1989: Some personal contemplations. *New Left Review.* **177**, 89-110.

Taylor, I. (1991). English football in the 1990s: Taking Hillsborough seriously. In J. Williams & S. Wagg (Eds.), *British football and social change* (pp. 3-24). Leicester: Leicester University Press.

Thompson, E. (1963). *The making of the English working class.* New York: Random House/Vintage.

Turner, B. (1988). *Status.* Minneapolis: University of Minnesota Press.

Vamplew, W. (1988). *Pay up and play the game: Professional sport in Britain, 1875-1914.* Cambridge: Cambridge University Press.

Veblen, T. (1953). *The theory of the leisure class.* New York: New American Library.

Vertinsky, P. (1990). *The eternally wounded woman: Women, exercise and doctors in the late nineteenth century.* Manchester: Manchester University Press.

Wilkinson, R. (1964). *The prefects: British leadership and the public school tradition.* New York: Oxford University Press.

Williams, J., Dunning, E., & Murphy, P. (1984). *Hooligans abroad: The behaviour and crowd control of English fans in continental Europe.* London: Routledge and Kegan Paul.

Williams, J., & Wagg, S. (Eds.) (1991). *British football and social change.* Leicester: Leicester University Press.

Williams, R. (1977). *Marxism and literature.* New York: Oxford University Press.

Willis, P. (1990). *Common culture.* Boulder & San Francisco: Westview Press.

# CHAPTER 2

# Ancient Athletic Motifs and the Modern Olympic Games

## An Analysis of Rituals and Representations

*Synthia S. Slowikowski*
*John W. Loy*

> *It is generally fairly difficult to know why and how an idea is born—emerges from the tide of other ideas which await realization—takes on substance and becomes fact. This, however, is not the case regarding the Olympic Games. The idea of their revival was not a passing fancy: it was the logical culmination of a great movement.*
>
> P. De Coubertin, T. Philemon, N. Politis, and C. Anninos,
> *The Olympic Games 776 B.C.-1896 A.D.: The Games of 1896*

The ancient Olympic Games represent the longest recurring sport event in the history of humankind; the modern Olympic Games "are the largest scheduled and regularly recurring event in the world" (Rothenbuhler, 1989, p. 138). Thus, in terms of both length and legacy, the "Olympic tradition" is the most notable sporting tradition in the Western world.

Given the many transitions of the modern Games during the past century, and granted the tremendous transformations in the Games from ancient to contemporary times, we recognize that it may make little sense to speak of the Olympic tradition. We also recognize, however, that a number of seemingly ancient athletic motifs are central features of the modern Games and that they serve to give some meaningful sense in modernity to the notion of an Olympic tradition.

We are interested in the vestiges and residues of ancient athletics in general, and of the original Olympic Games in particular, that remain attached to our modern Games—whether symbolically, or materially, in form and practice. Classical sportive motifs associated with competitors and contests—the core elements of the Games—are the main focus of our analysis. But we also examine ancient athletic motifs related to the peripheral elements of the Games. These latter elements include the rituals and representations that have historically surrounded the Games; as for example, the pilgrimages of contestants and spectators to the special place of contest, the awarding of prizes to the victors, and the primal images of fire and vegetation that have informed the traditions of both the ancient and modern versions of the Olympic Games.

We are intrigued by the fact that selected practices and traditions prominent in the ancient Games still exist in some form or manner in the modern Games. Accordingly, we seek to analyze the place of these vestigial elements in the contemporary framework of the Olympic Games. We question whether these vestigial elements are archaic or active, and we ask what is their use or place in today's Games.

Like the other contributors to this book, we draw on the work of Raymond Williams in our analysis, especially his work dealing with how certain cultures or aspects of culture are embedded in other worlds of meaning (e.g., Williams, 1977, 1982, 1983; Johnson, 1990; O'Connor, 1989; During, 1989; Eagleton, 1989; Brantlinger, 1990). In this essay, we specifically focus our attention on Williams's concepts of *archaic* and *residual* by highlighting how ancient athletic motifs have for various reasons been repositioned and revived in the present in special ways to guide the traditions and practices of the modern Olympic Games.

Past rituals and representations continue to be meaningful and are perpetuated as traditions because they may hold certain primal significance to humans. Primal elements, or significants, attached to the Olympic Games that we highlight in this essay include the agon motif, and the motifs of fire, pilgrimage, gift-giving, and vegetation. Our examination of these motifs stresses that such "ageless" elements illuminate the access to the past, but are, of course, not actually the past revived.

The past is active only in the sense that the present cultural context structures it to be active. In the case of fire and vegetation, for example, the motifs illuminate the access to the past because they recall what we consider to be "primal" universals. In Williams's (1977) words, these symbols were formed in the past, but remain active in the cultural process. In the present-day Olympic Games, such active symbols and actions are proffered in culture as "authentic." For instance, human competitiveness is seen as authentic when displayed in Olympic competition; the legendary flame that opens the Olympic Games is seen as an authentic rekindling of the sacred flame of Olympia, Greece.

## The Agon Motif

*Citius, altius, fortius.* (An Olympic motto)

The dominant thematic feature of both the ancient and modern Olympic Games is the agon motif. We refer to this motif in two senses throughout this chapter. First, we use the phrase in a rather specific sense to denote the pursuit of honor by means of demonstrated physical prowess and the achievement of bodily excellence. The comprehensive meaning of this sense of the agon motif was captured by Huizinga

(1955, p. 63), who noted that in all of civilization, one of the strongest incentives to perfection is the desire to be praised and honored for one's superiority. Huizinga demonstrates that many diverse forms of competition provide contexts for showing superiority, and he places particular importance on agonal contests as proving grounds for making merit manifest.

Second, we refer to the agon motif in a more general sense to connote the attitudes, actions, and vocabulary of agonal competition. With respect to the vocabulary of competition, we have chosen to use one of the most common Greek words for "contest," namely *agon*. Agon designates an assembly of competitors, spectators, and prizes in a special contest place (Scanlon, 1983, pp. 154, 158).

Morford and Clark (1976) have shown that

> the agon or spirit of rivalry and self assertion in the quest for personal fame describes a cultural *tour de force* in certain societies, especially in early Greek societies from whose language the term is derived. Within these societies war was the most prestigious avenue for displaying prowess, but, because it was limited and costly, athletic contests offered an acceptable substitute for displaying prowess between members of the same tribe or "in-group." (p. 164)

We propose that what was a substitute for true agon in the past is the substance of symbolic agon in the present. That is to say, within contemporary society, athletic contests provide the primary institutionalized and socially sanctioned competitive situations wherein contestants can excel in physical prowess and prove their bodily excellence. In the following sections, then, we examine the residues of the agon motif in the modern Olympic Games with a special emphasis on the social character of the competitors and the social structure of the contests.

## Agonal Competitors

Participants in agonal contests represent individuals engaged in active quests for excellence through physical prowess. In whatever particular contest, culture, or period, agonal competitors are readily characterized by their intense spirit of rivalry and competition; strong stress on individualism and self-assertion; and extreme emphasis on the pursuit of fame, glory, and honor (cf. Loy & Hesketh, 1984; Morford & Clark, 1976).

### The Homeric Warrior

With respect to the literature and ideals of Western civilization, the archetypal agonal competitor is the aristocratic Homeric warrior. Classical visions of the Homeric warrior vary somewhat in terms of the particular moral attributes and physical characteristics they emphasize, but virtually all accounts point to Homer's Achilles as the paradigmatic aristocratic warrior.

In a recent detailed analysis of Homer's hero, King (1987) shows how Achilles represents both the best and the "be[a]st" of the Achaians. With reference to the *Iliad*, King called Homer's Achilles the "best (*aristeuein*) and superior to others. . . . He is swiftest, the most beautiful, the youngest, and the most complex of the heroes who fight at Troy'' (pp. 2-3). The complex character of Achilles is evident in the dual nature he displays in battle. On the positive side, Achilles expresses concern and mercy for his opponents in his earlier fighting. On the negative side, Achilles expresses what King describes as a ''monomaniacal desire for vengeance'' (p. 14) during the Trojan War. His anger, brutality, cruelty, savagery, and wrath are seemingly without limit as highlighted in his killing of both Lykaon and Hektor.

Achilles' extended display of martial prowess throughout the *Iliad* characterizes his complexity and demonstrates the cost of being heroic. But as King (1987) well notes, Achilles' role in the *Odyssey* fails to feature his complexity and represents ''the classical stereotyping of Achilles as a warrior of quick anger, stark honesty, superlative prowess, and obsession with worldly honor'' (p. 2; cf. also pp. 45-49).

The latter attributes of prowess and honor are most often cited in ideal-typical descriptions of aristocratic warriors in ancient Greece. For example, Ossowska (1972, pp. 125-126) observes that Homer's warriors were always preoccupied with proving excellence (*aristeia*), and attempted to be first among equals. Similarly, Donlan (1981, p. 23) describes the aristocratic ideal in ancient Greece as being played out almost exclusively in the physical sphere, and in terms of prowess as a warrior. The endless aim of the aristocratic warrior was public recognition of his ability as ''best'' (*aristos*); his greatest fear was failure and communal humiliation.

This Homeric aristocratic ideal was reflected in athletics as well as warfare. For example, Odysseus is cajoled to display his physical prowess (and, thus, reveal his true aristocratic lineage), at the games of the Phaikians. Homer has Laodamos speak what has become a famous passage in sporting journalism:

> Come you also now father stranger, and try these contests, if you have any skill in any. It beseems you to know athletics, for there is no greater glory that can befall a man[1] living than what he achieves by speed of his feet or strength of his hands. (*Odyssey* 8.145)

Donlan (1981) traces the varied transitions in the Homeric aristocratic ideal from around 750 B.C., when the *Iliad* and *Odyssey* may have been composed, to the 5th century B.C. He clearly describes the marked transformations of the Homeric heroic ideal with the evolution of more complex social structures such as the *polis*, or city-state. However, he concludes that

> despite the enormous changes that took place within Greek culture during the four centuries covered by this survey, the upper-class Greeks of the late fifth century B.C., in their reflections concerning human behavior and the relations between men, continued to take as their assumptive starting point the complex of received beliefs embedded in the heroic ideal. (p. 3)

Similarly, such received beliefs served as the assumptive starting point of the ancient Olympic athletes; and remnants of such received beliefs are embedded in the ''heroic ideal'' of modern Olympic athletes.

## The Olympic Athlete

Throughout Homer, and particularly in Book 23 of the *Iliad*, and in the recounting of Odysseus' athletic feats in *Odyssey* 7.97-ff, examples of physical contests abound (e.g., Gardiner, 1930, pp. 18-27). In these examples, the character structure of the Homeric warrior and the athlete are isomorphic. This sentiment is echoed by Young (1984), who asserts: "In that quest for distinction through excellence we find the driving force behind Greek athletics. . . . And in the readiness of adult men to run the naked risk of public dishonor for the chance to achieve distinction" (p. 76).

The obsession to be first among equals is reflected in inscriptions carved in honor of legendary athletes of ancient Greece. For instance, one inscription boasts of a pancratiast who was a champion in all of the ancient Panhellenic Games (Olympic, Pythian, Isthmean, and Nemean Games):

I won all the contests in which my name was entered, defeating everyone. I issued no challenge nor was there anyone who dared issue a challenge to me. I was never in a tie match, never forfeited a bout, never protested a decision, never walked out of a contest nor entered a contest in order to please a king, nor did I ever win a fight that was started again, but in all the contests in which I entered I won the crown right there in that *skamma*, and I always qualified in the preliminaries. (*Iscrizioni Agonistiche Greche* 79.12-18)

An Olympic victory would, of course, eclipse all other forms of athletic competition in the Greek world. Indeed, the importance and prestige of the Olympic Games is indicated in the opening lines of Pindar's first Olympic ode:

Water is preeminent and gold, like a fire
　　burning in the night, outshines
all possessions that magnify men's pride.
　　But if, my soul, you yearn
　　　to celebrate great games,
　　　　look no further
　　　　for another star
　　　shining through the deserted ether
　　brighter than the sun, or for a contest
　　mightier than Olympia . . . (Pindar, *Olympian* 1.1-11)

Although the Olympic Games have undergone a marked transformation from an ancient, sacred festival to a modern, secular spectacle, they still constitute the most important and prestigious form of multisport competition in the world. Moreover, notwithstanding the fact that the modern Games are heavily commercialized and politicized, world-class athletes still strive to demonstrate their bodily excellence and to be first among their competitive peers.

The desire of modern Olympians to achieve distinction is illustrated by the following quotations from Olympic champions. Olga Connolly, the discus gold medalist in the 1956 Olympics, expressed her feelings of victory in stating:

Standing on the top of the Olympic victory is like stretching one's body to the top of the world. It is a moment where the individual man or woman gets introduced to the whole planet. It is a moment that is his or hers alone. (Staff, 1984b, p. 11)

Vince Matthews expressed his sentiments about winning the gold medal in the 400-meter race in the 1972 Olympics as follows: "Twenty years from now, I can look at this medal and say 'I was the best quarter-miler in the world on that day.' If you don't think that's important, you don't know what's inside an athlete's soul" (Staff, 1984a, p. 31). Ultimately, the modern Olympic Games offer an opportunity for gaining distinction in a uniform society. The Olympic athlete's achievement is highly valued because it represents action and devotion to a difficult goal that is unnecessary for life's sustenance (Lenk, 1985, p. 166). Lenk's observations highlight how the modern Games provide a competitive context for being recognized as the "best." But as the Ben Johnson case attests, the modern Games also provide a contesting situation wherein an individual can experience abject failure and its accompanying communal humiliation.

In summary, the Olympic athlete, like the Homeric warrior, adheres to the main tenets of agonistic conflict, namely: In order to excel one must prove one's excellence by demonstrated superiority of one's physical prowess; involvement in competition serves to give proof of superiority; and engagement in agonal contests is the major form of competition for displaying physical prowess and demonstrating superiority.

## Agonal Contests

Agonal competition is characterized by ritualized contests: (a) between peers; (b) played according to a specific set of rules; (c) emphasizing the display of physical prowess; (d) restricted to time and place; (e) having limited objectives; (f) involving "action"; (g) providing tests of moral character and social worth; and (h) offering a means of determining social rank, recognizing excellence, and according honor.

As previously noted, the purest examples of agonal contests, ranging from chivalrous warfare to athletic games, are found in archetypal warrior societies. In modern times, sports in general (and the Olympic Games in particular) are the primary avenues left for the expression of the agon motif in some residual manner.

### The Greek Contest System

In his classic sociological analysis of the Hellenic world, Gouldner (1965) stressed that a dominant cultural theme was "the active quest for fame through competitive achievement" (p. 45). He emphasized that early Greek society can be analytically viewed as a "contest system, essentially a mechanism of social mobility or a method for distributing prestige or public status among the citizen group: it is a 'game,' if you will, in which aliens or slaves do not play" (1965, pp. 45-46). Similarly, Poliakoff (1987, p. 104) and others argue that in comparison to other cultures, the Greeks oriented themselves significantly toward contest.

*Agon* then, was a ubiquitous feature of ancient Greek society. Athletic contest in particular became for the Greeks the most widespread expression of competition (Poliakoff, 1987, pp. 104-105), with the Olympic Games representing the crowning glory of athletic competition in the ancient Greek world.[2]

## The Olympic Games

At first glance the events and rules characteristic of the ancient and modern Olympic Games seem very dissimilar. However, we briefly show that there are some common elements in these historically varied forms of agonal competition.

*Events.* The first historic Olympic contest, and in fact the only event for the first thirteen Olympiads, was the *stade*—a foot race of about 200 yards. The *diaulos*, or double stade race, was introduced at the 14th Olympiad in 724 B.C.; succeeding Olympiads saw the introduction of the *dolichos* (long-distance footrace), pentathlon, wrestling, boxing, pancration, race-in-armour, chariot racing, various special events for boys, additional equestrian events, and even competitions for heralds and trumpeters (cf., e.g., Gardiner, 1930; Swaddling, 1980, p. 38; Sweet, 1987, pp. 6-7).

In contrast, the 24th modern Olympiad in Seoul was comprised of 23 sports (26 if the aquatics category is broken down into swimming, diving, synchronized swimming, and water polo), involving 237 different athletic competitions, not to mention a number of demonstration sports and events. Like the ancient Games, the modern Games include forms of foot racing, equestrian events, discus and javelin throwing, long jumping, and boxing and wrestling. Thus, there are some specific vestiges of ancient agon in the modern Games.

At an abstract level, the events of both the ancient and modern Games represent, singly or in combination, the efforts of individuals to demonstrate their superior physical prowess in five areas. For example, Weiss (1969) points out that contests pivot about the demonstration or performance of five attributes: "speed, endurance, strength, accuracy, and coordination" (p. 100). Weiss's typology is an interesting one, especially in the way in which he relates his five areas of athletic achievement to the causal forces of time, space, force, and energy.

Although the modern Olympic motto *Citius, altius, fortius* captures only a few of the areas of athletic achievement identified by Weiss (1969), one of the evident appeals of the Olympic Games is the fact that they involve unitary contests emphasizing the specific components of Weiss's typology; for example, speed in the 100-meter sprint, endurance in the marathon race, strength in the weightlifting events, accuracy in archery and shooting competitions, and coordination in diving and gymnastics events. (It is interesting to note that the ancient Games with few exceptions emphasized individual competition.) Admittedly, a number of individual and dual sports also preclude precise classification under Weiss's typology, as for example, fencing and the pole vault. Moreover, Weiss does not explicitly address the agonal component of versatility, that is, the demonstration of relative superiority in several areas. Certainly in antiquity's Olympic Games the winner of the pentathlon was most admired (Kinkead, 1984, p. 73). Within the modern Olympic Games the decathlon has replaced the pentathlon for purposes of identifying the world's best all-around athlete.

***Rules.***    Although all particular contests in the Games have specific rules, we suggest that vestiges of the agon motif can be found in a more generic set of rules applicable to all agonal contests. Gouldner's (1965) analysis of the Greek contest system set forth a set of implicit rules and conditions that we believe to be the basic regulations and circumstances that govern agonal contests in general and not just the Hellenic world in particular. With liberal paraphrasing of Gouldner's set of tacit instructions, we propose that the fundamental guidelines for agonal competition are the following:

1. The goal of the contest is for an individual to win more personal honor and prestige than other contestants.
2. Honor and prestige are won by means of demonstrated physical prowess.
3. The amount of honor and prestige that is won depends on several conditions, including
   - the importance of the contest to all members of a social system,
   - the importance of the contest to the particular peer group of participants,
   - the status and ability of opposing contestants,
   - the degree of difficulty associated with a given form of competition,
   - the value of the prizes (symbolic or material) to be gained in victory or lost in defeat, and
   - the value of the stakes that the contestant risks and the extent of the risk to which these are subjected. (Gouldner, 1965, p. 49)

The application of these rules and conductions is well documented in the context of the Olympic Games. For example, (a) an Olympic gold medal represents the most prestigious prize in all of sport; (b) the status and ability of opposing contestants is of the highest; (c) the Games are of utmost importance to the contestants because they can establish their relative ranking in the world; and (d) the Games are of importance to nation-states because they are held to reflect national character and to serve as an index of moral superiority (cf., Loy, 1981).

***Character contests.***    Finally, in concluding our account of the contest component of agon, we stress that agonal contests are "character" contests as well as "physical" contests because they involve Goffman's (1967) concept of action. By action, Goffman means engagement in activities that are consequential, eventful, fateful, and problematic; that are undertaken for their own sake; and wherein participants may place their very lives at risk (p. 185). Goffman contends that character is best displayed in the context of action; he argues that character contests represent "moral games" in which contestants' moral attributes and qualities are subjected to social evaluation. Every Olympiad illustrates the nature of character contests and offers to the world dramatic examples of the display of such valued moral attributes and heroic virtues as courage, gameness, integrity, and fair play (cf., Loy, 1981).

   Given the character-contesting component of agonal competition, it is not surprising that the Olympics have provided the Western world with a number of its heroes;

from Milo of Croton, called "the greatest Olympic victor of all time" by some (Umminger, 1963), to such modern Olympians of unforgettable achievement as Jim Thorpe, Paavo Nurmi, Mildred "Babe" Didrickson, Jesse Owens, Fanny Blankers-Koen, Bob Mathias, Emil Zatopek, Wilma Rudolph, Al Oerter, Rafer Johnson, Bob Beamon, Mark Spitz, Nadia Comaneci, Vasili Alexeyev, Carl Lewis, and Teofilo Stevenson. We honor such memorable athletes by making them our folk heroes; we give them immortality by casting their statues in bronze, enshrining them in sporting halls of fame, even by putting their faces on cereal boxes and trading cards, or by making dolls in their likenesses. The modern succession of heroic Olympians demonstrates that residues of the agon motif remain in contemporary sport and gives testimony that the embers, if not the fires, of agon burn forever within the human spirit.

# The Flame Motif

*Creatures of a day!*
*What is someone?*
*What is no one?*
*Man: a shadow's dream*
*But when god-given glory comes*
*a bright light shines upon us and our life is sweet.*
Pindar, *Pythian 8*

In *Greek Athletics and the Genesis of Sport* (1988), classicist David Sansone explains the existence and persistence of all sport by conceptualizing sport as a traditional ritual that has persisted outside the context within which it was once appropriate. The single origin for sport is to be found, according to Sansone, in primitive sacrificial ritual. Primordial hunting rituals such as camouflage and purification of the hunter's body before the hunt, the hunt itself, and the ensuing sacrifice and meals of the hunt, are imprinted behavior patterns that have endured as rituals. Specifically, these rituals became "sports" when the hunting, religious behavior arising from the hunt, and energy expended in the hunt were no longer imperative to survival.

## Ancient Fires

If we accept Sansone's (1988) thesis, we can define sport as "the ritual sacrifice of human energy" (p. 37). We recognize that there are problems with Sansone's supposition; namely, that sport cannot be attributed to one ecological origin, and that certain forms of sport, say women's ritual races in antiquity, could not have evolved from hunting ritual. But we are intrigued by the role that Sansone suggests fire played in ritualistic sport. Races to altars, as may have existed in ancient Greece, were "competitions among willing victims to select the best offering for sacrifice" (Kyle, 1988, p. 359).

Alongside these races, hunts, sports, and the rituals that consecrate these activities, can be found the torch, the burning altar, the fire images. Sansone (1988) discusses sport fire in a myriad of ways: Cherokee ball players purify themselves before games with fire; hunters living within the Arctic Circle perform fire rites before the hunt; before a footrace Zuni Indians of New Mexico engage in a ceremony in which a cigarette is passed around from one runner to another; and bonfires before football games are common on college campuses in the U.S. Sansone (1988) believes that the fire ceremony now connected with the opening of the Olympic Games is also a remnant of ancient fire rituals.

Influenced by Sansone's (1988) perception of sport-fire, and following Mircea Eliade's (1952) thought on images, we perceive the sport-festival flame representation to be an image that "precedes and informs cultures, remaining eternally alive and universally accessible," and that through representations such as the sport-flame ceremony, different "histories" can intercommunicate.

In its original form, fire, and later the torch symbol, was probably rooted to the home or hearth, the place where one was safe and satiated; the hearth fire was regarded in many cultures as sacred: ancient Egyptian, Greek, Roman, Gaul, German, Hindu, Japanese, and Aztec (Churchward, 1912; Raglan, 1964). It is likely, then, that fire came to be an attribute of the sacred, and that home, hearth, fire, torch, all were connected with this attribute. Within the context of the sport-flame ceremony, fire also came to be the dynamic element of both the ancient and modern torch runs (Slowikowski, 1982). In ancient torch relay races, never part of the ancient Olympic Games, the flame of the victorious torch was considered sacred and was used to set fire to the great sacrifice, which was the closing act of the ancient Greek festival (Sitlington Sterrett, 1901).

The ancient Greek *lampadephoria* (or, as we know it, "torch race") was originally part of various rituals that honored the deities Athena, Hephaestos, and Prometheus. It possibly originated at the end of the 9th century B.C. to honor these gods (who were in one way or another linked to fire or hearth mythologies), or to transfer "pure" fire from one altar to another. By the 6th century B.C., the *lampadephoria* ritual was included in state festivals inaugurated by leaders such as Peisistratus. Later, the *lampadephoria* was included in festivals all over the Greek world (Slowikowski, 1982). For example, Alexander the Great sponsored a torch race at Soli in 333 B.C., dedicating it to Athena (Slowikowski, 1988).

Where the torch race fire originated, who could carry it, and where its destination was, mirrored social reality of the time—the tradition of the *lampadephoria* was significant as an expression of hegemony at different points in time in the Athenian society. The transference of fire in the torch race expressed the domination of the village altar over the family hearth in the 8th century B.C., showed the ancient family religion predominant over state religion at the beginning of the 5th century, revealed the Athenian Empire's hold over her subjects at the end of the 5th century, and marked the introduction of foreign cults into polis religion through the 4th century. The *lampadephoria* directed peoples' gaze and behavior toward these ideas, giving shape to the Athenians' idea of their society. The concrete form of the torch race indicated to people the state of their society, and by indicating it, helped shape their view of the society (Slowikowski, 1982).

Rothenbuhler (1989) cites Durkheim's conception of modern secular religion as similar to the values, ideas, and sentiments that affirm the present-day Olympic tradition and mark it as different from professional sports. In the same way, the modern Olympic flame takes a place outside of the secular. Furthermore, in a similar manner, the ancient torch-relay was set aside from "athletics," never taking place in any of the great Panhellenic athletic festivals, including the Olympic festival. In smaller city festivals, the event was always separated from other races and athletic events, usually occurring the day before the traditional contests. For several centuries, it seems that the *lampadephoria* was not a contest; it was a sacred ritual act performed by an individual. When it became a relay race, and then a race between individuals, its "sacred" meaning remained. Ancient authors mention that it was considered a religious honor to run in the torch race.

## Modern Fires

Residual sacredness exists today, as is well illustrated by the Los Angeles Olympic Organizing Committee's (LAOOC) torch-run troubles. LAOOC committed itself to producing a "quality" Olympic Games, "quality" being revealed in LAOOC funding organizations like the Boy's Club of America, YMCA, and Special Olympics. The torch relay was created as one means for reaching that funding objective (Shaikin, 1988). Although it cost the bearer $3,000 to personally carry the Olympic torch for one kilometer, the IOC did not consider the program overly commercial (Shaikin, 1988). But there were objections to the money-making torch run venture. The Mayor of Olympia, Greece, asserted that he would prevent the Olympic flame from leaving his town if the sacred torch-relay was to become a money-making event.

The political crusades between and among the LAOOC and Greece that materialized around the torch-relay issue can be understood if we view the torch image as a prior, but still relevant hallowed representation common to humans. The fire of the torch was immediately proximate to the community members of Olympia, a small tourist town, but far removed from the LAOOC members. Although one can purchase anything from can openers and underwear to coins depicting the torch-relay at the kitschy Olympia stores, these items do not tender *real fire* to the customer—only the torch-relay run through the streets does. The actual torches used for the first leg of the relay can be bought for the right price at one of the finer stores in Olympia. What is for sale is the signified—the torch depiction; the signifier, fire, cannot be bought—until the Los Angeles Games, when the torch "buying" created an international stir.

Today's Olympic flame and torch runners, and the articulation of associated sport-fire images in culture, illustrate the transformation of an ancient symbol from its context of origin and of original interpretation—contexts that give the image modern-day authenticity—to a fabricated or invented authenticity. "Authenticity" often derives, in our present life, from conditions or things that evoke nostalgia. We are interested in nostalgia as a cultural form, for although nostalgia may be a private, intensely felt emotion, nostalgia may have a social side as well (Davis, 1979, p. vii).

What are the sources of nostalgic experience in group life? What relevance does nostalgia have in a cultural sense? To answer such questions as they address the sport-flame, we begin with a definition of collective nostalgia as forwarded by Fred Davis in his attempt to frame a sociology of nostalgia. Collective nostalgia is

> a condition in which symbolic objects are of a highly public, widely shared and familiar character, those symbolic resources from the past that under the proper conditions can trigger wave upon wave of nostalgic feeling in millions of persons at the same time. (Davis, 1979, p. 122)

One symbolic object that triggers such nostalgia is the sport-flame ceremony. Nostalgia in this sense is always ideological. In an extraordinary book, *On Longing: Narratives of the Miniature, the Gigantic, the Souvenir, the Collection*, Susan Stewart (1984) deals with the theoretical notion of nostalgia:

> The past that nostalgia seeks has never existed, yet longing for an impossibly pure context of lived experience at a place of origin, nostalgia wears a distinctly utopian face, a face that turns toward a future-past, a past which has only ideological reality. . . nostalgia is the desire for desire. (p. 19)

The longed-for place of origin appears ancient, linked to an immemorial past, yet it is the product of the current day, a selected tradition.

Identified with the sun, the torch and the flame are primordial symbols of purification, occurring in many allegories as the emblem of truth. As used in today's athletic festivals, the antiquity of the torch symbol confers on it a significance that eventually becomes more important than the original significance of the object itself. Whatever is old is authentic, unadulterated, true; old things do not deceive, therefore they stand for truth itself. Whatever is old is also primitive, closer to the "Golden Age" of humanity (Cirlot, 1962, pp. 13, 264, 326, 341; Luckiesh, 1920, pp. 17-18). Through the signifying process, the concepts are revived in culture at the moment one catches sight of the Olympic torch runner, or as millions of spectators observe the ignition of the Olympic flame itself.

Nostalgia may be one of the fundamental feelings (to be read also as powers, aesthetics, erotics) associated with ceremonial gatherings and in large gatherings of people; when the focus of the event is on the movement and ability of the human body, such as in the groupings at athletic festivals, an outlet for nostalgia is sought. When such ceremonies as the sport-flame ritual occur, that sought-after nostalgia is hypostatized. We hypothesize that if the origin of sport lies in its birth as the "ritual sacrifice of physical energy," and if the original rituals were laden with fire images, then modern sport-festival flame ceremonies surely induce nostalgia.

In relation to the modern Olympic Games, what is this nostalgia for? Nostalgia may exist for the solidarity it fosters with the strangers among whom we live (Murray, 1990, p. 213). In the mass society of modernity, we sense that we should be a community, yet even in our own neighborhoods we are strangers to each other. In Olympic Game gatherings, the world community is laid out in front of us in a sort of ideological solidarity. The ideologies become images that are in part constructed through reference to past traditions, such as fire rituals. Eliade (1952), points out that these images express the nostalgia for a "mythicized past"; regrets for a "vanished time"; the "sadness of existence"; and countless other meanings. One example of the archetypes of which Eliade speaks is the sport-festival flame ceremony. What is important about the flame ceremony is that it expresses more than the people who experience it could convey in words. Eliade says that images bring people together, and that images, if anything, activate an "ultimate solidarity" of the human race.

Our culture has absorbed the motif of the Olympic flame, creating around it the image of nostalgia for solidarity referred to above. We have paid too little attention to such nostalgias, and for this reason should study them.

The sport-festival flame ceremony may be one manifestation of a common universal image (Slowikowski, 1991). Within this realm, the sport-festival flame ceremony exists in different, yet also intertwined, contexts. These contexts are all defined by feelings and emotions, which are an important but usually unnoticed part of the momentum of public life and thought (Inglis, 1988).

The representation of the sport-flame can be recognized as a symbol—of authenticity, nostalgia—that has never disappeared from the human psyche. The aspect of symbols such as this may change, but their function remains the same; one has only to look behind their "latest masks" (Eliade, 1952). Moreover, the ceremony is just one example of the idealization of Classical Greece as reconstructed by contemporary society; that is, the image of the sport-flame ritual is a selected traditional ideal in our culture that has been variously blurred and interpreted away from its first representation.

Baudrillard and others tell us that Western culture has increasingly become a civilization of images (Baudrillard, 1983; Boorstin, 1967; Bungay, 1984; Kearney, 1989). The torch image, while it is nostalgic and authentic—an archaic residual— also, as it exists in the culture of the developed world, involves a stripping of its context and a reimmersion in a commercial nexus (Angus & Jhally, 1989). While the torch is a sign and symbol of the primal, nostalgic, and solidaristic, it is also a symbol used for selling copying machines, cereal, clothing, and other items.

The use of stylistic elements may be that of the advertiser, who simply plunders the art of the past for whatever superficial association it is thought will sell the product. Yet, at the same time, around this superficiality, we build up "worlds of culture and of meaning" (O'Hear, 1988, p. 162).

As the modern Olympic Game participants, sponsors, athletes, and spectators become increasingly conscious of their part in the making of history in the Olympic Games, ancient representations undergo a transformation that takes the images from the archaic to consumer good (Smith, 1988). It is in this consumer perception of antiquity, through, for instance, advertisements and T-shirts, that the modern Olympic Games remain surrounded by archaic residues. It is in this "postmodern" perception of antiquity that the ancient Greek world's athletics have impacted modern society, as residuals of an antiquity no one will really know. As Fredric Jameson (1983) reflects in a passage that has become infamous, "for whatever peculiar reasons, we seem condemned to seek the historical past through our own pop images and stereotypes about that past, which itself remains forever out of reach" (p. 118). In our own time, unrealized aspirations are projected, unconsciously or not, onto the screen of antiquity. As far as the Olympic Games go, this projection has been accomplished via archaic athletic symbols such as the torch, vegetation, and pilgrimage motif.

# The Pilgrimage Motif

> *I am amazed at the spectators who you say come from everywhere to the festivals, and are noble and prominent men but neglect their own urgent business for such things.*
>
> Lucian, *Anarcharsis*

Where do we travel and why? What places are important destinations to us? How does traveling change over time, in terms of where and why we travel? Once we arrive at a destination, what do we do?

James Clifford (1990) has recently asked such questions of cultures themselves, rethinking whole geographical areas and groups of people as sites of dwelling and travel. Others as well have contemplated travel experience as understood in relation to cultural and social features of shifting history. They detail, in Judith Adler's (1989) words "space and time—and the traveller's own body as it moves through both—as the baseline elements of all travel performance" (p. 7).

We find it valuable to reconsider the Olympic Games through the span of time by asking such questions as Clifford and Adler have of culture. Thus, we examine travel to the Olympic Games in terms of three themes, namely: the sites of the Olympic Games as pilgrimage centers; "touristic" authenticity; and the souvenir. Mostly, we are curious about the spectator, or traveler to the Games in relation to these themes, commenting on the athlete only in passing.

A pilgrimage center is a congregation area, set apart from the ordinary, drawing pilgrims from distances near and far (Moore, 1980, p. 207). Symbols and myths, understood by pilgrims, and common activities decorate the pilgrimage center. That travelers may perform ritual acts to enter and leave the center is best understood in reference to Van Gennep (1960) and Victor Turner's (1969, 1974) "rites of passage" and "liminality"; or in terms of the idea that pilgrimages are "calendrical rites which intensify the ordinary structure of the participants" (Moore, p. 210; cf. also Chapple & Coon, 1942). As such, the Olympic Game site, archaic and contemporary, is a pilgrimage center.

## Olympic Travels

When ancient Greeks traveled, they thought of who had come before them. The Greeks were concerned with lineage, corporally as well as geographically. In his

*Guidebook*, before telling of what he saw at and on the way to the Olympic site in Elis, Pausanias (himself a Roman tourist of the 2nd century A.D.), tells us of original inhabitants, of immigrants, of newcomers, of ancient kings that peopled the lands of Greece that lay beyond and around the Olympic site. Today, Olympic travelers are concerned with the area and inhabitants surrounding the Game site, but many times such interest and knowledge is defined by the media, who present us with visual and written "close-ups" and histories of the Olympic locale. While the highlight of a trip we make to the Games today probably surrounds the sojourn *within* and immediately surrounding the Olympic festival area, the ancient Greeks appreciated the journey *to* the festival area, which they made partially by boat, on foot, or by donkey.

Ancient literature mentions statues of import and cities in ruin that will be passed on the journey to Olympia; where to catch fish; where to find caves that cure leprosy. Upon leaving the Olympic Games site, the ancient texts speak of "Kyllene, fifteen miles from Elis" that gives good anchorage for shipping; "the river Larisos nearly twenty miles from Elis if travelling into Achaia"; and of territory beyond Elis that is productive and fruitful, "good for fine flax" (Pausanias 5-6).

At the start, the ancient Greeks traveled to the Olympic Games to participate in them as athletes, judges, or priests. There were few spectators. The Olympic stadium was a natural grass amphitheater—Pausanias (6.20.8) called it "a mound of earth" and not a very deep one at that. Constructed stone seats existed only for the ten to twelve *Hellanodikai*, judges of the Games; and a single altar seat for the priestess of Demeter (Slowikowski, 1989).

Athletes, judges, and trainers began the journey to Olympia months before the game in time to prepare for the festival, for athletes were required to enter a mandatory month-long training program under the eyes of the Olympic judges. Housing consisted of pitched tents and camping in the outskirts of the festival area. Later, from about the 5th century B.C. onward, the Games attracted thousands of visitors, among them "poets and sculptors, pilgrims and politicians, magicians and peddlers, and ordinary citizens looking for a good time" (Miller, 1990, p. 1).

In short, every four years for several centuries, crowds set out from all parts of the Greek world, suffering hardships on long and difficult journeys, to arrive at Olympia. Ancient literature mentions treacherous seas, precipitous mountains, long winding roads, "horribly displeasing water," "strong wild lions," and sand so silty that "even an athletic man can sink into it" (Pausanias, 5-6). Today, a traveler to the Olympic Games typically only suffers from the bureaucratic turmoils associated with a lost ticket or passport, or perhaps the temporary ills resulting from the consumption of foreign foods. Admittedly, however, there is the present danger of threats of terrorism related to Olympic travel.

But given the hazards confronted by early travelers to the Olympic Games, why did so many make the arduous journey to Olympia? Although we know a great deal about the production of the ancient Olympic Games, we know very little about the desire that attracted thousands to the games over many centuries. We know that people came to watch the contests, especially the equestrian events. Yet, we know virtually nothing about what spectators felt or did at the Games, beyond their rounds to sacrifice at the many Olympic altars.

Archaeological evidence does tell us that Olympia must have been filled with "tents and temporary hutches, stalls for peddlers, a continual din of animals and of human voices, and smoke from a thousand campfires and from the sacrifices performed almost continually" at various altars (Miller, 1990, p. 8). We know that Olympic visitors purchased food in nearby Elis, and wood at the Olympic grounds, to burn sacrifices of incense or meat. Ancient literature speaks of a "woodman" at ancient Olympia who provided timber at a fixed price to cities and private individuals for their sacrifices at such altars (Pausanias 5.13.3).

In summary, in the context of antiquity, Olympia was a sacred site and travel to the Games represented religious pilgrimages. We suggest that in the context of modernity, travel to the Games has latent overtones of religious pilgrimages to the extent that such travel redeems and transfigures the traveler. In any event, both ancient and modern travelers to the Olympics acknowledge the lure of the Games, and both leave with mementos.[3] However, each have differing prototypical tourist itineraries.

## Olympic Souvenirs

Today, the trip to the Olympic Games is no longer an experience of travel as it was for the Greeks; it is a touristic experience. In Culler's *Framing the Sign* (1988); MacCannell's *The Tourist* (1976); and Paul Fussell's *Abroad* (1972)—important books for the issues of concern here—it is pointed out that today "there is no more travel, only tourism" (Culler, 1988, p. 156). Fussell (1972) distinguishes tourism from travel, illuminating some of the issues we briefly explore in regard to athletic motifs. Fussell says that in tourism, the traveler seeks to raise social status at home; "realize secret fantasies of erotic freedom"; and to pose momentarily as a member of a social class superior to one's own—"to play a role of a shopper and a spender whose life becomes exciting only when one is exercising power by choosing what to buy" (p. 42). Seen in this light, travel to the Olympic Games ceases today to be an activity, experience, or undertaking, as it was in ancient Greece, and "becomes instead a commodity" (Boorstin, 1967, p. 84). One quests to obtain the best tickets for the best events, the closest hotel, the touch or word from an Olympic athlete.

Tourists, and the media associated with tourists, commodify travel into a quest for the authentic: As pointed out by Culler (1988), "authenticity is a major selling point in advertisements and travel writing. . . . Wanting to be less touristy than other tourists is part of being a tourist" (p. 158). For the world's billion sport fans, Olympic Game attendance is the ultimate *authentic* act of spectatorship, proved or commodified by securing "the" authentic souvenir (which varies from mass pro- duced Olympic flags, pins, T-shirts, programs, paperweights, and coins, to items— clothing, medals, sport implements, torches—meant for and once exclusively owned by the primary and secondary producers of the Olympic Games: the athletes, judges, and organizers.

These mementos, called "markers" by MacCannell (1973), represent the Olympic Game visit, make it valid, and recognize it. Markers frame and authenticate something as a sight for tourists. In this framing, the tourists may surround themselves with reproductions of the sight (Culler, 1988). The Olympic Game tourist (as well as other tourists) often continues to collect these markers, part of a seemingly human desire to possess objects.

In fact, James Clifford (1988) calls "some sort of gathering" around the self, "the assemblage of a material world, the marking off of a subjective domain that is not 'other'," (p. 218) universal. Remy G. Saisselin (1984) refers to this urge to collect as "bibelotization." Bibelotization is the democratization of possession, acquisition, and production; it is selling, buying, and finding a bargain. One example of the democratization of collecting is in collections created by Olympic-Game goers.

We may conceptualize the Olympic Game collection, whether it be pins, T-shirts, coins, flags, or programs, as echoing a longing for "inner" experience (Stewart, 1984). Collecting in this manner is part of "having a culture, selecting and cherishing an authentic collective property. Collecting, then, is the gathering up of possessions in arbitrary systems of value and meaning" (Clifford, 1988, p. 217). Furthermore, in discovering and acquiring Olympic related collections and "archaic" artifacts, like "old" torches, uniforms, or pins (which may actually be from the current Olympic Games), the authentic, nostalgic experience of the Olympic Games is deployed, circulated, and made valuable in culture.

Pins, which have been around the Olympics for decades, are a good example of the Olympic collection. In 1984, 30 million copies of one Olympic pin were produced, and as many as 20,000 "pinheads" (i.e., Olympic pin collectors) a day crowded into pin swapping and selling tents at the Los Angeles Olympic grounds. What the pins represent is imaginary: As one collector noted, "you devote yourself to collecting the teams you don't belong to and nations you've never visited" (Neff, 1988, p. 79). Baudrillard comments that such collecting is a dimension of our life that is both essential and imaginary (as noted by Clifford, 1988, p. 220).

What is remarkable, in terms of considering the ancient and modern festivals, the archaic and residual, is that modern Olympic markers are used to capture the past, for the past is viewed as authentic. But we have seen that modern markers of the Olympic visit cannot truly capture the authentic past. The past Olympic Games consisted, if we listen to the ancient writers, as much with getting to the games, performing appropriate libations at altars, and leaving the games, as it did in watching the games.

Today, the Olympic Games and site are structured commercially, broken up into parts to be consumed, including the stands, museums, and trading areas. Everyone mingled together at the ancient Games, nothing purposefully marked the site as authentic; spectators did not seek souvenirs labeled as authentic, or nostalgic. In contrast, MacCannell (1973, 1976) and Culler (1988) argue that Erving Goffman's (1967) front and back regions code authenticity for today's tourists. "There is a distinction between front and back, or between what is there to be shown to tourists and what is genuine" (Culler, 1988, p. 165). Listen to the voices in a crowd of

Olympic spectators today. Each feels superior to other Olympic travelers for having ventured into Olympic back regions: meeting athletes at a bar; getting in early to see a gymnast warm up; running a lap in the stadium; obtaining a pin through a trade with one of the track and field judges.

Although we have countered that past and present spectatorship and travel to the Games differ significantly, we have also suggested that symbols of the *past* are used in contemporary touristic markers to mark active sites as authentic. Such a marking of the ancient as authentic takes place in the present-day sport-flame ceremony, which is framed as ancient, but which is indeed modern; in the vegetation motifs associated with Olympic prizes; and in subtler ways, through traditions like the sport-flame ceremony, passed on to generations as an heirloom is.[4] We value these heirlooms, these motifs, and the practices associated with them, because they allow us experiences that are transcendent, that lift us up and make us feel a sense of awe. Experiences that take place at the Olympic Games that are framed as archaic, such as the flame ceremony, give us this feeling of awe.

Similarly, modern-day souvenirs with symbolically imbedded residuals of the past attached to them may "lift us up," make us feel a sense of awe. For example, Olympic T-shirts, coins, and advertisements depict the ancient Greek motif of the black running figure-outline of the classical Greek vase. Visually, the Greek black running figure is a paradigm of a mode of representation unique to the art of antiquity. Yet this perception of antiquity impacts the observer as an illumination of the past, thus attaching the authenticity that we have referred to throughout. Accordingly, the appearance on Olympic paraphernalia of motifs such as the Greek black-running figure have allowed the traditionally closed, select, elite audience of classical Greek art to have been broadened to mass or popular culture access by way of the exchange of souvenirs: Archaic representations from the past are borrowed and residually made part of the active present in things like Olympic T-shirts and reproductions of torches. We note also that beyond the Olympic realm, the sport-athletic and health theme has tended to be a vehicle by which classical Greek motifs are taken up in popular culture.

# Gift Giving and Social Exchange

> *Honored, they honor, decorated they decorate, the giver everywhere is glorified.*
>
> M. Mauss, *The Gift*, quoted from
> *Anucasanaparvan* Book 8, 1. 5850, of the *Mahabharata*

If we have been at all persuasive in our discussions of the agon, flame, and pilgrimage motifs, then the reader should be as intrigued as we are as to why selected Olympic traditions, albeit in altered forms, have survived for centuries. Although a variety of explanations might be offered, we speculate that the long-lasting influence of selected motifs and traditions is related to the phenomenon of gift giving.

To paraphrase Tumin's (1967) analysis of the phenomenon of social stratification, gift giving is (a) social, (b) ancient, (c) ubiquitous, (d) diverse in its forms, and (e) consequential. Gift giving is a universal behavior (Sherry, 1983) that involves processes of communication, economic exchange, social exchange, and socialization (Belk, 1979). Moreover, gift-giving generates identity, creates suspense, serves as a mechanism of social control, results in feelings of status anxiety, and develops attitudes of both gratitude and envy (Schwartz, 1967).

Huizinga (1955) has shown that the gift mode of social exchange has its origins in play and ritual. In turn, Marcel Mauss (1967), the classic discussant of gifts, has shown that the gift mode of exchange is founded on a set of moral obligations rising from religious origins, namely, the obligation to give, the obligation to receive, and the obligation to repay. Mauss wrote that in giving, a person gives himself or herself.

## The Fire Motif

To illustrate the nature of the gift mode of exchange within the context of the Olympic Games, we return to our analysis of the fire and agon motifs. We begin with Mauss (1967) who avowed that gift exchange is not only concrete, it is expressed in myth and imagery, symbolically and collectively. We look to Mauss's conception now, in first examining the ancient torch race as a type of gift exchange.

### Leitourgiai

Just as sponsorship is crucial for the existence of today's sporting spectacles, so too was it in ancient Greece, where the sponsorship of the torch race took the form of a particular type of gift exchange, the potlatch. This form of gift-giving involves feasting and heightened conspicuous consumption in which wealth is lavishly bestowed and sometimes actually thrown away or destroyed.

Some of the chief recurring expenses of the classical Greek city-state were for sacrifices and festivals, which had come to be magnificently elaborate. Festival expenses were met through the state treasury, and also through contributions by wealthy citizens. These contributions were called *leitourgiai*, and entailed providing a proper diet, instructors, torches, and oil for up to one hundred torch runners for a month, as well as decorating the scene of the contest and providing prizes for the race. Citizens who undertook such an exorbitant (and thus we have referred to this exchange as "potlatch"[5]) chore may have gained political and social credit, proved their patriotism, won the goodwill of the community, showed off their wealth, or maintained superiority.[6] Two ancient literary passages referring to the sponsorship of the torch race echo this sentiment: "[They] are burdensome to those to whom they are assigned, although conferring upon them a kind of distinction" (Isocrates, *Panathenaic Oration* 145), and, "He impaired his own livelihood for the public good" (*Inscriptiones Graecae* 4.2.65, 2.2.3206.12-15).

As a gift-mode of exchange, the reciprocity involved with the torch race *leitourgiai* persisted in the ancient Greek society from the 6th century B.C. through the 2nd century A.D. There is evidence that torch race *leitourgiai* were used as measures of character, that they occasioned the erection of commemorative monuments, and that they were included in official records issued by the state. Plutarch documents the politician Nicias's activities in the 5th century B.C.: "He tried to captivate the people by choral and gymnastic contests, and other like prodigality, outdoing in the costliness and elegance of these all his predecessors and contemporaries" (Plutarch, *Nicias* 111). In brief, the idea of torch races and gymnastic contests held at a noble's expense expressed an adaptation of the gift ethic in ancient Greek society.

In a related argument, Donlan (1981) suggests that the *leitourgia* was a means for aristocrats to suggest their superiority without antagonizing the sensibilities of their subordinates in society at large. Thus *leitourgiai* were especially important in the democratic Athenian society of the 5th century when every citizen was allegedly socially equal and when there was supposedly no "best" citizen.

## Modern Sport Flames

Ancient and modern "torch runs" differ in what they signify, in their context, in their practice, in how they are conceptualized, and in how they are experienced. On the other hand, past and present flame ceremonies denote and connote two forms of gift giving. First, the flame ceremony continues to express the giving of a social gift: Powerful donors designate who will receive the honor of carrying the Olympic flame. The norm of reciprocity underlying this gift mode of exchange serves to initiate relationships, as when South Korea's most renowned sports hero (Sohn Kee Chung, marathon gold medalist in the 1936 Games) handed the torch to Lim Chun Ae, a national heroine of the 1986 Games whose eardrum was ruptured in 1987 when her coach slapped her. It can also serve to sustain relationships or to heal relationships gone wrong, as evidenced in the selection of Jim Thorpe's grandson to carry the Olympic flame in 1984. Second, the flame ceremony serves as both a spiritual and erotic gift, as in the sense that gifts are a pattern of "spiritual bonds between things which are to some extent parts of persons" (Mauss, 1967, p. 11). Hyde (1983) and Murray (1990) also point out that gifts have an erotic force, erotic in the sense that gifts unite or bind people together.

The aesthetic and erotic power of the sport-flame as gift has elicited certain cultural dispositions, arrangements, and styles that favorably respond to, or complement, other elements of the society in question. Inglis (1988) urges us to ask how such cultural dispositions provide for the perpetuation of certain feelings, for cultural productions like the sport-flame ceremony "may exert a power going far beyond the warmth of individual responses, now aggregated, and convertible into a mass of unearthed energy whose force cannot be classified, organized or understood" (p. 54).

We have noted that the sport-flame ceremony constitutes both particular and general modes of gift-giving. The specific act of passing on the flame from one person to another reflects a gift mode of exchange, but also at a more abstract level the passing on of the tradition of the flame ceremony itself represents a type of gift-giving.

The sport-flame tradition is a type of symbolic gift that encompasses not only individuals, families, or ethnic groups, but entire cultures. In postmodernity, traditions like the flame ceremony connect cultures across space by way of their exchange as gifts in the active, present-day sense, and they connect generations across time, in the passive, past-period sense, as kinds of heirlooms. Of course, these cultural heirlooms are embellished to match the standards and styles of the particular period, as for example, the same spirit in which we reframe photos of our great grandfather, or remount our grandmother's ring in a contemporary setting. The sport-flame as cultural heirloom was first passed on as an ancient Greek brush torch; centuries later it appeared as a metal torch constructed by Krupps Steel Company for the 1936 Olympic Games; and today the torch appears as a vivid media image for a variety of commodities, including the Olympic Games.

## The Gift-Giving Motif

The gift mode of social exchange is especially characteristic of honor-sensitive and contest-based societies or social groups. Within modern societies, honor-sensitive, contest-based social groups are found among underclass ethnic youth gangs and within the institutional spheres of academic science, the military, performing arts, and sport. Each of these social formations reveals the active quest for excellence through competitive achievement, the need of individuals to determine their relative superiority, and the desire of individuals to have their superiority socially recognized. Because these social formations tend to emphasize status relative to wealth or power as the primary form of social recognition, the gift mode of social exchange is a particularly appropriate mechanism of social control.

To illustrate the nature of the gift mode of exchange in terms of the agon motif, we give four comparative examples of the athlete in action. First, like a "macho" member of an ethnic youth gang, the athlete self-assertedly displays physical prowess in an effort to receive enhanced status from peers. In the case of either a gang member or an athlete, the demonstration of physical prowess under conditions of top class competition or high risk is especially valued.

Second, like the military, sport holds up certain ideal heroic virtues such as bravery and courage; the athlete, like the soldier, is admired for acts (gifts, if you will) of gallantry. In exchange for these gifts of gallantry, the athlete and soldier are honored by both peers and the public at large.

Third, like the performing artist, the athlete gives creative performances in exchange for public recognition. The athlete, like the performing artist,

> must produce a final, instantaneous and temporal image of the world as embodied in the score without error, with full mastery of highly developed technical means of performance, and with sufficient warmth, spontaneity, and freshness to induce an audience to suspend its awareness of all other worlds but the world framed by the score and created by the performance. (Bensman & Lilienfeld, 1973, p. 61)

The greater the level of difficulty of the performance, the greater the social recognition of the athlete or performing artist.

Fourth, the athlete, like the scientist, exchanges original contributions for peer and public recognition. The normative structure of science is based on the exchange of social recognition for the contribution of original knowledge; the normative structure of sport is based on the exchange of social recognition for contributions of original athletic feats.

> In science, the acceptance by scientific journals of contributed manuscripts establishes the donor's status as a scientist—indeed, status as a scientist can be achieved only by such gift giving—and it assures him of prestige within the scientific community. (Hagstrom, 1965, p. 13; cf. Collins, 1968; Storer, 1966)

Similarly, in sport, public recognition of contributed record-breaking performances establishes the donor's status as a true athlete and assures the athlete status within the sporting community and a degree of prestige with the public at large.

We suggest that the desire to demonstrate bodily excellence in return for social recognition is the heart of the social exchange process between athletes and spectators within modern sport in general, and within the modern Olympic Games in particular. This is not to say that all athletes are motivated by the desire to demonstrate bodily excellence, nor to say that social recognition is always the primary reward for athletic performance. We believe, however, that the quest for bodily excellence is a sport ideal and that the normative structure and ideology of the Olympic Games is oriented toward this ideal, or agon motif.

## Prizes and the Vegetation Motif

We have argued that it is the desire for status in the form of peer prestige or social honor rather than wealth or power per se that distinguishes participants in agonal contests. Of course, a competitive game may be a competition for power or wealth, not merely for status. Yet, there are countless examples "where status and only status" is what the game is about (Runciman, 1968, p. 40). Or, as Huizinga (1955, p. 50) emphasized in his analysis of the civilizing functions of play and contest, the competitive "instinct" may not be a desire for power. The important thing may be to outperform others and be honored for that. Granted the primacy of status relative to wealth or power in agonal contests, it is not surprising that symbolic rewards often outweigh material rewards for successful performances.

It is difficult to think of an institutional sphere other than sport (save perhaps the military) wherein so much is made of such symbolic awards as medals, prizes, ribbons, trophies, and honorific offices. Perhaps these symbolic rewards (gifts for outstanding performances) are merely a historical legacy carried over from a time when athletic performance did not provide much material advantage for successful athletes. Nevertheless, they still serve as a means of celebrating heroes and as a mechanism of social control (Goode, 1978).

Goode (1978) has noted that the importance of symbolic awards is that they (a) sift and evaluate the participants, and thus furnish information about how each individual ranks in his or her area of achievement; (b) indicate that one's talents are worthy of respect; (c) provide proof that one has achieved a certain level of performance; (d) greatly influence the future careers of the individuals who receive them; (e) are public announcements that attract a far wider audience than just the winners; (f) give prestige to achievements that seem so outstanding that not honoring them is to deny some supposed values of society; (g) give prestige primarily to activities that do not pay off very well materially; and last, but not least, (h) enhance the social identity of both individuals and groups (pp. 156-171).

Interestingly, many of the symbolic awards associated with sport in general, and with the Olympic Games in particular, have a vegetation motif; for example, bouquets of flowers, garlands, and wreaths. One ritual connected with victory in the ancient game for which we have a good deal of evidence is that of the decoration of the victorious athlete with woolen fillets, long strips of wool dyed red that were tied around the athlete's head, arm, or legs to mark him as a victor in various events in the days or hours before he was awarded the actual crown of olive (Thucydides 4.121.1, 5.50.4; Pausanias 6.1.7, 6.22.2, 6.20.19; Plutarch, *Pericles* 28.5; Sansone, 1988). For example, Pindar calls "take up his crown, his fillet of fine wool; and send him this winged new song!" (Pindar, *Isthmian* 5.61-63, as quoted by Sansone, 1988, p. 83).

The crowning of the victorious athlete with leaves or feathers may be related to the original purpose of crowning the head with vegetation: The primitive hunter disguised or camouflaged himself with vegetation to blend in with his surroundings. Sansone (1988, p. 82) asserts that the woolen bands were the last vestige of the primitive hunting practice of dressing up in the hide of the victim. According to Sansone, the victorious athlete of antiquity wore a crown of vegetation and held branches in his hands as a token of his sacrificial character (pp. 86-88).

The ancient athlete himself, then, was a gift of a sacrificial nature, identified symbolically by the vegetation he held or wore. The vegetation that he held and was adorned with represented, according to Mauss's (1967) "theory of alms," "on the one hand a moral idea about gifts and wealth and on the other of an idea about sacrifice" (p. 15). Whatever the original meaning of the fillets, vegetation, and branches worn or held by victorious athletes, the ancient symbol of the practice has persisted. Modern athletes often receive bouquets of flowers and are crowned or beribboned with vegetation, or subtle imitations of vegetation, as can be found in advertising and television examples.

The vegetation motif within contemporary sport has come to concretize a different set of relationships and circumstances than it did within ancient Greek athletics, yet one might argue that the athletic vegetation props act as a bridge to displaced meaning. To this extent, the vegetation crownings tell us not who we are, but who we wish to be. That is, meaning that is relocated in time or space is a fundamental strategy that cultures and individuals use to deal with discrepancy between the "real" and the "ideal" (McCracken, 1988, p. 117).

The palm or vegetation as expressions of fulfillment, elevation, and exaltation are the two traditional attributes of victory. Within the realm of sport today, the victory leaves imprinted on Olympic medals, programs, T-shirts, and so on, are means of tradition by which we commune with the myths of our society, with the link to our ancient past. Postmodernists suggest that there is in industrialized societies a growing interest in "primitive" art, the search for authentic experiences, and a nostalgia for the past. Through props such as the vegetation, sport-flame, or agon motifs, modern society attaches itself to the archaic. At the same time, the traditional history of one society—in our example, ancient Greece—is absorbed into the universal heritage history of the present and more powerful society.

The discovery of long-lived traditions, then, not only highlights the human relation to the past and to imperial powers (Hobsbawm & Ranger, 1983), but, more importantly, such discovery reveals continuing nonchanging human need, such as the need of warmth from a fire, the need for the solidarity gained through community, and the need to know how one measures up to the very best.

# Conclusion

*As is the generation of leaves, so is that of humanity. The wind scatters the leaves on the ground, but the live timber burgeons with leaves again in the season of spring returning. So one generation of men will grow while another dies.*

Homer, *Iliad*

In our analysis of the ancient athletic motifs associated with the Olympic Games, we have attempted to demonstrate how archaic representations from the past are borrowed and residually made part of the active present. We have tried to understand, in a cultural intendment, why the need for such images has come to be felt.

We have tried to highlight both the differences and similarities between the ancient and contemporary agon motifs as they are revealed in culture through athletics. In so doing, we have emphasized that not only in athletics, but in culture as a whole, these motifs have been created, transformed, and contested, and continue to be so at this very moment.

Two motifs connected to agon—fire and vegetation—have been shown to be cultural complexities, chameleons that selectively represent such ideals as patriotism or authenticity (Slowikowski, 1991). We may even consider such images to be icons, special images intended to put us in relationship to the sacred. When we study icons as they appear within patches of culture—such as Olympic Games—we are led to what a society values. Some of modernity's values associated with the present-day Olympic Games are woven into the cultural concepts of tourism. We have illuminated the differences between ancient and modern travel to and from the Olympic Festivals, demonstrating that one *traveled* to the ancient Games, but that one *tours* the modern Games. We have discussed the postmodernist concepts of authenticity and nostalgia as they inform travels to Olympic Games, and we have tied these concepts to the topic of collecting by arguing that the human desire to possess "markers" of where one has been is part of a cultural tradition of gift exchange, of passing something down or handing something on.

Lévi-Strauss (1966, p. 233) contends that the West is a "hot" society, one committed by ideological principle to its own transformation through continual change. We have tried to illustrate that the symbolic senses of some archaic motifs associated with the modern Olympic Games have served the purpose of tempering our hot society, of reminding our hot society, in a nostalgic way, of its past, of its bonds to the worth of community, of its gift exchanges.

Our perception of the past is today often an artificial script of what we believe to be the past, and the motifs, the peripherals found in association with our great Olympic fest today, serve our culture as a kind of access to a past that is otherwise inaccessible to us. The motifs allow us to participate in, and even in a sense to take possession of, the meaning of a past that we have created through the selection of particular archaic traditions. The motifs illuminate the access to the past because they recall, in both an affective and cognitive way, what we have invented or selected to be primitive universals such as agonistic competitions, material fires and symbolic flames, and religious pilgrimages to sacred sites.

Perhaps the ancient athletic motifs that we have described are in fact primitive universals, reflecting Becker's (1973, 1975) general principle of "immortality-striving." Becker argues that everyone seeks immortality, identifying with any kind of self-expression that he or she believes gives immortality. Immortality is "sacred"; an icon of all times. Homeric heroes, athletes, and the humanity of modernity value immortality.

Becker (1971) uniquely defined culture as a "structure of rules, customs and ideas which serve as a vehicle for heroism" (p. 78). He asserted that every individual wants to know where he or she ranks as a hero, that is, how outstanding they are relative to their peers and "significant others" (p. 76). He further contended that the determination of heroic rank is governed by artificial edifices that he called *cultural hero systems*, "the channels culture affords the individual for making a secure contribution to the world despite the realization that his contribution is a finite one" (Scimecca, 1979, p. 63).

We tentatively propose that modern sport in general, and Olympic Games in particular, constitute self-contained cultural hero systems, and that individuals actively and vicariously identify with such systems in order to achieve some semblance of immortality. The athletic motifs associated with these systems—themselves the immortal symbols of contest, fire, vegetation—serve to reinforce Becker's notion that immortality-striving is a universal icon of humankind.

# Notes

1. Although we have used nonsexist language in our chapter, many of the original Greek documents and other classic works we cite are sexist in terms of present-day conventions. We acknowledge that these quotations may, in the words of the *APA Publication Manual*, be interpreted as "biased, discriminatory or demeaning"; however, we have quoted the originals as they stand, lest our essay become overburdened with *sics*.

2. Yalouris (1976, p. 80) points out that *Agon* (Contest) had already assumed a concrete form by the beginning of the 5th century B.C., and a statue of him holding jumping weights in his hands was set up in the sanctuary at Olympia. There was also a representation of him, in relief, on the gold and ivory table

on which the crowns intended for the Olympic victors were laid. The coins of Peparethos (modern Skopelos), dated 500-480 B.C., also have a picture of *Agon*.

3. As they do today, travelers to the pilgrimage center may also have bought trinkets and souvenirs as symbols of their journey. In and on the perimeter of the Olympic grounds, archaeologists have unearthed thousands of small bronze animals—mostly deer and bulls that are thought to have been "souvenirs" purchased at vendor stands set up for the tenure of the games. These souvenirs were most likely good luck charms, and also proved that one had made the journey to Olympia.

4. Dorst (1989, pp. 132-134) discusses tradition that is like gift-giving, saying that "the affinity of gift giving and tradition appears most vividly, perhaps, in the heirloom, which is often given as a gift but represents a link between generations" (p. 133). Dorst cites "Thomas Mann's *The Magic Mountain* as a meditation on the affective properties of the heirloom, of the sense it gives 'of change in the midst of duration, of time as flowing and persisting, of recurrence in continuity'." We used the same idea as Dorst (see "Modern Sport Flames" and "The Gift-Giving Motif" later in this chapter) without being aware of his work until the final draft of our essay.

5. Modern Olympic Games themselves are a form of potlatch undertaken by the nations and cities that sponsor them. The host city attempts to make its games bigger, better, and more expensive; also, the hospitality involved reflects a giving.

6. See Donlan, 1981, for discussion of other ancient Greek aristocratic gifting practices.

# References

A. Modern Authors

Adler, J. (1989). Origins of sightseeing. *Annals of Tourism Research*, **16**, 7-29.

Angus, I., & Jhally, S. (Eds.) (1989). *Cultural politics in contemporary America*. New York and London: Routledge.

Baudrillard, J. (1983). *Simulations*. New York: Semiotext(e) Inc.

Becker, E. (1971). *The birth and death of meaning* (2nd Ed.). New York: Free Press.

Becker, E. (1973). *The denial of death*. New York: Free Press.

Becker, E. (1975). *Escape from evil*. New York: Free Press.

Belk, R. (1979). Gift-giving behavior. In J. Sheath (Ed.), *Research in marketing* (Vol. 2, pp. 95-126). Greenwich, CT: JAL Press.

Bensman, J., & Lilienfeld, R. (1973). *Craft and consciousness*. New York: John Wiley and Sons.

Boorstin, D. (1967). *The image*. New York: Atheneum.

Brantlinger, P. (1990). *Cruesoe's footprints: Cultural studies in Britain and America*. New York and London: Routledge.

Bungay, S. (1984). *Beauty and truth*. London: Oxford University Press.

Chapple, E., & Coon, C. (1942). *Principles of anthropology*. New York: Henry Holt.

Churchward, A. (1912). *Signs and symbols of primordial man*. Edinburgh: Riverside Press Limited.

Cirlot, J.E. (1962). *A dictionary of symbols.* New York: Philosophical Library.

Clifford, J. (1988). *The predicament of culture: Twentieth-century ethnography, literature and art.* Cambridge and London: Harvard University Press.

Clifford, J. (1990, April). *Traveling others, traveling selves.* Paper presented at conference, Cultural Studies Now and in the Future, Urbana, IL.

Collins, R. (1968). Competition and social control in science. *Sociology of Education,* **41,** 123-140.

Culler, J. (1988). *Framing the sign: Criticism and its institutions.* Oxford: Basil Blackwell.

Davis, F. (1979). *Yearning for yesterday: A sociology of nostalgia.* New York: The Free Press.

De Coubertin, P., Philemon, T., Politis, N.G., & Anninos, C. (1896). *The Olympic Games 776 B.C. - 1896 A.D.: The Olympic Games of 1896.* Athens: Charles Beck.

Donlan, W. (1981). *The aristocratic ideal in ancient Greece.* Lawrence, KS: Coronado Press.

Dorst, J.D. (1989). *The written suburb: An American site, an ethnographic dilemma.* Philadelphia: University Press.

During, S. (1989). After death—Raymond Williams in the modern era. *Critical Inquiry,* **15,** 681-703.

Eagleton, T. (Ed.) (1989). *Raymond Williams: Critical perspectives.* London: Polity Press.

Eliade, M. (1952). *Images and symbols: Studies in religious symbolism.* New York: Sheed and Ward.

Fussell, P. (1972). *Abroad.* New York: Oxford University Press.

Gardiner, E.N. (1930). *Athletics of the ancient world.* Chicago: Ares.

Goffman, E. (1967). *Interaction ritual.* Garden City, NY: Doubleday.

Goode, W.J. (1978). *The celebration of heroes.* Berkeley: University of California Press.

Gouldner, A.W. (1965). *Enter Plato.* New York: Basic Books.

Hagstrom, W.O. (1965). *The scientific community.* New York: Basic Books.

Hobsbawm, E., & Ranger, T. (Eds.) (1983). *The invention of tradition.* New York: Cambridge University Press.

Huizinga, J. (1955). *Homo Ludens: A study of the play element in culture.* Boston: Beacon Press.

Hyde, L. (1983). *The gift: Imagination and the erotic life of property.* New York: Vintage.

Inglis, F. (1988). *Popular culture and political power.* London: Harvester Wheatsheaf.

Jameson, F. (1983). Postmodernism and consumer society. In H. Foster (Ed.), *The anti-aesthetic essays on postmodern culture.* Port Townsend, WA: Bay Press.

Johnson, R.W. (1990, February 8). Moooovement. *London Review of Books,* pp. 5-6.

Kearney, R. (1989). *The wake of imagination. Toward a postmodern culture.* Minneapolis: University of Minnesota Press.

King, K.C. (1987). *Achilles.* Berkeley: University of California Press.

Kinkead, E. (1984, July). The original Olympiads. *The New Yorker* (pp. 72-74, 77-79).

Kyle, D.G. (1988). Essay review. [Review of *Greek athletics and the genesis of sport*]. *Journal of Sport History,* **15,** 356-361.

Lenk, H. (1985). Towards a philosophical anthropology of the Olympic athlete and/as the achieving being. In *Report of the twenty-second session of the International Olympic Academy, July 11-25, 1982* (pp. 163-177). Lausanne: International Olympic Committee.

Lévi-Strauss, C. (1966). *The savage mind.* Chicago: University of Chicago Press.

Loy, J.W. (1981). An emerging theory of sport spectatorship: Implications for the Olympic Games. In J. Segrave & D. Chu (Eds.), *Olympism* (pp. 162-204). Champaign, IL: Human Kinetics.

Loy, J.W., Jr., & Hesketh, G.L. (1984). The agon motif: Prolegomenon for the study of agonetic behavior. In K. Olin (Ed.), *Contribution of sociology to the study of sport. Festschrift in honor of Professor Kalevi Heinila* (pp. 31-50). Jyvaskyla: University of Jyvaskyla Press.

Luckiesh, M. (1920). *Artificial light.* New York: Century.

MacCannell, D. (1973). Staged authenticity: Arrangements of social space in tourist settings. *American Journal of Sociology*, **79**, 589-603.

MacCannell, D. (1976). *The tourist: A new theory of the leisure class*. New York: Schocken Books.

McCracken, G. (1988). *Culture and consumption: New approaches to the symbolic character of consumer goods and activities*. Bloomington and Indianapolis: Indiana University Press.

Mauss, M. (1967). *The gift*. New York: W.W. Norton.

Miller, G. (Ed.) (1990). *Nemea: A guide to the site and museum*. Berkeley and Los Angeles: University of California Press.

Moore, A. (1980). Walt Disney World: Bounded ritual space and the playful pilgrimage center. *Anthropological Quarterly*, **53**, 207-217.

Morford, W.R., & Clark, S.J. (1976). The agon motif. *Exercise and Sport Sciences Review*, **4**, 163-193.

Murray, R.F. (1979). *An overture to social anthropology*. Englewood Cliffs, NJ: Prentice Hall.

Murray, T.H. (1990). The poisoned gift: AIDS and blood. *The Milbank Quarterly*, **68**, 205-225.

Neff, C. (Winter, 1988). Pining for those pins. *Sports Illustrated* (Special Issue), pp. 74-79.

O'Connor, A. (1989). *Raymond Williams: Writing, culture, politics*. London: Blackwell Press.

O'Hear, A. (1988). *The element of fire: Science, art and the human world*. London: Routledge.

Ossowska, M. (1972). *Social determinants of moral ideas*. London: Routledge & Kegan Paul.

Poliakoff, M.B. (1987). *Combat sports in the ancient world: Competition, violence and culture*. New Haven and London: Yale University Press.

Raglan, L. (1964). *The temple and the house*. London: Routledge & Kegan Paul.

Rothenbuhler, E.W. (1989). Values and symbols in orientations to the Olympics. *Critical Studies in Mass Communication*, **6**, 138, 147.

Runciman, W.G. (1968). Class, status and power? In J.A. Jackson (Ed.), *Social Stratification* (pp. 25-61). Cambridge: Cambridge University Press.

Saisselin, R.G. (1984). *The bourgeois and the bibelot*. New Brunswick, NJ: Rutgers University Press.

Sansone, D. (1988). *Greek athletics and the genesis of sport*. Berkeley: University of California Press.

Scanlon, T.F. (1983). The vocabulary of competition: *Agon* and *aethlos*, Greek terms for contest. *Arete*, **1**, 147-162.

Schwartz, B. (1967). The social psychology of the gift. *American Journal of Sociology*, **73**, 1-11.

Scimecca, J.A. (1979). Cultural hero systems and religious beliefs: The ideal-real social science of Ernest Becker. *Review of Religious Research*, **21**, 62-70.

Shaikin, B. (1988). *Sport and politics: The Olympics and the Los Angeles Games*. New York: Praeger Publishers.

Sherry, J.F., Jr. (1983). Gift giving in anthropological perspective. *Journal of Consumer Research*, **10**, 157-168.

Sitlington Sterrett, J.R. (1901). The torch race. *American Journal of Philology*, **22**, 393-419.

Slowikowski, S.S. (1982). *The cultural context of the torch race in ancient Greece*. Unpublished Master's thesis, University of Washington, Seattle, WA.

Slowikowski, S.S. (1988). *Sport and culture in ancient Macedon*. Unpublished Ph.D. thesis, The Pennsylvania State University, University Park, PA.

Slowikowski, S.S. (1989). The symbolic *Hellanodikai. Aethlon. The Journal of Sport Literature*, **7**, 133-141.

Slowikowski, S.S. (1991). Burning desire: Nostalgia, ritual and the sport-festival flame ceremony. *Sociology of Sport Journal*, **8**, 239-257.

Smith, B. (1988). *The death of the artist as hero: Essays in history and culture*. Oxford: Oxford University Press.

Staff. (1984a, Summer). *Life*, (Special Issue), **7**.

Staff. (1984b). *Official Olympic Guide to Los Angeles*. Los Angeles: ABC Publishing.

Stewart, S. (1984). *On longing: Narratives of the miniature, the gigantic, the souvenir, the collection*. Baltimore: Johns Hopkins University Press.

Storer, N.W. (1966). *The social system of science*. New York: Holt Rinehart & Winston.

Swaddling, J. (1980). *The ancient Olympic Games*. Austin: University of Texas Press.

Sweet, W.E. (1987). *Sport and recreation in ancient Greece. A sourcebook with translations*. New York and Oxford: Oxford University Press.

Tumin, M. (1967). *Social stratification*. Englewood Cliffs, NJ: Prentice Hall.

Turner, V. (1969). *The ritual process: Structure and anti-structure*. Chicago: Aldine.

Turner, V. (1974). *Dramas, fields, and metaphors: Symbolic action in human society*. Ithaca, NY: Cornell University Press.

Umminger, W. (1963). *Superman, heroes and gods*. New York: McGraw Hill.

Van Gennep, A. (1960). *The rites of passage*. Chicago: University of Chicago Press.

Weiss, P. (1969). *Sport: A philosophic inquiry*. Carbondale, IL: Southern Illinois University Press.

Williams, R. (1977). *Marxism and literature*. Oxford: Oxford University Press.

Williams, R. (1982). *The sociology of culture*. New York: Schocken Books.

Williams, R. (1983). *Keywords: A vocabulary of culture and society*. New York: Oxford University Press.

Yalouris, N. (1976). The importance and prestige of the Games. In *The Olympic Games in ancient Greece* (pp. 77-81). Athens: Ekdotike Athenon S.A.

Young, D.C. (1984). *The Olympic myth of Greek amateur athletics*. Chicago: Ares Publishers.

## B. Latin and Greek Authors

Homer. *Iliad*. Translated by Richmond Lattimore. Chicago: University of Chicago Press, 1951.

Homer. *Odyssey*. Translated by Richmond Lattimore. New York: Harper & Row, 1965.

Isocrates. *Panathenaic Oration*. Translation. New York: Penguin Books, 1948.

*Inscriptiones Graecae*.

*Inscrizioni Agonistiche Greche*. Translated by Luigi Moretti, English translation by Waldo Sweet. Oxford: Oxford University Press, 1987.

Lucian. *Anarcharsis*. Translated by Stephen G. Miller. Chicago: Ares Publishers, 1979.

Pausanias. Translation. New York: Penguin Books.

Pindar. *Victory Songs*. Translated by Frank J. Nisetich. Baltimore: Johns Hopkins University Press, 1980.

Plutarch. *Pericles. Nicias*. Translation. New York: Penguin Books.

Thucydides. Translation. New York: Penguin Books.

# CHAPTER 3

# Sport and the Victorian Gentleman

*W. Robert Morford*
*Martha J. McIntosh*

The universal addiction to sport that characterizes life in the 20th century is generally acknowledged to have had its origins in the Victorian era. Late in the 19th century, sport emerged as a uniquely English institution ready to be exported around the world. How did this come about? And why in England of all places? For answers to these questions, our study of the process whereby sport became fully institutionalized in Victorian England must focus less on the sport forms per se and more on the value systems imbedded in sporting practice. These values sustained an adherence to sport as a way of life; the practices of sport took on new forms in new social environments.

The social history of the Victorian age (1837-1901) is fascinating because of the complexity and intricacy of its class structure and the changing nature of its interclass relationships. We cannot hope to do justice to this period in history and the multiplicity of its unfolding elements. A historical snapshot that freezes a particular period in time tends to stress only those dominant cultural elements that appear as obvious images. Williams (1977) advocates that the dominant events of a given period are not only representations of social antecedents, but are themselves at the point of analysis in constant motion. Hence, the historical analysis of a cultural process such as sport must also take into account marginal and incidental evidence because it may portray the seeds of transformation. Although the dominant elements are the hegemonic influences in a given period, Williams claims that ''we have also to speak . . . of the residual and the emergent, which at any moment in the process are significant both in themselves and in what they reveal of the characteristics of the dominant'' (p. 122).

Accounts of the dominant and emergent social elements surrounding sport at any period will differ depending on the approach taken. Here, the approach is from the class-bound social perspective of the Victorian gentleman.

The industrial revolution of Victorian England may be viewed as the most important event of the era, changing forever the nature of English society. Industrialization and urbanization gave birth not only to a new kind of gentleman whose economic power derived from a manufacturing rather than an agricultural economy, but also to new kinds of sports. The sports emerging at the end of the era were not those of rural England at the beginning of Victoria's reign.

We owe the development of modern sport to the Victorians. In their sport, the Victorians displayed before the world the exercise of manly Christian virtues. The masculine dominance and presumed ethnic superiority inherent in their system was unconsciously absorbed by generations of youthful players. To this legacy of the Victorians in sport can be traced much of our contemporary confusion about amateurism, sexism, and racism in sport.

In this study, we take a look at the Victorian gentleman and Victorian sport. On the English scene in particular, they are intricately linked. During Queen Victoria's reign both were in a state of dynamic change.

# Members of a Chivalrous Institution

As a concept the term *gentleman* requires some explanation. For the Victorians, it described a man given to an idealized code of behavior. Because conduct rather than class per se was at the heart of the concept, the term has remained vague and ambiguous (Mason, 1982). Money and ownership of land were initial prerequisites in the social classes that made up the bulk of the gentlemanly ranks. Although land was always an important aspect of membership, its importance diminished as the Victorian era unfolded. Members of the clergy, military officers, industrialists, and some civil servants were among those eventually able to claim gentlemanly status, provided they emulated the proper conduct becoming a gentleman.

Foremost among the gentlemanly ranks by virtue of birth were the aristocracy of nobility. As members of the House of Peers, however, the aristocracy were frequently in attendance at court and so might well be absent from (and indeed might not even live on) their estates. On the other hand, the squire was not a noble by birth, but was in every respect a gentleman living entirely on his land. On the English country scene, the squire not only devoted his life to the pursuit of sport, but he was also the backbone of the English system of civil administration. As Longrigg (1977) has portrayed him in *The English Squire and His Sport*, the squire was the "master of sport."[1] Together, the aristocrat as lord of the estate and the squire as master of his manor or hall formed the landed gentry. Only a small minority of the English gentry was noble by birth. As the lesser gentry, the squires were a much larger subclass of landowners. Unique to England, the ranks of the squirearchy swelled significantly during the reign of Henry VIII (1509-1547) as wealthy yeomen (a tenant or freehold farmer, generally independent economically but not a member of the gentlemanly ranks) and townsmen bought church lands put up for sale by the monarch following his dissolution of the English monasteries. As a result, many yeomen moved into new manor houses and many wealthy townsmen moved to the countryside, thereby swelling the ranks of the gentlemen (Longrigg, 1977).

The predominantly rural sports of the turn of the 19th century were under the patronage of a country gentry and squirearchy and consisted of hunting, horse racing, cricket, and pugilism. By the end of the century, however, these sports were superseded in large part by new forms of sport preferred by the new industrial middle classes, whose urban environment favored football and rowing. However, the value system imbedded in the ethos of the country gentleman was deeply ingrained and widely respected in Victorian society; so much so, perhaps, that it gained a hegemonic hold over the values and sporting practices of the games cult that was firmly in place by the end of Queen Victoria's reign.

The physical isolation of an island from its nearby continental counterparts permits the emergence of unique cultural practices. Of the many cultural variants in the island nation of Britain, the variant most closely associated with fostering sport as cultural practice in Britain was the notion of the English Gentleman. The concept of gentleman in English society took on features that separated the class from its continental counterpart. It was among the gentlemanly elite of England that the pursuit of sport attained a dominant place in social life. As emulation of gentlemanly behavior became widespread, so the pursuit of sport as a manifestation of this behavior came to exert a hegemonic influence over the rest of the nation. It was the gentleman's concept of sport that inspired Pierre de Coubertin's ideals for his "Movement" and the revival of the Olympic Games.

Britain's industrial age produced a spectacular revival of interest in the medieval knight and above all in his code of behavior (Gies, 1984). Walter Scott's novels of knightly heroism, fair play, and courtly reverence for women were enthusiastically received. "Heroic myth was as popular as heroic biography and was a 19th century phenomenon" (Houghton, 1987, p. 305). In *The Return to Camelot*, Girouard (1981) stated,

> Scott gave his thousands of readers a Walter-Scott version of the Middle Ages that captured their imagination because it was presented so vividly, was so different from the life they themselves lived, and yet seemed to express certain virtues and characteristics which they felt their own age was in need of." (p. 34)

"Scott created a type of character which not only was to be imitated in innumerable later novels, but was to become a model for young men in real life" (Girouard, 1981, p. 37). The moral vigor of the hero, his individuality, and his will to action were perceived to be counteracting forces to the democratizing influence of the new industrial age in Britain. The heroic model reinforced the ideals of gentlemanly conduct and strengthened, for a while at least, the foundations of the English country gentry. In precisely this conservative-aristocratic environment, "where the dread of bourgeois democracy was strongest, heroic literature acquired the value of a political symbol" (Houghton, 1987, p. 325). However, the Victorians selected only those qualities of chivalry that they admired and then adapted them to their own use. Nowhere did this remodeled code find greater expression than in sport. "Being a sportsman, being a gentleman and being chivalrous were totally overlapping concepts" (Girouard, 1981, p. 238).

The chivalrous gentlemanly ethos of the Victorians, however, downplayed as vulgar three important aspects of medieval agonal behavior: competitiveness, assertiveness, and self-interest. Instead, the adapted ethos emphasized unselfishness, modesty, fair play, magnanimity in victory, and disinterest. Caught up in a neo-romantic wave of adulation for the medieval troubador's ideal model of chivalrous knight errantry, the Victorians overlooked the simple fact that chivalry was at best only a thin veneer and, in reality, was largely unsuccessful in controlling the contentious behavior of the medieval knight (Keen, 1984). "On the field of honor it is not virtue but might that prevailed" (Peristiany, 1974).

The enthusiasm for gothic culture was not limited to fiction, poetry, and art. Real knights in armor also made their appearance at a lavishly staged tournament in Scotland[2] at the castle of Lord Eglington on August 28, 1839. Lord Eglington staged his tournament according to all the protocols, trappings, and ordinances of a medieval tournament, or at least in keeping with Scott's description of a tournament in *Ivanhoe* (the tournament at Ashby de la Zouch in Scott's novel *Ivanhoe*, published in 1819). Thousands of spectators—some estimates claim as many as a hundred thousand— filled the specially constructed stands surrounding the lists (Girouard, 1981). The knights who were to engage in combat, and who were all to have observed periods in training for this event, adopted coats of arms and medieval names such as the "Knight of the Black Lion" (Anstruther, 1963).

However, what should have been a grand occasion full of pomp, glitter, and romance fizzled dismally. The tournament's opening feature, a parade of participants escorting the "Queen of Beauty," began three hours behind schedule, due, apparently, to poor organization. The delay was disastrous as a torrential rainstorm struck the tournament site. Within minutes, umbrellas replaced lances, and what might have been a spectacle ended up a mere debacle (Anstruther, 1963).

> When the tournament finally ended, a scene of appalling chaos ensued as tens of thousands of stumbling, slithering people looked in vain for their bogged-down carriages or started to make their way through rain and mud to the nearest available shelter. (Girouard, 1981, p. 102)

Beyond their interest in the romantic notion of honor and chivalrous adventure, the Victorian English, along with much of western Europe, reawakened a long-standing interest in ancient Greece, especially its literature, art, and archaeology (Jenkins, 1981). However, as with their romanticized concept of chivalry, the Victorians adapted their interests in Hellenic subjects to conform to their own categories of thought, culture, and morality (Jenkins, 1981). For example, Greek pederasty (so closely associated with athletic practices in the classical period) was thoroughly suppressed as an unnatural practice in the Public Schools. In describing this tendency, Turner (1981), in his study of *The Greek Heritage in Victorian Britain*, wrote, "Across the Western World Victorian authors and readers were determined to find the Greeks as much as possible like themselves and to rationalize away fundamental differences" (p. 8). Such idealism was not lost on de Coubertin; searching for a model for his scheme to revitalize the educational system of his own country, he settled on the athleticism of the Ancient Greeks. In doing so he was acting perfectly in accordance with the practices of his time. Thus, with one eye on the Ancient Olympic Games but with his other firmly riveted on the gentlemanly and chivalrous conduct of Victorian sport, de Coubertin adopted a Victorian idealization of Greek athletic practices. In doing so he ignored the intense rivalry and spirit of self-assertion that underlay the Greek agonal system. Similarly overlooked by de Coubertin and the Victorians was the fact that, even very early in the history of the Ancient Olympics, the internal rewards of honor, self-interest, and prestige had already given way to an emphasis on external rewards based on goods and money. This was, of course, far removed from the amateur ideal of the Victorians.

It is not entirely fair to say that the Victorians were ignorant of the capacity of agonal practices (especially those of the Ancient Greeks) to change over time. However, in keeping with Victorian standards of morality, they viewed these changes as morally bad (Gardiner, 1930). Thus, to safeguard what they perceived to be the uplifting and ennobling spirit underlying sport's purity, and to offset the forces of such corrupting influences as commercialism, the Victorians invoked the notion of chivalry.

The Victorian gentleman saw in his chivalrous characterization of sportsmanship a means of distancing himself from the worker and the professional. However, de Coubertin went a step further and saw in this concept of chivalry a means of protecting the moral purity of sport. "The spirit of chivalry is the last summit and supreme goal of sporting activity" (Diem, 1967, p. 103). In his opening remarks before the 1894 Paris Congress, de Coubertin said:

> Firstly it is necessary to preserve the noble and chivalrous character which distinguished athletes in the past, in order that it may continue effectively to play the same admirable part in the education of the modern world as the Greek masters assigned to it. (p. 107)

These Greek masters may have been none other than the games masters who were behind the athleticism of the English Public Schools that de Coubertin admired so much, an athleticism saddled by the gentlemanly ethic that Gilmour (1981), in his book *The Idea of the Gentleman in the English Novel*, described as the "elevation of respectability and good form over talent, energy and imagination." Gies (1984) summarizes this 19th century penchant for overlooking reality by remarking that the Victorians evoked an illusive and beguiling past and found in it a code of behavior for their own time. "But the past had grown far remote, not only with the passage of centuries but through the vast metamorphosis of western society" (p. 207).

Another reason behind the very real difference in the Victorian attitude to agonal contests stems from different meanings attached to the concept of honor. For the Greeks and the Medieval Knights, honor was bestowed through competitive modes; for the Victorian gentlemen, honor was derived from respect due to social rank and the accompanying right to precedence (Peristiany, 1974; Goode, 1978).

Failure to distinguish between such vastly different meanings for honor in different periods of history and in different cultures can easily confuse the best intentions of the unwary reformer. It was the goal of reforming education in France that triggered de Coubertin's interest in sport as a manly education, especially as it appeared in the English Public Schools—the primary breeding ground of the gentleman (Gilmour, 1981).

## The Aristocratic Sporting Tradition in Pre-Victorian England

Sport was widespread in 18th-century England (Strutt, 1834). It was a prominent feature in the daily lives of the aristocratic and landed elite, and it was a popular occurrence, in many forms, among the peasantry and laboring classes. Although the rural and urban working classes lacked the resources to indulge themselves to any extent in recreational sporting pursuits as a way of life, these sports were, nonetheless, important to them as a form of traditional celebration and festival jollity. In all parts of the world, the harsher realities of a laborer's life left little time for the cultivation of recreational interests. Hence, the many distinctly local and regional sports and games described by Joseph Strutt in 1801 owed their longevity and survival to the numerous festival occasions throughout the year.

England in this period was still largely rural, but the industrial revolution was already on the horizon. It would shortly transform English society, in Hall's (1986, p. 8) terms, from a land of rural laborers to industrial workers, from a land of villages and parishes to one of cities and suburbs, from government by accepted custom and common rights to one based on law, principle, and property rights, from local sanctions to public order. This transformation would bring a drastic reshaping of English popular culture (p. 23) and a realignment in class relationships. Naturally these changes would also transform sport.

The coming industrial revolution was to take place primarily in the cities. However, another revolution was already underway in the 18th century, this one in the English countryside. The agrarian revolution was about to alter the interclass relationships underlying the pursuit of sport in rural England.

Throughout the 17th century, rural England had gradually evolved from its feudal past into a state of agrarian capitalism. By the late 18th century, it was clear that the nature of the social relationship between landowners and peasants was forever altered (Newby, 1987).

Agricultural practice had changed from farming for the subsistence of a local rural population into a planned scheme for supplying the growing urban marketplace. Hence, profit replaced subsistence as the landowner's rationale for farming. Increased production to meet market needs became possible with advances in farming technology. Farm workers and peasants became increasingly displaced. Formerly, the peasantry was guaranteed by tradition access to common land and the security and benefits of a mutually obligatory relationship to a paternalistic landlord. In time, however, the peasant was replaced by an agricultural laborer freed from feudal obligations but also disenfranchised from common land by new enclosure laws. These changes in rural society created widespread unrest and increasing poverty among the lower classes. The landed classes, on the other hand, increased their wealth and hold over the land. The course of these historic events favored the rise of the gentlemanly classes, and sport flourished among their ranks in both rural and urban settings. At the same time, the traditional culture of the rural peasantry was increasingly blocked, and their games and sports gradually diminished in importance. But we are getting ahead of ourselves. Let us return to look at sport in 18th century rural England, when the world was divided into those who were gentlemen and those who were not.

An account of 18th-century English sport by Brailsford (1982) sets aside the widely perceived notion that sport prior to the industrial revolution lacked organization and was confined to strongly traditional modes of recreation associated with parish and harvest activities. On the contrary, at least three popular sports were relatively well organized in the 18th century. Although horse racing, boxing, and cricket were the products of upper class pleasure, they flourished within the context of a wider popular support. Along with hunting, these sports generated great interest and came to acquire a rich literary heritage revealing their importance in English rural life. By contrast, the popular recreations of the day—associated with the traditions and customs of village and parish life—left few such remains after their passing (Malcolmson, 1973).

Sport, whether under the direct sponsorship of the dominant landed classes or merely the folk expressions of a local subordinate peasantry, was widely perceived to have been a unifying factor cementing relationships between classes. As Malcolmson (1973) points out, the participation of the local gentry was an essential ingredient of these festivities during the first half of the 18th century, and ''gentlemen were not entirely disengaged from the culture of the common people'' (p. 68). The country squire, a prominent member of the English scene, was widely known as the ''booby squire'' because of his addiction to rural sports. His crude country manners were in marked contrast to the refinements of London court society.

Squires were the backbone of fox hunting and coaching (a form of racing across country roads driving a coach and four). In close association with their social superiors, the aristocracy, this landed elite was dependent on the members of their households, retainers, and the peasantry from the villages encompassed by their estates and manorial properties to care for and sustain their passion for sport. Lower class members of the household and nearby villagers provided the labor to maintain the horses and hounds for hunting and racing. They watched over and took care of the game stocks and helped in the driving of game. The gentry and their social inferiors shared a common love in judging hunting and riding prowess, protocol, and ritual in the hunt along with an understanding of game lore, husbandry, and the art of ''venerie.'' Beyond the actual performance of jobs according to social rank, all shared a common sporting terminology generated over the centuries and rendered into language and customs that set the rural sporting community aside as a relatively unified and interdependent whole.

Others outside this sporting community were thrown into its embrace on the occasion of race meets, cricket matches, and bouts of pugilism. Race meets in particular attracted crowds of several thousand, and in their midst small businesses flourished; lesser sports such as cock fighting flourished as side shows between gentlemen of different houses or estates (Armitage, 1977). Cricket in particular is a rural sport whose early history is often cited as an example of a sport encouraging interclass coexistence. Cricket clubs were established by gentlemen who organized teams composed of their retainers or others in their employ. It was the usual practice for those gentlemen to play for and captain their own team against similarly established teams. Harris (1975) refers to these players, as opposed to their gentlemanly captains and patrons, as being, in effect, the first "broken" time professionals. However, there was no social significance or stigma attached to such status. In spite of its complexities, social class was a fact of life and accepted by those from beneath as such. One's social position as a gentleman was always plain for all to see. At the races the gentry had their paddocks while the rest had the rails (Armitage, 1977).

One's station in life was an established fact. The days of conflict between amateurs and professionals in sport were still a long way off. For the time being sport patrons could mix and play freely with those who depended on patronage for the opportunity to play. And nowhere was this patronage more evident than in pugilism. A certain pugnacity had become an admired trait in the personality of the squires and gentlemen who took lessons in boxing (Armitage, 1977). However, gentlemen were the sponsors rather than the participants in the extended bouts promoted throughout the period (Morsley, 1979). The company of successful pugilists imparted a reflected glory on their noble patrons (Armitage, 1977).

By the end of the century, horse racing and cricket had become institutionalized to the extent that both sports had well-established rules and were supervised by an authoritative body. The M.C.C. (Maryleborne Cricket Club) was formed in 1787 as the White Conduit Club and became the authority behind the game with its revised laws published in 1788. In thoroughbred racing, the Jockey Club was formed in 1750 at Newmarket and became the guardian of the "turf." As Brailsford (1982) has shown, the crowds attracted to some sporting venues created all the problems facing modern spectator sport today, including such issues as admission charges, spectator facilities, crowd control, payment of players, and betting. The arrangement of such popular events was geared to take advantage of the tempo of the working week; at the time, Monday and Tuesday were the most popular days for spectator events.

## Members of the Sporting Elite

Until recent times, the pursuit of sport as a way of life was possible only among the socially elite or aristocratic class. As a primary feature in life, traditional sport required certain preconditions, because its pursuit typically produced no economic benefit. It was, in fact, a consumption pursuit requiring relatively large amounts of energy, resources, and time. Hence, as a way of life its pursuit was limited to a small segment of society. They were a privileged elite freed from the necessity of labor and in possession of the necessary power to control those of less privileged status, typically by holding them in their employ. In some instances, and for brief periods in time, relative harmony was achieved between those of the privileged classes and their subordinates. Such would appear to be the case in 17th- and 18th-century rural England.

The absolute power of the monarch had been broken by Cromwell's revolution, with the result that it was the nobility who ruled the nation and the lesser gentry, or the squires, who ruled the countryside as local magistrates (Mason, 1982). In fact, "the aristocracy who ruled the nation and the local gentry were both part of the nobility," they shared a common passion for sport, and they all considered themselves to be gentlemen (Castronovo, 1987, p. 18). Dunning and Sheard (1979) suggest there was good reason why this love of sport was so strong in England. The majority of the nobility preferred to live close to the land rather than at court. For some time following Cromwell's revolution, the court scene of the restored English monarchies was not popular among the realm's nobles. Further, George I, who came to the English throne from Hanover in 1714, sought to embellish his English court with the courtly customs of his former European neighbors. Hence, French courtesy and manners were glorified. The English nobility, with their penchant for rough and tumble rural sports (Dunning and Sheard, 1979) were, by comparison, rather crude (Mason, 1982).

In living close to the land, the English nobility lived in relative isolation from one another, and hence became dependent to some degree on interaction with their servants and villagers (Mason, 1982). Interaction across class barriers was especially apparent in the realm of sport. Hunting, blood sports (e.g., cock fighting), and cricket particularly fostered a sense of participation and mutual dependence between the classes. Prior to the end of the 18th century the rural classes mixed well; there was an understanding among the lower classes about the differences in social standing between them and their social superiors that made it unnecessary for the elite to assert their rank and status and insist on deference (Mason, 1982).

> Because customary standards were set and power over their practice dispensed locally, a landlord and his tenant could meet individually at a "cocking" without either presuming for a moment that he could really bridge the immense vertical distances separating the landed and the labouring classes. (Hall, 1986, p. 25)

Unique in this rural environment was the concept of the gentleman. In the 18th century only those who possessed the necessary wealth and land could rightly call themselves gentlemen. A gentleman's manners, his sense of morality, his speech, and his dress had been the standard in effect for a long time prior to the Victorian age. Despite a certain outward appearance that always set a gentleman apart (especially from his social inferiors) he was always, by presence alone, an identifiable figure to the average working-class Englishman. It was a concept that resided in the mind of the peasant and villager.

The origins of the gentleman lie deep in feudal society and the qualifications for noble birth. Gilmour (1981) explains that the social refinements imposed on the knightly classes during the renaissance brought to the concept a certain degree of social rank combined with some of the qualities that such rank ought to imply. At the turn of the 18th century the dominant perspective of a gentleman was still largely derived from its earlier roots. It was essential that a gentleman should live without engaging in any manual labor or too visible an attention to business (Gilmour, 1981) and without displaying too much desire for victory in sporting contests. Clearly then, a life of leisure enabled a gentleman to cultivate both his style and his pursuits. Among some, style denoted a sense of frivolous snobbery, idleness, and social elitism. For others, style was displayed in the mastery of horses and hounds, or the rugged determination of the possessed hunter, or the love of chase and contest. Gilmour (1981) stresses that "the notion of a gentleman lay at the heart of the social and political accommodation between the aristocracy and the middle class" (p. 2).

## The Emergent Industrial Gentleman

In time, and especially in the early stages of the industrial revolution, the ranks of the gentleman of blood became increasingly penetrated by a new gentleman of means. The social distinction between the dominant perspective of a gentleman because of his birth increasingly gave way to an emergent perspective based on his wealth. Wealth eventually took precedence over birth in defining eligibility for gentlemanly status (Castronovo, 1987). Hence, as Gilmour (1981) states, the association of gentleman with rank was replaced by an association with class. The broadening base of power that accompanied this shift in association had widespread effects (Mason, 1982). As opportunities to acquire wealth increased it became an overwhelming reality of English life that there would be more people who wanted to, and indeed did, become gentlemen (Castronovo, 1987). This accommodation of a concept to incorporate a larger segment of society demonstrates, as Castronovo suggests, the essential fluidity of English society.

This fluidity—which had to some extent always been in place, because the concept of a gentleman was an upwardly mobile one—is seen by historians such as Castronovo to have served the English aristocracy and landed elite well in an era of widespread social unrest at home and social revolution on the European continent. In effect, the unique feature of English life lay in a whole class of men whose status was widely admired and whose behavior, morality, and manners were widely emulated even by those without the means to support the lifestyle and whose social existence was balanced between the two extremes of social class. Hence, "the English gentleman was able to pose himself between the world of privilege and the world of democracy" (Castronovo, 1987, p. 17). In Europe, gentlemen remained inextricably tied to their rank and birth and were by contrast despised for it. Again Castronovo summarizes the distinction in a quote from de Tocquiville: "gentleman in English applies to any well educated man, regardless of birth, whereas in France gentilhomme can only be used of a noble by birth" (p. 18).

Mason (1982) has summarized the qualities of the Victorian gentlemanly ideal. These included generosity, openheartedness, magnanimity, responsibility, leadership, disinterestedness, and an all-abiding courtesy to women. Mason also describes the Victorian gentleman as being sporting and pugnacious, and it was the qualities of combativeness and the genuine love of fair play in particular that attracted the reluctant affection of "ordinary" people. "Toughness of muscle and toughness of heart. In the Victorian mind the ideal of strength is a combination of force and firmness'' (Houghton, 1987, p. 198). The Victorian gentry were admired for their manliness, for being redblooded, aggressive, and virile. This widespread admiration of physical strength and prowess also resulted in the condemnation of weak, intro-spective men as effeminate.

Assimilation into the ranks of gentlemen of a man whose wealth derived from industrial labor and the making of money through exchange practices did not take place without social conflict. Only a portion of the urban middle class rose to become wealthy industrial barons, creating, in effect, an upper middle class. These men had the capital to purchase sufficient land and the accompanying leisure lifestyle considered appropriate to the status of a gentleman. Conflict between the dominant and emergent forms of gentlemen occurred on many fronts; of interest here is the conflict that arose over access to the residual values that were at the heart of a gentleman's lifestyle and that the emergent industrial gentleman sought to emulate.

Central to this lifestyle was sport, especially those sports focused on the horse. As practiced on a daily basis, the rural gentleman's attachment to sport was embedded in tradition. The horse was vital to the hunt and to racing. The maintenance of fine stables was a key factor in country life (Longrigg, 1977). Although game birds and animals required large tracts of land and were more the domain of the landed aristocracy, riding to hounds, the steeplechase, and coaching were the primary pursuits of the large squirearchy who lived throughout rural England. Traditions that span centuries are cultivated in the individual through exposure and practice from an early age. Conventions, rituals, and practice with attendant language, tools, and dress surround such long-established traditions and keep the outsider at bay. The uninitiated masquerading in this environment are threatened by exposure through their ignorance of custom.

While the industrial gentleman could purchase the land, the horses, and the servants, penetrating the gentry's customary lifestyle to become an equal proved more difficult. However, ''as professional and business people found their way into the ranks of the gentry in the 18th and 19th centuries, many periodicals and novels rushed to provide guidance, uplift and service on the nature of the gentlemanly ideal'' (Castronovo, 1987, p. 62). The sudden wave of published material treated the new gentleman to a plethora of didactic texts that accelerated this assimilation into the ranks of the gentry. However, the emergent gentleman, even as he pursued and acquired the trappings of gentlemanly virtues and values, was to alter the very practices to which these customs had always been applied.

A gentleman of industrial wealth rather than landed and private means had to attend to his business interests in the city. Hence, life could only be lived in leisurely style periodically. The dominant country lifestyle of the squirearchy had always engaged in sport on a daily basis. However, this was not practical for the emergent gentleman. Traditional sports that required a span of several days for their pursuit gave way to sports that required briefer amounts of time. Even in instances where the dominant forms survived, as in the case of fox hunting, they did so with the added help of a more efficient transport system of railways and in altered forms as weekend pursuits.

Even though such traditional sporting pastimes as riding to hounds were modified to meet the time constraints of the urban gentleman, the practices and rituals associated with the hunt remained relatively unchanged. However, changes of a much larger magnitude were soon to occur in the incorporation of team games, especially football, into the emergent urban middle-class lifestyle. Football, once a rough and tumble free-for-all played by local yokels, was, in a span of three decades, thoroughly modernized.

The modernization of sports such as football and cricket began in the 1830s. This process came about through the interplay of middle-class values with those of the aristocratic class. Dunning and Sheard (1979) have referred to this unplanned process as the incipient modernization of sport or the unintended consequence of social change wrought by industrialization.

# External Factors Influencing Reform

Dunning and Sheard (1979) take the position that by the middle of the 19th century, the industrialization of England had resulted in an imbalance of power in favor of the bourgeoisie or the newly emerged middle class over that of the aristocracy and gentry. In other words, a power base derived from the relatively dynamic sphere of industrial production was more powerful than one derived from the ownership and control of land, which was a relatively static resource. Girouard (1979) expressed it differently, noting that "growing urbanization and industrialization meant that an aristocracy based on land had no hope of preserving a monopoly of power" (p. 5). Arnstein (1975), however, has argued that the triumph of the Victorian middle class is largely a myth. He contends that

> the increase of the wealth of the middle class, and their intermarriage with their social superiors have caused them to assimilate the tastes and prejudices of their new connections . . . the holders of property naturally take the color of their views from those who are above them and not from those who are below. (p. 219)

For the industrialist, social prestige and acceptance among the gentry did not come from newly acquired wealth alone but rather from a gradual assimilation through appropriate behavior and the adoption of gentry practices. In fact, according to Arnstein (1975), there is ample evidence to show that the middle-class values of industriousness and respectability had more of an impact on the lower classes than they did on the aristocracy. A case in point, with respect to sport, is the directional impact of middle-class attitudes toward cruelty and the improper treatment of animals.

Animal protection lobbyists, made up largely of middle-class reformers (Ritvo, 1987), formed the Society for the Prevention of Cruelty to Animals in 1824; in 1840 it became the Royal Society for the Prevention of Cruelty to Animals (R.S.P.C.A.) under Queen Victoria's patronage. Ritvo, in *The Animal Estate* (1987), says that "the Victorian critique of inhumanity . . . confounded two missions: to rescue animal victims and to suppress dangerous elements in society'' (p. 131). From time to time, the R.S.P.C.A. may have directed harsh words to upper-class sporting practices, but its actions were entirely directed against the sports of the working class. A part of the Society's mandate was the elevation of lower-class moral responsibility toward animals.

> If cruelty to animals represented, in general, the triumph of humankind's baser nature, the kind of cruelty that individual humanitarians found most distressing was likely to signal what they considered the most dangerous threat to social order. In the view of the R.S.P.C.A. and its supporters, that threat came from the uneducated and inadequately disciplined lower classes, and it was their duty, once the source had been identified, to counter it. (Ritvo, 1987, p. 135)

From 1835 onward a series of parliamentary acts banned such animal sports as bull, bear, and badger baiting, dog and cock fighting, and ratting—all sports that attracted the lower classes and criminal elements to various and sundry seamy establishments. ''The R.S.P.C.A.'s efforts at social engineering were explicitly directed at the lower social orders of society'' (Ritvo, 1987, p. 155). The Society's reforms had no impact on the blood sports of the country gentry. In fact, fox hunting and steeplechasing, in particular, were becoming increasingly attractive to the ''nouveau'' gentleman anxious to be assimilated into the social setting of the country gentry.

The ongoing assimilation of the monied urban middle classes into the gentlemanly ranks was bound to affect what it meant to be a gentleman. Nowhere was this more apparent than in that very special Victorian institution—the public school. It was in the Victorian public school that the potentially conflicting values of two very different social systems were accommodated to create the new gentleman. And it was in the reformed public school that the process of incipient modernization of sport primarily took place (Dunning & Sheard, 1979).

Industrialization was a prime mover behind the extensive and all-encompassing social changes wrought on English society. Every social institution was affected. In the same manner that pressure grew for reform of the government and the church, pressure grew for reform of the public schools. ''From the fall of Napoleon until the middle of the thirties, all aspects of Public School boy life were the subject of continual comment by all shades of British opinion'' (Mack, 1938, p. 156). The rebellious and lawless conditions rampant in these schools had reached such a level by the early 1830s that it resulted in a public outcry for a school system free from state interference, in which the hand of the masters was strengthened, yet the autonomy of the boys was preserved (Dunning & Sheard, 1979). Woodward (1962) has suggested that the public schools ''would not have outlasted the age of reform if they had not been remodelled under the direction of a few remarkable men'' (p. 485). One of the more successful efforts at reform was achieved at Rugby School under the headship of Thomas Arnold.

The cult of games (especially rowing, cricket, and local variants of football) was widespread in the public schools before the reform period (Mangan, 1981). However, the place of sport in the life of the schoolboy was unregulated and unsystematic. It was not until after the reforms that games evolved into a social institution within the school; they were rationalized as contributing to the educational process itself.

The rationalization of games within the structure of the reformed public school resulted in numerous modifying factors unintentionally derived from the ever widening influences of the urban middle class elite. Central to the process of sport's bourgeoisification are the following trends noted by Dunning and Sheard (1979).

- The civilizing process resulted in expectations of greater self-control and emotional restraint among players along with less socially tolerated physical violence.
- Rules of play were codified and rules of conduct for players were enforced.
- Formal organization and the complex division of labor among players increased.
- Fairness in playing conduct was emphasized.
- The degree of central control increased, often outside the game itself; games were increasingly used to encourage status rivalry among the public schools.

These factors affected the organizational and regulatory structure of games playing and it is not hard to see the influence of the industrial model expressed in these modifications. However, sport itself continued to be dominated by a value system that was thoroughly aristocratic. Arnstein (1975) noted that in spite of extensive reform in the way public schools were run, the curricula relied heavily on nonutilitarian subjects. Further, the schools continued to stress tradition and noblesse oblige, the acceptance of social hierarchy, the cult of the amateur, and the air of indifference and disinterestedness—all qualities, incidentally, of the gentleman (Mason, 1982). Thus, Arnstein (1975) in citing Rupert Wilkinson, concludes that "the reformed public school system captured middle class talent in the promotion of gentry class power" (p. 220). Finally, Arnstein (1975) points out that the public schools, labeled by Mason (1982) as "factories for gentlemen," produced few if any noted merchants and businessmen, but rather "turned out country gentlemen, army officers, imperial administrators, civil servants, members of Parliament and cabinet members" (p. 161).

# The Victorian Public School as a Major Agent of Reform

We turn now to an examination of life in the Victorian public school as it relates to the expression of gentlemanly values in the realm of games, or, perhaps more accurately, the use of games by public school masters as a tool in the civilizing process. Prior to the 18th century, it had been the custom for young gentlemen to be privately tutored at home. However, during the second half of the 18th century and the beginning of the 19th century it became increasingly fashionable among the upper echelons of English society to send their sons off to the top public schools.[3] The term *public school* increasingly came to mean private as these schools were transformed into educational establishments for the upper classes. Schools such as

Harrow and Rugby, originally created to educate the local youth, became the providers of a classical education for the sons of the gentry and the nouveau riche (Chandos, 1984).

Through the public school experience young boys were schooled in the qualities of moral character, social adaptability, and self reliance (Chandos, 1984), all virtues fundamental to the gentlemanly ideal of the early Victorian period.

Thus, partly due to habit and fashion and despite criticism and divided feelings, and a severe contradiction of the liberal seventeenth century range of studies, a public school came to be widely accepted as the place where boys destined to be bred as gentlemen might conveniently be initiated into the life of a community of their peers and contemporaries. (Chandos, 1984, p. 28)

During the Victorian era ''these schools acquired a reputation among their supporters of being able to give [their students] a foretaste of real life, of 'licking into shape' the recalcitrant, of providing a training in manliness, resolution and true-blue English fair play'' (Warner, 1945).

However, the reality of life in the public schools at the start of the 19th century left much to be desired in the way of gentlemanly upbringing. The young boy, sent away from parental supervision into an institutional environment lacking adequate supervision, formed a character that was far from gentlemanly. An imbalanced master-to-student ratio (Chandos, 1984) and the proximity of many public schools to the open countryside (Mangan, 1981) provided the perfect motivation for young boys to roam free and engage in mischief. Free from any confines—except those that may have existed among the boys themselves—opportunities to create trouble abounded. Concrete evidence of this undisciplined behavior by young gentlemen can be found in many of the written accounts of the boys' adventures in the schoolyard and the countryside.

In Carleton's *Westminster School* (1965) references are made to the frequency with which fights took place in the Cloister garth, a place so often used by the boys for their confrontations that it was known as the ''fighting green.'' The fights ''were regular affairs with rounds and seconds, and the clash of the combatants and the applause of the onlookers often disturbed the service in the Abbey but a few yards away'' (p. 45). The records of events at Rugby School also highlight instances of boyish exuberance. A confrontation between the students and a landowner, Boughton Leigh, over fishing, an activity that the boys regarded as an ancestral right but technically belonged to the landowner, almost led to open rebellion when students were identified and expelled for being involved in an off-limits activity (Bamford, 1960).

Not only was life in the public school Spartan; it was unruly and bordered on anarchy. This naturally led to declining enrollments and threatened the existence of the schools. Nonetheless, the families of new middle-class wealth spawned by the Industrial Revolution were quick to recognize the opportunities afforded by the public schools for increased contact with their social superiors—the landed gentry (Newsome, 1959). However, like their rural counterparts, the urban professional middle class was not ready to send its sons off to schools where vice and violence were rampant (Mangan, 1981). Calls for radical reform and strong action (Carleton, 1965) were widespread. Gradually, the environment within the public school became more civilized.

The prefect-fagging[4] system was the first element to come under attack. While educational reformists fought to change the system, the schoolboys fought equally hard to retain their system. Whether it was officially recognized—as in the case of Winchester, where the system had been included in the 1382 founding charter of the school (Warner, 1945)—or was merely treated as a given by the masters and the schoolboys, the prefect-fagging system was regarded by the boys as a tradition and a closely guarded right (Chandos, 1984). When criticisms over the cruelty and vice of the system led to the initial threats to take away what was regarded as a traditional right the students resorted to open rebellion at the public schools— Winchester in 1770, 1774, 1778, 1793, and 1818; Eton in 1818, 1819, and 1832 (Honey, 1977); Charterhouse in 1821 (Warner, 1945).

The potential use of the system as a tool of character formation could not be disregarded by the reformists or by the "old boys" who still wanted their sons to gain from a tradition they had experienced and believed had some merit (Chandos, 1984). Incentive to use the system was also derived from the fact that where no prefect fagging existed "the most savage elements in the school were free to indulge without restraint" (Chandos, 1984, p. 104). The headmasters had to develop a solution that was acceptable to the students, parents, and educational reformists—a solution that improved on rather than eliminated tradition.

The headmasters tried several solutions. One solution that eventually contributed to improving the problem of internal control was the division of the boys into houses, in effect creating several smaller living units within the school, with each house under the leadership of an assistant master. Wright (1977), however, maintains that the real answer to the problem of control turned out to be much simpler. "Like the late Roman emperors the Victorian headmaster, faced with the inevitable, loaded the leaders of his little Goths and Vandals with titles and responsibilities and hoped for the best. Unlike the last Roman emperors he got it" (p. 11). This combination of smaller living units with the prefect system placed the "house masters" in position to at least minimally supervise the boys under their charge.

As early as the 1820s the headmaster of Rugby, Dr. Thomas Arnold, was promoting prefect fagging as an improved instrument of Christian principles (Haigh, 1985). What Dr. Arnold did was to take the prefectorial system attributed to Drs. Goddard of Winchester, Heath of Harrow, and Drury of Harrow (Haigh, 1985) and infuse it with little more than a new moral tone. The system of prefects and fags was still left to be run by the boys, giving them the opportunity to develop the leadership skills necessary in their future careers.

As it was, Arnold's work at Rugby turned the stream back into its old channel. It set new standards of discipline and moral tone and showed that it was only necessary for the public schools to set their house in order for them to regain their hold on the affections of the upper classes. Reform was in most cases the prelude to renewed popularity, and by the middle of the century not only were most of the schools again full, but new ones were everywhere springing up to meet the demand. (Carleton, 1965, p. 55)

"For the boys as a whole, the new regime was a mixed blessing. While protected from the more arbitrary despotism of their elders, they lost much of their old freedom outside the classroom" (Wright, 1977, p. 11). What the headmasters introduced were not new games but a new attitude to those games already being played. Nowhere was this more apparent than in the realm of play.

## Sport and Games in the Public Schools

The physical pursuits that would eventually become the competitive sports played by the public-school boys were already in place in the 1700s. Students were participating in rowing at Westminster by the 1740s and playing cricket at Harrow by the 1760s, and by 1800 cricket was at Rugby (Haigh, 1985).

The early transition of school games into a competitive sport form, which began to appear in public school accounts of the late 1700s, was also influenced by the progressive changes occurring in British sport at large. Outside the realm of school the world of organized sport was beginning to take shape. The founding of the Marylebone Cricket Club in 1788 (Mitchell & Leys, 1950) was soon followed in 1796 by a cricket match played between Westminster and Eton (Carleton, 1965), marking the first interschool sport competition of any kind. By 1829, the popularity of cricket in society was mirrored by the tradition of annual cricket matches between Eton and Harrow, Harrow and Winchester, and Winchester and Eton (Haigh, 1985). In other public-school sports such as rowing, Westminster and Eton also led the way with the first interschool contest in 1829 (McIntosh, 1952). Interschool matches in football were slower to develop due to the different set of rules used by each school (McIntosh, 1952) and by the fact that the game had to be accepted as suitable to be played by young gentlemen (McIntosh, 1952).

The importance with which the students treated games and competitive sport and the amount of time they spent at it eventually made it the perfect medium through which to instill character and the gentlemanly characteristics. The educational system itself moved to make the most of this medium.

Games became something more than mere games; they became institutions, both absorbing the energies of growing boys living in a boys' world and preparing for real-life situations by inculcating "games values" and team spirit—values as important to the gentleman as were competitive values to Smiles's businessman or skilled laborer. (Briggs, 1954, pp. 152-153)

Much has been made of Thomas Arnold's influence in this area. However, it was not until the 1850s and 1860s—a quarter of a century after Arnold—that newly established schools such as Marlborough and Uppingham led the way in recognizing sport as an educational tool (McIntosh, 1952). Lessons of courage and leadership experience gained on the playing field were increasingly accepted among the new definers in the continuing evolution of the gentlemanly ideal. As *Westward Ho!* author Charles Kingsley wrote in 1874:

> In the playing fields boys acquired virtues which no books can give them; not merely daring and endurance, but, better still, temper, self restraint, fairness, honor, unenvious approbation of another's success, and all that "give and take" of life which stand a man in such good stead when he goes forth into the world, and without which, indeed, his success is always maimed and partial. (McIntosh, 1963, p. 77)

Circumstances surrounding the joining and intertwining of the gentlemanly ideal and games-playing into a mutually beneficial relationship were different for the various public schools. The introduction and rate of development of this new tool of character formation was directly linked to such factors as a headmaster's attitude, the availability of facilities, provision of adequate play time, and student initiative. Games as school-boy play were slowly being transformed into organized school sport.

Changes in the masters' attitudes toward games was a slow progression: from disapproval, to toleration as a method of dissipating excess energies, to approval as an exercise from which some merit could be derived. While the starting point for this progress is usually attributed to Dr. Thomas Arnold, it was actually other headmasters who made the changes. The myth of Dr. Arnold's involvement results largely from Thomas Hughes's best selling novel *Tom Brown's Schooldays*—a literary description of public school life as it supposedly was in Arnold's time that did more to promote sport than Thomas Arnold ever did (Bamford, 1960; Haigh, 1985; Mangan, 1981). The true innovators in both established and new public schools were headmasters such as Cotton of Marlborough, Thring of Uppinham, Vaughan of Harrow, and Almond of Loretto. These educators saw games not only as a means of infusing character in the boys (Mangan, 1981), but also as a means of monopolizing the boys' time and energies, which would otherwise have been spent on rebellious pursuits (Honey, 1977; Simon & Bradley, 1975) and sexually immoral conduct (which horrified the Victorians and against which the Victorian school masters were constantly on guard [Mangan, 1981]).

In a few decades, the unchanneled and unruly pursuits of youthful school boys metamorphosed into a formidable institution within the public schools. By the closing decade of the century the impact of the games cult was widely felt throughout the public schools, the universities, and English social life generally.

There was nothing novel about the "institution of sport" in English life; it was the extension of this institution into education that was novel. An old tradition was being refashioned in a new environment. Sport as a long-standing tradition of English country life had taken the form of hunting, horse racing, pugilism, and cricket. What emerged as the new tradition through the public schools was focused on football, cricket, and rowing. These three sports were particularly suited to the emergent urban gentry. Hunting and racing, however, remained on the countryman's calendar. Further, public school pupils, once their free and lawless activities had been curtailed, continued to find expression for their youthful spirits and energy in games that could be enjoyed within the restraints of a school's grounds. Cricket, established throughout the country, filled a seasonal void at school. Football, once a village rough-and-tumble with many local forms, emerged on the school campus in variant forms. Rowing became popular among those schools with access to rivers.

The growth of games as an important facet of school life was very much a student-driven movement, because the schoolmaster's responsibility usually ended at the classroom door. However, most headmasters were quick to recognize the powerful hold that games had on their youthful charges. Sporting prowess displayed on the football field and cricket pitch created natural prestige hierarchies among the students that resulted in a unique system of internal control. Those who exhibited skill and courage in hard-fought games of football, or displayed coolness of nerve and accomplishment in cricket, not only gained the respect and adulation of younger and less skilled players but became their heroes as well. Where better, then, for a headmaster to find his prefects than among the athletically elite? Sports heroes became leaders. Once school authorities became aware of the inner workings of the games cult among the schoolboy peerage they were quick to forge games to the educational process and the mission of the reformed public school. As organized games among the young became increasingly encouraged and sanctioned by their elders, the necessary trappings of institutionalized sport fell quickly into place. Specialized clothing and marks of distinction (colors), codes of behavior, interschool fixtures, codified rules of play, a rationalized role in school life, and appropriate goals and outcomes were added to the basic accoutrements of the game itself. It was not long before the vocabulary of sport and an array of sporting cliches entered the everyday language of the schoolboy, and subsequently the gentleman, the soldier, the merchant, and the clergy. Phrases such as "it's not cricket," "play the game," and "letting the side down" were absorbed into the common language. Many contexts in life, business, and religion could be expressed by sport metaphors.

Formalized games, then, informed the lives of the English schoolboy of the late Victorian period to such an extent that "the way of sport" became an indelible part of his being. Even those who were not good at games, or actively sought to avoid them altogether, were nonetheless surrounded by them.

## Sporting Virtues

It was only natural that in games the population saw the very virtues that made England great, that won her an empire, that brought her army and navy triumph after triumph in battle. Courage, coolness under fire, respect for the enemy, Spartan tolerance for pain and discomfort were daily manifested on the field of play, or so it was believed. No wonder the reformers and schoolmasters were quick to take the next step. If these were the virtues that were displayed and admired in sport, then the process could be reversed. Through sport these qualities could be encouraged and developed. This was the step that led to legitimizing games as a laboratory for character building. The English public saw games in every facet of their lives and facets of their lives in every game. The popularization of the schoolboy novel and adventure stories that glorified the exploits and athletic prowess of youthful heroes fueled the passion and fervor of the nation in the belief that games were the ultimate testing ground for manly virtue and the ideal preparation for the game of life.

Of the schoolboy novels, perhaps the best known was *Tom Brown's Schooldays*, written by Thomas Hughes and published in 1867. In his introduction to a contemporary reprint of the novel, Andrews (1968) wrote:

> There are no really bad boys here, no saints. For the most part these are boys who, while young, will violate seemingly every rule in the book of morals and manners—and then will grow up to be like their fathers—landed gentry, merchants, rectors and deacons and members of parliament. For these are members of upper-middle-class families who have been sent to Rugby not to be scholars—although some boys became scholars—but to become "brave, helpful, truth-telling Englishmen, and gentlemen, and Christians." (p. 5)

By the middle of the 19th century, generations of schoolboys had experienced the Spartan system of the public school and the process of growing up from homesick freshman to senior and prefect. Hughes eulogized the system in his widely imitated novel of life in the public school (Quigley, 1982). In his description of the novel's hero, Tom Brown, the author framed Tom's athletic exploits with allusions to significant events and institutions in English history. Tom's confrontation with another schoolboy rival, ending in a fistfight with Slogger Williams, is likened to a medieval "passage at arms" where heroic knights challenged each other to combat in the lists. Tom's first exposure to the violence of football comes early in his life at Rugby School when as a new boy he is permitted to stand and defend the goal line along with all the other nonplayers. Of course, in his recklessness he rushes out to dive on the ball to save a touchdown from being scored by the opposition. Here is how Hughes describes the scene as the opposing players rush toward Tom. "Reckless of the defence of their own goal, on they came across the level big side ground, the ball well down amongst them, straight for our goal, like the column of the Old Guard up the slopes at Waterloo" (Hughes, 1968, p. 96). For a moment, the reader is transported back to the advance of Napoleon's elite corps against the British line. Every schoolboy knew enough of the battle tactics of the French and British armies to recognize the analogy: the French advanced in columns; the British stood their ground in lines and squares. Football players, however, do not advance in columns. Nonetheless, such famous examples of heroic courage under enemy fire burned brightly in the minds of countless schoolboys, who were themselves eager to emulate the gallantry of enshrined heroic action so that they too might bask in the admiration of their peers for their gallant deeds.

The reference to cricket as a veritable institution in English life comes in the final chapter in Tom's last game at school. In a conversation with one of the masters, the master comments, "What a noble game it is too!" "Isn't it?" replies Tom, who goes on to say, "But it's more than a game. It's an Institution." A third voice then adds, "Yes, the birth right of British Boys, old and young, as habeas corpus and trial by jury are of British men" (Hughes, 1968, p. 270). Strong stuff with which to swell the hearts of future schoolboys.

The promotion of games would not have been successful without the involvement of the schoolboys themselves, who organized and participated in sport at the public schools. For the students, however, the games took on new meaning with the rise of the cult of athleticism, rather than because of the gentlemanly virtues they could gain on the playing fields. The athletic heroes of *Tom Brown's Schooldays* became the models to imitate (Simon & Bradley, 1975), and success in competition became paramount for sport (Honey, 1977) in the eyes of the schoolboys. The English public school system had become the nurturer of young gentlemen and games had become the key instrument through which to instill all the necessary characteristics.

By the end of the Victorian period a school was to be judged not just by the caliber of its headmaster—though this was important—but also by the quality of the whole staff, the characteristics of its clientele, its buildings and playing fields, its successes at work and play, its traditions, the loyalties of its "old boys," and those aspects of its moral collectivity that were known to the Victorians as "tone" (Honey, 1977). The success of the method was evident by the number of schools that, seeking to become established, copied the sport structure and made it a priority of the school to turn out young gentlemen (Simon & Bradley, 1975). The public schools turned out an identifiable human product—a ready-made gentleman immediately identifiable by his alma mater, his distinctive public school accent, and his record of athletic prowess. "To the men who interviewed candidates for executive government posts, a public school accent and public school mannerisms spelt 'quality' " (Wilkinson, 1964, p. 11).

By the turn of the century, the public schools had not only increased in number; they had become factories churning out Christian gentlemen who would in turn go on to the universities, the professions, and the world at large. The term *Christian gentlemen* suggests the close association between sport and religion and is an interesting and important feature of the Victorian period. The two primary means of transmitting cultural values in Victorian society were education and the Christian church. Sport was an important interactive agent between them.

## Muscular Christians

Most headmasters of the great public schools were also ministers of the cloth ordained in the Church. Further, a central platform of the public school reform movement had emphasized the importance of Christian values in education. Arnold at Rugby, who was a minister and an important figure in framing school reform, felt his primary purpose was to educate his charges to become Christian gentlemen. Arnold may not have contributed to the promotion of games at Rugby school, but his overriding belief in the importance of instilling Christian virtues into his pupils may have affected some of his students. According to Mack (1938), such one-time games players as Thomas Hughes (author of the best-selling novel *Tom Brown's Schooldays*) and others who later became headmasters of several of the important public schools provided the real impetus to the games movement as a "useful instrument in effecting Arnold's moral purposes, to teach loyalty, honourableness, graciousness in defeat, self sacrifice and cooperation" (p. 335). Mack goes on to suggest that since these were highly desirable ends, these disciples of Arnold gave their "support to a movement which without aid from authority, might never have grown to the proportions which it later assumed" (p. 336). Within a few decades it was apparent that the importance of games as a central feature in school life, when coupled with an emphasis on morality and Christian virtues, had created a generation of muscular Christians.

As an expression, muscular Christianity began to circulate in relation to Kingsley, Hughes, and others about 1857. "It represents, not only fairly but favourably, a school of feeling rather than thought, which, though small is becoming very influential in the hands of zealous and eloquent teachers" (Fitz-James Stephen, 1858, p. 190). Muscular Christianity espoused a vigorous, manly, straightforward, self-reliant, honest kind of man who used his "strength and power under god in the service of others" (Mack and Armytage, 1952, p. 96); it may have been a reaction to the flabby effeminacy of some Oxbridge undergraduates (Kendall, 1946). Team games, it was said, developed moral character, patriotism, and the courage to stand up for what was right; to defend the underdog, to champion fairness, and to exercise self-control. If a young man was strong in body; pure in heart; faithful and loyal to friend, family, and country; knew his duty before God; put service to the team ahead of himself; and adhered to the rules of the game, he was a muscular Christian. Epitomizing just such qualities, the heroes of Thomas Hughes's and Charles Kingsley's novels were indeed muscular Christians.

These novels displayed an "admiration of athletic, upper middleclass, somewhat Christian youngmen which inspired the term 'Muscular Christianity' " (Martin, 1953, p. 219), an expression that, when it was applied to Charles Kingsley, irritated him considerably. Occasionally he would try to shrug the label off. "I have to preach the divineness of the whole manhood, and am content to be called a muscular Christian, or any other impertinent name" (Kendall, 1946, p. 54).

Kingsley, who claimed not to know the meaning of the expression, is quoted by Martin (1953) as saying "Its first and better meaning may simply be a healthful and manly Christianity; one which does not exalt the feminine virtues to the exclusion of the masculine" (p. 219). E.F. Johns, in his *Words of Advice to School-Boys* (1912), admonished, "Be manly boys. If you will be manly, if you will be Christian men, you will attain the highest point that God gives man to gain . . . play well, and above all work well; work heartily and play heartily" (p. 6). There were "few men," according to Boardman (1931), who "lived more wholeheartedly and more manfully than Charles Kingsley. By nature he was hot tempered, frank, energetic and combative. His 'muscular Christianity' was cheerful and robust, and his whole life was one of strenuous endeavour to better ennoble mankind" (p. 5).

Sport as it developed and flourished in the public schools and found expression in the social life of the country was a means to an end, a tool for achieving the higher ethical purposes dear to the hearts of men like Hughes, Kingsley, and many others, including the new generation of public school headmasters. The church—many of whose leaders were the product of the public schools—recognized the importance of sport in the lives of the young and the importance of the Christian sport hero as a bridge in communicating the Christian message (Scott, 1970). Sport served ably as a proving ground for the exercise of Christian virtues; the stout-hearted Christian fought a good fight and maintained a straight bat.

However, an excess of virtue can become a vice (Ballard, 1896). The promotion of games that began and flourished under the auspices of liberalism and religious revival underlying the public-school reform movement was, by the 1860s, compromised by the conservatism and materialism of the rising industrial and mercantile middle class, whose sons entered the public schools in ever-increasing numbers. Subtly, old ideals were bent to fit the needs of a new age; from the glorification of games emerged the cult of athleticism. In Mack's (1938) view, athleticism "meant the gradual obliteration in boys' minds of the moral purposes for the sake of which masters had originally encouraged games" (p. 337). And, "an athlete quietly learned that only by strength and self assertion could he win a place on his own team and help conquer rival teams" (p. 338).

A new breed of athletic musclemen gradually displaced the muscular Christian.

The only point in common between the two being that both held it to be a good thing to have strong and well exercised bodies. Here all likeness ends for the muscleman seems to have no belief whatever as to the purposes for which his body has been given him. (Brown, 1880, p. 39)

Like Arnold, Hughes suffered the ironic fate of having prepared the ground for practices which he abhorred (Mack, 1938). The excessive emphasis on athleticism in the schools and universities concerned Hughes greatly, and he sought, repeatedly, to clarify the meaning behind his concept of true manliness. His writings on the subject were collected by Brown (1880), who quoted Hughes as commenting that "athleticism is a good thing if kept in its place, but it has come to be very much over praised and over valued among us" (p. 18).

Mack and Armytage (1952) claim that the message Hughes attempted to convey in *Tom Brown's Schooldays* was one of nourishing crusaders for the Christian life. However, his intention was misinterpreted by his middle-class readers. In place of Tom Brown, the knightly champion of Christian virtues, they saw only Tom Brown the proconsul. Thus, instead of nurseries for social servants, the public schools became, instead, training ground for sahibs. With the rise of *Victorian imperialism*

what was wanted were . . . honest, patriotic, unthinking young men to man Britain's outposts around the world. The better discipline and esprit de corps that Arnold had helped establish in order to effect liberal moral ends, became fetters binding the average public schoolboy to the worst of idols—good form and a reverence for things established. (Mack and Armytage, 1952, p. 101)

Thus the public schools came to furnish a new gentleman for an imperialistic age. By the turn of the century, the interdependent triangle of education, sport, and religion had become instrumental in exporting both the new gentleman and his sport around the world. Mangan (1986) has ably documented this process and its impact in his *The Games Ethic and Imperialism*.

In his paper "Sport, Cultural Imperialism and Colonial Response in the British Empire," Stoddart (1988) argued that, as a central feature in the public school system, sport was a powerful although largely informal social institution that created shared beliefs and attitudes between rulers and ruled while also maintaining the social distance between them.

> These people from the public schools and the old universities went into the city as bankers or lawyers, the civil service as diplomats or policy formulators, the world of politics as masters of power, and the military as officers; or they returned to education as teachers as perpetuators of the system or went into the established church, where many of them became 'muscular christians' with a belief in the good of games. Many of them, too, went as servants of empire to Africa, Asia, the Pacific or the Caribbean, taking with them their ingrained acceptance of the social power and importance of games. (Stoddart, 1988, pp. 653-654)

# Conclusion

The public school created a new gentleman for a new age, an age in which sport as a central feature of aristocratic life transcended its simple beginnings and the boundaries of gentlemanly society to become a powerful tool in the process of empire building, a civilizing agent, and a unifying force among the diverse cultures of the world. However, what was produced in this conjunctive has imposed on the world a hegemonic definition of one way of sport, a definition that has provided hegemonic masculinity, hegemonic cultural imperialism, and hegemonic conceptions of race and gender.

## Notes

1. See also the writings of: "Nimrod" (Charles James Apperly). *Nimrod's Hunting Days* and *Nimrod's Hunting Reminiscences*, republished by Bodley Head, London, 1928; and Robert Smith Surtees, *Handley Cross*; or *Mr. Jorrock's Hunt*, London: Bradbury & Evans (1854).
2. Gothic fever also overran the southern states of America during the 1840s and '50's during which time many tournaments were held in the "Old South." See Osterweis, R.G. (1949). *Romanticism and Nationalism in the Old South*. Yale Historical Publications: Vol. 39.
3. The top public schools have been recognized by modern historians as those examined by the 1861 Clarendon Commission, which included Charterhouse, Eton, Harrow, Rugby, Shrewsbury, Westminster, and Winchester. The rank label was also defined by the parents' view of the schools as fashionable and scholarly, as well as by the schoolboys' definition of a public school in relation to a clearly defined social hierarchy (Chandos, 1984, p. 22; Wilkinson, 1964, p. 9).

4. Prefects were senior boys, usually in their final year or two at the school and therefore seventeen or eighteen years of age. Prefects were responsible for discipline and virtually all organizational responsibilities within the boarding school system. A "fag" was the term given to entering freshman students, usually thirteen or fourteen years in age. The term *fag* could be translated as *gopher* as these freshmen were required to fetch and carry at the prefect's will.

# References

Andrews, C.A. (1968). Introduction. In Thomas Hughes, *Tom Brown's School Days* (pp. 3-7). New York: Aimont.

Anstruther, J. (1963). *The Knight and the umbrella.* London: Geoffrey Bles.

Armitage, J. (1977). *Man at play.* London and New York: Frederick Warne.

Arnstein, W.L. (1975). The myth of the triumphant Victorian middle class. *The Historian, 37.2,* 205-221.

Ballard, F. (1896). *Sports from the Christian standpoint.* London: James Clarke.

Bamford, T.W. (1960). *Thomas Arnold.* London: Cresset Press.

Boardman, J.H. (1931). *Notes on Kingsley's Hereward the Wake.* London: Normal Press.

Brailsford, D. (1982). Sporting days in eighteenth century England. *Journal of Sport History, 93,* 41-54.

Briggs, A. (1954). *Victorian people.* London: Odhams Press.

Brown, E.E. (1880). *True manliness: From the writings of Thomas Hughes.* Boston: D. Lothrop.

Castronovo, D. (1987). *The English gentleman.* New York: Ungar.

Carleton, J.D. (1965). *Westminster school.* London: Rupert Hart-Davis.

Chandos, J. (1984). *Boys together.* London: Hutchison & Company.

Diem, C. (Ed.) (1967). *The Olympic idea, discourses and essays.* Carl-Dian Institute, Stuttgart: Verlag Karl Hofmann.

Dunning, E., & Sheard, K. (1979). *Barbarians, gentlemen and players.* New York: New York University Press.

Fitz-James, S.L. (1858). Tom Brown's Schooldays. *The Edinburgh Review,* **107,** 172-193.

Gardiner, E.N. (1930). *Athletics of the ancient world.* Oxford: Clarendon Press.

Gies, F. (1984). *The knight in history.* New York: Harper & Row.

Gilmour, R. (1981). *The idea of the gentleman in the Victorian novel.* London: Allen and Unwin.

Girouard, M. (1979). *The Victorian country house.* New Haven: Yale University Press.

Girouard, M. (1981). *The return to Camelot.* New Haven: Yale University Press.

Goode, W.J. (1978). *The celebration of heroes.* Berkeley: University of California Press.

Haigh, A.P. (1985). *Thomas Arnold: A man of fact or fiction?* Unpublished graduate thesis, University of British Columbia, Vancouver.

Hall, S. (1986). Popular culture and the State. In T. Bennett, C. Mercer, & J. Woodacott (Eds.), *Popular culture and social relations* (pp. 22-49). Open University Press, Milton Keynes.

Harris, H.A. (1975). *Sport in Britain.* London: Stanley Paul.

Honey, J.R. de S. (1977). *Tom Brown's universe.* Toronto: Fitzhenry & Whiteside.

Houghton, W.E. (1987). *The Victorian frame of mind 1830-1870.* New Haven and London: Yale University Press.

Hughes, Thomas (1968). *Tom Brown's schooldays.* New York: Airmont.

Jenkins, R. (1981). *The Victorians and ancient Greece.* Cambridge: Harvard University Press.

Johns, E.F. (Ed.) (1912). *Words of advice to school-boys.* London: Simpkin.

Keen, M. (1984). *Chivalry*. New Haven: Yale University Press.

Kendall, A. (1946). *Charles Kingsley and his ideas*. London: Hutchinson.

Longrigg, R. (1977). *The English squire and his sport*. London: Michael Joseph.

McIntosh, P.C. (1952). *Physical education in England since 1800*. London: Bell and Sons.

McIntosh, P.C. (1963). *Sport in society*. London: Watts.

Mack, E.C. (1938). *Public schools and British opinion 1780-1860*. London: Methuen.

Mack, E.C., & Armytage, W.H.A. (1952). *Thomas Hughes: The life of the author of Tom Brown's Schooldays*. London: Ernest Benn.

Malcolmson, R.W. (1973). *Popular recreations in English society 1700-1850*. Cambridge: The University Press.

Mangan, J.A. (1981). *Athleticism in the Victorian and Edwardian public school*. New York: Cambridge University Press.

Mangan, J.A. (1986). *The games ethic and imperialism*. Harmondsworth: Viking.

Martin, R.B. (1953). *The dust of combat. A life of Charles Kingsley*. London: Faber and Faber.

Mason, P. (1982). *The English gentleman*. London: Andre Deutsch.

Mitchell, R.J., & Leys, M.D.R. (1950). *A history of the English people*. Toronto: Longmans, Green.

Morsley, C. (1979). *News from the English countryside 1750-1850*. London: Herrap.

Newby, H. (1987). *Country life: A social history of rural England*. London: Weidenfeld and Nicholson.

Newsome, D. (1959). *A history of Wellington College 1859-1959*. London: John Murray.

Peristiany, J.G. (Ed.) (1974). *Honour and shame*. Chicago: Midway reprint.

Quigly, I. (1982). *The heirs of Tom Brown*. London: Chatto and Windus.

Ritvo, H. (1987). *The animal estate*. Cambridge: Harvard University Press.

Scott, P. (1970). Cricket and the religious world in the Victorian period. *The Church Quarterly*, **3**, 134-144.

Simon, B., & Bradley, I. (Eds.) (1975). *The Victorian public schools*. Dublin: Gill and Macmillan.

Stoddart, B. (1988). Sport, cultural imperialism, and colonial response in the British empire. *Comparative Studies in Society and History*, **30**, 4.

Strutt, J. (1834). *Sports and pastimes of the people of England*. London: Thomas Tegg.

Turner, F.U. (1981). *The Greek heritage in Victorian Britain*. New Haven: Yale University Press.

Warner, R. (1945). *English public schools*. London: Collins.

Wilkinson, R. (1964). *The prefects*. Toronto: Oxford University Press.

Williams, R. (1977). *Marxism and literature*. Oxford: Oxford University Press.

Woodward, Sir Llewelyn (1962). *The age of reform* (2nd ed.). Oxford: Clarendon Press.

Wright, C.J. (1977). Before Tom Brown: Education and the sporting ethos in the early 19th century. *Journal of Education Administration and History*, **9**(1), 7-14.

# CHAPTER 4

# Transforming Into a Tradition: Rugby and the Making of Imperial Wales, 1890-1914

*David L. Andrews*
*Jeremy W. Howell*

> *Rugby engages a nation in need of an identity. From childhood onwards, it holds the imagination.*
>
> Gerald Davies,
> Welsh Rubgy International Player

> *I would rather have played for Wales at Cardiff Arms Park than Hamlet at the Old Vic.*
>
> Richard Burton

Wales is the smallest nation in Britain, with a population of approximately 4 million living within 8,000 square miles. However, what is lacked in acreage is made up for in national *hwyl*. This volatile spirit, this affective mood, desire, and fervor helps distinguish the Welsh from their immediate neighbors and longtime oppressors, the English. In Wales rugby commands the national gaze, and it is at the rugby arena where Welsh *hwyl* is most evident. To the popular imagination rugby is as Welsh as coal mining, male voice choirs, *How Green Was My Valley*, Dylan Thomas, and Tom Jones. As the noted Welsh rugby coach Bill Samuel (1986) commented, "Rugby is our national game" (p. 152).

There are few more nationalistic moments in British sport than when 50,000 or so Welsh men and women sing their national anthem, *Hen Wlad Fy Nhadau* (Land of My Fathers), before an international rugby game at Cardiff Arms Park. The trepidation that such a unified voice strikes into opposing teams is legendary. Within a rugby context the anthem acts as an emotional and nostalgic documentary of what being Welsh is all about. Rugby brings out the sparkle in a proud and historically downtrodden people. Feelings of joy and melancholia, pride and prejudice, community and memory, heritage and self-expression, politics and passion all come together as one, framed in a few moments of intense nationalistic fervor.

Only in the last 100 years has rugby acquired such a prominence in Wales. Contrary to popular mythology and romanticism, there is no God-given decree that makes rugby inherently Welsh. The connection between rugby and Wales is neither law nor an essential or absolute fact of life. This articulation required specific conditions to appear and had to be composed and sustained by specific sociocultural processes.

The period of Welsh ascendancy (1890-1914) created a historical conjuncture later dubbed "the High Noon of Edwardian Wales" (Morgan, 1982). By the start of this period, Wales had begun to assert its influence within economic, religious, and political realms. However, it was rugby that was to play a major part in consolidating the modern Welsh nation. The game had become an emergent feature of Welsh popular culture by the early 1890s. In the ensuing years, the ambitious industrial bourgeoisie thrust rugby onto the agenda of Welsh cultural consciousness and made it resonate with the ideological and structural precepts that constituted the emergent definition of Wales.

The frequent outpourings of the Welsh media agencies, as well as numerous symbolic practices and actions, were the avenues through which the professional class was able to manufacture and consolidate the relationship between rugby and an unfolding Welsh nationality. These mechanics of articulation were comparable to what Gareth Williams (1988) described as the "literary bread and literal circuses" (p. 132) that promoted the nationalist ideology of the Welsh industrial bourgeoisie. Between 1890 and 1914 the interpretive actions of the Welsh populace transformed rugby into a nationally popular social activity. Rugby came to represent a significant site at which the ascendant power group asserted its influence on an expanding populace. Our purpose in this chapter is to analyze this period and reconstruct the context in which the articulation between rugby and the Welsh nation first occurred.

# The Making of Imperial Wales

*There was no concealing the disconcerting newness of the South Wales society of the last quarter of the nineteenth century.*

D. Smith and G. Williams,
*Fields of Praise*

The second half of the 19th century witnessed the development of Wales into a thriving industrial nation. This growth was in stark contrast to the rest of the stagnating British industrial economy. The South Walian annex of the Imperial productive force was the one British region where growth was still "breakneck and full of promise" (G.A. Williams, 1985, p. 222). While the tinplate, copper, and zinc industries paved the way, the expansion of anthracite mining resulted in "King

Coal'' (Morgan, 1982), conveying Wales to the center of the world economic stage. To boost the flagging British economy the Anglo-architects of the British Empire gazed expectantly at the physical and human resources of Wales. Wales became a prime target for the predatory economic impulses of British inner colonialism.

The rapid maturation of Welsh industrial capitalism had a profound effect on Wales. The expanded mining industry, centered on South Wales, polarized the country into depressed northern and thriving southern regions. Entering the last quarter of the 19th century, the overwhelming majority of the Welsh population lived in the new towns and cities of the narrow southern industrial belt.

Industrial capitalism proved divisive in Welsh society, creating markedly different social groupings with contrasting values, beliefs, and aspirations. Thus migrant workers from rural Wales, immigrant workers predominantly from the southwest of England, and a flourishing industrial bourgeoisie produced an uneasy coalition within Welsh society. These disparate groups clashed, denying Welsh society any cohesion or unity. Even the domain of popular culture was fragmented between practices and identities that reflected the diverse backgrounds of the Welsh populace. And there was growing dissatisfaction among the industrial population as they began to experience the oppression and exploitation that accompanied industrial capitalism.

New industrial communities sprang up whose very existence challenged the accepted definition of the nation. For this reason, the later Victorian era was marked by a crisis of ''conscience of the Welsh people, as they are forced to reassess themselves, and readjust to a new world'' (Morgan, 1986a, p. 34). In short there existed a definitive ambiguity affecting the Welsh nation, a clear example of a crisis of national identity. On the threshold of a period of visible economic prosperity, Wales was faced with a distinct lack of homogeneity that threatened to disrupt any impending advances.

It was left to a new and dynamic social coalition to assuage the stark variance afflicting the Welsh condition. According to Morgan (1982), ''Economic expansion provided the coalfield indirectly and other parts of the Principality, with a new prosperous mercantile and professional class such as it had previously lacked'' (p. 94). This group was primarily concerned with administering and overseeing their vested interests in the growth of Welsh industrial capitalism. Consequently, the ambitious industrial bourgeoisie concerned themselves with their own (and, indirectly, Welsh national) advancement within the British Imperial economic framework.

The path to an Imperial Wales was reached through the promotion of a Welsh cultural nationalism, which proved a potent agent of social cement, cohesion, and legitimation, in the midst of the trauma of industrialization. As Rawkins (1983) pointed out, Welsh cultural nationalism was a compensatory reaction to industrial expansion: It was ''a response to the development and diffusion of the modern, capitalist, industrial economy'' (p. 215). Rearticulating rather than rejecting the residual national traditions and activities of earlier periods of Welsh history, the Welsh middle class sought to formulate a Welsh culture and identity more relevant to the requirements of consolidating and capitalizing on ''the most buoyant and expansive economy in Britain'' (G.A. Williams, 1985, p. 221).

# Rugby and the Imperial Welsh Nation

*Amidst the silence that could almost be felt, the Colonials stood in
the centre of the field and sang their weird war-cry. Teddy Morgan
acted as conductor while the Welsh team sang their national anthem.
The great crowd joined in the chorus. The effect was electrifying.*

An observer, Wales versus New Zealand

By the last quarter of the 19th century Wales was involved in a bourgeois-led
ideological struggle over the popular understanding of the Welsh nation. This conflict
involved the winning over of the Welsh populace to a new image of themselves.
As Hall (1981) informs us, this is a very complex procedure; cultural change is a
process whereby some cultural practices and activities are replaced by others. It is
within the realm of cultural struggle that rugby, a distinct form of Welsh popular
culture by the 1890s, came to represent a significant site on which the ascendant
middle class sought to impose its hegemonic will on the Welsh populace. Rugby
became firmly entrenched in a larger field of social forces that engaged the Welsh
people, within the ideological boundaries of a new Imperial Wales, a Wales that
was simultaneously classless and democratic, progressive and historic, Welsh and
British (G.A. Williams, 1982, 1985).

## Classless and Democratic

Within the emerging Imperial nation considerable emphasis was placed on the
apparent democratic and classless nature of Welsh society. This conception of Wales
was expressed within the notion of the *gwerin*. A complex and almost untranslatable
Welsh term, the *gwerin* referred to the common people but only in the sense that they
were not the nobility or *bonedd*. However, the *gwerin* cannot be simply translated as
the working class. Rather, the *gwerin* can be described as the Welsh middle and
lower classes who came to prominence in the 1830s and 1840s, after centuries of
passive obedience to the Welsh squirearchy and the Anglican clergy (Morgan,
1986b). The *gwerin* emerged from ''the religious upheavals of the eighteenth, and
the political and social upheavals of the early nineteenth centuries'' (Morgan, 1986b,
p. 135). Evidently the concept of the *gwerin* can be traced back to the period of
Welsh history when the radicalism of Welsh religious nonconformity first began to
hold the national consciousness in a vicelike grip.

Despite being the product of a small section of Welsh society, this preacher-
based ideology had an influential effect on the popular imagination. Through nonconformity the Welsh created an identity for themselves, which was promoted by a
populace ''united in their Welsh self-consciousness as expressed in the life of the
chapel'' (Morgan, 1986a, p. 35). This movement of Protestant dissent united working
and middle class people around a classless and democratic populism, effectively
camouflaging a social structure that was anything but classless and democratic. To
the popular imagination Wales had become the nation of the *gwerin*.

With the concerted industrial capitalist development of the late 19th century,
the populism of nonconformity lost its all-embracing grip on the Welsh people.

Nonconformist Wales was undermined by the harsh social realities that accompanied the development of industrial capitalism and by a new professional class that was more concerned with its own and Welsh national advancement. However, the vision of Wales as a land of the *gwerin* did not simply disappear. Instead, the concept of the *gwerin* was rearticulated into a new fused discourse of "democracy, radicalism, nonconformity and literacy in the later nineteenth century" (Jones, 1984, p. 211).

As previously mentioned, industrialization created deep rifts and divisions within Wales. A partial remedy to this splintering of Welsh society was a reaffirmation of the traditional, if fallacious, idea of Wales being a united nation of the *gwerin*. In times of national instability it was an astute step to connect the expressions of contemporary Welsh progress to the unique (especially when compared to the class-based cleavages within English society) classless democracy that was believed to exist in Wales.

Predictably, rugby football became connected to the reworked understanding of the *gwerin*. The 1890s witnessed a marked growth in the number of working-class participants in the game. In 1895 there were 23 clubs affiliated with the Welsh Football Union (W.F.U.); by 1900 there were 50. The bulk of the new clubs were situated in the southern mining industrial valleys. One such valley, the Rhondda, grew from a population of 1,000 in 1851 to over 113,000 by 1901. From such rapid proletarian expansion surfaced the near-mythical Rhondda forward.[1] This generic term effectively referred to any blue-collar forward who emerged onto the Welsh international scene during the 1890s. And it was not long until "the Rhondda Forwards—a readily employed euphemism for any collier, tinplateman, steelworker or docker—were fully united with 'clever'—generally middle class—backs" (Smith, 1984, p. 107). By successfully embracing manual laborers for their physical strength and white-collar professionals for their skill and creativity, Welsh rugby was promoted as transcending the social divides that had characterized the development of rugby and football in England (G. Williams, 1988). The Welsh middle class successfully diverted attention from the inherently class-ridden nature of the Welsh game. This was achieved by promoting the idea that regardless of socioeconomic background, being a gentleman was a prerequisite of participation, and gentleman status was arrived at through an individual's skill and attitude as opposed to social background. Thus the Rhondda forward was a gentleman on the pitch, but a collier off it. The archetypal middle-class backs were gentlemen wherever and whenever.

Evidently, rugby was in no sense of the word a classless practice; indeed, it painfully reflected the class divisions existing within Welsh society. Similarly, the game could scarcely be described as being democratic. The working class made up an ever-increasing proportion of the rugby-playing fraternity but was distinctly underrepresented in the upper echelons of the games administration. Regardless of Dunning and Sheard's (1979) claims to the contrary, the Welsh middle class was significantly involved in the running of the game. However, as a classless and democratic practice, rugby was successfully grafted onto a rearticulated version of Wales as a democratic and classless modern nation of the *gwerin*. As one contemporary commentator saw it:

Wales possesses in Rugby Football a game which is immeasurably more valuable than the popular code of the other countries. . . . It has made a democracy (i.e., the common man) not only familiar with an amateur sport of distinguished rank but is in reality a discovery of democracy which acts as participant and patron. . . . A game democratic and amateur is a rare thing—a unique thing to be cherished, and therefore the concern of thinking men who value the complex influences working for higher levels of citizenship. (Smith, 1980, p. 228)

## Progressive and Historic

The Wales of the early 1890s was a vibrant and progressive (if somewhat divided) nation. Dominated by a southern industrial region that revitalized Britain's Atlantic economy, Wales strutted cockily into the Edwardian era. In the persona of its national representatives, Wales excelled in politics, religion, education, and sport. During this time of fleeting euphoria surrounding the temporally prosperous and progressive Welsh nation, the onset of concerted and consistent success in international rugby was viewed as an almost inevitable result of national advancement. Welsh progress in rugby was successfully articulated with Wales's emergence as a progressive society (Smith & Williams, 1980). In this vein, Wales's first home victory over England, the accompanying Triple Crown, and the endless stream of victories of the "First Golden Age" (1900-1911) were all related to and expressed in terms of the wider national progress.

The giddy heights of national progress created a swelling tide of self-belief among the general population. In the face of the array of expressions of Welsh national advancement, which came to the fore during the last quarter of the 19th century, the Welsh became convinced they were reaping the benefits that their God-fearing existence merited, both on and off the rugby field. Although it seemed to contradict the notion of national progress, the coinciding creation of a historical demeanor was in reality very much a part of the advancement made by the Imperial Welsh nation. Indeed, progress as a nation could only be fully realized if a historic element to Wales was assembled. The unifying properties of a progressive Wales were furthered by the promotion of the supposedly historically founded elements of the contemporary Welsh condition. The historical legitimation of the Imperial nation authenticated and reinforced the progress being made.

The ideological manufacturing of Wales as a historic nation was expedited by the way in which progress was articulated to the Celtic heritage of the people. References to Wales as a nation of the Celts gave the dynamic Welsh nation a historic view of their past while offering a popular interpretation of the present. Welsh development as an economically self-confident, culturally creative, and nationally self-aware entity became linked to the supremacy of the Celtic race. The Celts were not the first inhabitants of Wales, but they were widely regarded as being racially representative of the Welsh. By perpetrating this interpretive sleight of hand, the professional classes created historic and traditional aspects to the Imperial nation.

In spite of rugby's English origins, the Welsh evidently lost their short-term memories as the game became increasingly immersed in the ideology of Welsh Celticism. This connection was advanced by racial theorists of the day and by the emerging popular commercial press (see Smith, 1981). Nowhere is this more evident than in the coverage of the 1905 international game between Wales and New Zealand. The liberal *South Wales Daily News* (December 18, 1905) provided interesting explanations for the Welsh victory:

> The men that represented Wales embodied the best manhood of the race. . . . We all know the racial qualities that made Wales supreme on Saturday: but how have they been obtained? Wales has a more restricted choice of champions than the other nations. She has had fewer opportunities in the exercise of some of the mental and physical powers than the nations with ancient universities and wider fields of training. It is amazing that in the greatest of all popular pastimes she should be equally distinguished. . . . The great quality of defence and attack in the Welsh race is to be traced to the training of the early period when powerful enemies drove them to their mountain fortresses. There was developed then those traits of character that find fruition today. "Gallant little Wales" has produced sons strong of determination, invincible stamina, resolute, mentally keen, physically sound.

Without specifically mentioning the Celtic link, the commentary explicitly adopts the hypothesis as explanation for the Welsh triumph. The more conservative national daily newspaper, the *Western Mail* (December 18, 1905), was even more forthright in its explanatory zeal, declaring that "the prestige of Wales has been enhanced tremendously as a nation possessed of those splendid [Celtic] qualities—pluck and determination."

The Welsh daily press was by no means the sole patron of the notion of Celtic supremacy. The 1906 edition of George Borrow's popular travelogue *Wild Wales* (first published in 1856) included a much-needed explanatory forward, written by Theodore Watts-Dunton. The Wales of 1906 was far different from that which Borrow's original prose described half a century earlier; rugby was barely visible in the 1850s. To address what had become a glaring oversight, Watts-Dunton related Borrow's preoccupation with the "Cymric athlete" (p. xxi) to the emergence and success of Welsh rugby. Watts-Dunton expressed regret that Borrow never lived to see the "great recrudescence of Cymric energy" that was currently being displayed on the rugby field (1906, p. xxii). Predictably Celtic athletic prowess became viewed by the Welsh populace as a major factor in Welsh rugby's successes against those of Anglo-Saxon descent. Within this context the Welsh constructed the rugby field as a site of struggle on which a battle of races, and hence nationalities, was symbolically reenacted.

The widespread rereading of George Owen's 16th century *Description of Pembrokeshire*, published in standard form in 1892 (see Howells, 1973), also had a conspicuous influence on the historical signification of Welsh rugby. Owen's account of 16th century southwest Wales detailed a version of Tudor folk football known as *cnappan*. The inherent similarities between rugby and *cnappan* provided many commentators with a direct line of historic Welsh descent for the modern game. In all probability the origins of the rugby code lay with the popular, if poorly defined, phenomena of folk football and its subsequent appropriation and standardization by the English public schools. However, as engaging as this genealogical fantasizing may be, it is wrong to claim that Welsh rugby descended directly from this singularly Welsh version of folk football. Nevertheless, many connected rugby in this way. In doing so an instant yet historic Welsh lineage was created for rugby that could rival its equally dubious Celtic pedigree.

## Welsh Indigenous and British Imperial

Rugby was ascribed a traditional demeanor through its articulation within the discourses of Welsh nationalism and British Imperialism. As stabilizing entities within the popular consciousness, the connecting of rugby to British and Welsh identities reaffirmed and consolidated its position as a Welsh game. Of course rugby was not the only fresh-faced component of an emerging Welsh cultural nationalism. The last quarter of the 19th century saw the *eisteddfod* (a festival celebrating the practices and traditions associated with Welsh cultural identity), which had been revived as an annual event at Llangollen in 1858, firmly establish itself as a festive expression of cultural distinctiveness.

The patriotic enthusiasm of the 1880s and 1890s resulted in the emergence of a proliferation of Welsh institutions. Rugby football entered into the institutionalization of Welsh life relatively early, with the founding of the W.F.U. in 1881. Other concrete manifestations of nationhood included the University of Wales (chartered in 1893) and the National Library and Museum (both chartered in 1907). Part of the motivation for founding these national institutions was the widely felt Welsh craving for parity with their more established British neighbors, the English and the Scots. These seemingly indispensable trappings of modern nation status demonstrated to the rest of the world that the modern Welsh nation had arrived.

In conjunction with tangible national institutions, the Welsh also promoted symbolic nationally representational signs in order to express and consolidate their existence. A Welsh national flag, anthem, and emblems were all brought to the fore in the late Victorian era. They indicated a nation attempting to demonstrate the progress it had made in creating an autonomous identity. Such an obvious identity out of difference to its British counterparts was hopefully going to aid the unification of the Welsh agglomeration of cultures and experiences. Rugby played a central role in this process.

The popularity and symbolic meaning of *Hen Wlad Fy Nhadau* (written in 1856 by two Pontypridd brothers, Evan and James James) resulted in the song becoming the Welsh national anthem during this period. Additionally, Wales acquired a number of national emblems and symbols that were to represent the new nation. The leek, the three-plumed motif of the Prince of Wales, the dragon of Cadwaladr, and later the daffodil were all publicized as having symbolic Welsh meanings.

These Welsh national "badges of membership" (Hobsbawm, 1983, p. 11) were transposed to the rugby arena where leeks, red dragons, and daffodils were commonly used to distinguish national allegiance. At the celebrated international match against New Zealand in 1905, the Welsh rugby team chose to sing *Hen Wlad Fy Nhadau* in response to the *haka*, a Maori war dance and symbol of New Zealand nationalism. Significantly, one of the earliest and most publicized airings of the Welsh national anthem was in a rugby context.

The Wales being constructed at this time was no less pro-British, in an Imperial sense, than it was aggressively Welsh. As G.A. Williams (1985) commented, "Welsh identity has constantly renewed itself by anchoring itself in variant forms of Britishness"; in doing so the marginal Welsh have done little more than live within "the interstices of other people's history" (p. 194). Nowhere is the duality of the Welsh condition better exemplified than in the Welsh placement within the British Imperial structure of the late 19th century.

To exploit the Welsh economy to the full, the English needed to provide the Welsh with some sort of cohesive British identity. In short, Wales needed to be connected to the triumphs of British colonial expansion so that the growing workforce would willingly contribute to the consolidation and expansion of the Empire. This coveted Welsh Imperialism increasingly penetrated the faltering Nonconformist Welsh condition throughout the last quarter of the 19th century. This can be seen from the sales returns of Wilkins, the workman's booksellers in Merthyr. In 1850 this outlet was selling 189 copies of the newspaper *News of the World* to every 12 copies of the Chartist *Northern Star*. This figure is particularly significant when one considers that *News of the World* was promoting a "British jingoism proper to an imperial working class, a music-hall in print" (G.A. Williams, 1985, p. 202).

It would be wrong to think that the English power elite merely imposed an Imperial British consciousness on the Welsh population. Rather, Imperial British capitalism developed such a hegemonic positioning that the Welsh actively sought a position of prominence within the Imperial framework. The industrial middle class clearly wished to connect the glorious Empire to the headway made by Wales. As Smith (1980) stressed: "The new Wales was, in important respects, profoundly pro-imperialist—the Empire of nations was, after all, its own highest justification for within the imperial framework could be made the Welsh contribution" (pp. 225-226). Welsh developments and successes were thrust onto the world stage. Their profile was heightened by articulating them as constituent components of the British Empire.

The emergence of Wales into the Imperial economy meant a reconstruction of Welsh identity. Wales became a vibrant, if junior, partner in the British Empire. By entering the discourse that subsumed the new nation, rugby was able to bridge the gap between an emergent and fully established aspect of Welsh popular culture. Moreover, the popularity of rugby was such that as a high profile aspect of Welsh life, successes associated with the game helped to constitute and consolidate the Imperial nation. Like the majority of the Welsh populace, the W.F.U. actively chose to emphasize the British identity of Wales by articulating Welsh rugby to symbolic elements of British culture. Indeed, there are numerous examples whereby rugby was connected to an Imperial discourse. The rejection of the leek and the subsequent adoption of the Prince of Wales's three plumed insignia as the motif worn on Welsh international jerseys, along with his motto *Ich Dien* (''I Serve''), represented a move by the Welsh rugby administration to demonstratively underline its loyalty to and place within the British Imperial state formation. The pro-Imperialist sentiments of the W.F.U. were further demonstrated on the occasion of the death of Queen Victoria in 1901. Rugby grounds were closed for 2 weeks throughout Wales until after the state funeral, as a mark of respect for their Queen and an expression of their allegiance to British sovereignty.

Far from dismissing any notion of Welsh individuality, these expressions of loyalty signified a contemporary need to express Welsh nationalism within a distinctly British context. Thus, the Welsh national rugby team represented the sporting equivalent of the Welsh Guards, the Royal Welsh Fusiliers, and the Royal Regiment of Wales. These military units were nationally associated elements of the British army. Similarly, rugby became a prominent Welsh torchbearer within a wider context. The national side vied in competition with its British adversaries in the British Home International Championship, which Wales first won in 1893.

Welsh players who were selected as members of British touring teams to the far reaches of the Empire reinforced the British identity of the Welsh. Prominent players such as Gwyn Nicholls (1899 tour to Australia) and R.T. Gabe and P.F. Bush (1904 tour to Australia and New Zealand) truly were British Lions and their exploits as such were followed with great interest throughout the Principality.

The W.F.U. was also prepared to support its more combative nonsporting national representatives abroad. The £250 donation in 1899 to the dependents of South Walian volunteers to the Boer War, and the considerable gift in 1900 to the ''Welsh hospital'' in South Africa, bore witness to the commitment to this British conflict (Smith, 1980). Such a feeling of Britishness also permeated through most of the Welsh social spectrum:

> That January (1900) in Swansea the crowd of almost 40,000 who had come to see Scotland sang ''God Save the Queen'' with some feeling—the immediate news of the war had been of General Warren's bloody retreat from Spion Kop. (Smith & Williams, 1980, pp. 121-122)

It seems clear that most Welsh were concerned yet wholehearted supporters of their involvement in the Boer War, demonstrating a Welsh vindication of both Britain and a British identity.

Rugby played a major role in reinforcing the British Imperial identity of Wales, and nowhere is this better exemplified than in the media coverage of the Pyrrhic international match played against the All-Blacks in 1905. So important was this meeting that the renowned Welsh rugby journalist J.B.G. Thomas (1970) was moved to describe it as ''the most historic match ever to be played in the game'' (p. 10). It occurred on December 16, toward the end of the first New Zealand All-Black tour of the British Isles. These ''All-Conquering Colonials'' (*Daily Mail*, September 22, 1905) went into the game having won all 27 previous games on the tour, including conclusive international victories against Scotland, Ireland, and England.

During the course of their triumphs the All-Blacks amassed a staggering point tally of 791-22. As a result of All-Black supremacy over the rest of British rugby, the international against Wales was increasingly viewed as the last chance for the humiliated home countries to gain some sort of revenge against the upstart colonials. Wales, holder of the Triple Crown, unbeaten at home for 6 years, was undoubtedly the strongest of the home rugby nations. And yet on the eve of the game, confidence in Welsh fortunes was scarce:

> Wales is the only portion of the United Kingdom in which Rugby Union football is the national game (as it is in New Zealand), and it would be a kind of poetic justice if the victorious progress of the New Zealand team were checked at Cardiff today. . . . None of the Welsh teams . . . has the faintest chance of scoring a victory, and the only consolation for the players of Rugby Union in this country will be found in the inability of the "silver fern" to score a full thousand points in the course of their tour. (*The London Times,* December 16, 1905)

Despite the skepticism of many commentators, the game was enthusiastically anticipated by the Welsh.

The great public interest shown toward this rugby war created an atmosphere of incredible expectancy: "The match is eagerly looked forward to and, although the Cardiff Arms Park can accommodate 40,000 people, it is estimated that almost double that will want to witness the game" (*The London Times,* December 16, 1905).

On a dry and windless day, a record crowd of 47,000 (the gate receipts amounted to £2,600) watched a rugby spectacle that has rarely, if ever, been matched. An ultimately victorious Welsh national team became the proud representatives and saviors of the honor of Great Britain. This is illustrated by the following quote from the *South Wales Daily News:* "Wales has won! What the other nations of these islands have failed to do has been achieved by those sons of the Ancient Britons" (December 18, 1905). On the same day, the *Western Mail* reiterated the Imperial nature of the victory by stating that in beating the undefeated All-Blacks, Wales "came to the rescue of the Empire."

The great popularity of rugby meant it was in a unique position to satisfy the seemingly diverse needs of a Welsh society that was committed to developing a legitimate Welsh national ideology within the wider British Imperial structure. As the final defenders of Britain, the Welsh rejoiced in their victory over the colonial upstarts, just as they had supported the Imperialist cause during the Boer War. As Smith (1981) concludes: "Neither of these public sentiments was contradicted by the emphasis on Welshness, for it was, in those heady days, seen as the passport to complete equality within the British Empire" (p. 32).

# Resistance to Rugby in Wales

> *Even an ape . . . would not disgrace itself by seeking its pleasures in kicking a football. . . . If young and middle-aged men wish to*

> *frequent pubs, theatres and football fields, then let them in the name*
> *of the living God remain outside the Christian pale.*
>
> Reverend John Rees

Despite the remarkable growth in Welsh interest in rugby, it would be wrong to think there was a harmonious link between popular interest in the game and its potential for national cohesion. The industrial bourgeoisie were clearly the most powerful group within Welsh society at this time. They had appropriated rugby and sought to secure its ever increasing popular appeal to their ideological vision of Wales as an Imperial nation. While most in the working class enthusiastically embraced the game, conflicts of interest arose that reflected a working-class dissatisfaction with the ideological baggage being promoted by rugby's middle-class sponsors.

## Social Contradictions Within Welsh Rugby

As Welsh rugby entered the popular realm it became an increasingly important focal point for local community interest and involvement. The growth and standardization of club fixture lists and the emergence of Cup and League competitions enhanced the competitive element. However, the creation of community loyalties exacerbated and in some cases provoked local and regional rivalries. There evolved a keen competitive edge between teams and communities from a particular locality (e.g., Neath and Swansea) and those from particular regions (e.g., the rivalry between Swansea from the west and Cardiff from the east).

With popular class involvement came popular class practices that were often violent and robust. Incidents of serious player violence were reported, most notably during knockout competition cup games. The size of the crowds watching South Wales Challenge Cup games regularly surpassed those watching early internationals, and although this competition played a major part in popularizing rugby, the heightened rivalries expressed themselves in the increasingly violent nature of the game.

The Swansea-Cardiff game of 1892 was particularly violent. Cardiff won despite vehement and heated appeals by Swansea players to the referee. The unfortunate official was attacked after the game, a stone intended for him actually taking out a spectator's eye. In the ensuing uproar, newspaper offices in Swansea were attacked for printing the Cardiff victory (Smith & Williams, 1980). Welsh rugby was, as Gareth Williams (1988) so correctly described, not "the tranquilizer of unruly proletarian crowds any more than it was the sedative of industrial militancy" (p. 132).

Another middle-class ideal of sporting behavior openly flaunted by many working-class rugby players was the ethos of amateurism. This ideology so lauded by bourgeois promoters of the new sports conflicted with the traditional mores of popular behavior. The whole ideology of amateur sport was based on the altruistic notion of playing games for the games' sake, not for monetary reward. This did not fit comfortably with the traditional forms of recreation that dominated working-class existence, many of which encouraged gambling and were unashamedly pursued for financial reward (cock fighting, footraces, bare knuckle fights, etc.). Moreover, expecting the working classes to indulge in organized physical activity without receiving some sort of financial reward was wholly unfair and unrealistic, considering the economic deprivation that dominated proletarian existence.

The threat of professionalism came both from within and outside the amateur game of rugby union. The heightened interest in rugby resulted in the charging of an admission fee to improve club facilities. These investments subsequently attracted more paying spectators and hence more revenue. Working-class players, mindful of the loss of wages incurred due to their involvement in the game and fully aware of the profits being made as a direct result of their exploits, began to demand some sort of financial recompense. As the turn of the century approached the modest financial payments that had habitually "lubricated the cogs of Welsh club rugby" (Gareth Williams, 1985, p. 130) escalated into a glaring aberration in the Welsh game. The "shamateur" nature of rugby in Wales had long been suspected by the other Rugby Unions of the Home Countries. They were keenly aware of the strength and success the working class had brought to the Welsh game. There seems no plausible reason to deny that the following scenario from Newport Rugby Club was anything but commonplace:

> Rugger teams were supposed to be amateur but if Newport spotted a promising young man in a team up the valley, they'd find a job for him in Newport, in the docks, the timberyard, a factory, even in the workhouse, and it was always arranged that he didn't have to work the Saturday morning before a match. (Paget, 1985, pp. 120-121)

By the Edwardian era, under-the-table financial arrangements such as these were an almost universal aspect of the Welsh game.

The prominence of rugby was also threatened by the emergence of rival football codes that openly adopted professionalism and provided an alternative to the dominance of rugby union. Although predating rugby in Wales, association football came to the fore following its "reawakening" in 1890 (Lile & Farmer, 1984, p. 193), when the South Wales Football League was formed. Welsh soccer was essentially semiprofessional. It relied heavily on promotional visits made by top English clubs to arouse local interest. Soon the attraction of open financial reward resulted in soccer taking hold in some predominantly working-class valley towns such as Aberdare, Ebbw Vale, Merthyr, and Rhondda. In the process rugby was displaced as the premier sport within many of these districts. Soccer's emergence was illustrative of a working-class rejection of the middle-class sporting ethos of amateurism; a conflict similarly exhibited by the illicit professionalism present within the rugby code in Wales. However, due to the solid foothold established by rugby, as well as its bourgeois sponsorship, soccer was never likely to usurp the national prominence of a practice that was well on the way to becoming *the* Welsh game.

The Welsh bourgeoisie clearly appreciated the importance of popular culture, particularly rugby, to the manufacturing of a new nation. This meant care had to be taken when tackling conspicuous acts of working-class resistance, such as the overt violence and illegal payments that were plaguing Welsh rugby. It was vital not to jeopardize popular support for the game if the link between rugby and national consciousness was to be maintained, enhanced, and the middle-class vision of Wales popularized and ultimately realized. A direct assault on popular feeling could have resulted in hostility toward the bourgeois position of leadership. Hence, the middle class could not ignore the growing popularity of rugby and the game's embedded position within the national consciousness. Only through compromise and negotiation could the Welsh power bloc consolidate its hegemonic ascendancy. Consequently, the administrative machinery of the W.F.U. imposed little more than token punishments designed to reprimand but not alienate the working class.

Concerning the increasingly violent nature of rugby, the W.F.U. was almost compelled to suspend the South Wales Challenge Cup. This happened in 1897. It was hoped that such a development would diffuse the competitiveness and violent acts prevalent both on and off the field. Motivated by unruly crowd behavior, the W.F.U. also temporarily closed grounds, including Neath (1895), Aberavon (1896, 1899), and Abertillery (1897). The W.F.U. even erected placards in grounds warning spectators of the punishments for disturbing the peace and distributed game rules intended to educate the volatile crowds. Although violent behavior remained an aspect of Welsh rugby, the Welsh administration had publicly declared that violence was definitely not an acceptable aspect of the modern game. By doing so, rugby was promoted as a pursuit that was to be played and watched by Welsh "gentlemen" of whatever social class.

The abuses of the amateur ethos were more immediately threatening, and they stung the W.F.U. into some positive action. In April 1900 the W.F.U. agreed with its English counterpart to clamp down on the specter of professionalism. As a result, in 1901, the Aberaman club was expelled from the W.F.U. for alleged financial irregularities. In reality this and similar gestures were little more than token acts designed to appease the Home Unions. The administrators of rugby in Wales were powerless to completely eradicate the professional element involved in the game, simply because it was such a prevalent aspect of it. A compromise of sorts was arrived at in which open professionalism was officially abhorred by the W.F.U. The payment of players' expenses, sometimes generous in the extreme, became an overlooked but prevalent anachronism of the amateur ethos. This shamateur settlement seemed to suit all parties. It was an acceptable response to the antiprofessional sentiments of the Welsh middle class while still accommodating the more financially oriented working-class participants. Gareth Williams (1985) posed a valid question in asking just "How Amateur Was My Valley?" during the period from 1890 to 1914.

## Nonconformism and Welsh Liberalism

While the Welsh working class represented the most potent threat to the hegemony of the industrial bourgeoisie, there were factions within the Welsh middle class that displayed a revulsion toward rugby and the industrially oriented Imperial nation. The middle-class dissent vented toward rugby in Wales came from the religious and political wings of the residues of Nonconformity. Although a prominent practice by the 1890s, rugby had yet to confirm its traditional pedigree and was viewed with paranoid skepticism by some sections of Welsh society:

> Although rugby would become a touchstone of Welshness, especially in the eyes of the non-Welsh world, it was lacking any such unequivocal lineage in the 1890's. Rugby, in the eyes of those who thought they were leading a national renaissance in politics . . . was of foreign origin and dubious influence. (Smith & Williams, 1980, p. 99)

To the leaders of Nonconformist Wales, the Chapel dignitaries and Welsh Liberal politicians, rugby was a touchstone of a new and threatening way of life imported from England. It represented the heathenous and sin-laden industrial existence. The religious and political resistance against rugby was indicative of two cultures in conflict, one residual and one emergent, vying for supremacy in the popular representation of the Welsh nation.

Religious dissent had dominated Wales since the middle of the 19th century, when the Welsh became a very religious people whose social lives were focused around preaching, Chapel societies, choirs, temperance movements, and Sunday schools. And yet it was toward the end of the century, just when the hegemony of Chapel culture seemed most overpowering, that conspicuous signs of decline appeared (G.A. Williams, 1985). Many aspects of social behavior (including marriage, attitudes toward law and order, education, and leisure pursuits) evolved in ways that resisted the overbearing stringencies of Chapel culture. Such developments also reflected a shift from a religious to a more secular Welsh existence that accompanied the maturity of the capitalist economy.

Rugby was thrust into this cultural struggle as representing the profane culture associated with the new industrial world. To further damn rugby in the eyes of the Chapel, early clubs were often sponsored by, and used the facilities of, the local public house, thus linking the game to the evils of alcohol. The Chapel displayed a strident hostility towards rugby that manifested itself in a number of ways. In 1890 the members of a Chapel at the head of the Swansea valley narrowly lost a public debate concerning the future of the village rugby club. In response to their defeat—on the day before the team's first game—the Chapel representatives sawed down the goalposts and took them to the local police station. The loosening of moral standards and religious adherence that became associated with the game resulted in Chapel members viewing rugby as a disruptive threat to the religiously devout nation they had created.

The religious revival of 1904 and 1905 was clear response to the threat posed by rugby. It was an act of resistance by an established, if increasingly residual, definition of Wales against the threatening modernity of an industrialized upstart Wales. This "cry of anguish from a people torn between two cultures . . . singled out rugby as a rival deserving of condemnation. It had some success" (Smith & Williams, 1980, pp. 120, 126). There were ritual burnings of international tickets and rugby jerseys; many clubs disbanded, including Morriston, Ammanford, and Loughor.

Despite its widespread significance and impact, the revival represented little more than the final throes of a doomed culture. Rugby was engendering more fervor and passion than ever before. Nonconformity had little option but to acquiesce to the swelling tide of popular support for rugby. As one preacher put it, "What was the use of preaching against football" (reported in the *South Wales Daily News*, January 7, 1901). Rather than following their predecessors and displaying an open hostility to the game, later preachers were at pains to place rugby, as an accepted element of Welsh popular culture, firmly within the context of their Welsh religion. A Presbyterian minister in 1910 publicly rejected "the rigid system under which he had been brought up (that) had led him to believe that football matches were of such a character that it was wrong for Christian people to support them" (reported in the *South Wales Daily News*, January 6, 1910). The minister (in accord with many of his colleagues) realized that the survival of his religion required its acceptance of the constituents of the Imperial nation. Thus the Chapel was compelled to conspicuously support rugby if it was to maintain its popular status and establish a foothold within the new Wales.

From a political standpoint, rugby as a product of urban and industrial Wales was viewed with hostility by the leaders of Welsh Liberalism. This social group was keen to preserve Nonconformist Wales and strove to promote a separatist agenda for the nation. David Lloyd George, the leader of the *Cymru Fydd* (Free Wales) movement, was dismayed by the grip rugby had on the imagination of the Welsh populace. In a letter written to his wife in 1895, he commented that the people of Tredegar had "sunk into a morbid footballism" (quoted in Smith & Williams, 1980, p. 66).

By the 1980s, the population of Wales was clearly more interested in Welsh rugby than in Welsh radicalism. Consequently, the Welsh Liberals had little option but to accommodate the game within their agenda. Interestingly, it was David Lloyd George who led the way. He attended his first match in 1907, commenting, "It's a most extraordinary game. I never saw it before and I must say it is more exciting than politics" (Smith & Williams, 1980, p. 66). By 1913 his son was a regular within the London Welsh side. Lloyd George's conversion to rugby football mirrored the rejection of extremist Welsh isolationism by a socially aware Welsh Liberal party attempting to secure a successful future.

The Welsh Liberals were coerced into discarding their isolationist ambitions in the wake of the potency of the new national ideology of the industrial bourgeoisie and the oppositional proletarian culture that accompanied the maturation of industrial capitalism. The rejection of separatism was a prerequisite for radical politics to play a definitive role within Imperial Wales. The Welsh Liberals needed to be sensitive to popular feeling to avoid being discarded as a remnant of an earlier age.

The threat to rugby from radical political thought never really materialized. The game's widespread popularity rendered it a dominant practice that compelled the evolving Welsh Liberal movement to accommodate the game. Welsh politics took a definite step toward a modified compromise and popularity by positively encouraging and incorporating emergent popular cultural phenomena such as rugby. In doing so, Welsh Liberalism provided Wales with a political identity that was aligned with mainstream British Liberalism.

Rugby did experience resistance from a number of sources in its ascent to nationally popular status. That rugby football was able to sidestep the threats posed by working-class, religious, and political resistance, its Welsh identity greatly enhanced, demonstrated the adroit maneuverings of the hegemonic leadership of the Welsh industrial bourgeoisie. Through the processes of incorporation, negotiation, and either rejection or compromise, rugby was firmly articulated to the discourse of Imperial Wales.

# Conclusion

> *Wales is a process. Wales is an artifact which the Welsh produce.*
> *The Welsh make and re-make Wales day by day, year by year, genera-*
> *tion after generation.*
>
> Gwyn A. Williams,
> *When Was Wales?*

In less than three decades, rugby experienced a relatively smooth transition from being an emergent pastime to becoming a traditional and dominant popular practice "stitched into the pattern of Welsh life forever" (Smith & Williams, 1980, p. 172). The connection between rugby and the literal and literary elements of Imperial Wales played a major part in the rearticulation of the popular image of Wales. In turn, this confirmed and consolidated rugby's sociocultural prominence within the "new" nation. As Gareth Williams (1983) stated, "Rugby football, along with coal, hymns and Lloyd George, signalled the full blown arrival of Wales into the modern world" (p. 339).

The immediate aftermath of the 1905 Welsh victory over New Zealand was a period that could be described as the zenith of Welsh Imperialism. Wales was temporarily united by a popular national discourse that successfully sutured together the residues of earlier traditions with the emergent activities and practices of an industrial Wales. The rapidity of rugby's articulation into the new Imperial discourse is exemplified by the following reference to a group of Welsh students standing on Southampton Docks, January 23, 1906. Decked in leeks and red, and singing *Hen Wlad Fy Nhadau* as a gesture of farewell to Dave Gallagher's First New Zealand All-Black touring side, these Welsh supporters had no inclination that:

> Neither their sporting passion nor their colours and favours would have seemed
> representative of Welshness to their grandparents. The song they sang was, an
> anthem, even younger. Their marks of Welshness, apparently so venerable,
> were almost as young as they were themselves. (Smith, 1984, p. 28)

In discussing rugby's articulation to a new vision of Wales as an Imperial nation, we have tried to provide the context in which rugby was inserted. By context we do not mean some preconstituted context into which rugby was simply stitched. Contexts are actively produced, requiring work and effort. A context cannot exist before the elements that constitute it (Grossberg, 1989), and rugby is one such constituent of the Imperial Welsh conjuncture.

Rugby's rise to nationally popular status helped cement the hegemonic relations in the Wales of this period. Hegemony refers to all those political, economic, and ideological practices and processes whereby a power bloc (not a whole class but an alliance of class fractions) has control over society. The power bloc controls a nucleus of economic activity and can expand that control into a moment of political leadership and social authority throughout the cultural sphere of life. In Wales it was a leadership that attempted to unify and reconstruct the vision of society through a series of national themes: classless and democratic, progressive and historic, Welsh and British. Rugby clearly played a part in that reconstruction.

There were other elements and discourses at play in the formation of a middle-class hegemony at this time: the workplace, the economy, the struggle over the Welsh language, the rise of the union and the Labour movement. Many aspects we admittedly omit. Our point has been to concentrate on the nationally popular status of rugby, to emphasize its crucial place in the ideological realm of late Victorian and Edwardian Wales. Rugby was part of a broader process that created a new understanding of Wales by which people organized themselves and came to make sense of their lives and the society in which they lived. For as Gramsci (1971) noted, it is through the popular that things pass into the realm of common sense.

According to Hall (1988), it is the conceptions that organize the people that are worth struggling over. Social subjects can be won over to new positions and to new views of themselves and their nation. This interpretive victory was not about the Welsh being duped by a stream of dominant ideas passed down by some consolidated ruling class. Like Hall, we do not believe organic ideologies are quite so consistent or homogeneous. We need to take seriously the fact that the Welsh do produce their own history even if it is not under conditions of their own making. We have tried to show that the making and remaking of Imperial Wales was made up of a number of sometimes competing discourses. In the process creating the new nation these discourses seem to fracture along particular lines, get stitched up, and articulated into a new national agenda and leadership where all Welsh people, the *gwerin* and the *bonedd*, minister and congregation, capital and labor, rich and poor, rugby player and spectator can be represented.

The process of articulation is what ideology is all about. To return to our introduction, there was absolutely nothing that guaranteed the connection of rugby, the game, to Wales, the nation. That articulation was socially, culturally, and politically produced.

## Acknowledgments

We would like to acknowledge the great debt we owe to both Gwyn A. Williams and Gareth Williams. The work of these outstanding scholars directed us toward the problematic addressed within this chapter. Gwyn A. Williams has produced many indispensable monographs relating to the historical understanding of Welsh culture and society. His Gramscian-oriented cultural Marxism has been important in shaping our own sociopolitical commitment and concerns. Gareth Williams has produced excellent studies that represent the logical starting point for anyone interested in the history of Welsh rugby. It was never our intention to develop or enhance Gareth Williams's work; this would prove an impossible task. Rather, we have used many of the products of his meticulous historical probing to substantiate and, we hope, enliven our more critical and culturally focused concerns.

## Note

1. The positions in rugby are broadly divided into the forwards and the backs. During the formative years of rugby football, forward play was dominated by the combined physical commitment required within the scrum and the lineout, whereas back play was more reliant on individual creativity and finesse.

## References

Billot, J. (1970). *History of Welsh international rugby*. Ferndale: Ron Jones.

Bragg, M. (1989). *Rich: The life of Richard Burton*. London: Hodder and Stoughton.

Davies, G. (1983). *Welsh rugby scrapbook*. London: Souvenir Press.

Dunning, E., & Sheard K. (1979). *Barbarians, gentlemen and players*. New York: New York University Press.

Gramsci, A. (1971). *Selections from the prison notebooks* (Q. Hoare, & G. Nowell-Smith, Trans.). New York: International.

Grossberg, L. (1989). The formation of cultural studies: An American in Birmingham. *Strategies*, **2**, 114-149.

Hall, S. (1981). Notes on deconstructing "the popular." In R. Samuel (Ed.), *People's history and socialist theory* (pp. 227-240). London: Routledge & Kegan Paul.

Hall, S. (1988). *The hard road to renewal: Thatcherism and the crisis of the left*. London: Verso.

Hobsbawm, E. (1983). Introduction: Inventing traditions. In E.J. Hobsbawm & T. Ranger (Eds.), *The invention of tradition* (pp. 1-14). Cambridge: Cambridge University Press.

Howells, B. (Ed.) (1973). *Elizabethan Pembrokeshire: The evidence of George Owen*. Pembrokeshire Record Society Series 2.

Jones, G.E. (1984). *Modern Wales: A concise history c.1485-1979*. Cambridge: Cambridge University Press.

Lile, B., & Farmer, D. (1984). The early development of Association Football in South Wales, 1890-1906. *Honourable Society of Cymmrodorion Transactions*, 193-215.

Morgan, K.O. (1982). *Rebirth of a nation: Wales 1880-1980*. Oxford: Oxford University Press.

Morgan, P. (1986a). Keeping the legends alive. In T. Curtis (Ed.), *Wales: The imagined nation* (pp. 17-42). Bridgend: Poetry Wales Press.

Morgan, P. (1986b). The gwerin of Wales: Myth and reality. In I. Hume & W.T.R. Pryce (Eds.), *The Welsh and their country: Selected readings in the social sciences* (pp. 134-152). Llandysul: Gomer Press.

Paget, M. (1985). *Man of the valleys: The recollections of a South Wales miner*. Gloucester: Alan Sutton.

Rawkins, P. (1983). Uneven development and the politics of culture. In Glyn Williams (Ed.), *Crisis of economy and ideology: Essays on Welsh society, 1840-1980* (pp. 217-230). London: S.S.R.C./B.S.A. Sociology of Wales Study Group.

Samuel, B. (1986). *Rugby: Body and soul.* Llandysul: Gomer Press.

Smith, D. (1980). Wales through the looking glass. In D. Smith (Ed.), *A people and a proletariat* (pp. 215-239). London: Pluto Press.

Smith, D. (1981). People's theatre—a century of Welsh rugby. *History Today,* **31** (March), 31-36.

Smith, D. (1984). *Wales! Wales?* London: Allen & Unwin.

Smith D., & Williams, G. (1980). *Fields of praise: Official history of the Welsh Rugby Union 1881-1981.* Cardiff: University of Wales Press.

Thomas, J.B.G. (1970). And in the beginning. In J.B.G. Thomas & R. Harding (Eds.), *Rugby in Wales* (pp. 13-17). Llandybie: Christopher Davies.

Watts-Dunton, T. (1906). Introduction. In G. Borrow, *Wild Wales* (pp. vii-xxiii). London: Dent.

Williams, Gareth. (1983). From Grand Slam to great slump: Economy, society and Rugby Football in Wales during the Depression. *Welsh History Review,* ix(June), 338-357.

Williams, Gareth. (1985). How amateur was my valley: Professional sport and national identity in Wales, 1890-1914. *Proceedings of the Third Annual Conference of the British Society of Sports History* (pp. 127-140). June-July 1985. Jordanhill College of Education. Glasgow: Scotland.

Williams, Gareth. (1988). From popular culture to public cliche: Image and identity in Wales, 1890-1914. In J.A. Mangan (Ed.), *Pleasure, profit, proselytism: British culture and sport at home and abroad 1700-1914* (pp. 128-143). London: Frank Cass.

Williams, Gwyn A. (1982). *The Welsh in their history.* London: Croom Helm.

Williams, Gwyn A. (1985). *When was Wales?* London: Penguin.

# CHAPTER 5

# Sport and Social Change in Latin America

## Joseph L. Arbena

Latin America, defined here as everything in the Western Hemisphere south of the United States, is physically and culturally complex. Among some 30 countries, populations reach from Caribbean microstates of 100,000 to Brazil's nearly 150 million. Economic activities encompass primitive subsistence agriculture, extensive commercialized farming, and sophisticated mechanized industry. Similarly, standards of living range from Venezuela's oil-financed $4,000 annual per capita gross national product to Haiti's impoverished $300. Argentina, Cuba, and Costa Rica boast literacy rates of 90% or higher, while many struggle to stay above 50%. The majority of Latin Americans speak Spanish, but Brazil's legions communicate in Portuguese, and significant minorities speak French, Dutch, English, and various Amerindian languages such as Quechua, Aymara, Guaraní, and distinct Mayan dialects. In recent years political systems have covered the spectrum from open democracies (e.g., Costa Rica and Venezuela) through military dictatorships (e.g., Chile and Panama until 1989-1990) to the socialist states of Cuba and Nicaragua (the latter 1979-1990) and even Paraguay's personalist dictatorship, which ended in 1989 after some 35 years (James & Minkel, 1986).

In the world of sports, variety is also the name of the game. Of course, across the region in the 20th century, soccer (*fútbol* in Spanish, *futebol* in Portuguese) remains the preferred participant and spectator sport. But its popularity is not unchallenged nor evenly distributed, either by place or by social group. For example, in the Spanish-speaking circum-Caribbean area, including Mexico's Yucatán, baseball (*béisbol*) has been "the king of sports" for almost a century (Joseph, 1987; Krich, 1989; Oleksak & Oleksak, 1991; Ruck, 1984; Wagner, 1984), while in the Anglophone Caribbean cricket holds sway (Burton, 1985; James, 1983). In Argentina, rugby is widely played on the club level (Llistosella, 1977), and polo enjoys high status among a wealthy elite (Bugler, 1969). Boxing, as in the United States, is often a means of escape from poverty for all ethnic groups from Mexico to Argentina

(Gammon, 1980), while two mechanized sports—cycling and auto racing—have produced large crowds and national heroes in several countries: the former, for example, in Colombia and Costa Rica, the latter in Argentina and Brazil (Fangio & Carozzo, 1987; Medina Pérez, 1986).

As demonstrated at the 1987 Pan American Games, Brazil is an international basketball power, and Latin American tennis stars have increasingly populated world rankings since the glory days of Maria Esther Bueno (Brazil) and Pancho Segura (Ecuador). The 1988 Olympic Games likewise displayed the continuing prowess of the Peruvian women's silver medalist volleyball team (Salcedo & Sánchez León, 1982). Depending on location, Latin Americans also support track and field, horse racing, field hockey, swimming, handball and related court ball games, chess (which is considered a sport in the region), and, more recently, recreational activities such as hiking, camping, survivalism, boating, sport fishing, and so on. And this does not include *patolli*, *pato*, cockfighting, bullfighting, and other preindustrial games and sports that have either disappeared or survived regionally but in modified forms.

This essay illustrates, through selected examples across the temporal and spatial sweep of Latin American history, the interactions among these many forms of sport and recreation and other spheres of social control, conflict, and change.

# Historical Overview

Despite many significant internal variations, Latin American history, both general and sportive, displays enough shared experiences that we can tentatively trace some parallel processes and propose some potentially fruitful areas for comparative inquiry and theorizing. In broad terms, virtually all of Latin America has passed through several long epochs, with marked transitions between. Several thousand years of Amerindian civilization was truncated by the arrival of European conquerors in the early 1500s, and within less than a century the long Latin American colonial era—mostly under Spanish or Portuguese control—was firmly in place.

With the impact of the European Enlightenment and, in the Spanish kingdoms, the introduction of the so-called Bourbon Reforms, serious political, economic, and social dynamics were unleashed. The result for much of the region was an outbreak (around 1810) of often bloody struggles aimed at achieving political independence, such that by the mid-1820s the formal Iberian presence was gone from all but Cuba and Puerto Rico—separation from Spain for those two islands coming only in 1899—whereas other European colonial regimes would persist in several small Caribbean zones until after World War II.

For those nearly twenty countries that experienced self-government through most of the 1800s, the next major historical transition was primarily economic. The last decades of the 19th century drew them closer into the expanding North Atlantic capitalist system, mainly as exporters of primary products (unprocessed agricultural and mineral products) and as consumers of European and (later) North American manufactured goods, technology, and capital. Latin America was frequently the target of outside military intervention and heavy diplomatic pressure, often on behalf of the economic interests of foreign states. In some areas, especially the Southern

Cone (comprised principally of Argentina, Chile, and Uruguay), Latin America became a destination for substantial European migration, both seasonal and permanent. These processes continued well into the 20th century, when they were paralleled and then to a degree displaced by domestic urbanization, industrialization, rising nationalism, and the growth of mass culture—the combined effects of which were sometimes social unrest, sometimes increased repression, and sometimes both (Burns, 1986; Pike, 1973).

## Society and Culture

These broad historical periods were accompanied, perhaps even defined, by dramatic social changes. In brief, the imposition of European rule after 1492 brought not only profound political changes to what became Latin America, but extensive biological and cultural upheaval as well (Crosby, 1972). While Iberian institutions were imposed on the native populations, the New World gene pool expanded and mixed dynamically, as brown, white, and, soon thereafter, black populations engaged in rampant miscegenation. The cultural sphere was at first no less unstable, as Amerindian, European, and African customs and traditions—under a veneer of dominant Iberian traits—interacted to produce a syncretic culture whose character was original (though uneven) across the hemisphere. It was a society that at times even allowed, perhaps paternalistically, the mass of "folk" to practice their culture with a degree of independence and dignity, even when their economic and political positions remained marginal.

By the time of nominal political independence, it was clear that distinct regional cultural types were emerging, despite the long history of somewhat uniform Spanish or Portuguese institutional domination. With independence came further splintering and, given different environmental circumstances, the pursuit of different paths of national cultural development. The influx of 19th-century European capitalism and its classical liberal ideology would universally challenge the older elite and folk cultures, often with devastating social consequences. The pursuit of profit in the capitalist world market provoked assaults on traditional communities, values, and relationships, as well as attempts to rob the lower classes not only of their land and labor but also their culture (Burns, 1980).

The political and demographic disruption that followed was often profound. Expanding populations sought to raise their political voice, improve their economic welfare, and define their sociocultural niche. Simultaneously, by the mid-20th century, most Latin American governments were struggling to build national cohesiveness for purposes of domestic control and development and international status and leverage. To these ends they overtly or covertly manipulated cultural sources—at times, paradoxically, in concert with foreign allies—through the expanding structures of mass communications and agencies of mass mobilization. The content and long-term objectives of the messages, of course, depended on the nature of the controlling regimes (Dorfman, 1983; McNeill, 1986).

Such social changes were, in turn, marked by or reflected in changes in sport, recreation, and leisure activities at different levels of the social hierarchy. Despite limited research on Latin American sport (Arbena, 1986, 1989; Wagner, 1985), there is evidence to suggest that, just as in other cultural (and political and economic) spheres, the sport-recreation complex became an arena for conflict between those groups seeking to impose or maintain their dominance and those that resisted all or part of the hegemonic cultural system (Arbena, 1988). The sport-recreation-leisure realm was not always the main issue at stake, but at the time, or with hindsight, it was and is perceived to have social (and, thus, political) meaning beneath its surface appearance.

Sport, like all forms of culture, is both produced and consumed, so its role must be understood in both those dimensions (Da Silva, 1980; García Canclini, 1984). Sport is more than just a reflector of society; it is a part of society, interacting with other parts often in a dialectical fashion. At times, sport may be a mechanism by which the hegemonic sectors, consciously or not, manipulate the factors of production and consumption to maintain their unequal control of those resources and, by implication, power. Similarly, sport appears to give underrepresented elements a mechanism for organization and movement in the struggle for social and psychological survival, the struggle to maintain "social space" in a system they may be unable or unwilling to destroy, but within which they aspire to function with some degree of comfort and dignity (Stein, 1987, 1988).

# Conquest and Domination, 1492-1700

Columbus and his successors encountered in the New World, especially in Mesoamerica (the culture hearth of central and southern Mexico, Yucatán, and parts of Central America), people who engaged in various games, physical activities, and athletic competitions (Piña Chán, 1969). It is unlikely that any of these were sport in the modern sense (Guttmann, 1978), though in the case of the ubiquitous ball games—with or without permanent courts—there was certainly a level of training, skill, institutional structure, and spectator enthusiasm reflecting extensive community involvement and support (Taladoire, 1981). Surely the sacred content of such games was dominant, making them more ritualistic than instrumentally rational. (Rational is applied in this chapter in the sense of depending on detailed and continuously refined rules and methods that are allegedly based on choice rather than tradition, that consciously relate the means to the ends, and that are more or less universally applied in the game's formal practice.) Yet with their possibly professional player class, bureaucratization, and associated gambling, they were not totally unlike some 20th-century sports. They likely served a "distinctly recreational function" as well (Leyenaar, 1978; Scheffler, Reynoso, & Inzúa C., 1985).

On one hand, the Spanish were impressed by the skill with which the Amerindian athletes performed. On the other hand, they perceived in the religious content/context of the ball games and other recreational activities expressions of a culture they sought to suppress. Some of their motivation was narrowly spiritual—the sincere desire to root out the vestiges of pagan worship and related behavior. Yet, as Padden (1970) argued, for Spanish and Amerindian alike the conflict was as much over power (read political sovereignty) as over religion and culture, for the ability to choose one's god or one's customs, including leisure pursuits, implied a degree of freedom from the domain of the conquering authority. And, as the Spanish also saw in their Jewish and Moorish minorities back home (a view heightened by the Protestant Reformation), religious (and cultural) pluralism threatened to bring political division: Heresy was religious/cultural and political at the same time.

In principle, the Spanish set out early to impose cultural orthodoxy in their new kingdoms. The results, though substantially successful, were not totally so, and residual forms of some (many?) pre-Columbian games and sports persisted even into the present century. As Bushnell (1978) has shown, in Spanish Florida in the late 1600s, government and Church authorities "became convinced that a certain game of ball played by the Christian Indians was detrimental to their bodies, their souls, and the [local] peace" and initiated a campaign demonstrating "the identification of conversion with sovereignty long past contact and conquest" (p. 1).

In Mexico (which was called "New Spain" in the colonial era) it is clear that, despite periodic attempts over 450 years to eliminate these "diabolical" customs, in many isolated communities the games went on. As a result, there are reports of "a modern, peripheral survival either of an archaic form or of a simplified version of the classical [ball] game" in northwest Mexico (Kelly, 1943) and of variants of patolli, a "board" game (similar to parcheesi) with strong religious/mystical content, often accompanied by high-stakes gambling (Caso, 1924-1927; Kendall, 1980).

In reference to the ancient ball games, such recent expressions, in rural and also urban areas, appear as a

defensive element to conserve self-identity. . . . Besides being a mechanism which reinforces and sustains social relations, it may also be a form of survival among [internal] migrant groups defending their traditional identity while being absorbed by values of an urban culture. (Scheffler et al., 1985, pp. 59, 94-95)

And, simultaneously, it can provide some degree of relaxation and pleasure.

The important thing is not that these remnants of indigenous games and athleticism pretend to become again the dominant forms of play, nor that they have influenced the nature of modern sports in Mexico or elsewhere in Latin America. Rather, they illustrate that, in maintaining some degree of their cultural heritage, indigenous and even mestizo communities could retain a degree of dignity, independence, and social space in societies that in most ways restricted their freedom. These games/sports held special meaning for their practitioners long after their original ritualistic symbolism had disappeared. And, more recently, the belief that such practices continued in the face of overwhelming odds has become itself a source of Mexican national pride (Perdomo Orellana, 1986-1987).

# Colonial Rule and Cultural Adaptation, 1700-1850

Across the Latin American realm during the centuries of colonial rule, perhaps more important than the lingering residual expressions of indigenous culture was the process of regional (often local) development, which saw, in varying degrees, Amer-indian, European, and African peoples and their cultures both mix and evolve in the context of new circumstances. Concerning games, recreation, and sport, the result was a tremendous variety of activities that came to express particular class and environmental conditions. Thus appeared a kind of "traditional" culture that, by the mid-19th century, would provide the social pattern with which the imported, modernizing culture—games, sports, and all—would clash. In sum, this new domi-nant system was surely less Christian and homogenous than either Crown or Church might desire, but it was, on average, more European than indigenous or African in origin and form. Also, in a surprising way, it was, in the aggregate, a culture that allowed for the reasonable expression of needs and values of a good percentage of the population.

For example, in Argentina, while indigenous games/sports persisted among rela-tively unconquered tribes (Magrassi, Berón, & Radovich, 1982), in the gradually expanding areas of European contact there emerged a mestizo culture adapted to the physical and economic landscape of the humid pampa. Centered around a life of cattle and horses, the so-called gaucho society developed recreational activities that reflected not just the demands of work, but mirrored a total lifestyle that valued mobility, dexterity, and skills associated with an equine-oriented existence. By the early 1800s the fiercely independent gauchos were most adept at a variety of vigorous and, often, violent games/sports such as *pato* (try to imagine a type of basketball on horseback!), bullfighting, *la corrida de sortija*, and horse racing (Sáenz, 1951; Slatta, 1983).

In the cities, particularly the port of Buenos Aires, Iberian-derived contests and diversions, along with some residues of African and mulatto social life, were more common: bullfighting (until about 1819), cockfighting, cards and other games of chance, literary societies (*tertulias*), and, in the Afro-Argentine realm, ritualistic music, dance, and religious ceremonies. These Iberian and African forms would, of course, partially decline as British and French influences increased, and such amusements as cricket, rowing, fencing, croquet, horse racing, and golf occupied more time and space. With a new wave of Spanish immigration would also come an infusion of the ancient Basque-based sports of jai alai and varieties of handball (Llanes, 1981; Troncoso, 1982).

In colonial Chile one sees a similar pattern of uneven fusion and distribution of indigenous and Iberian games and recreational practices. Because of Iberian tradition and the colonial economy, equine and other animal-based sports played a central role: racing, jousting, parading, and other activities (both ceremonial and practical) involving horses; and bullfighting and cockfighting, which drew large crowds. Reflecting the indigenous heritage were the Araucanian *chueca* (similar to field hockey and also played in Argentina) and various ball games, some of which merged with Iberian ball games. In one of the best studies available on colonial games, sports, and recreation in Latin America, Pereira Salas (1947) describes these Chilean physical games and sports along with street games such as hopscotch and a wide range of games tied to gambling (e.g., dice, cards, lotteries, board games), an affliction officially considered so widespread that it was a long-term source of serious governmental and clerical concern.

In Mexico and Peru, two powerful centers of Spanish colonial rule and of continuing conservative allegiance to Hispanic values even after independence, the bullfight retained broad appeal through the 19th century, though not without criticism. Eventually the break from Spain separated the Americas from regular contact with Iberian bulls and fighters. Nationalism, however weak, led to partial rejection of Spanish traditions, and currents of secular and Christian liberalism perceived the bullfight as brutal and corruptive. Nevertheless, in town and city alike, the festival of bulls retained a place in both popular and elite culture, at least in these two traditional centers (Flores Hernández, 1986).

In sum, by around 1850 the sport scene across Latin America, like the entire cultural landscape, was diverse by region and class. Sport and recreation (older and newer types combined) of general European origin were most common, but geographical isolation and the weakness of most institutional sources of potential control (e.g., police, army, schools) allowed numerous indigenous residuals and mestizo, mulatto, and even creole hybrids to thrive, a condition which reflected the poorly integrated and heterogeneous social systems.

# Diffusion and the New Hegemony, 1850-1930

Theoretically, as Williams (1982) observed, cultural export "is a function of relative political or commercial dominance, with especially clear cases in the political empires and many related cases in general international competition" (p. 230). Cultural export through political dominance was achieved partially within Latin America's various colonial empires. But cultural export/import through commercial competition and dominance has become more the case over the last century, as new technologies, monopolistic structures, and power imbalances have given rise to "general processes of cultural dominance and then of cultural dependence." While Williams does not comment on sport per se, he notes correctly the extensive impact of such cultural exports on the recipient societies, potentially permeating the entire culture and affecting even such areas as language and ideology. After 1850 this combined economic and cultural penetration in Latin America is seen in various examples that relate to sports and recreation as cultural forms.

With industrialization and more rapid modes of communication in Europe and North America came the spread of Western industrial and financial capitalism to Latin America. Capitalism, in turn, brought trade, investment, technology, and immigration, all of which carried a new European culture and with it new European sports, sport technology, and such presumed sporting forms or values as gentlemanliness, discipline, and cooperation. For Latin America, as with the rest of the world, the center of modern sport innovation was principally England, and secondarily France and the United States (Bale, 1984, 1989). The result was a serious confrontation between the traditional sport /recreation complex and the forms, organization, and values of the imported sports, values that ultimately had as much to do with the needs of modern industrialism and commercialism as with the practice of sport alone. In other words, most of Latin America, in its relations with the metropolitan countries of the North Atlantic, found itself in an increasing state of economic and cultural dependency, with those two dimensions being functionally intertwined.

Whether they were imposed or adopted, it appears that these modern sports, especially soccer, "spread through the world on the wide-ranging tentacles of British capitalism," or of United States capitalism in the cases of baseball and later basketball and volleyball. Soccer, in particular, and other organized professional sports with a mass following in general, "are peculiarly appropriate recreational patterns for modern, urban societies." This is because such sports (may) teach, to players and spectators alike, such values as discipline and order, acceptance of limited and specialized roles, diligence, the need for training, and teamwork, all of which are "virtues in terms of learning a place in a hierarchical society and an industrial process" (Allison, 1978, pp. 218, 223, 207). Not that these values and characteristics were totally lacking in premodern or traditional games, but in modern sports they are relatively more intense and universal. Surely some Latin Americans embraced imported sports with those relationships in mind, though others had reasons far different from seeking to legitimate their own domination through the creation of a set of symbols and institutions in support of a new hegemony. No doubt, many just found these sports physically and emotionally appealing: They were "fun" (Arbena, 1990a). Consequently, as Guttmann (1988) recognized, in evaluating the motivations behind sport diffusion, it is difficult to untangle the interaction between internal ludic properties and external cultural associations.

Specifically, as Beezley (1983, 1987, 1988) discussed, in late 19th-century Mexico, during the Porfiriato (1877-1911), the growing popularity of both competitive and recreational cycling paralleled and reinforced the acceptance of values and behavior associated with industrialization and so-called modernization in Europe and the United States. Part of this was mere imitation of a European fad, aimed at proving that Mexicans could behave like the "best" people of the civilized world, but some of it derived from cycling's connection with technology, physical fitness, precision in measuring time and distance, and commercialization. Similarly, in a sweeping analysis of sport's growth and of its value in promoting individual physical and mental development, social progress and cohesiveness, national identity, and international recognition among civilized nations, Sola (1914) described with optimism and pride the positive accomplishments of Cuban athletes in the arena of modern sports clubs and competitions.

Perhaps more graphic is the case of Argentina (and, to a degree, of neighboring Uruguay). Even before the mid-1800s, British technology, capital, personnel, and culture were penetrating the urban areas on both sides of the Río de la Plata estuary, a process that would intensify and geographically spread as the British played an ever greater role in the region's import-export economy, in its banking and transportation sectors, in its emerging educational system, and in its evolving recreational and leisure activities. Above all, through the founding of schools and of athletic and social clubs, the British introduced sports that back home had become rationalized and popularized as part of the larger pattern of industrialization: cricket, rugby, soccer (association football), polo, horse racing (clockwise on grass), fencing, rowing, cycling, gymnastics, and track and field.

In part through their friendships with local British citizens and in part through a desire to imitate the admired British behavior, Argentines and Uruguayans alike designed school curriculums and organized clubs based on British models. By 1900, Buenos Aires, Montevideo, and corresponding environs were the sites of frequent sporting competitions among national populations, resident foreign communities, and visiting European athletes. At the same time, at least the upper echelons of these South American areas were adopting broader European economic and social values associated with so-called modernization (Buzzetti & Gutiérrez Cortinas, 1965; Troncoso, 1982). And, as these modern values and institutions spread from city to country with the force of the state in support, the relative freedom and regional culture (including authentic popular sports) of pampean society were gradually destroyed: The gaucho was forced into a dependent labor relationship and became a consumer of someone else's culture (Slatta, 1986).

Similar processes of implantation and parallel geographical and social diffusion are seen in the case of baseball in Yucatán, introduced via Cuba in the 1890s, eventually spreading from the elite downward and from the cities outward (Joseph, 1987, 1988); that of soccer in Paraguay, introduced in Asunción by a Dutch physical education teacher around 1900, played first by clubs in the capital, later taking hold in the interior and among other social groups (Bestard, 1981); and that of boxing in Chile, introduced late in the last century, mainly by British sailors, through Valparaíso, continuing on to Santiago, and quickly drawing support across the socioeconomic spectrum (González, 1973).

The example of soccer in early 20th-century Lima is interesting because it further illustrates the processes and conflicts noted and because it also suggests a change that marks the evolving transition from traditional through amateur to professional sport. When soccer first became absorbed into the Peruvian cultural panoply, it conformed to the mold of various other elite, exclusivist sports and institutions of the era. Later, as soccer filtered through Lima's middle and lower socioeconomic strata, it became increasingly a form of amusement, escape, identification, expression, class/race consciousness, and a source of role models for the popular sectors—in sum, a means to personal fulfillment and social survival for the weak and poor, as these developed their own style of play, organized their own teams, and programmed their own parallel system of social activities (Stein, 1987, 1988).

At times, Limeño soccer provoked working class violence and, in turn, fear within the upper classes. In reaction, the latter sought to regulate the game by organizing leagues, charging admissions, paying ''tips'' to players, moving into international competition, and imposing governmental regulations, making the game increasingly structured and eventually professional. For a while, though some resisted, many workers/players did not try to escape the system but exploited it for their own benefit. By the 1930s, although institutionalized soccer became more popular, at least in terms of audience, it ultimately became an effective mechanism of social control, its role as valid popular expression greatly diminished. In short, institutional control of competition, space, and resources, co-optation through payments of salaries and other benefits, and the promotion of divisions among the working class based on team and neighborhood rivalries all combined to rob soccer of its earlier spontaneity and autonomy (Deustua Carvallo, Stein, & Stokes, 1984; Stein, Deustua Carvallo, & Stokes, 1986).

One illustrative consequence of soccer's limitations as an effective means of social organization and expression is seen among Lima's large and variegated communities of migrants from Peru's interior highlands. Especially since the 1960s, such groups have deliberately chosen to employ music instead of sports to differentiate themselves from other regional and social groups and to challenge the dominant social consensus by seizing control of a unique cultural form and, at least symbolically, asserting their own sense of power (Turino, 1988).

## The Popularization of Sport, 1930-Present

The diffusion of modern sports throughout Latin America from the mid-19th century on is characterized by two parallel and interconnected processes: geographically outward and socially downward. As described previously, in *most* cases these sports entered Latin American countries through a capital or major port city and via middle- to upper-class foreigners or locals who had traveled in Europe or the United States (Arbena, 1990a). Thanks to radio, television, cheap printed matter, population migrations, and the spread of education, these processes continue to the present (Escobar M., 1969).

Also, as in the case of Limeño soccer, most of these imported sports began as amateur activities. The emerging hegemonic form centered first in a relatively small, elite segment of the population, thereby mixing class values with the symbolism of the larger modern culture. But in virtually every sport in every country, amateurism gradually gave way to professionalism, in most cases as a result of bringing the masses into the games both as players and as spectators. Of course, the amateur level continued, though even there in many cases the sports became highly institutionalized, commercialized, and technologically based—in effect, becoming professional in all but the narrowest sense. While such changes were met with some resistance, particularly by those who wanted to preserve certain class privileges, the more truly capitalist and commercial forces tended to support this evolution as a means both to earn profits and to inculcate across the social spectrum values they believed would strengthen their dominant status. Clearly, in the larger context, modern amateur and modern professional sports mostly represent the same symbolic construct.

In a very real sense, sport (including physical education and recreation) has become big business, whether on the professional or so-called amateur level. Be it equipment for athletes, facilities and entertainment for spectators, souvenirs and pulp reading materials for fans, education for coaches and officials, broadcast rights for listeners and viewers, the control of players (the raw material of sports) by clubs or Olympic committees, salaries for administrators, transportation and related services for all involved, and so on, sports create huge expenditures of money that need to be justified and that tend to create both institutions and implicit or explicit belief systems that are ostensibly self-perpetuating (Sebreli, 1981).

The parallel processes of institutionalization, commercialization, and professionalization of imported, modern sports began early, though the timing, in the short run, varied notably from sport to sport and place to place. Those countries with the closest ties to the North Atlantic capitalist system (e.g., Mexico, Cuba, Brazil, the Southern Cone) and those sports with the broadest appeal among the masses (e.g., boxing, horse racing, baseball, soccer) combined to produce the earliest forms of professionalism. Soccer's evolution no doubt caused the most trauma, as white, European-oriented elites sought to maintain their class preserve in the face of both rising skills among the masses and the joint desire to win and make profits on the part of some club members and administrators (Rachum, 1978).

The result was several decades of quasi-professionalism until open salaries for soccer players were permitted around 1930. However, several Latin American countries (Colombia, for example) refused to sanction the change until after World War II. Other sports have become mainly professional (e.g., auto racing, tennis) or remained primarily amateur (e.g., polo, volleyball, rugby) or both (basketball), depending on tradition and market potential. Not surprisingly, the self-proclaimed socialist states of Cuba and (until 1990) Nicaragua have made the elimination of formal professional sports a part of their ideology and programs.

Not everyone over the last century has found these "new" sports, amateur or professional, adequate for their psychological or social needs. As described previously, in Mexico a number of residual forms of indigenous games have persisted even into this century. Similar situations have been noted in other Latin American areas, especially among geographically or socially marginal communities. Smith (1987) described a ritualistic, traditional "festival" of fistfighting (*tinku*) among peoples of the Laimes and Pampas tribes carried out annually in a small village near Cochabamba, Bolivia. Though there may be some deep emotional link between this "sport" and the appeal of world-class professional boxing—"People fight, and people watch them fight, to feel"—the performance style and context also reflect the persistence of traditional cultural identity and a degree of alienation from the dominant society.

In a more positive tone, in a situation reminiscent of Stein's soccer players and fans in Lima before 1930, Mandle & Mandle (1988) evaluated basketball among poor blacks in Trinidad and Tobago in the mid-1980s. Though the sport is imported from the United States and its presence is reaffirmed by the reception of NBA games on local television, basketball is important to these people

because it is theirs—it constitutes a community in which they initiate and influence what goes on. . . . Basketball is thus an arena—chosen by the participants—where they can express themselves, where they can exercise some degree of control, and where they find important personal and social meaning. (pp. 18-19, 20)

In other words, basketball in this case, and no doubt other sports in other locations, "represents a realm of freedom and creativity, a form of their own cultural articulation, and this despite basketball's foreign origins."

In an even more ambiguous situation, Klein (1989, 1991) describes how the presence of American major-league teams in the Dominican Republic has a deleterious effect on the autonomy and quality of local baseball. In attempting to develop the game, United States interests—like other types of multinationals—are underdeveloping the game. Simultaneously, baseball is an American popular cultural form that functions to soften hostile responses of Dominicans to American political and economic domination of their country. Thus, while serving to reproduce United States control, baseball takes on the appearance of a benevolent, even helpful, cultural institution. Nevertheless, it may also promote Dominican national pride— and eventually anti-Americanism—by offering Dominicans a rare way of beating the foreigners and of becoming better than they are at their own game on their own soil (Ruck, 1991).

The lesson is that even sports introduced by dominant or imperialist forces, including corporate-sponsored mass institutions, may be manipulated by elements within the recipient society to forge, if not a truly residual or emergent subculture, at least an enclave or conditioning atmosphere that permits the fulfillment of needs or the expression of values at variance with some of the hegemonic structure, and not necessarily by people who consciously reject the dominant system (Lears, 1988). But, in a manner of speaking, it is usually the hegemonic culture that defines the limits and terms within which these variants can, even must, develop.

Although, as noted previously, bullfighting declined following Latin American independence, it never disappeared, especially in Mexico, which remains today the world's second center for that ancient festival (Cahill, 1988). Certainly in Mexico, as in Peru, Venezuela, and other places where the *corrida* persists, the sport has changed, clearly influenced by trends seen in other modern sports: for example, big stadiums (*plazas de toros*), fan clubs, media promotions, and generally greater commercialization. In fact, some of the renewed interest in bullfighting in the late 19th century may even be related to the tendency to borrow things European, even if that meant the less developed Spanish (Beezley, 1983). Nevertheless, there is evidence to suggest that in some circles the continued appeal of this "traditional" activity from the Hispano-colonial era embodies resistance to both modernization and non-Hispanic Europeanization, while it continues to embody certain qualities of the larger society (Garland, 1948; Zurcher & Meadow, 1967).

Perhaps less dramatic, but compelling nonetheless, are today's "revived" or stylized versions of sports/games whose roots also lie in an older, preindustrial age. In Argentina, for example, the imported polo (Levene, 1988) and the reemergent gauchesque pato appear as attempts to perpetuate a rural, equine tradition in the face of mechanization and urbanization. That these two sports are now almost exclusively elite activities does not negate their importance to some Argentines as a source both of resistance to cultural change, however psychic and symbolic, and of pride in national cultural and athletic distinctiveness and achievement; though what we see here, in Williams's (1977) terms, *may* be more truly archaic than residual. Polo, of course, like West Indian cricket, allows the former "colonials" to beat the former "masters" at their own game, while highlighting one of Argentina's richly unique features—the grassy pampa. Pato, more clearly a product of the pampa and its hybrid culture, offers the pride of invention and the display of unrivaled skill (Grenón, 1956). Both help maintain Argentina's reputation for superior horsemanship.

At the same time, it can be argued that the current class features of polo and pato represent a type of reverse residualism, as the oligarchy seeks to retain its class identity in the face of the rising mass culture exemplified musically (in an earlier age) by the tango, athletically by soccer, and politically by Peronismo, the working-class movement that has unsettled Argentine society since the 1940s (Ciria, 1983).

In some cases, residual cultures express themselves not so much in different (premodern?) games and sports, but in the "deviant" manner in which they shape the playing of so-called modern or dominant games. As Smith (1986) demonstrates, at first the game appears to be the same, but as it is played out in its specific context, the game proves to have characteristics and meanings for its local participants far different from those anticipated by the outside player or observer. It could even be argued that the application of the term "national" to styles of soccer and other sports reflects the persistence of older, perhaps traditional, cultural values and forms that, to some, are inconsistent with the aspirations of the dominant culture. Such an accusation has been made concerning the attempts by the Brazilian military governments to reform their national soccer team (by "whitening" the squad and Europeanizing its style of play) despite the victory in the 1970 World Cup in Mexico City (Shirts, 1988).

Perhaps because 20th-century Latin American societies in general have been less "modern"—that is, less industrialized and rationalized—the region's sport network has likewise been less institutionalized or rationalized—and, consequently, less able on average to serve as a rigid indoctrinating mechanism for hegemonic cultures. In some ways this may work to the good in that by default it leaves more space for the operation of residual and emergent forms.

But it also has its drawbacks, at least in some Latin American eyes, in that it means that there have been fewer real resources, both human and capital, available and mobilized for the enhancement of physical culture. This is a two-edged sword: Some enthusiasts of pure play and spontaneous games may applaud the lack of structure. Still, in an increasingly urbanized environment, the lack of space, facilities, equipment, coaching, and some level of organized competition deprives many people of opportunities for recreation, physical fitness, and the pleasures of sportive participation. In many marginal sectors of Latin America's rapidly growing cities, such limitations on participation in play, games, and sport retards individual socialization and hampers the emergence of a sense of community, cooperation, and respect for authority; self-identification and self-esteem often remain low with serious dysfunctional consequences for the society (Picón Cardona et al., 1984).

Not surprisingly, demands for more sport and recreational resources have come from different directions, with different means and aims in mind. Surely, the degree of popularization of sport and recreation that has occurred throughout Latin America in this century is a product, in part, of the cry from proponents of physical education that national health, morality, and overall development would be aided by raising physical culture through the schools, the clubs, or the national sports programs, though the role of commercial forces in support of similar trends cannot be neglected.

As early as 1912, the Argentines organized a national institute for physical education, and in 1922 a founder of the Argentine Olympic Committee pronounced sporting development a step toward "the perfection of the race and the glory of conquering what is noble, worthy, and beautiful" (Viale, 1922, p. 10). A half century later an Ecuadorian physical educator argued that sport, properly practiced, can be an important agent in the formation of the individual and societal personality (Silva Romo, 1973).

Frequently, these same experts criticize concentrating on elite and professional sports. Consequently, a debate is sometimes heard between the proponents of "popular sport" and those who appear to focus on producing those international "stars," most often for the soccer field, who will bring glory to their respective and beloved country (*patria*). Not that the two objectives are always mutually exclusive, but in societies with scarce resources, choices must be made, and that means setting priorities (Ponce, 1979). Cuba may be the only Latin American country that in recent years has made progress on both fronts, but at a cost that critics find politically unacceptable. Yet in this debate at least there is agreement that more physical education, sport, and recreation is good for something, as long as it's the "right" kind.

Promoters of broader sociopolitical reform—or alternative systems—have not always agreed on the potential role of sport in their dreams. Some believe that sport, at least professional and other structured varieties in both its organizational framework and its actual performance context, is so tainted or corrupted by the hegemonic domain that it is irrelevant to popular liberation movements. There is no denying that, overtly or covertly, sport in some Latin American contexts has served to strengthen the claims of the dominant political culture and that competing styles have been subject to varying degrees of exclusion or suppression. In two well-known cases, Brazil in 1970 and Argentina in 1978, incumbent military regimes sought to exploit the emotional and nationalistic sentiments that followed their country's victories in soccer's World Cup in order to divert attention from their own failings or to "prove" the capability of their own leadership and the degree to which they deserved patriotic loyalty (Cernadas Lamadrid & Halac, 1986; Lever, 1983). But, in both cases, the long-term results were not nearly so effective as the regimes had hoped or their critics feared (Arbena, 1990b; Larsen, 1983).

In Chile, following the coup d'état of September 1973 that overthrew the government of Salvador Allende, the new Pinochet-led junta was especially harsh in its attacks on amateur youth sports clubs and their leaders on the grounds that they were centers of Communism—all part of a larger policy of suppressing or controlling forms of cultural activity associated with the previous regime: theater, movies, book publishing, and music (Calabrano, 1975). Under these relatively strong military regimes it might appear unnecessary to take such measures, but "dominant groups can ill afford to assume their own society is wholly pacified, although of course it is in their interest to have others think that all opposition has been successfully precluded or contained.'' Hence the effort to legitimate the dominant ideology and leadership by blotting out obvious or even perceived sources of contrary thought (Lipsitz, 1988, p. 147).

In other contexts, sport has proven to be either a haven for residual cultural traditions or a basis for expressing potential or real alternative modes. Even nonacademics in Latin America have recognized that, if sport is not an inherent characteristic of all human societies, it has become such a pervasive and appreciated quality of the mass and folk cultures that to ignore it is to deny a valuable, perhaps necessary, means to social and political change. Evanson (1982) concludes, after examining various expressions of contemporary Brazilian popular culture, that soccer ''may be one of the sources of an authentic Brazilian nationalism, at once popular and liberating, and more immediately potent than polemical campaigns of the Left against multinational corporations'' (p. 408). If soccer thus expresses ''the people,'' revolutionaries who must work from and through such people can use soccer as a means to know them and to allow them to communicate their wants and needs.

Following a decade of repressive military rule in Chile, during which the government sought to suppress various popular sports institutions, Ossandón (1982) noted the resultant contradictory character of mass soccer. On the one hand, the regime can use soccer to divert the attention of the people from more important issues and channel their energies into harmless cheering. Simultaneously, however, mass soccer can have a liberating effect, in that the match offers the people a chance to cultivate a sense of solidarity based on a shared experience and a real opportunity to choose sides (to elect) in a contest and to express their vocal support in a way that makes them feel they can have influence. And for opponents of the military junta, just the right response emerged spontaneously, as recounted by an exiled Chilean poet, when the scoring of an important goal in Santiago's National Stadium produced a cry of ''*venceremos*'' (''we will triumph''), an emotional phrase that in the 1960s and 1970s had been a battle cry of Chile's political left (Epple, 1977).

## Twentieth-Century Revolutionary Alternatives

Given this pattern of linking sports and politics, the role of sports in the process of revolution in Latin America likewise offers interesting insights. As early as the first decades of the institutionalized Mexican Revolution, which followed the violent phase of the 1910s, there is evidence of a conscious attempt to use sport to promote political, social, and even foreign policy goals on behalf of a government that professed to be revolutionary. Driven in part by nationalism and in part by developmentalism—and perhaps only marginally by radicalism—post-1920 Mexico saw at least some calls, though even fewer actions, aimed at using sport and physical education as ways to raise Mexico's international stature and the quality of its society and polity. As an anonymous writer in *El Nacional* (August 17, 1939) argued, sport teaches organization, cooperation, solidarity, working for an end and seeing results, and controlling passions and vices, which aids in fighting for ''the greatness and the liberty of the nation'' and the well-being of all. Also, it was

Mexico that organized and hosted the first Central American and Caribbean Games in 1926, an act that paralleled its efforts not only to promote those domestic aims, but also to expand its influence among its Middle American neighbors (Arbena, 1991).

In 1950 Guatemalans cited the completion of their national sports complex, the Ciudad Olímpica, in preparation for hosting the VI Central American and Caribbean Games, as both a point of national prestige and testimony that their "Revolution [of 1945] continues its forward march, maintaining itself to the rhythm of labor and social construction . . . eloquent demonstration of what can be achieved by a people and government [acting] in perfect harmony" (Paniagua S. et al., 1950, p. 5).

More extreme than either the Mexican or Guatemalan cases are the later experiences of Latin America's two Marxist states: Cuba (since 1959) and Nicaragua (1979-1990). Cuba started down the road to socialism shortly after Fidel Castro led the overthrow of the Batista regime in January 1959; Nicaragua was guided by the Sandinista movement after the Somoza family was driven into exile in July 1979. In neither case did sport play a significant role in mobilizing the successful revolution. But in both cases sport became a definite area of policy concern—perhaps more so in Cuba—after the revolutions began.

Almost from its establishment the Castro regime sought to use sport for several domestic and international objectives. Broad programs of physical education and sports could raise the level of physical well-being (in part for potential purposes of national defense), promote discipline and social solidarity, and win popular gratitude for the regime in return for providing free recreational, participant, and spectator activities. The end of formal professional sports proclaimed the end of "exploitation" of athletes; expanded opportunities for female participation allegedly ended sexism.

International triumphs in sport have served two ends: to make Cubans feel proud of their country and supportive of their revolutionary leaders and, above all, to prove to others, especially in Latin America, that the Cuban model is truly a success and potentially applicable elsewhere (Arbena, 1990c; Pye, 1986). It may be questioned, however, given the control over international sports structures by first- and second-world powers, whether small countries like Cuba can ever generate a genuinely anticolonial movement merely by amassing more medals in "Western" sports played under Western rules (Eichberg, 1984).

The Nicaraguans, while sharing some of the Cubans' ideals and emulating some of their programs, had less time and fewer resources to develop a truly revolutionary sports program. Though professionalism was generally abolished, sports investment and bureaucratization lagged far behind the Cuban experience, and international triumphs were rare. Still, it is apparent that the Sandinistas recognized that sport can be reformed and promoted in various ways to achieve revolutionary political and social ends (Wagner, 1988). In both the Cuban and Nicaraguan cases, however, anecdotal evidence suggests that at least a minority in both countries have felt that the new programs have failed in that, for example, Cuban sport remains elitist and to a degree sexist and that Nicaraguan sport has progressed hardly at all. Some likewise argue that contacts with professionals in the United States (say in baseball, basketball, and boxing) would be a good thing. Old ways die hard! Thus, it will be interesting to see how the end of Sandinista control in April 1990 affects Nicaraguan sports policy.

The charge has been made, of course, that (in moral and functional terms, at least) the Cubans, like the former Soviets and East Germans, are no better than the Argentine, Brazilian, and Chilean military, or any capitalist society for that matter, in that they are merely manipulating sport for "political" objectives that solidify the power of the incumbents and exclude alternative systems or contenders for control (Arbena, 1990c). In fact, the Cubans have been quite honest about their political intentions in shaping a revolutionary sports program. Consequently, while some Latin Americans express admiration for Cuban athletic achievements (Ellacuría, 1970), others reject equally the United States and Cuban-Soviet systems and contemplate the replication in their countries of a third, more liberating (or less manipulative) alternative, based possibly on a "Scandinavian" pattern (i.e., socialist but not high-pressured) or on some ideal model thus far not seen in practice (Cadavel, 1979).

## Conclusion

In Latin America, if sport has not constituted one of the major battlegrounds on which the hegemonic culture—or, over time, cultures—has struggled with residual or emergent deviations, it certainly has been a social realm in which the implications of such struggles, though centered elsewhere, have manifested themselves. However, since hegemony is not a static state, today's hegemonic style, in sport as in other cultural areas, may be tomorrow's residual anomaly and, given enough time, the future's (re)emerging alternative. Latin America, as we have observed, offers examples of this across a broad sweep of time and space; nowhere in the region can it be argued that sport or any cultural hegemony was ever absolute (Prieto Castillo, 1985). Latin America also illustrates that in recent years proponents of both social control and varieties of social change have increasingly seen in sport an attractive technique for achieving their objectives.

Yet, throughout, it is important to remember that sport and recreation, like many cultural forms, "can also have a vigorous and complex life apart from accommodation or resistance to the dominant social order" (Lears, 1985, p. 588). Though certainly shaped by cultural context, the human spirit is so creative, human emotions so expressive, human needs and fears so intense, that people often speak and act in ways that defy easy explanation or fail to conform to even the most sophisticated theoretical models.

## References

Allison, L. (1978). Association Football and the urban ethos. In J.D. Wirth & R.L. Jones (Eds.), *Manchester and São Paulo: Problems of rapid urban growth* (pp. 203-228). Stanford: Stanford University Press.

Arbena, J.L. (1986). Sport and the study of Latin American history: an overview. *Journal of Sport History*, **13**, 87-96.

Arbena, J.L. (Ed.). (1988). *Sport and society in Latin America: Diffusion, dependency, and the rise of mass culture*. Westport: Greenwood Press.

Arbena, J.L. (Ed.). (1989). *An annotated bibliography of Latin American sport: Preconquest to the present*. Westport: Greenwood Press.

Arbena, J.L. (1990a). The diffusion of modern European sport in Latin America: A case study of cultural imperialism? *South Eastern Latin Americanist*, **33**(4), 1-8.

Arbena, J.L. (1990b). Generals and *goles*: Assessing the connection between the military and soccer in Argentina. *The International Journal of the History of Sport*, **7**(1), 120-130.

Arbena, J.L. (1990c). Sport and revolution: The continuing Cuban experience. *Studies in Latin American Popular Culture*, **9**, 319-328.

Arbena, J.L. (1991). Sport, development, and Mexican nationalism, 1920-1970. *Journal of Sport History*, **18**(3), 350-364.

Bale, J. (1984). International sports history as innovation diffusion. *Canadian Journal of History of Sport*, **15**, 38-63.

Bale, J. (1989). *Sports geography*. London: E & FN Spon.

Beezley, W.H. (1983). El estilo porfiriano: Deportes y diversiones de fin de siglo. *Historia Mexicana*, **130**, 265-284.

Beezley, W.H. (1987). *Judas at the Jockey Club and other episodes of Porfirian Mexico*. Lincoln: University of Nebraska.

Beezley, W.H. (1988). Bicycles, modernization, and Mexico. In J.L. Arbena (Ed.), *Sport and society in Latin America: Diffusion, dependency, and the rise of mass culture* (pp. 15-28). Westport: Greenwood Press.

Bestard, M.A. (1981). *[Ochenta] 80 años de fútbol en el Paraguay*. Asunción: Litograf.

Bugler, J. (1969). A gentleman's game. *New Society*, **13**, 846-847.

Burns, E.B. (1980). *The poverty of progress: Latin America in the nineteenth century*. Berkeley: University of California.

Burns, E.B. (1986). *Latin America: A concise interpretive history*. Englewood Cliffs, NJ: Prentice-Hall.

Burton, R.D.E. (1985). Cricket, carnival and street culture in the Caribbean. *The British Journal of Sports History*, **2**, 179-197.

Bushnell, A. (1978). "That demonic game": The campaign to stop pelota playing in Spanish Florida, 1675-1684. *The Americas*, **35**, 1-19.

Buzzetti, J.L., & Gutiérrez Cortinas, E. (1965). *Historia del deporte en el Uruguay (1830-1900)*. Montevideo: Talleres Gráficos Castro & Cía.

Cadavel, A. (1979). *El deporte visto por los universitarios*. México, D.F.: Universidad Nacional Autónoma de México.

Cahill, L. (1988). Horns, capes, & courage. *Américas*, **40**(6), 38-41.

Calabrano, D.A. (1975). La cultura, el deporte y la juventud chilena. *Cuadernos Americanos*, **200**(3), 55-68.

Caso, A. (1924-1927). Un antiguo juego mexicano: El patolli. *El México Antiguo*, **2**, 203-211.

Cernadas Lamadrid, J.C., & Halac, R. (1986). *Los militares y el Mundial*. Buenos Aires: Editorial Perfil.

Ciria, A. (1983). *Política y cultura popular: La Argentina peronista, 1946-1955*. Buenos Aires: Ediciones de la Flor.

Crosby, A.W., Jr. (1972). *The Columbian exchange: Biological and cultural consequences of 1492*. Westport: Greenwood Press.

Da Silva, C. (1980). Indústria cultural e cultura brasileira: Pela utilizacão do conceito de hegemonia cultural. *Encontros com a Civilização Brasileira*, **25**, 167-194.

Deustua Carvallo, J., Stein, S., & Stokes, S.C. (1984). Soccer and social change in early twentieth century Peru. *Studies in Latin American Popular Culture*, **3**, 17-27.

Dorfman, A. (1983). *The empire's old clothes*. New York: Pantheon Books.

Eichberg, H. (1984). Olympic sport—Neocolonization and alternatives. *International Review for the Sociology of Sport*, **19**, 97-105.

Ellacuría, I. (1970). Medallas para Cuba. *ECA; Estudios Centro Americanos*, **25**(259), 228.

Epple, J.A. (1977). Noticias del fútbol. *Literatura Chilena en el Exilio*, **1**(3), 12.

Escobar M., G. (1969). The role of sports in the penetration of urban culture to the rural areas of Peru. *Kroeber Anthropological Society Papers*, **40**, 72-81.

Evanson, P. (1982). Understanding the people: *Futebol*, film, theater and politics in present-day Brazil. *The South Atlantic Quarterly*, **81**, 399-412.

Fangio, J.M., & Carozzo, R. (1987). *Fangio: Cuando el hombre es más que el mito*. Buenos Aires: Sudamericana/Planeta.

Flores Hernández, B. (1986). *La ciudad y la fiesta: Los primeros tres siglos y medio de tauromaquia en México, 1526-1867*. México, D.F.: Instituto Nacional de Antropología e Historia.

Gammon, C. (1980). Cradle of champions. *Sports Illustrated*, **53**(22), 86-100.

García Canclini, N. (1984). Gramsci con Bourdieu: Hegemonía, consumo y nuevas formas de organización popular. *Nueva Sociedad*, **71**, 69-78.

Garland, A.G. (1948). *Lima y el toreo*. Lima: Librería Internacional del Perú.

González, R. (1973). *El boxeo en Chile*. Santiago: Editora Nacional Quimantú.

Grenón, J.P. (1956). El juego de pato. *Historia*, **1**, 121-146.

Guttmann, A. (1978). *From ritual to record: The nature of modern sports*. New York: Columbia University Press.

Guttmann, A. (1988). ''Our former colonial masters'': The diffusion of sports and the question of cultural imperialism. *Stadion*, **14**(1), 49-63.

James, C.L.R. (1983). *Beyond a boundary*. New York: Pantheon Books.

James, P.E., & Minkel, C.W. (1986). *Latin America*. New York: Wiley.

Joseph, G.M. (1987). Documenting a regional pastime: Baseball in Yucatán. In R.M. Levine (Ed.), *Windows on Latin America: Understanding society through photographs* (pp. 76-89). Coral Gables, FL: North-South Center, University of Miami.

Joseph, G.M. (1988). Forging the regional pastime: Baseball and class in Yucatán. In J.L. Arbena (Ed.), *Sport and society in Latin America: Diffusion, dependency, and the rise of mass culture* (pp. 29-61). Westport: Greenwood Press.

Kelly, I. (1943). Notes on a west coast survival of the ancient Mexican ball game. *Notes on Middle American Archaeology and Ethnology*, **26**, 163-175.

Kendall, T. (1980). *Patolli: a game of ancient Mexico*. Belmont, MA: Kirk Game Co.

Klein, A.M. (1989). Baseball as underdevelopment: The political-economy of sport in the Dominican Republic. *Sociology of Sport Journal*, **6**(2), 95-112.

Klein, A.M. (1991). *Sugarball: The American game, the Dominican dream*. New Haven: Yale University.

Krich, J. (1989). *El béisbol: Travels through the pan-American pastime*. New York: Atlantic Monthly.

Larsen, N. (1983). Sport as civil society: The Argentinian junta plays championship soccer. In N. Larsen (Ed.), *The discourse of power: Culture, hegemony and the authoritarian state* (pp. 113-128). Minneapolis: Institute for the Study of Ideologies and Literature.

Lears, T.J.J. (1985). The concept of cultural hegemony: Problems and possibilities. *American Historical Review*, **90**, 567-593.

Lears, T.J.J. (1988). Power, culture, and memory. *Journal of American History*, **75**, 137-140.

Levene, G. (1988). Hoofbeats from the pampas. *Américas* **40**(6), 26-31.

Lever, J. (1983). *Soccer madness*. Chicago: University of Chicago.

Leyenaar, T.J.J. (1978). *Ulama: The perpetuation in Mexico of the pre-Spanish ball game ullamalitzli*. Leiden: EJ Brill.

Lipsitz, G. (1988). The struggle for hegemony. *Journal of American History*, **75**, 146-150.

Llanes, R.M. (1981). *Canchas de pelotas y reñideros de antaño*. Buenos Aires: Municipalidad de la Ciudad de Buenos Aires.

Llistosella, J. (1977). *Los Pumas*. Buenos Aires: Ediciones Match.

Magrassi, G.E., Berón, M., & Radovich, J.C. (1982). *Los juegos indígenas*. Buenos Aires: Centro Editor de América Latina.

Mandle, J.R., & Mandle, J.D. (1988). *Grass roots commitment: Basketball and society in Trinidad and Tobago*. Parkersburg, IA: Caribbean Books.

McNeill, W.H. (1986). *Polyethnicity and national unity in world history*. Toronto: University of Toronto.

Medina Pérez, P. (1986). *Veintún años de la Vuelta a Costa Rica*. San José: Editorial Costa Rica.

Oleksak, M.M., & Oleksak, M.A. (1991). *Béisbol: Latin Americans and the grand old game*. Grand Rapids: Masters Press.

Ossandón, C.A. (1982). Las dos caras del fútbol. *Araucaria de Chile*, **20**, 192-194.

Padden, R.C. (1970). *The hummingbird and the hawk: Conquest and sovereignty in the Valley of Mexico, 1503-1541*. New York: Harper & Row.

Paniagua S., B., et al. (1950). *Guatemala*. Guatemala City: Tipografia Nacional.

Perdomo Orellana, L. (1986-1987). The prehispanic ballgame tradition. *Voices of Mexico*, **2**, 64.

Pereira Salas, E. (1947). *Juegos y alegrías coloniales en Chile*. Santiago: Editora Zig-Zag.

Picón Cardona, L., et al. (1984). *La importancia de la educación física en el area marginal de la ciudad capital*. Unpublished seminar report, Escuela Normal de la Educación Física, Guatemala City.

Pike, F.B. (1973). *Spanish America, 1900-1970: Tradition and social innovation*. New York: Norton.

Piña Chán, R. (1969). *Games and sport in Old Mexico* (J. Becker, Trans.). Leipzig: Edition Leipzig.

Ponce, F. (1979). Ocio y deporte. *Revista Mexicana de Ciencias Políticas y Sociales*, **25**(95-96), 79-90.

Prieto Castillo, D. (1985). Cultura dominante y alternativas. In H. Cerutti Guldberg (Ed.), *El problema de la identidad latinoamericana* (pp. 61-76). México, D.F.: Universidad Nacional Autónoma de México.

Pye, G. (1986). The ideology of Cuban sport. *Journal of Sport History*, **13**(2), 119-127.

Rachum, I. (1978). Futebol: The growth of a Brazilian national institution. *New Scholar*, **7**, 183-200.

Ruck, R. (1984). Dominican real fan and talent hotbed. *Baseball Research Journal*, **13**, 3-6.

Ruck, R. (1991). *The tropic of baseball: Baseball in the Dominican Republic*. Westport, CT: Meckler.

Sáenz, J.P. (1951). *Equitación gaucha en la pampa y Mesopotamia*. Buenos Aires: Ediciones Peuser.

Salcedo, J.M., & Sánchez León, A. (1982). Voleibol peruano: Matar por amor al arte. *Quehacer*, **18**, 67-83.

Scheffler, L., Reynoso, R., & Inzúa C., V. (1985). *El juego de pelota prehispánico y sus supervivencias actuales*. Tlahuapan, México: Premiá Editora.

Sebreli, J.J. (1981). *Fútbol y masas*. Buenos Aires: Editorial Galerna.

Shirts, M. (1988). Sócrates, Corinthians, and questions of democracy and citizenship. In J.L. Arbena (Ed.), *Sport and society in Latin America: Diffusion, dependency, and the rise of mass culture* (pp. 97-122). Westport, CT: Greenwood Press.

Silva Romo, J. (1973). *Teoría y práctica del deporte*. Quito: Imprenta Cevallos.

Slatta, R.W. (1983). *Gauchos and the vanishing frontier*. Lincoln: University of Nebraska Press.

Slatta, R.W. (1986). The demise of the gaucho and the rise of equestrian sport in Argentina. *Journal of Sport History*, **13**, 97-111.

Smith, G. (1986). A letter from South America. *Sports Illustrated*, **65**(27), 94-99.

Smith, G. (1987). The fiesta in the town of ghosts. *Sports Illustrated*, **67**(15), 76-84.

Sola, J.S. de (1914). El deporte como factor patriótico y sociológico; Las grandes figuras deportivas de Cuba. *Cuba Contemporánea*, **5**(2), 121-167.

Stein, S. (1987). Miguel Rostaing: Dodging blows on and off the soccer field. In W.H. Beezley & J. Ewell (Eds.), *The human tradition in Latin America: The twentieth century* (pp. 15-25). Wilmington: Scholarly Resources.

Stein, S. (1988). The case of soccer in early twentieth-century Lima. In J.L. Arbena (Ed.), *Sport and society in Latin America: Diffusion, dependency, and the rise of mass culture* (pp. 63-84). Westport, CT: Greenwood Press.

Stein, S., Deustua Carvallo, J., & Stokes, S.C. (1986). Soccer and social change in early twentieth century Peru. Part II. *Studies in Latin American Popular Culture*, **5**, 68-77.

Taladoire, E. (1981). *Les terrains de jeu de balle*. México, D.F.: Mission Archeologique et Ethnologique Francaise au Mexique.

Troncoso, O. (1982). *Juegos y diversiones en la Gran Aldea*. Buenos Aires: Centro Editor de América Latina.

Turino, T. (1988). The music of Andean migrants in Lima, Peru: Demographics, social power, and style. *Latin American Music Review*, **9**(2), 127-150.

Viale, C. (1922). *El deporte Argentino (contribución a su desarrollo y prosperidad)*. Buenos Aires: Librería de A. García Santos.

Wagner, E.A. (1984). Baseball in Cuba. *Journal of Popular Culture*, **18**, 113-120.

Wagner, E.A. (1985). Sport. In H.E. Hinds, Jr. & C.M. Tatum (Eds.), *Handbook of Latin American popular culture* (pp. 135-150). Westport, CT: Greenwood Press.

Wagner, E.A. (1988). Sport in revolutionary societies: Cuba and Nicaragua. In J.L. Arbena (Ed.), *Sport and society in Latin America: Diffusion, dependency, and the rise of mass culture* (pp. 113-136). Westport, CT: Greenwood Press.

Williams, R. (1977). *Marxism and literature*. Oxford: Oxford University Press.

Williams, R. (1982). *The sociology of culture*. New York: Schocken Books.

Zurcher, L.A., & Meadow, A. (1967). On bullfights and baseball: An example of interaction of social institutions. *The International Journal of Comparative Sociology*, **8**, 99-117.

# CHAPTER 6

# Subcultures in Sport: Resilience and Transformation

*Peter Donnelly*

Over 100 years of anthropological and sociological research has revealed the almost infinite diversity of human patterns of living. The principal taboos of western society (cannibalism, incest, homosexuality, etc.) may all be found at some time, in some place, as a normal part of social organization. Many principle western values—status systems, competition, private property, the sanctity of human life, male dominance, the nuclear family, and so on—may be shown to be an alternative but not an exclusive set of values. They are alternative precisely because, at some time, in some place, social groups have organized themselves without any recognizable status system, without competition, without private property, with little regard for human life, with female dominance, and with domestic arrangements different from the nuclear family.

These varying patterns of beliefs, meanings, behaviors, and symbolic systems constitute the culture of a social group. Tylor's (1871) classic definition of culture as "that complex whole which includes knowledge, belief, art, morals, law, custom, and any other capabilities acquired by man as a member of society" (p. 1) still has some relevance. However, modern definitions are more likely to propose that culture is "produced" as well as "acquired" and that it is "a constitutive social process, creating specific and different 'ways of life' " (Williams, 1977, p. 19).

Despite the potential diversity of culture, a hegemonizing tendency results in certain "meanings and ways" (Pearson, 1979) being preferred by specific social groupings to create a *dominant* culture. Because the selection is made from such varied and contradictory possibilities (e.g., hunting is favored, pit sports are not), the questions of *who* determines aspects of the dominant culture and *in whose interests* the selections are made become significant. In North American society, the dominant culture reflects primarily the interests of whites, males, the wealthy and powerful, and the able-bodied (cf. Loy's account of moral stratification in North American society in Loy, McPherson, & Kenyon, 1978, pp. 406-410).

A complete description of the dominant culture in a complex society such as North America is, of course, well beyond the scope of this paper. However, it is possible to take one aspect of the dominant culture as an indication of this complexity. Williams (1970) identified the major value orientations of American society as achievement and success; activity and work; moral orientation; humanitarian mores; efficiency and practicality; progress; material comfort; equality; freedom; external conformity; science and secular rationality; nationalism and patriotism; democracy; individual personality; and racism and related group-superiority themes. The order and exact content of this list is likely to have changed somewhat over time, and it is quite likely that the list would be somewhat different in Canada. But the common-sense, taken-for-granted nature of the list indicates the successful hegemony of the dominant culture, and both the confidence and the complexity of the dominant culture are revealed in the ability to hold contradictory values (e.g., equality vs. racism).

This American dominant culture is particularly significant globally in the second half of the 20th century. Americanization, a process that involves the cultural, economic, and political diffusion or domination of American ideas, values, and social forms, is evident on every continent. In Europe, for example, Americanization is taking a number of forms. Americanisms may now be found in all of the European languages (*le drugstore*, *le hamburger*). Since the Second World War, there has been American control of many aspects of the European economy, such that American-based multinationals (e.g., Esso, Singer, Heinz, Ford, IBM) are household names in most countries. Through NATO and through American bases in non-NATO countries (e.g., Spain), the defense and destiny of Europe have become inextricably linked with the United States. And in terms of cultural and leisure pursuits, American domination of the film and television industries has a powerful impact on European thought and lifestyles (cf. Hepworth & Featherstone, 1982); American-style consumer culture is also prevalent, and American sports and the American style of sport are spreading rapidly.

These arguments about a dominant national culture or the dominance of an international culture evidenced by Americanization have been made frequently. In its 1947-49 report, the British Royal Commission on the Press noted the momentum of the dominant culture toward a fixed state: "Among the most powerful forces in national life today are the centripetal forces making for centralization and uniformity in government, in education, in amusement, and in standards of taste" (cited by Whitson, 1983, pp. 149-150). Levi-Strauss (1978) similarly recognized the homogenizing effects of various forms of cultural hegemony and took the idea to its extreme when he suggested that: "We can easily conceive of a time when there will be only one culture and one civilization on the entire surface of the earth" (p. 20).

But these homogenizing tendencies should not be thought of as static or monolithic. Levi-Strauss (1978) also felt that one culture was unlikely since the process has a dialectical aspect: "The more a civilization becomes homogenized, the more internal lines of separation become apparent; and what is gained on one level is immediately lost on another . . . . I don't see how mankind can really live without some internal diversity" (p. 20). These contradictory tendencies became apparent in western society during the 1920s and 1930s. During this period, despite several years of economic depression, increasing leisure time and spending power were closely associated with the widespread commercialization of sport and leisure. When combined with "the growth of the media, it was part of the development of a more uniform and homogeneous society, partaking of an increasingly common culture" (Stevenson, 1984, p. 381). Simultaneously, personal sport and leisure interests began to diversify markedly, reflecting greater freedom of choice for many people and an expansion of home-based recreation. Recently, research and theoretical work in the area of cultural studies has taken this dialectic between homogeneity and heterogeneity as its focus. In the case of sport and other aspects of popular culture, cultural forms are seen less as a totally incorporated aspect of the dominant culture[1] and more as a field in which values, ideologies, and meanings may be contested. In terms of this type of analysis of cultural production, reproduction, and transformation, the hegemony of the dominant culture "has continually to be renewed, recreated, defended and modified. It is also continually resisted, limited, altered, challenged by pressures not all its own" (Williams, 1977, p. 112).

In other words, there are continual challenges to the dominant culture that must be answered or accommodated. Williams's (1977, 1980) view of the dynamic nature of culture—the hegemony of the dominant culture that is continually opposed (or at least shown to be alternative) by both residual and emergent aspects of culture, which the dominant culture in turn attempts to incorporate or suppress—provides the basis for the following discussion of sport subcultures. As cultural units that share in the dominant culture and maintain and produce a number of alternative cultural forms and ideologies, subcultures provide an ideal model with which to explore dominant, residual, and emergent aspects of culture. Gruneau (1981) proposed that we need to know how "subcultures, with their various 'establishment' and 'countercultural' emphases, have been constitutively inserted into the struggles, the forms of compliance and opposition, social reproduction and transformation, associated with changing patterns of social development" (p. 10). Bishop and Hoggett (1987) noted that "[leisure] subcultures are the means by which the dominant values of wider society are transmitted, resisted or negotiated" (p. 32). Subcultures may range, therefore, from resilient and conservative maintainers of tradition (i.e., residual culture) to the most active sites of cultural production (i.e., emergent culture).

# Sport Culture and Sport Subcultures

In this section I explore the issue of resilience through several examples of sport subcultures that held on to older meanings and ways until they fell out of step with the dominant sport culture. As such, they were residual culture providing both resistance and an alternative to the dominant sport culture. Then I examine the transformation of those sport subcultures as they became incorporated by the dominant sport culture. And, finally, I consider examples of emergent sport subcultures that have had a transformative effect on the dominant sport culture. But first it is necessary to consider the nature of the dominant sport culture.

## Dominant Sport Culture

The dominant sport culture in western society involves materialism, achievement, the work ethic, dehumanization of athletes, and a win-at-all-costs attitude. Gruneau (1984) succinctly described contemporary sporting practice as

> completely open, achievement based activity, conducted for the purposes of sporting careers and economic reward. Within this definition is the notion that enjoyment in sport is tied to skill acquisition, that specialization is the basis for excellence, and that some form of economic reward is justified and necessary in order to achieve at the highest levels. (p. 14)

Similarly, McPherson, Curtis, & Loy (1989) examine the occupational orientation of youth sport with its particular patterns:

- Behavior—Only the highly skilled play and get rewarded
- Values—Winning is all that counts, be aggressive, deviate from the rules when necessary
- Beliefs—An elite career must begin early in life and include extensive competition, including more games per year than some professional teams
- Symbols—Trophies, uniforms, jackets, bonuses for playing for a specific team (p. 255)

These definitions indicate the selective and exclusive nature of the dominant sport culture, and it is not difficult to think of alternatives to such things as skill acquisition, specialization, and extrinsic rewards. That these aspects of sport appear natural and normal attests to the successful hegemony of the dominant sport culture.

These cultural characteristics are American in origin and are supported by several content-analysis studies conducted in the United States. Edwards (1973, p. 69) identified the dominant American sports creed and outlined 12 categories divided into 7 central themes characteristic of the sport culture at the time: character, discipline, competition, physical fitness, mental fitness, religiosity, and nationalism. Many of these are still relevant characteristics. Snyder (1972) felt that locker-room slogans used by coaches would also be a good indicator of American values in sport; his study identified slogans relating to physical and mental fitness, the idea that pain is a desirable and inevitable part of sport,[2] aggressiveness and competitive spirit, acceptance of strict discipline, and subordination of self to the team. Similar categories were evident in an analysis of American university athletic department press guides (Snyder & Spreitzer, 1989). These content analyses compare favorably to Williams's (1970) set of major value orientations of American society (noted previously).

The Americanization of international sport is clearly supplanting the Europeanization of sport that occurred in the latter part of the 19th century. The earlier European (initially English) values of strict amateurism, sportsmanship, generalization rather than specialization, and the valuing of participation over success (a means rather than an ends orientation) are disappearing, even in Europe. Win-at-all-costs attitudes are shifting sportsmanship into a residual category in Britain, and *le fairplay* is suffering a similar fate in France. Raphael (1985) noted that the three games regarded as "national" by the British (cricket, rugby, and soccer) all can result in a draw or tie. This is assumed to have a strong relationship with the principles of balance and compromise that were long an aspect of the dominant British political culture. The recent introduction of means for achieving a winner in 1-day cricket and in some soccer games (the shoot-out) may be associated with the Americanization of sport. In English professional soccer it is no longer even possible to "share the points" in a tie, because three points are now awarded for a victory and only one for a draw.

The Americanization of European sport is also proceeding through the popularity of North American sports on television, particularly American football, and through growing participation in the principal North American sports (football, baseball, basketball, and ice hockey). In 1983, there were only two fully equipped and operational American football teams in Britain. By 1986 there were 150 teams and an apparently viable and well-sponsored intercity league. "Gridiron" football has continued to be popular (although there are signs that a plateau of interest may have been reached), and now there is further international expansion with the World League of American Football (W.L.A.F.) (cf. Maguire, 1990). Interest in baseball is also expanding, and North American players have been welcome in the semiprofessional basketball and ice hockey leagues in Europe. Together with the sports themselves, the American-style "hoopla" has also been adopted and is spreading to the traditional European sports (cf. Maguire, 1988). In British professional soccer, for example, there is a preference by some for a "super league" playing in all-seat stadia to a middle-class spectatorship, rather than the "stands" and working-class support of the game as it now exists.

Despite the prevalence of the Americanized model of sport, lip service is still paid to the older model when coaches and administrators talk about sportsmanship and playing for the sake of playing. And a great many people find themselves harking back to a romanticized earlier version of sport when faced with much of the over-commercialized hype of modern sport, or with such events as drug scandals. Reactions to Eddie "The Eagle" Edwards, the one-person British ski-jumping team at the 1988 Calgary Olympics, indicate the transitional state between the European and American sport models in the public consciousness.

In most of the United States and parts of Canada, Edwards was a joke of the "bad is good" variety. But in the United Kingdom and other parts of Canada there was a genuine and nostalgic affection for his apparent representation of some type of "authentic" amateurism that has almost disappeared from the dominant sport culture. The contradiction lies in the fact that, while admiring those aspects of his performance, people tended to applaud the fame and wealth that he achieved for a time because of his "amateurism."

In addition to such nostalgic challenges to the dominant sport culture, challenges in the form of residual and emergent sport subcultures also exist; these are discussed in terms of the resilience and transformation of sport subcultures.

# Resilience

Resilience, in this case, is not concerned only with sports that have survived for a long time in an apparently unchanged form. Sports such as track and field, horse racing, soccer, baseball, and cricket appear to meet this criterion, but though the forms of the sports are the same, their meanings and ways (Pearson, 1976) have changed over time in order to conform to the dominant sport culture. Resilience here refers to instances of sport subcultures where the form and the meanings and ways of the sport have survived to become anachronistic and possibly oppositional to the dominant sport culture. In other words, the sports began in conformity but did not change as the dominant sport culture changed, and they became aspects of residual culture.

For example, Metcalfe (1987) has examined the survival of folk games in mining villages in a region of England. Such activities as pigeon and sparrow shooting, rabbit coursing, and a form of bowling were in complete accord with pre-19th-century sport culture in England, but by the late 19th century they had largely been displaced by the newly organized amateur sports. In the mining villages under study the older activities with "unwritten rules, no formal organizational structure and indeterminate time and spatial boundaries" were "tied to the taverns and gambling [and] were the antithesis of amateur sport" (Metcalfe, 1987, p. 38). Despite a great deal of condemnation and external pressure (a clear indication of the oppositional nature of the activities) they survived until 1914. Numerous examples of this type exist, but I want to concentrate specifically on three sport examples of interest because they have recently undergone, or appear to be undergoing, a transition from residual status. These are rugby, climbing, and boxing.

## *Rugby*[3]

The crystallization of rugby (and soccer) from the earlier forms of folk and public-school football has been well documented (e.g., Dunning & Sheard, 1979; Mason, 1980). The game gradually "civilized" out of extremely violent origins. While the older and more established public schools favored the soccer forms of the game and banned the practice of hacking (kicking another player in the shins) quite early, Rugby school only banned the use of iron-shod boots for hacking in 1845. The game continued to be rough, and in an era when citizens were far more accustomed to viewing public acts of violence than today, "spectators of a game among Old Rugbeians in Liverpool in 1855 were asked if 'this new sport was a worthy manner for gentlemen to employ themselves on a Saturday afternoon' " (Walvin, 1978, p. 86). Such criticisms increased, and it was only with the formation of the Rugby Football Union (R.F.U.) in 1871 that hacking was reluctantly abolished.

Between 1871 and the mid-1960s rugby in England remained relatively unchanged in both cultural and technical terms. The conservatism of the participants (in terms of resistance to change) was signalled by their slowness to adopt civilizing constraints on player violence. And this conservatism is exemplified by the wholehearted manner in which rugby embraced the growing amateur movement, a movement that had been developing since the 1860s as a deliberate class barrier to participation.

Of the three major British sports, the response of rugby to professionalization was by far the most conservative. While cricket, with some modifications, was able to accommodate an open game involving both amateurs and professionals, and soccer was able to maintain both amateurs and professionals under the same governing body, rugby was unable to tolerate any semblance of professionalism and the potential democratization of the game that might result.

Dunning and Sheard (1979) determined that the rugby establishment—in contrast to the cricket and soccer establishments—was derived largely from the bourgeoisie, including graduates of newer and lower status public schools. As a consequence, their conservatism (in contrast to the more liberal attitudes of their socially secure social superiors) may have derived from "status insecurity," in which the marginality of those involved in rugby "made them anxious lest contact of too close or too direct a kind with members of the working class should contaminate their status" (Dunning & Sheard, 1979, p. 198). In 1895, the R.F.U. forced clubs in the north of England, who were making broken-time payments to working class players, to break away and institute the separate game of Rugby League.

By the end of the 19th century, rugby had become *the* winter sport of the upper and middle classes in England. A combination of the bourgeoisification of the upper classes and a continual series of defeats of upper- and upper-middle-class soccer teams by amateur and professional working-class teams during the last decade of the 19th century eventually resulted in "more and more public and grammar schools [beginning] to renounce [soccer] and switch to the 'simon-pure' amateurism of the increasingly class-exclusive Rugby game" (Dunning & Sheard, 1979, p. 197).

The sport had also become the epitome of the dominant sport culture at the turn of the century. The game was played with courage and abandon, but this behavior was tempered with a deep concern for the values of gentlemanly amateurism and sportsmanship. Most of the players had other athletic interests (e.g., cricket in the summer), and most were convinced that the manner in which the game was played was far more important than the outcome.

The combination of conservatism and lack of democratization, together with the strict amateurism, resulted in the game in England being frozen into a relatively static state until the 1960s. Despite a number of humiliating losses by the national team to better prepared and more professionalized teams from the "colonies" (e.g., New Zealand and South Africa), there was little coaching or organized practice; there was a sense that it was somehow unsportsmanlike to train, and post-game drinking and rowdy (men only) social behavior was highly valued. In 1965, the sport was an embattled conservative bastion, actively resisting all of the trappings of modern rationalized sport. And yet, this resistance[4] also had the effect of preserving, for a time at least, some of the more admirable characteristics of the earlier sport culture. These include the pleasure of participation and consideration for one's opponent and for the rules (written and unwritten) of the game.

## Climbing

Climbing[5] emerged as a sport in the European Alps in the mid-19th century. It resulted from the presence in the Alps of tourists seeking adventure and natural scientists seeking data, many of whom were imbued with the new spirit of athleticism. The sport eventually developed into a series of "climbing games" (Tejada-Flores, 1967), and met all of the criteria for being considered as a legitimate sport except that there was no institutionalized competitive structure (the situation in the USSR was somewhat different). In other words, notwithstanding the fact that climbing had no governing bodies, no formal competition or competitions, no written rules, and no means of enforcing rules, it adopted the prevailing sport culture of the late 19th century and functioned exactly like any other sport.

The system of rules and conventions that existed in climbing (termed *ethics* by climbers) are socially constructed and socially sanctioned. That is, the rules are created by consensus among climbers (both verbally and through climbing journals), transmitted by the same means of communication, and enforced by self-discipline and social pressure. Ethics are based on the premise that, given enough time and resources (human, financial, and technical), anything can be climbed. Therefore, some guidelines are needed to give the mountain or cliff a "sporting" chance (i.e., introduce an element of uncertainty to the outcome) and not to beat it into submission. The ethics also permit competition by ensuring that climbers attempting similar types of ascent employ similar means.

Ethics take the form of a series of proscriptions based on the difficulty and the danger of the ascent being attempted. In the "bouldering game," ascents of boulders or low cliffs usually not more than 10 metres in height, everything is proscribed. As climbers proceed through the hierarchy of climbing games—rock climbing, big-wall climbing, alpine climbing—more and more equipment (ropes, karabiners, pitons, etc.) and techniques are allowed until the ultimate "expedition game" is reached. Because the chance of reaching a Himalayan or high Andean summit is extremely limited, any resources that climbers can muster are permitted.

Because there are no referees or formal sanctions to ensure compliance with ethics, the only sanctions are derision and public denouncements. For example, despite the "anything goes" attitude in expedition climbing, when an Italian Everest expedition in the 1970s ferried men and supplies to a fairly high point on the mountain by helicopter before undertaking the final ascent, the act was widely condemned in climbing journals. Both tradition and ethics have it that the whole mountain should be climbed and supplies carried. Despite the prestige that nations attach to belonging to the "Everest Club" (i.e., being among those countries who have placed at least one citizen on the summit of Everest), the sanctions appear to have been adequate since the act has not been repeated. Climbers cannot prevent someone from building scaffolding against a section of cliff and claiming a first ascent, and they cannot prevent individuals from carrying compressed air drills to drill bolt holes to aid an ascent. But the fact that the first has never happened and the second is extremely rare (and was initially met with widespread condemnation and derision) attests to the success of the informal system of sanctions.

The type of competition facilitated by the ethics depends on record keeping, either in the climbing literature or in the oral history of a particular locale. Record keeping makes it possible to engage in direct competition for first ascents (of a mountain, a new route on a mountain, or a new route on a cliff), which may also include first solo, first female, and first winter ascents. Record keeping also makes indirect competition possible—competition for the style or quality of an ascent—which may refer to the speed of an ascent but is usually considered in terms of how closely an ascent conforms to prevailing ethical standards. For example, if an ascent has been accomplished using two pitons, and a subsequent climber manages to ascend the route with only one or no pitons, that becomes the new best standard for the route. Special praise is reserved for those individuals who bring the ethics of a lower game in the hierarchy to a new level (e.g., soloing a rock climb or big-wall climb means that bouldering ethics have been brought to a more difficult game), and this has recently created a new game. The use of alpine ethics on mountains previously climbed only with expedition ethics has created the "super-Alpine game," which is rapidly becoming the new standard for Himalayan and high Andean ascents.

The resilience and significance of climbing lies in the fact that it existed for so long as an alternative to mainstream sport, as an unincorporated and self-governing parallel to the dominant sport culture. The sport has been anarchic in the best sense of the term, the sense that "all forms of government are oppressive and undesirable" (*American Heritage Dictionary*, 1971). And climbers have, in recent years, been very conscious of the difference from other sports and have acted to maintain that difference.

For example, any type of certification has been anathema to most climbers. There was strong resistance to going the way of hang gliding, scuba diving, and sport parachuting, where certification programs and competency ratings are associated with status and reinforced by badge wearing. Where bureaucratic organizations do exist (national Alpine Clubs, British Mountaineering Council, Union Internationale des Associations d'Alpinisme) any attempt on their part to step beyond the mandated bounds of publishing guidebooks and journals, maintaining mountain huts, conducting equipment tests, or fighting access battles was usually met with strong criticism from the climbing community. When, in the mid-1970s, the Soviets proposed some international speed-climbing competitions with a view to introducing the sport to the Olympics in 1980, there was an international outcry from the climbing community. The concern was not so much with speed climbing per se but with the inevitable development of a governing bureaucracy, organized competitions, restrictions, and commercial involvement.

This resilience appears to be coming to an end, as noted in the next section. But for well over 100 years the subculture of climbers managed to conduct a sport that was open to all who wished to be involved, was created, re-created, and transformed by the participants in face-to-face interaction, with a set of rules that was sensitive to individual, local, regional, and national differences and was able to direct and contain the behavior of members by consensus. The resistance and resilience of climbing makes it a worthwhile model for consideration as an alternative to the dominant sport culture.

## Boxing[6]

Whereas the resilience of rugby was based on its anachronistic nature, and climbing is of interest because of its resilience as an alternative, the resilience of boxing is of a different order. The sport survives, and even appears to flourish, despite an extended period of criticism and marginalization.

For the first half of the 20th century boxing, and particularly amateur boxing, was a significant part of the dominant sport culture, receiving support and participation from across the entire social spectrum. Boxing was a university sport in Britain and North America (the first Oxford-Cambridge boxing meet took place in 1897); it became an Olympic sport in 1904; it was taught at public, state, and private schools; it was an activity at exclusive summer camps in North America; it was a mainstay at youth clubs and YMCAs; and it was an essential part of military training. It was considered to be significant for the development of character and for promoting sportsmanship and the gentlemanly art of self defense.

There was some public criticism of professional boxing, and the "punch drunk" syndrome was first identified in 1928. But in general terms, the sport had full establishment support, and the Joe Louis—Max Schmelling fights in the late 1930s came to symbolize, for Americans, the confrontation between democracy and fascism. It was after the Second World War, in the 1950s, that the sport began to be the target of significant public criticism, and this criticism took a number of forms.

Summerskill (1956) began what might be termed the women's critique of boxing, and drew attention to the brutalizing and degrading aspects of the sport. This argument has been refined to single out boxing as the only sport in which the object is to inflict physical punishment on an opponent, and to suggest that this practice has no place in modern society. A United States Senate Subcommittee in 1960 drew attention to the corrupt aspects of the sport—gambling, fixed bouts, and links with organized crime. Corruption and exploitation are still apparently widespread in the sport, and the various administrative bodies (e.g., State Boxing and Athletic Commissions, the three world title sanctioning bodies (WBA, WBC, IBF), the British Boxing Board of Control, etc.) appear to be characterized by incompetence.

Medical concerns about boxing, which tend to peak after deaths in the ring, have now become the principal critique of the sport.[7] Death, brain damage, and blindness are all concerns (although the immediate death rates in boxing are far lower than in a number of other sports), and these concerns have resulted in a ban on professional boxing in Norway and Sweden and calls for a ban on the sport from such organizations as the American, British, and Canadian Medical Associations, the American Public Health Association, and the British Safety Council. There are even rumors that a powerful group in the International Olympic Committee is working to abolish boxing as an Olympic sport.

Because of these critiques, boxing began to lose its establishment support. In Canada, for example, the Canadian YMCA dropped boxing in 1954, the Canadian Armed Forces in 1955, and by the 1960s boxing was no longer a part of the school physical education curriculum or an interuniversity sport. The sport was virtually abandoned by the middle and upper classes, and it became marginalized to the working class and racial minorities. As a consequence, the meanings (character and gentlemanly self defense) attributed to the sport by the middle- and upper-class participants—those with the most power to define what is appropriate in the dominant sport culture—could no longer hold, and boxing began to be defined as an inappropriate form of physical activity.

The resilience of boxing, despite over 40 years of ongoing and increasing criticism, is remarkable. It has survived the criticism, it has survived a series of tragic ring deaths in the early 1980s, and it has survived international amateur judging (cf. the Seoul Olympics) that may be even more biased than figure skating and gymnastics. The sport appears to be more popular than at any previous time, with an ongoing series of "richest fights in history," most recently Hagler-Leonard in 1987 and Tyson-Spinks in 1988, indicating that promoters are able to accumulate increasing amounts of money for "purses" and profit. Major fights may be held in 20,000-seat arenas, outdoor stadia of more than twice that capacity, or even Las Vegas parking lots. These are invariably full, and spectators pay up to $1,500 for ringside seats. However, the large television audiences produce the greatest revenue, not only through the commercial networks but also through pay-cable sports networks, closed-circuit performance, pay-per-view cable, and satellite broadcast to other countries.

The promotion and entertainment appeal of the sport clearly account, in part, for its resilience, as does the commercial viability of boxing that results from its entertainment appeal. But this does not explain why boxing continues to entertain people, or why it has not been made illegal. All of the sports in which animals are constrained to fight each other (e.g., cock and dog fighting) have been made illegal in most parts of North America, but the same concessions have not been made for humans because of the voluntarist assumptions that are made. However, boxing is clearly approaching a paradoxical and untenable position, and the first signs of transformation are evident.

## Transformation

Transformation refers to change in a society, as in "transformation of capitalist social relations" or "transformation of gender relations." In this case, the transformation from a European-style to an American-style dominant sport culture has been noted previously, but the specific concern is with transformation in sport subcultures and specifically in the meanings and ways of those subcultures.

Transformations are often thought of in terms of the development of emergent cultures or as a shift to a more progressive position in an established subculture. For example, Manning (1981) and Patterson (1969) have shown how cricket in the West Indies, originally a major symbol of white British colonialism, changed in both style and meaning as it came to represent anticolonialism and nationalism. Similar transformations occurred with cricket in Australia and rugby in New Zealand, while in northern and northeastern Spain in the 1960s soccer came to symbolize Basque and Catalan resistance to Franco's dictatorship (Shaw, 1985). In the first two cases presented here the transformations are toward the dominant sport culture—sports that had a residual and alternative nature but are now being incorporated. In the case of boxing, the apparently pending transformation is of a somewhat different order. As an additional aspect of transformation, countercultural changes are also considered.

## Rugby

English rugby since the mid-1960s has seen the introduction of scientific coaching and training methods; increasing levels of violence in the game; the introduction of league play (as a more rational competitive structure than the previous club-arranged "fixtures"); the introduction of organized mini-rugby, which parallels in almost every way the North American little league sports; increasing commercialization and television coverage; a quadrennial World Cup; and a change to a less rowdy social life.

This dramatic transformation from a bastion of amateurism and playing for fun to the epitome of rationalized nonprofessional sport in England has not occurred without a substantial amount of internal resistance. For example, despite the new professionalized attitudes, the old antagonism to Rugby League (the professional game) persisted until very recently, because anyone who had played the game was not allowed admission to R.F.U. clubhouses (a ban that was not applied to professionals from other sports). The R.F.U. still refuses to move to a more rational refereeing system with the promotion of linesmen to assistant referees, despite the increasing violence in the game, which is seen as a refusal to model themselves on such professional games as soccer. Some national team players in Scotland were recently obliged to avoid commercial display by using black shoe polish to hide the Adidas stripes on their shoes, and to purchase generic track suits rather than wear suits that identified a manufacturer. The R.F.U. belligerently attempted to assert its independence from the dominant sport culture, and put the Olympics at risk, by maintaining ties with apartheid South Africa when all other sports had agreed to a boycott. Also, there are still examples, even at the highest levels of the game, of the old post-game rowdy behavior.[8]

The professional approach to rugby is part of a widespread change in the meaning of sport in the United Kingdom. Despite the resistance of some of the "old guard," the game is again becoming incorporated as part of the dominant sport culture, and this transformation is occurring for a number of reasons. These include the desire to overcome the humiliating losses to better prepared teams from the Commonwealth; the introduction of direct government involvement in amateur sport through the founding of the Sports Council in the late 1960s, which provided an impetus (financial and administrative, and in terms of accountability for funds received) to achieve success in amateur sport; the further democratization of the game to the lower middle class, which resulted in an additional loss of the old elite values and a greater emphasis on winning; and the shift from a player-centered to a spectator-centered game (Dunning & Sheard, 1979), which resulted in further financial dependence and commercialization and the motivation to produce a quality (spectator) product. Given these circumstances, the incorporation of the game into the dominant sport culture was inevitable.

## Climbing

Since the 1960s, growing public interest and participation and the increasing techno-logization and commercialization of climbing have had a significant influence on the transformation of the sport. Climbers have discovered an increasing number of ways to make a living at their activity, not just as guides and instructors, or in other aspects of the outdoor education scene (both public and private), but also as photographers, authors, film and video makers, and film stunt men/women and coordinators. Some climbers have been able to obtain enough sponsorship and other sources of income to become full-time professional adventurers. Many more have managed this on a part-time basis, and an increasing number of sponsorship opportunities have become available to individual climbers as well as to expeditions.

As with rugby, training had been considered unsportsmanlike by climbers. However, professionalization has been associated with a major movement towards training, particularly on indoor artificial walls, and also in basement gyms and weight rooms. This has been associated with the appearance of numerous articles and books about fitness and training (e.g., Hurn & Ingle, 1988).

This increasing commercialization and professionalization is another way that the development of climbing has been parallel to that of the mainstream sport culture, but incorporation had always been avoided by the rejection of formal competition. However, the first organized competition outside eastern Europe took place at Bardonecchia in Italy in 1985, and a growing number of professional competitions have been held each year since then to the point where there is now an apparently viable series of World Cup competitions. These have occurred because of the interest of a number of top rock climbers who saw competitions as another source of income and who have argued that such competitions would not affect the essentially anarchic nature of the sport, because of the interest of sponsors and television companies in Europe and North America, and because the majority of climbers who were against both competitions *and* what little there is of a bureaucratic structure in the sport had no way to prevent them from occurring.

Most climbing organizations have now adopted an "if you can't beat them, join them" attitude. In an attempt to ensure some control, to govern environmental concerns, and to prevent the formation of parallel organizations that, as legislative bodies in a competitive sport, would inevitably become more powerful than the current service organizations, the Union Internationale des Associations d'Alpinisme (UIAA) has developed an internationally acceptable set of rules for the sport.[9]

The consequences of this transition are not yet apparent. On one hand there are many climbers who are fearful that competition and the development of legislative bodies will lead to restrictions, certification, and testing throughout the sport—the full incorporation of climbing. On the other hand, there are many others who have accepted competition as an inevitable development in the sport, accepted the argument that this is just another "game" and will not have an impact on the sport as a whole, or that the two types of climbing (now widely referred to as "adventure" climbing and "sport" climbing) will coexist. While the latter outcome is the most likely possibility at this time, this significant shift toward the dominant sport culture has the potential to cause a major transformation in the sport replete with both intended and unintended consequences. For example, the use of power drills to make bolt holes, which earlier met with derision, is now widely accepted among sport climbers.

## Boxing

Boxing is clearly a sport in transition. Two relatively distinct views of the sport prevail internationally, with little in the way of neutral opinions. In the first, boxing is a popular and profitable form of mass entertainment; it provides an opportunity for social mobility for the disadvantaged; it is a useful outlet for those who may otherwise turn to delinquent activities; and it is practiced by individuals who freely choose to participate and who are aware of the risks. It may well be a "celebration of individualism," and it certainly provides a forum to test and display character in "America's tragic theatre" (Oates, 1987).

In the second, the sport is brutal, uncivilized, and medically unjustifiable; as the only sport in which the explicit object is to inflict punishment on an opponent, it is an anachronism; social mobility is available to so few, and is so short-lived, that the sport functions as a form of social control for the many who attempt to achieve it; the participants may not be "cultural dupes," but they are certainly not fully informed about the risks to health that may result from participation; and the sport propagates ideas about gender, race, and conflict resolution that have no place in modern society.

There are a number of striking parallels between the present-day status of boxing and the status of prize fighting (bare knuckle boxing) in the mid-19th century (Donnelly, 1989). No cultural form can survive intact in such a contradictory state, and the resolution in the case of prize fighting was an outright legal ban. This had two immediate consequences: first, the sport went underground; second, the Queensberry Rules were devised in 1867 for the new and middle-class sport of boxing. With the introduction of gloves, three-minute rounds alternating with one minute rest periods, and the 10-second knockout, the sport was appropriated and re-created by the middle class. A professional version of boxing soon developed, providing a legitimate outlet for the prize fighters.

The contradictory state of boxing has already had a number of consequences, the most obvious of which is the fact that there have been more rule changes in the last 10 years than at any time since the introduction of the Queensberry rules. Among the various rule changes that have been considered, implemented (not always on an international basis), or experimented with for boxing in recent years are the use of protective headgear, thumbless gloves, and heavier (more padded) gloves; tighter medical supervision and better record keeping, including the introduction of a boxer's passport in some places in which the date, opponent, and outcome of every bout are officially recorded, along with medical reports; the reduction of title fights from 15 to 12 rounds, and the imposition of a standing eight-count when a boxer appears defenseless. In addition there are the bans in the Scandinavian countries, the calls for bans from various organizations, and the threat to Olympic boxing. An outright ban on boxing (in English-speaking countries) in the near future seems unlikely. If it were to occur it would have a number of negative consequences for the participants, who would almost inevitably continue to box underground for smaller reward and with less medical supervision. But a continuing civilizing transformation of the sport seems inevitable, particularly with respect to the administration and supervision of boxing.

## Countercultural change

In addition to these specific examples, other more widespread transformations have occurred in association with and often in opposition to the growing Americanization of sport. A number of these have been short-lived, or have been totally or partially incorporated, but they provide some insight into the richness of cultural production and confirm that hegemony is not easily won.

These transformations are all associated with the major social movements that began in the 1960s and early 1970s, and all have their basis in specific subcultures. They include the fitness movement, the environmental movement, the countercultural and new games activities that have also affected the conduct of physical education and youth sport, and the folk revivial.[10]

*The fitness movement.*    The success of the fitness movement is partly rooted in the women's movement, and in action by women to take the control of their health away from the male-dominated medical establishment. Along with the environmental movement and other aspects of the counterculture concerned with health and lifestyle, the fitness movement has had widespread consequences with regard to diet, drinking, smoking, and exercise, and has affected the conduct of physical education in schools. There have been several setbacks resulting from the patriarchal nature of society and from new right political movements. For example, Donnelly (1988) and MacNeill (1988) have noted the patriarchal exploitation of women's aerobics and bodybuilding; Ingham (1985) has shown that the fitness movement is being used to support reductions in state intervention in health care by personalizing the issue of health. But the fitness movement has enabled a great many individuals, particularly those previously excluded from fitness opportunities (e.g., women, the disabled, and the aging), to enjoy a more active life, and has created a number of noncompetitive alternatives to mainstream sport.

*The "greening" of sport.*    The environmental movement led to a significant increase in participation in outdoor sports and activities (Donnelly, 1977; Wilson, 1977). In addition to specific interest in the environment evidenced by such sports as birding, Wilson (1977) has proposed that the "growth of these sports offers evidence of a dissatisfaction with modern American life and suggests that the source of this discontent was excessive technology and urbanization" (p. 54). Paradoxically, some environmentalists have indicated that this growth in participation is damaging the environment in some sensitive areas, but it is clear that the overall effect of the outdoor activities has been to conserve and protect wilderness areas from threatened government and commercial exploitation. That is, the presence in national parks and other wilderness areas of large numbers of active users who are taking pleasure in the environment forestalls consideration of alternative uses (cf. Donnelly, 1987, in press). Unused areas that are maintained for environmental conservation are far more vulnerable. Although some outdoor activities have been partially incorporated by the dominant sport culture (e.g., cross-country skiing; see the previous discussion of climbing), these sports largely exist, because of their differences in form and meaning, as an alternative to mainstream sport.

*Countercultural activities.*   Beginning in the 1960s a number of countercultural activities were developed in direct opposition to the dominant sport culture. These include activities such as surfing, skateboarding, frisbee, "hot dog" skiing, and the various cooperative and "new" games. Such activities were informal, playful, and expressive precisely because the dominant sport culture in North America was (and is) rationalized, technologized, bureaucratized (Ingham, 1975), and patriarchal. Some of the activities have since been partially incorporated, but the long-term effects have been significant. For example, cooperative and new games are now a major part of the physical education curriculum in many places; and the critique of an overemphasis on competition, which resulted in the development of cooperative games, also resulted in the development of "house" leagues in youth sports in Canada (in which all participants have an equal amount of playing time). A continuing sensitivity to the excesses of the dominant sport culture, whether it be sexist and racist or condoning of violence and drug abuse, has also resulted from this countercultural movement, and the effect is widespread in Western society. As Schulke (1984) recently noted with regard to student sports in West Germany, they "appear more as the *avant garde* of a democratic sports culture, a culture which will embrace all people and contribute to their personal development" (pp. 580-581).

*Folk revivals.*   Finally, the social movements of the 1960s and early 1970s took a far more cosmopolitan view of culture, and various groups began to search around the world and into the past for alternatives to aspects of the dominant culture. For example, there has been a revival of folk games and dances in places such as Belgium, England, and Portugal;[11] the revival and development of expressive activities such as dance and musical-gymnastic performances; and increasing involvement in martial arts such as aikido (cf. Clement, 1984), and in meditative exercises such as yoga and tai chi. All of these aspects of physical culture provide legitimate alternatives to the dominant sport culture.

When examining these various transformations, whether they involve the incorporation of an activity or a shift toward an alternative or oppositional position, both the form (text) of the activity and its cultural meaning (context) have to be taken into account.[12] Practices having alternative meanings in one culture or at one time may be fully incorporated into dominant social relations in another culture or at another time. It is this question of context, together with the dynamic nature of culture, that is crucial to the better understanding of resilience and transformation in sport subcultures.

# Discussion

Williams (1980) proposed that we have to see

> a temporal relation between a dominant culture and on the one hand a residual and on the other hand an emergent culture. But we can only understand this if we can make distinctions, that usually require very precise analysis, between residual-incorporated and residual not incorporated, and between emergent-incorporated and emergent not incorporated. (p. 41)

The preceding discussion of resilience and transformation highlights the need for this "very precise anlaysis."

## Rugby

In the case of rugby, its resilience was almost entirely of the residual-incorporated type. The game never posed a direct threat to the dominant sport culture in England and, in fact, the vast majority of the values and meanings associated with the game were in complete accord with mainstream sport even as it changed. However, for a short period of time after the Americanized model of sport had begun to assert itself completely on most other sports, the resilience of rugby preserved some ideas about sportsmanship, playing for fun, respect for an opponent, and notions of "the well-played game" (DeKoven, 1978). The effect of this was not very important in England where the game attained a rump status in its assertion of ideas that were only receiving lip service in other sports.

The transformation of rugby during the 1970s and into the 1980s was in no sense emergent—it represented the incorporation of rugby into the new dominant sport culture. But the older ideas had been preserved long enough to have an effect in North America. The growth of rugby in North America since the mid-1960s is interesting since it did not develop as another incorporated sport. Instead, just as English rugby began to adopt all of the trappings of Americanized sport, the game reappeared in North America replete with all of the old characteristics and values of the English game. Donnelly and Young (1985) proposed that the game was emergent in North America in that it provided the perfect countercultural alternative for those who enjoyed the contact and action of American or Canadian football but wished to distance themselves from the ideological overtones. Without the resilience of the game in England it is unlikely that it could have had this effect in North America.

## Climbing

The resilience of climbing resulted in the preservation of the idea that nonrationalized/nonbureaucratized sport could exist. Climbing was an example of "residual not incorporated" sport that did not oppose the dominant sport culture but survived as an alternative. It may be likened to a worker-controlled industry. As long as it does not appear as a better alternative to the majority of industrial workers, and as long as its product is not in direct competition with the product of capitalist-owned industries, it is not a direct threat. However, as an alternative it is always an impending threat because it preserves the notion of a different way of organizing the relations of production (or sport). The aim of dominant cultures is to present themselves as the normal and natural, commonsense way of doing and thinking—the only choice. The survival of residual cultures and the appearance of emergent cultures continually demonstrates the existence of choices.

The apparently impending transformation of climbing is predicated on the emergence of a new form of the sport. But that form appears to be emergent-incorporated, and the fact that it may take the rest of the sport with it is an indication of the pervasiveness of the dominant sport culture. Maintaining a worker-controlled industry involves more effort on the part of individuals than is required in typical capitalist-controlled industries; maintaining a community-controlled sport requires similar effort. The benefits of such individualism may have been perceived as not worth the effort by climbers who have contributed to the potential incorporation of their sport.

Apparently innocent links with government, such as the British Mountaineering Council's acceptance of funds from the Sports Council to maintain its office and carry on its educational, access, and conservation work, result in accountability and a certain amount of implicit control; climbing on publicly owned lands also has had a controlling effect as governmental supervision of parks increases; climbers promoting and seeking careers in outdoor education have also led to government regulation (e.g., certification and safety standards); but the sporting goods industry has been the major force in incorporation via a growing number of individual and expedition sponsorships as the number of climbers (and therefore the market) has increased in recent years, and by organizing and funding competitions. The need to make a living, when combined with the opportunity to climb on a full-time basis (as a bureaucrat, educator, or professional) has great appeal to many individuals. When these are combined with the acceptance of organized competition, they may have the effect of assuring the full incorporation of climbing into the dominant sport culture. However, the richness of debate still evident in the sport may be an indication of the continuing strength of the anarchic and community-controlled ''adventure'' climbing.

## Boxing

The case of boxing, as noted previously, is of a different order. The idea of the gentlemanly art of self defense appears to be largely irrelevant today; boxing survives because of its appeal as entertainment, and because it remains a legitimate form of physical expression in a particular class culture. But its residual incorporated nature preserves a cultural form that is questionable.

The questions need to be asked and the abuses and excesses evident in boxing need to be controlled, but legal restraints on the sport would fit into the realm of state control of working-class activities and state constraint of the physical (policing the body). An outright ban on boxing may not be appropriate, not only because it would drive the sport underground, but also because it is unwarranted. As the Ontario Amateur Boxing Review Committee concluded:

> We believe those persons who dislike boxing have no right to *prohibit* the activity among those who wish to enjoy it. Canadians cherish the right of individuals to pursue recreational and cultural activity without state interference. In the absence of any compelling evidence boxing violates human dignity, the abolition of boxing would be an unfair abrogation of that right. (Kidd, Corner, & Stewart, 1983, p. 34)

The transformation of boxing to increase the rights and safety of the participants is warranted. But boxing remains a residual and important form of cultural expression while social and economic circumstances continue to limit and frame the choices available to the working class, and it will only disappear when its relevance and meaning as a cultural practice disappears.

## Counterculture

The various transformations associated with the countercultural social movements of the 1960s and early 1970s are difficult to classify because, although the vast majority of them are emergent not incorporated in nature, they are also often rooted in residual cultural practices. For example, the fitness movement has predecessors in a variety of mass gymnastic and health movements in the late 19th century and in the 1920s and 1930s; the environmental movement was preceded by rambling and cycling as mass sports in the 1920s and 1930s; and the folk revival of games and dances are more explicitly residual. However, if both text and context are taken into account, there has certainly been a search for the authentic form of folk activities, but the original meanings cannot be re-created. The revival of English Morris dancing provides a case in point. The form of dancing practiced by 16th- and 17th-century farm laborers and tenant farmers can be reproduced fairly accurately together with the original form of dress and music. But the present-day dancers cannot possibly re-create the original meanings and values, and they have, in fact, frequently turned the activity into a rather exclusive liberal middle-class social club. Public performances are frequently mocked by farm laborers and by the working-class youths who would have been participants 200 years ago.

The countercultural and new games activities are far more emergent in nature, although even in these cases there may be elements of a residual form (e.g., surfing is an ancient Polynesian activity, and a number of the new games derive their inspiration from older game forms). But the time, place, and structural location of all of these activities resulted in a new set of alternative or oppositional meanings that were in accord with the new context, and it is therefore far more appropriate to classify the activities as emergent. Many of the new cultural forms have now lost their alternative oppositional nature, and some were rapidly incorporated (e.g., hot dog or freestyle skiing and skateboarding), but their effect in shifting the base of and posing a challenge to the dominant sport culture is still evident.

# Conclusions

It is possible now to identify and summarize some of the conditions associated with resilience and transformation in sport subcultures.

## Resilience

The basic defining condition for resilience is a changing dominant sport culture that results in the condition of resilience and residualness. But resilience, to the extent of becoming residual, also appears to be associated with the following nondiscrete factors:

### Limited democratization

Both rugby and climbing, when they were confined to the middle classes, tended to be extremely conservative carriers of tradition and meaning, particularly those associated with amateurism, not training, and so on. Both held out against a changing dominant sport culture. Tennis and golf showed similar conservative tendencies, but in all important respects they embraced the new order in sport very rapidly. Conservatism is not confined to the middle class; the one consistent element in boxing has been working-class involvement, despite the periodic involvement of the middle and upper classes, and the sport depends on its capacity to remain meaningful in working-class culture. Similarly, the survival of the folk games described by Metcalfe (1987) depended on their rootedness in a particular class culture.

### Relative isolation

Existence outside mainstream metropolitan culture can certainly aid in the survival of residual forms. Folk games and dances are almost always thought of as rural rather than urban forms although this is not necessarily the case—they just survived longer in rural settings. Whitson's (1983) study of shinty and Metcalfe's (1987) isolated mining villages provide examples of this. Relative isolation may also be considered in other than geographical terms. Activities that are limited to particular class, gender, racial, or ethnic cultures may also become residual because of their relative isolation.[13]

### Immigration

Immigrant groups tend to form "cultural bubbles." That is, old-country values tend to become fixed at the time of migration such that, within a few years, ethnic groups no longer reflect the changing culture of their country of birth or the values of their adopted country. In the case of colonization, the residual culture may be passed on to the native population, and commentators have noted that it is necessary to go to India, for example, in order to see "English" cricket as it used to be played. Sometimes the cultural forms may be deliberately maintained by immigrant ethnic groups to preserve solidarity and resist assimilation (e.g., LaFlamme, 1977; Pooley, 1981).

### Response to threat

In the previous condition assimilation may be perceived as a threat that results in the determination to preserve cultural forms, but threats may take other forms. For example, boxing is currently under threat, and has been on previous occasions. An embattled state, as in the case of Metcalfe's miners, may result in a hardening of the determination to survive, and may promote resilience. Climbing has anticipated a threat to its existence ever since Queen Victoria inquired if it was possible to ban the sport after the Matterhorn accident in 1865,[14] and its resistance to incorporation can easily be understood in terms of fear of the regulation that would result.[15]

### Deliberate search for authenticity

As noted previously, folk revivals may recreate the form but not the meaning of earlier activities. The search for authenticity may come close to original meanings— as in the serious practice of martial arts involving both mental and physical discipline—but it is more likely to be on the order of the Society for Creative Anachronism, which stages medieval tournaments and the like. The search for authenticity may also be an anti-high-tech backlash that becomes fashionable because it creates a new level of difficulty. Telemark skiing using cross-country skis on downhill slopes and a return to the longer and heavier surfboards are both examples of this type of action, but these are more easily interpreted as transformation than resilience.

## Transformation

The basic defining condition for transformation in cultural forms such as sport is transformation in the larger society. Nationalist movements, for example, in colonized societies are likely to result in a change in meaning in the sports played as they are co-opted into the nationalist movement. Similarly, the complex of social changes that resulted in the counterculture of the 1960s and early 1970s involved a wide range of popular cultural forms including sport. A change in the dominant sport culture will result in the incorporation (at different rates and to different extents) of most forms of sport, but it is also likely to spawn new alternatives to challenge the hegemony of the mainstream. Transformations are also associated with the following nondiscrete conditions:

### Democratization

With regard to democratization, evidence from one case study (of climbing) suggests that when a sport democratizes to the extent of involving the working class it is likely to undergo significant cultural changes (Donnelly, 1982). Similarly, the further democratization of rugby in the 1960s appears to have resulted, in part, in the changes that occurred in the game in England. This type of transformation is intuitively correct because the traditional values of sport are essentially upper- and middle-class values, and the involvement of a different class culture inevitably involves the introduction of new values. In both of the cases noted previously this resulted in the incorporation of the sports into the dominant sport culture. But democratization may also involve race and gender as well as social class, and there are indications that more progressive transformations have resulted. For example, anticolonial (on the basis of race) transformations of cricket have occurred in the West Indies and the Trobriand Islands, and Birrell and Richter (1987) have documented the feminist transformation of softball.

## Exportation/importation

The transformative effect, worldwide, of the European model of sport in the late 19th century has been noted previously, as has the more recent Americanization of sport. However, on a more subcultural level, the cross-border spread of sports can have transformative effects. In North America, several attempts to introduce soccer as a spectator sport have failed, but the game has become a mass participation sport with more players than Little League Baseball. This unintended effect resulted from the appropriateness of the game at a time when an inexpensive alternative to football was being sought by many school boards and communities, one that would promote participation and fitness, was not gendered, and had a lower risk of injury. Also, the transformations associated with the spread of rugby in North America since the mid-1960s, and its adoption as a countercultural activity, have been noted previously.

## Commercialization and new technologies

The development of new technologies and the growth of commercial potential in various sport subcultures can have a major transformative effect. The case of climbing has been noted previously, but we might also note the development of heli-hiking, heli-hunting, heli-skiing, fly-in fishing, changes in skiing and fishing equipment, new lightweight cycling and camping equipment, new materials that permit winter participation in a number of activities with some degree of comfort, better designs for sails and for parachutes, ultralights, and hang gliders. An interesting contradiction is evident in that the "greening" of sport has frequently depended on the development of such new and synthetic materials. Commercialization has also resulted in the transformation of a number of sports to render them more acceptable to live and television audiences (e.g., golf, squash).

## Growth of dependency

Transformations may also result from the loss of independence. The acceptance of money and other forms of support from government agencies or private sponsors results in dependency, the need to be accountable for aid received, and an emphasis on success by whatever means are available because lack of success may result in withdrawal of support. Dependency also results in the loss of control by the participants and voluntary administrators, because government and private sponsors are able to assert policy, strategy, and changes in the form and possibly the meaning of an activity.

Two final notes of caution are in order. First, I have, for convenience, treated sport subcultures as homogeneous entities, when they are far more likely to be heterogeneous. The martial arts subculture ranges from authentic participants attempting to re-create the mental disciplines of the Far East, through Ninja cultists, professional kickboxers, and feminist self-defense groups, to survivalists and even wife-beaters and rapists (Roberts, 1988). Transformations taking place at the leading edge of a sport may take a long time to affect the entire subculture. It is still possible to find "coarse" rugby (Green, 1967) being played in England, and most climbers cannot conceive that their particular manner of participation will be affected by the advent of competition climbing. And in boxing, there are frequent rumors of bare-knuckle prize fights being staged privately. Also, rapid transformations are likely to produce a backlash in which some participants make a fetish of preserving or re-creating an earlier style of participation (cf. surfing and telemark skiing noted previously). While such heterogeneity is a complicating factor, it also attests to the richness and diversity of cultural forms and the active cultural production that occurs in subcultures.

Second, Gruneau (1988) has noted that some researchers "seem to have discovered resistance virtually *everywhere* in capitalist consumer cultures" (p. 25). The discussions of resilience and transformation presented here indicate that these characteristics, normally considered to be reflections of resistance, may have quite the opposite effect. This again points to Williams's (1980) distinction between the incorporated and nonincorporated aspects of culture. Also, the concern with incorporation and the dominant (sport) culture needs to be qualified. "Hegemony is not domination in any direct sense; rather it is an ongoing process of accommodation and apparent compromise" (Gruneau, 1988, p. 24). Finally, the dynamic nature of culture and subcultures must be kept in mind, together with the specific spatial, temporal, and structural contexts.

# Notes

1. In this case, serving to reproduce the values of capitalist and state socialist systems; in earlier analyses, acting as an "opiate of the masses" to deflect attention from political action.
2. This is evident in the T-shirt slogan, "No Pain, No Gain," worn by many athletes, and in its more recent manifestation in reference to the Barcelona Olympics, "No Pain, No Spain."
3. The following discussion of rugby is drawn largely from Donnelly and Young (1985) and refers only to English rugby because of the existence of distinct national variations in the meanings and ways of the rugby subculture.

4. While there is a tendency to think of resistance movements as progressive, many are quite conservative in nature (cf. Thompson, 1980). Of course, what is conserved may eventually come to be seen as progressive, as is the case with some aspects of residual culture.

5. The following discussion of climbing is drawn largely from Donnelly (1980). The term *climbing* is used here in a generic sense to refer to a whole series of climbing "games."

6. The following discussion of boxing is drawn largely from Donnelly (1989).

7. I have argued elsewhere (Donnelly, 1989) that while the medical critique of boxing has become the most prominent argument against the sport, it is somewhat biased and tends to mask other more cultural critiques.

8. The following report appeared after an international game between England and France in 1982: "Celebrations at the post-match banquet in Paris last Saturday began with the customary throwing of bread rolls and went on to include the drinking of after-shave lotion presented to the guests by the French Rugby Federation, the dousing of a French official with sauce, and the upsetting of a fruit table" (*Manchester Guardian Weekly*, February 28, 1982).

9. During the embryonic stage of competition (1985-1989), climbers were often presented with a set of rules on the first day of competition and, as problems became apparent, were given a revised set on the second day. Competition was characterized by "off the cuff" rulings and all-night judges' meetings, and even the UIAA rules have not resolved all the problems (see Berkhout, 1991). However, the rules have ensured that no more competitions will be held on outdoor natural cliffs (because of environmental problems), and their acceptance supports the high aspirations of the sport (e.g., acceptance as an Olympic event).

10. Several of these have been developed from Eichberg (1984).

11. These revivals are often associated with nationalist and independence movements in colonized societies or among aboriginal groups (e.g., native North American games).

12. For a recent example of the distinction between text and context, see Whiting (1989) on professional baseball in the United States and Japan. While the way that the game is played (text) is essentially the same in both countries, the cultural meaning (context) of the game is substantially different.

13. The survival of cock fighting in Cajun, Louisiana (DelSesto, 1980) originally met the condition of relative isolation, but now seems to be retained in response to the threat of assimilation (noted subsequently).

14. There was a major public outcry in England after the deaths of Douglas Hadow, the Reverend Charles Hudson, and Lord Francis Douglas during the first ascent of the Matterhorn. This and subsequent accidents inspired Queen Victoria to write to Gladstone to ask if there was anything she could do to mark her objection to the number of accidents in the Alps. Gladstone replied that he did not think there was any action she could take, noting that there were less "respectable" sports that were equally destructive.

15. Of course, another response to threat could be transformation through incorporation into the dominant sport culture or into a self-regulating and "safer" activity. The latter option was chosen by hang gliding after it came under threat from the American Federal Aviation Authority (McDougall, 1979).

# References

Berkhout, K. (1991). Competitive sport climbing: The social construction of a sport. Unpublished Master's thesis, University of Western Ontario, London, Canada.

Birrell, S., & Richter, D.M. (1987). Is a diamond forever? Feminist transformations of sport. *Women's Studies International Forum*, **10**, 395-409.

Bishop, J., & Hoggett, P. (1987, Summer). Clubbing together. *New Socialist*, 32-33.

Clement, J.P. (1984). La pratique de l'aiki-do en France: "Contre-culture" ou "avant-garde" culturelle. In *Sports et sociétés contemporaines* (pp. 375-380). Paris: Societé Francaise de Sociologie du Sport.

DeKoven, B. (1978). *The well-played game: A player's philosophy*. New York: Anchor Books.

DelSesto, S.L. (1980). Dancing and cockfighting at Jay's Lounge and Cockpit: The preservation of folk practices in Cajun Louisiana. In R.B. Browne (Ed.), *Rituals and ceremonies in popular culture* (pp. 270-281). Bowling Green, OH: Bowling Green University Press.

Donnelly, P. (1977). Vertigo in America: A social comment. *Quest*, **27**, 106-113.

Donnelly, P. (1980). *The subculture and public image of climbers*. Unpublished doctoral dissertation, University of Massachusetts, Amherst.

Donnelly, P. (1982). Social climbing: The changing class structure of rock climbing and mountaineering in Britain. In A. Dunleavy, A. Miracle, & R. Rees (Eds.), *Studies in the sociology of sport* (pp. 13-28). Fort Worth: Texas Christian University Press.

Donnelly, P. (1987, December). Creating national parks—"A grand, good thing?" *Tourism Management*, 349-351.

Donnelly, P. (1988). Sport as a site for "popular" resistance. In R. Gruneau (Ed.), *Popular cultures and political practices* (pp. 69-82). Toronto: Garamond Press.

Donnelly, P. (1989). On boxing: Notes on the past, present and future of a sport in transition. *Current Psychology: Research & Reviews*, **7**(4), 331-346.

Donnelly, P. (in press). The right to wander: Issues in the leisure use of countryside and wilderness areas. *International Review for the Sociology of Sport*, **28**(2/3).

Donnelly, P., & Young, K. (1985). Reproduction and transformation of cultural forms in sport: A contextual analysis of rugby. *International Review for the Sociology of Sport*, **20**(1), 19-38.

Dunning, E., & Sheard, K. (1979). *Barbarians, gentlemen and players: A sociological study of the development of rugby football*. New York: New York University Press.

Edwards, H. (1973). *Sociology of sport*. Homewood, IL: Dorsey Press.

Eichberg, H. (1984). Olympic sport—Neocolonization and alternatives. *International Review for the Sociology of Sport*, **19**(2), 97-105.

Green, M. (1967). *The art of coarse rugby*. London: Arrow.

Gruneau, R. (1981). Review of *Surfing subcultures of Australia and New Zealand*. *ICSS Bulletin*, **21**, 8-10.

Gruneau, R. (1984). Commercialism and the modern Olympics. In A. Tomlinson & G. Whannel (Eds.), *Five ring circus: Money, power and politics at the Olympic Games* (pp. 1-15). London: Pluto Press.

Gruneau, R. (1988). Introduction: Notes on popular culture and political practice. In R. Gruneau (Ed.), *Popular cultures and political practices* (pp. 11-32). Toronto: Garamond Press.

Hepworth, M.S., & Featherstone, M. (1982). *Surviving middle age*. Oxford: Basil Blackwell.

Hurn, M., & Ingle, P. (1988). *Climbing fit*. England: Crowood Press.

Ingham, A. (1975). Occupational subcultures in the work world of sport. In D.W. Ball & J.W. Loy (Eds.), *Sport and social order* (pp. 333-389). Reading, MA: Addison-Wesley.

Ingham, A. (1985). From public issue to personal trouble: Well-being and the fiscal crisis of the state. *Sociology of Sport Journal*, **2**, 43-55.

Kidd, B., Corner, F., & Stewart, B. (1983). *For amateur boxing: Report of the Ontario Amateur Boxing Review Committee*. Toronto: Government of Ontario.

LaFlamme, A.G. (1977). The role of sport in the development of ethnicity: A case study. *Sport Sociology Bulletin*, **6**, 47-51.

Levi-Strauss, C. (1978). *Myth and meaning: Five talks for radio*. Toronto: University of Toronto Press.

Loy, J.W., McPherson, B., & Kenyon, G. (1978). *Sport and social systems*. Reading, MA: Addison-Wesley.

MacNeill, M. (1988). Active women, media representations, and ideology. In J. Harvey & H. Cantelon (Eds.), *Not just a game: Essays in Canadian sport sociology* (pp. 195-211). Ottawa: University of Ottawa Press.

Maguire, J. (1988). The commercialization of English elite basketball, 1972-1988: A figurational perspective. *International Review for the Sociology of Sport*, **23**(4), 305-324.

Maguire, J. (1990). More than a sporting touchdown: The making of American football in England, 1982-1990. *Sociology of Sport Journal*, **7**(3), 213-237.

*Manchester Guardian Weekly*. (1982). Report on France vs. England rugby match. February 28, p. 24.

Manning, F. (1981). Celebrating cricket: The symbolic construction of Caribbean politics. *American Ethnologist*, **20**, 616-632.

Mason, T. (1980). *Association football and English society, 1863-1915*. Brighton: Harvester.

McDougall, A. (1979). *The subculture of hang gliders: Social organization of a high risk sport*. Unpublished Master's thesis, University of Western Ontario, London, Canada.

McPherson, B., Curtis, J., & Loy, J. (1989). *The social significance of sport*. Champaign, IL: Human Kinetics.

Metcalfe, A. (1987). Resistance to change: Folk games in the mining communities of Northumberland, England, 1880-1914. *HISPA Bulletin*, **26**, 38.

Oates, J.C. (1987). *On boxing*. Garden City: Dolphin/Doubleday.

Patterson, O. (1969, June 26). The cricket ritual in the West Indies. *New Society*, 988-989.

Pearson, K. (1976). Subcultures, drug use, and physical activity. Paper presented at the International Congress of Physical Activity Sciences, Quebec City.

Pearson, K. (1979). *Surfing subcultures of Australia and New Zealand*. St. Lucia: University of Queensland Press.

Pooley, J.C. (1981). Ethnic soccer clubs in Milwaukee: A study in assimilation. In M. Hart & S. Birrell (Eds.), *Sport in the sociocultural process* (pp. 430-447). Dubuque, IA: Brown.

Raphael, F. (1985, August 23). Not so fair play. *New Society*, 267.

Roberts, Y. (1988, March 4). Survival of the species. *New Statesman*, 12-13.

Schulke, H.J. (1984). Student sport: Sub-culture or the *avant garde* of a new sport-culture? In *Sports et sociétés contemporaines*. Paris: Societé Francaise de Sociologie du Sport.

Shaw, D. (1985, August) The politics of "futbol." *History Today*, 38-42.

Snyder, E.E. (1972). Athletic dressing room slogans as folklore: A means of socialization. *International Review of Sport Sociology*, **7**, 89-102.

Snyder, E.E., & Spreitzer, E.A. (1989). *Social aspects of sport* (3rd Ed.). Englewood Cliffs, NJ: Prentice Hall.

Stevenson, J. (1984). *British society, 1914-1945*. Harmondsworth: Penguin.

Summerskill, E. (1956). *The ignoble art*. London: Heinemann.

Tejada-Flores, L. (1967, May). Games climbers play. *Ascent*, 23-25.

Thompson, E.P. (1980). *The making of the English working class*. Harmondsworth: Penguin.

Tylor, E.B. (1871). *Primitive culture*. London: John Murray.

Walvin, J. (1978). *Leisure and society, 1830-1950*. New York: Longman.

Whiting, R. (1989). *You gotta have wa: When two cultures collide on the baseball diamond.* New York: Macmillan.

Whitson, D. (1983). Pressures on regional games in a dominant metropolitan culture: The case of shinty. *Leisure Studies,* **2**(2), 139-154.

Williams, R. (1970). *American society.* New York: Alfred A. Knopf.

Williams, R. (1977). *Marxism and literature.* Oxford: Oxford University Press.

Williams, R. (1980). *Problems in materialism and culture.* London: Verso.

Wilson, W. (1977). Social discontent and the growth of wilderness sport in America, 1965-1974, *Quest,* **27**, 54-60.

# CHAPTER 7

# Sexual Oppression in Sport: Past, Present, and Future Alternatives

*Alison Dewar*

Women in sport. These words mean different things to different people. For some they are a contradiction in terms. For others they are evidence and cause for celebration of women's achievements in a progressive and equitable age. There is enormous diversity in both academic and popular literature in the images of women's relationships to the sporting world. The debates about the images are often lively and intense.

In this chapter I analyze sexual oppression in sport, an arena of popular culture in which gender representations (as well as those of class, race, and age) are played out in potent and powerful ways. This means that sporting practices are not simply representations of the here and now. They are developed and articulated as a result of historically developed and socially produced limitations and possibilities. Sporting practices are not static reflections of the past, nor are they clear visions of the future. They are practices that have been contested and negotiated within the dominant structures and systems of meaning that define the social relations of power and dominance in society.

I begin with an analysis of mainstream or orthodox research and scholarship on gender issues in sport, exploring how this work defines and represents gender relations within sport. I examine the assumptions underlying, and ideological positions adopted in, this work and the political agendas they imply; I also investigate how particular representations of gender relations help produce and reproduce hegemonic sporting structures and practices.

*Note.* A much shorter version of this chapter appeared in the *International Review for Sociology of Sport* (26)1, pp. 15-22, 1991.

Following this analysis and critique of orthodox work I argue for critical feminist analyses of gender relations in sport, locating relational work on gender in sport within the tradition of cultural studies. This tradition emerged in Britain in the 1950s and was articulated and developed from the work of Raymond Williams, Richard Hoggart, and E.P. Thompson. The Centre for Contemporary Cultural Studies at the University of Birmingham, England, has been primary in sustaining and developing work in this tradition (Hall, 1981). Examples are Paul Willis's (1977, 1978) critical ethnographies of working class "lads," Angela McRobbie's (1978) study of the lives of working class adolescent girls, Phillips Corrigan's (1979) work on working-class boys' responses to schooling, and Dick Hebdige's (1979) study of youth subcultures. There are also examples of North American work in this tradition. Michael Brake's (1985) examination of youth culture and subcultures in America, Britain, and Canada is one example.

Put simply, British cultural studies explore how cultural practices are implicated in producing and maintaining societal relations of power and dominance. The promise for feminists of a cultural studies approach to sport is its framework for understanding how sporting practices sustain male power and privilege. The recognition that hegemony is contested and won, rather than given, allows us to examine how alternatives to dominant sporting practices may challenge or defend the systems and structures of male power and privilege. The contradictions and processes of these hegemonic struggles are key questions in cultural studies.

Concluding with a brief examination of alternatives to sexual oppression in sport, I explore the American struggles over the definition and control of women's collegiate sport. When these struggles are seen in the context of their social, political, and historical moments, we can develop questions that may illuminate the complex and often contradictory relations between dominant, residual, and emergent sporting forms and structures.

# Different Perspectives of Analysis:
# The Case of Florence Griffith Joyner

One example of multiple representations is Florence Griffith Joyner, an American track star who has become a media symbol not only for her performances on the track but also for her style and presentation off the track. We are as likely to find reports of the designs of Griffith Joyner's running outfits or the color of her fingernails as we are to discover theoretical analyses of male power and privilege in the sporting world.

Many celebrate Florence Griffith Joyner as a symbol of attainment of equality for women and blacks in the United States. She symbolizes excellence not only in terms of her incredible strength, speed, and power but also in terms of heterosexual femininity and beauty. For this group, Griffith Joyner is living proof that we have come a long way, that women and African Americans really can have it all. However, this is only one interpretation of her successes in sport. For others, Griffith Joyner symbolizes how strong, powerful, and fast women, whose performances are potential challenges to hegemonic representations of the "weaker" sex, are trivialized, marginalized, and sexualized in an attempt to diffuse any threat to male power and privilege. She is, in this view, yet another black female athlete who has become a symbol not of liberation but of the oppression still prevalent in mainstream, white American male–defined sport.

Thus, as this example shows, it is possible to have considerable theoretical and ideological diversity about issues of women in sport. Much of what is proclaimed about this relationship can be conflicting and contradictory.

The fact that there is theoretical and ideological diversity in the ways we analyze women in sport is not problematic. The difficulty is that this diversity is rarely acknowledged and frequently misunderstood. Complex issues are often presented in simplistic frameworks that juxtapose extreme positions in either/or relationships. Discussants then are frequently forced to defend these extremes, rather than promoting dialogue and debate about the political and ideological implications of viewing the relationships between women and sport in multiple ways.

# Interpreting "Facts":
# Giving Context to Hegemonic Perspectives

The uneasiness about multiple perspectives means that only certain narrowly defined analyses of women and their relations to the sporting world are viewed as valuable and useful. Orthodox (and hegemonic) means of judging the worth of knowledge tend to be defined as correct because they appear to provide clear answers to the questions being posed. These judgments define as "good" work that appears to provide politically and ideologically objective or neutral descriptions of facts. But the appearance of neutrality is possible only because those who claim to present "just the facts" in fact subvert their ideological positions and political agendas in the name of "good science." Others who instead explicitly articulate their ideological positions in their work risk being labeled biased, reactionary, and unrepresentative. Why? Because to break the silence in the hegemony of orthodox, Western, masculinist sociology is to do "bad" or unreliable work.

To return to my earlier example of Florence Griffith Joyner, it is often argued that in her case the "facts" are clear and speak for themselves. Her performances, which can be reduced to supposedly objective numbers or facts, and her subsequent rise to fame as a world-class athlete and media darling are touted as incontrovertible evidence of equality for women in sport. It can be difficult to dispute "the facts"; Griffith Joyner is the fastest woman in the world, and she is being rewarded. But this approach—letting the facts "speak for themselves"—gives the impression that they say all that needs to be told. They do not. The performance statistics alone mask many other stories of the incredible racism and sexism Griffith Joyner has faced in her rise to fame. When the facts are assumed to speak for themselves, the view is promoted that there is only one possible interpretation of the data. But the data or facts must be interpreted within particular contexts to be rendered meaningful.

Running 100 meters in 10.54, for example, needs a context to be meaningful. We have to locate this fact in a particular historical and social conjuncture. The 100-meter race is of special significance in American track, a significance that is socially and historically constructed. Florence Griffith Joyner is a woman and an African American; these are also significant in interpreting this fact. Ten-point-five-four seconds cannot speak for itself. It appears to only because we assume the context that allows its interpretation and move on to claim this bit of data as a neutral, objective representation of reality—a gold-medal Olympic performance. When we know that an African American woman has run the 100-meter race in 10.54 seconds we are able to interpret this as a world class performance. We do not stop there. We also use the context to give meaning to our interpretations. This is a woman's performance; thus it may be seen as suspiciously fast and achievable only with the aid of performance enhancing drugs. This is also an African American woman's performance; thus it may be assumed to be fast because of her natural abilities rather than as a result of years of hard work, accumulated knowledge, and commitment to the sport. When we foreground such facts, sporting practices can cease to be seen as socially constructed, historically produced cultural forms that are negotiated and contested in ways that reflect and serve the interests and needs of privileged groups. There are many possible interpretations of the facts, but those that challenge the status quo are often silenced.

Despite the suggestion that facts speak for themselves, they are not always left alone to do so. In certain cases this seems too risky, leading to multiple and perhaps conflicting interpretations of what the facts represent. This appears to have occurred with Florence Griffith Joyner's performances. Explanations of her success range from steroid use (to resolve the problem that no real woman could be that fast and look that good) to natural athletic ability (reproducing racist stereotypes of African Americans as natural athletes). We select and promote explanations that reinforce stereotypes so that we can assimilate "the facts" into our existing frameworks without challenging hegemonic representations of women or blacks.

In reality, facts must be interpreted to be meaningful. When we assume that facts speak for themselves, we present one interpretation as "the truth." This reductionist process has a definite ideological agenda—one that defends hegemonic relations of power and privilege. So allowing the facts to speak for themselves is to let only some facts speak, and in a certain way. To claim that this is objective and neutral is simply one way in which hegemony presents itself as the orthodox consensus. Yet, if one suggests that Florence Griffith Joyner not only is being oppressed but also is supporting the very systems that oppress her because she has accommodated to and become incorporated in the structures of white, masculinist, heterosexist sport, the response is often anger, disbelief, and ridicule. As a student once asked, "What do you feminists want? I don't understand you; here is someone you should be excited about, an awesome woman, and all you want to do is criticize her. I just don't get it." I'm concerned that this person is not the only one who doesn't "get it." The struggles that become apparent in trying to analyze the various "isms" in sport make it clear that the social analysis of sporting practices is complex and often difficult.

# Mainstream Work: Incorporation in and Accommodation to Masculinist Sport

Within the sociology of sport, the scholarship that falls under the rubric of women in sport is diverse in its methods and its questions. Rather than write another review of this work,[1] I criticize existing work on gender issues in terms of its accommodation to, incorporation of, and resistance to dominant frameworks for defining sport. I examine the assumptions underlying work in this tradition and their political and ideological implications.

## Categoric Research

Most gender work in sport sociology has framed gender as a categoric issue, with the primary focus on quantifying and empirically studying differences in abilities and behaviors between males and females. Put simply, categoric study documents sex differences in sporting performance and attempts to explain them in terms of biology and socialization. It is categoric work that attempts to isolate and identify "facts" and to present them in formats designed to convince us that they can and do speak for themselves.

Typically, categoric research uses psychological theories and models for behavior and focuses on individual traits and behaviors. This work falls into three broad categories, which Hall (1981) calls femininity studies, sex role socialization studies, and androgyny studies.

### Femininity Studies

Femininity studies have attempted to show that female athletes remain psychologically "feminine" despite their participation in a "masculine" activity (see, e.g., Metheny, 1964; Money & Ehrhardt, 1972). There are a number of problems with this approach. First, it assumes that the problem lies with women who choose to participate in sport rather than with the sporting practices they choose. Sports are depicted in this work as naturally masculine, and women, who are not naturally masculine, risk losing their femininity if they are serious participants in sport.

This work also is methodologically and conceptually flawed. As Birrell (1988) explains in her review of this genre, "Methodologically, the research suffers from problems of poor operationalization, inadequate sampling, use of inappropriate instruments, poor statistical analysis, generalizing beyond the data, and inferring causal relationships from weak correlational patterns" (p. 464). She suggests that femininity studies have conceptualized the relationship between women and sport in ways that isolate women's sport experiences from their social and cultural contexts. In other words, female athletes are defined as the problem and are depicted as "victims" who are personally responsible for any deficiencies they are judged to have in personality, motivation, or femininity. This approach translates socially defined, culturally produced standards for women's behaviors into immutable categories; the standards themselves and the relations they create are never examined.

Rather than question the ways that culturally produced notions of femininity are used to constrain and control women, this research describes and evaluates the degree to which female athletes display "appropriate" feminine attitudes and behaviors.

## Sex Role Studies

The second group of categoric research focuses on sex roles. This work attempts to explain differences in women's and men's involvements in sport in terms of sex role socialization patterns for boys and girls (see, e.g., Allison & Butler, 1984; Anthrop & Allison, 1983; Bell, 1980; Greendorfer, 1978; Harris, 1980; Hart, 1976). The assumption is that being an athlete and being a woman are incompatible and the theory is that women are less likely than men to participate in sport because they are taught that sporting involvement and femininity conflict. Girls in North American culture learn to define involvement in sport as problematic because they are receiving powerful messages that being feminine means exhibiting certain values, behaviors, and dispositions that appear natural and inevitable.

A kind of perverse logic is evident here. If we agree that women are likely to experience debilitating role conflicts when they become involved in sport, we place them in a no-win situation. By accepting role conflict theory we blame the victims for failing to meet the standards defined as appropriate for the roles of feminine women and athletes. In so doing, we offer women three choices: remain in sport, live with the conflict, or be seen as unfeminine anomalies. They can leave sport and resolve the conflict. Or they can stay in sport and become apologists[2] for their involvement by downplaying their athletic abilities and emphasizing femininity both on and off the court or playing fields. These are hardly enabling choices.

What remains unexamined and unexplained are the contexts in which we negotiate and develop our gender identities.[3] Not all children learn and accept "appropriate" sex roles. The ways in which we learn and articulate our gender identities are not uniformly prescribed. We negotiate our identities as men and women within the contexts of the structures that define our lives. The reduction of this complex and often contradictory process to the learning of a predetermined sex role obscures the fact that socialization is neither absolute nor inevitable.

The view this research presents is very narrow. The concept of sex role is presented as a universal script. In reality what it represents is one white, middle-class, heterosexual definition of femininity and masculinity—not the only legitimate one. Sex role researchers ignore questions about how sporting practices are used in our culture to legitimize and reinforce cultural stereotypes about women. Instead, they focus on individuals' attitudes and behaviors. This encourages us to define problems or conflicts among women athletes as personal troubles rather than as social issues of the ways in which sporting structures and practices create and maintain social relations of power and domination.

## Androgyny Studies

Androgyny studies differ from the femininity and sex role approaches in using measures of "psychological androgyny" (the possession of a combination of both masculine and feminine behavioral characteristics) rather than measures of so-called masculinity and femininity (see Bem, 1984; Duquin, 1978; Myes & Lips, 1978).

Despite the use of different measures, androgyny studies reflect many of the same problems as the femininity and sex role studies. This work does not challenge the stereotypes of masculinity and femininity perpetuated by sex role research; it simply reframes them by using them to develop measures of androgyny. Like other categoric work, androgyny studies assume that gender issues are troubles personal to individuals. Women, then, are encouraged to become androgynous and to display masculine and feminine behaviors in appropriate situations.

Although this work claims to value traditional male and female behavior characteristics equally, it celebrates male behavior at the expense of female (Birrell, 1988). This happens through a focus on the kinds of behaviors appropriate for success in sport rather than on the ways that sporting practices have been created to reinforce and reward traditional masculine behaviors and traits. In this analysis, women are seen as deficient, and the onus is placed on them to reduce any conflicts between being a woman and being an athlete by becoming androgynous—a lesser male. It is assumed that if women want to fit into sport, it is women, rather than sport, that must change.

The message in this research is clear: Only men's behaviors and experiences count in our culture. Because this work does not examine how sporting practices legitimize society's relations of power and privilege, the solutions offered to women commit them to existing structures and practices. Androgyny research says that women who want to play sport have to play by men's rules.

Categoric research is not limited to femininity, sex role, and androgyny studies. In the exercise and health sciences, for example, categoric research accounts for performance gaps between men and women with biological rather than behavioral differences (see Baker, 1987; Dyer, 1982; Wells, 1984; Wyrick, 1974). Any differences in categoric research are of degree rather than kind; irrespective of the focus of categoric research, its assumptions are the same—and make it flawed.

Categoric research views gender relations as based on differences in individual traits rather than in socially and historically produced patterns of social relations. This view falsely separates individuals' behaviors from their social and historical contexts. Any sex differences related to sport are treated as problems for individuals, solvable at the personal level. If women want to achieve equality and close any gaps between themselves and men, they must alter their behaviors and socialization. Equality is defined as catching up with the men. But where sex differences are attributed to biology rather than behavior, women have little hope of change, so they must simply accept their difference, which in sporting terms means accepting biological "inferiority." Categoric work never questions why our sporting practices are defined to allow men to display their physical strength, speed, and power. Nor does it question why the performance gap in sport is given so much attention in our society or how it is used to bolster images of male power and dominance as natural and immutable.[4] Cultural stereotypes about the body, masculinity, femininity, and sexuality are presented in a framework that reproduces them. Despite its claims of objectivity (Let the facts speak for themselves) and apoliticism (How can we dispute the facts?), categoric research has a clear political stance. It supports and legitimates prevailing relations of inequality.

## Distributive Research

When gender is defined as a distributive issue, the major focus of the research is directed away from the description of individual differences and toward documenting and describing the nature and extent of the opportunities available to different categories of individuals. Researchers who ask distributive questions are concerned with identifying the underlying material and symbolic factors that contribute to social ranking and inequality (Gruneau, 1975). In other words, distributive researchers understand that there are groups or categories of individuals in our society who, because of their access to material and symbolic rewards, are more privileged than others. These groups, because of their prestige and status, have access to resources and opportunities denied to less privileged groups. Distributive research allows them to investigate who gets what and why. Questions such as numbers of programs, funding, facilities, and opportunities for mobility to leadership positions that exist, for example, for women and men, for African Americans and whites, or for the middle classes and working classes are typical of this kind of research.

Distributive research defines inequality in the same ways. This work sees inequality within liberal democratic societies as a problem of equality of opportunity. The assumption is that if all individuals are provided with the same opportunities to develop their talents and skill the sport system, as well as other agencies and institutions in society, will select and allocate rewards to individuals on the basis of merit (hard work and talent) or universalistic criteria rather than ascriptive, categoric differences or particularistic criteria. In short, equality in this work means equality of opportunity, rather than equality of condition. This means that individuals are afforded an equal chance to be unequal or to compete for limited or scarce rewards. The problem for distributive researchers is not the number or nature of the rewards available but how they are allocated, to whom, and why.

There are many examples of distributive research on women in sport. Researchers have examined a variety of different issues. For example, there are studies comparing women's and men's participation rates in sport (Fasting & Sisjord, 1985; Howell & McKenzie, 1987; Vickers & Gosling, 1984), leadership and administrative opportunities for men and women in sport (Abbott & Smith, 1984; Carpenter & Acosta, 1985; Hart, Hasbrook, & Mathes, 1986; Inglis, 1988; Theberge, 1984; White & Brackenridge, 1985), media coverage for women's sport (Bryant, 1980; Fasting & Tangen, 1983), athletic scholarship opportunities for women and men (Coakley & Pacey, 1984), and the impact of Title IX legislation on women's sport (Acosta & Carpenter, 1985; Chu, Seagrave, & Becker, 1985; Hult, 1976).

These studies are important and useful because they provide evidence that allows researchers to document the patterns that exist in the allocation of resources and opportunities for women and men at different levels of the sporting system. The evidence from these studies presents a fairly gloomy picture, especially when it is situated within the social context of the period. These data have been collected in a historical period that is seen by many as one of increasing opportunities for women, not only in sport but in all areas of public and private life. Federal legislation—specifically Title IX—designed to ensure equality of opportunity for women under the law may have sparked much optimism of the dawning of a new, progressive age, but the data have certainly dampened if not totally extinguished that initial optimism.

These data show that women have lost more ground than they have gained since the enactment of Title IX legislation in 1972. Although women's participation rates in sport have increased exponentially since 1972, other opportunities have declined significantly in this same period. Birrell (1988) captures these trends in this comment:

Although the growth of women's programs created greater opportunities to coach women athletes, the number of women in those positions began a precipitous decline. A similar trend was occurring in administrative positions: As men's and women's athletic programs merged, men were invariably named to head the programs. (p. 473)

Birrell's (1988) review of research trends on women's sport in the 1980s summarizes much of the evidence gained from distributive research. The data she reports reconfirm the failure of the promise of equality embodied in legislation such as Title IX. Data show that men rather than women seem to have been the primary beneficiaries of this legislation. For example, Birrell (1988) cites evidence to show that the percentage of women coaches of women's sports declined from 81% in 1974 to 51% in 1986, and the percentage of women's athletic programs directed by women has fallen from 79% in 1973-1974 to 15% in 1985-1986. She also reports data by Abbott and Smith (1984) that show there is a changing face of women's athletics, but it is one where men rather than women are achieving power and control. What is clear from most of the distributive research on women's sporting programs is that distributive equity is an ideal rather than a reality in American collegiate (where most of the data have been collected) sport.

Critiquing distributive research is a difficult yet necessary task. Distributive research provides important evidence of the results of both individual and systemic sexual discrimination. This evidence frequently lays the foundation for change and has created the impetus for challenges to systems that perpetuate sexual discrimination. Any criticism of this may be interpreted as antiwomen, a step backward rather than forward, and letting men off the hook. Despite the risk of such interpretations, it is important to examine the assumptions underlying distributive work and to identify their consequences. It is the nature of the questions asked and the strategies for change that are implied in distributive work that are open for discussion, debate, and criticism, not the actual data it provides.

The great strength of distributive work is perhaps also its great weakness. Documenting patterns of inequality provides immediate evidence of problems, and as such it appears to hold the promise of real solutions. Title IX is one attempt to achieve, through legislative means, solutions to distributive inequity. But the promise of action and solutions is counterbalanced by the pitfalls of trying to change the system from within. By working within the system one is forced to accommodate to it and become incorporated (even if reluctantly) within dominant frameworks for defining sporting structures and practices. Striving for equality, which is the basis of distributive analyses, means striving for equal access to what white men have and control. But are dominant sporting programs and practices worth gaining access to? The assumption is made that hegemonic sporting practices are worth keeping and that women will be happy if they can "benefit" from them like men have.

By viewing equality in this way, distributive research cannot account for what are often referred to as the unintended consequences of moves designed to equalize access, opportunity, and reward. Distributive work lacks an analysis of power and the ways in which sporting practices are used to privilege white men and their interests and needs, which in turn legitimizes and reinforces power relations in our culture.

Without an analysis of power, distributive research may become ineffectual, because it will continue to promise equal opportunity for women in a sporting system that is designed to oppress and suppress us. If the promise of equity in distributive work is to be realized, the data need to be interpreted in different ways. Seeking equal opportunity sounds wonderful but delivers little. Evidence of distributive inequities can be useful if it is used to document how sporting practices are negotiated and contested in our culture. Such analysis may set the stage for the transformation of hegemonic sporting practices and the demise of sexual oppression in sport.

In summary, distributive research analyzes structural barriers to inequality and seeks, through collecting appropriate evidence, to identify and eliminate obstacles to full equality for women in the sporting world. The fact that distributive research focuses on structural rather than individual impediments to equality does not mean that it challenges hegemonic representations of gender. It simply presents another kind of fact that is assumed to speak for itself in a different way. Distributive researchers assume that when facts are identified and patterns of distribution and allocation ascertained, equality can be achieved by altering the patterns.

Much like categoric work, distributive research works within or accommodates itself to existing frameworks for defining sporting structures and practices in our culture. This incorporation and accommodation achieves, at least in the short term, the promise of pragmatic and immediate solutions to sport's distributive inequalities. What it does not and cannot do is address the very real dangers of short-term gains, which ultimately change very little and may (as in the case of Title IX) result in long-term losses for women, because the bases for male power and control remain unchallenged.

## Alternatives to Mainstream Work: Relational Analyses of Gender

Although mainstream categoric and distributive research on gender continues to flourish, critics are becoming more vocal (at least in sport sociology). The form and substance of the criticism vary considerably with the theoretical positions of their protagonists. These critiques form the basis for alternative, relational analyses of gender.

There is considerable debate among feminist and critical sport sociologists about the desired forms and functions of feminist relational social criticism. Critcher (1986), Deem (1988), Hall (1985, 1988), Sparks (1988), and Willis (1982) all present different perspectives on how relational analysis—or, as Sparks (1988, p. 355) calls it, "the critical project of sport and leisure"—ought to proceed. Despite their differences, the authors are all critical of dominant idealist paradigms in sociology generally and sport sociology specifically. It is these idealist paradigms that attempt to reduce social relations to neutral and objective facts that, once identified and manipulated, are assumed to represent "the truth" about or the "natural order" of the social world.

In contrast to this search for independent facts, relational work begins with very different assumptions about the social world. Relational analyses, in my view, begin with the assumption that sporting practices are historically produced, socially constructed, and culturally defined to serve the interests and needs of powerful groups in society. This means that sport is a cultural representation of social relations—not neutral, objective, and ahistorical, but a set of selected and selective social practices that embody dominant meanings, values, and practices that create and maintain hegemony. Understanding how this hegemony is negotiated and contested is crucial in relational analyses. The recognition that hegemony is won rather than given provides a framework for viewing how individual and collective responses to dominant sporting policies and practices may defend or challenge masculinist (or any other kind of "ist") sport.

The key in relational work is to find ways to make the unspoken spoken and the invisible visible. If we can do this, then it may be possible to understand how mainstream, hegemonic representations of sport can present themselves to us as natural and inevitable. Hegemony is secure if we continue to believe that the facts really can and do speak for themselves. Recognizing that all facts need to be interpreted and that there are many possible interpretations is the first step toward challenging hegemonic representations of sport. The easiest way I know to do this is to ask two questions: Whose interpretation of the facts is being presented? Whose interests does it serve?

These questions allow for alternative explanations and interpretations of sporting practices. They suggest that what is left unstated is as important as what is said. Relational work is not only interested in these silences and who and what they represent; more importantly, it examines the processes involved in the negotiations and struggles over whose voices are heard, by whom, when, where, and in what ways. Questions like these move beyond the analysis of actions and patterns. They locate these actions and patterns within their respective contexts, and do so in ways that link them to the patterns of domination and subordination in sport and in society. Paul Willis (1982) captures the essence of relational work in this statement:

> This approach is different because it is concerned with meaning, and values, and social explanation, without attempting positivistic rigor. It accepts differences in

sports performance between men and women, accepts that cultural factors may well enlarge the gap, but is *most* interested in the manner in which this gap is understood and taken up into the popular consciousness of our society. (p. 120)

He goes on to argue that

The analytical sociocultural task is not to measure these differences (between the sexes) precisely and explain them physically, but to ask why some differences, and not others, are taken as so important, become so exaggerated, are used to buttress social attitudes and prejudice. (p. 120)

Willis suggests that it is more important to understand how sporting performances are used to present male power and domination as natural and immutable than to measure and record the performances themselves. The fact, for example, that the fastest woman in the world is slower than the fastest man is not of interest in relational analysis. What is important is why this fact is deemed important, what it symbolizes, and how it is implicated in the reproduction of the social relations of gender or male power and privilege in society.

It is difficult to provide a complete synthesis or review of relational work because, as Birrell (1988) suggests, "The shift in the field is so recent and the insights so exciting that it is difficult to capture all the trends in recent research" (p. 483). Despite these difficulties, Birrell provides an excellent analysis centered on four themes she identifies as central to the critical feminist project: (1) the production of an ideology of masculinity and of male power through sport; (2) the media practices through which dominant notions of women are reproduced; (3) the centrality of issues of physicality, sexuality, and the body for defining gender relations; and (4) the resistance of women to dominant sport practices as they create women-centered sporting practices or seek to transform sport into a more humane activity. Rather than restate Birrell's analysis, I will outline what I believe are the strengths and weaknesses (or, perhaps more accurately, the promises and pitfalls) of existing relational work.

## Strengths of Relational Analyses

Perhaps the greatest strength of existing relational work is its diversity. This diversity is particularly useful because it raises important questions and debates about appropriate theoretical, methodological, and epistemological frameworks for feminist relational work. Although these debates appear at times to be divisive and potentially counterproductive, they illustrate the importance of developing good critical work in sport and leisure studies. The debates redefine the terrain for critical work—an exciting and stimulating (if somewhat frightening) experience (Hall, 1988). The real promise of this dialogue is in forcing feminist scholars to read outside of sport sociology to develop an interdisciplinary consciousness for understanding how the social relations of domination and subordination are created, recreated, and changed. It is this critical consciousness that forms the basis for feminist cultural studies (of which sport and leisure are an extremely important part).

Another strength of existing relational work is the detailed evidence it provides (often from critical ethnographic studies) of the various ways in which male hegemony is articulated, negotiated, and contested in a variety of sporting and leisure activities and structures. For example, Elizabeth Wheatley's (1988) subcultural analysis of women rugby players illustrates how women can and do challenge the dominant male sporting practices that characterize rugby. The women in her study show how women can win cultural space in a sport that is closely guarded as the terrain of white, middle class, heterosexual men.

Other examples provide similar insights into the negotiations involved in the struggles over the production and reproduction of gender relations in creating and recreating sport and leisure: Lois Bryson's (1987) analysis of Australian sport and the ways in which male hegemony is constructed and reconstructed; Nancy Theberge and Alan Crank's (1986) study of the structures and processes of systemic discrimination in newspaper coverage of women's sport; Susan Birrell and Diana Richter's (1987) and Cheryl Cole's (1988) studies of the struggles of women softball players to critique and transform dominant, male-defined sporting forms and practices. These are only a few of the studies integral to the feminist critical project.

## Weaknesses of Relational Analyses

Despite the promise of relational feminist work, it is not without weaknesses. The most obvious and serious weakness is that it focuses almost exclusively on white, middle-class, Western women. Despite its efforts to develop emancipatory theories and practices, this work perpetuates "a continuing racist bias" (Birrell, 1988). Drawing on work by Cole and Birrell (1986), Birrell argues that

> as a field, we have yet to deal with issues of race in any profound theoretical manner. The experiences of women of color differ from those of white women in significant ways, yet, while our models for analysis provide space for dealing with race as a relation of domination and subordination, we have not made the commitment necessary to begin to explore that dynamic. (p. 491)

The challenge is to develop our work in ways that allow us to explore this dynamic. Simply adding women of color to our work is not enough, just as adding women to male-defined theories is inadequate. We must strive to understand the experiences of all women, not just those privileged by race and class.

Although the racist bias is a serious problem in much of the relational feminist work on sport, it is not the only one. There are other silences to be broken. Much needs to be understood about how women's lives are structured—not only by race, class, and gender, but also by age, sexual identity, ethnicity, and health. The list could go on. The point is to avoid the idealist, positivist trap of piling variable upon variable to explain women's lives and instead to develop a commitment to critical feminist work that is inclusive rather than exclusive. We must embrace the challenge and develop theories and methodologies that are sensitive to difference and the powerful ways that these differences come together in systems of domination and subordination in women's and men's lives.

# Future Directions: Possibilities for Examining Sexual Oppression in Sport

There is the danger in an attempt to outline future directions for work on sexual oppression in sport that a suggested direction is taken as the only way to proceed. I don't intend this section for use in this way. It is impossible to know where future research might take us or where it ought to be going; I will simply present some ideas and raise some questions about the directions of my own work and thinking.

Debates over the forms and functions of feminist critical work on sport and leisure will probably continue to shape future work. This is one of the field's greatest strengths. However, it is in the context of these debates that empirical and theoretical work develops and thrives.

Although theoretical analysis is crucial to feminist cultural studies, we must go beyond theorizing and make the difficult move from intellectual discourse to action. (I am reluctant to make explicit the forms of action that may arise out of this work, because part of linking theory and practice is that they develop together and are informed by each other. Given this, my suggestions begin with possible avenues for inquiry that I hope will also lead to strategies for challenging and changing dominant sporting practices.) It is one thing to critique dominant sporting frameworks and practices; it is quite another to challenge and change them. Women who challenge dominant sporting practices encounter an array of responses, most of them unpleasant and frustrating.

Taking on the status quo is no mean feat, and the consequences can be devastating. But the consequences of silence are worse. The challenge is to try to understand the short- and long-term implications of different strategies for changing sport. We must understand more clearly the consequences of individual and collective acts of accommodation, incorporation, and resistance to mainstream sporting programs, practices, and policies if we are to gain insight into the ways that the struggles over the contested terrain of sport are played out. It may not simply be a question of calling for resistance by all people at all times. Challenging hegemony is more complex and contradictory than it may appear. Perhaps we must begin work that allows for continual debate, dialogue, and reassessment of strategies and their relative successes and failures.

One starting place might be to closely examine how different women have challenged the dominant power relations of sport. This approach holds the potential for a greater understanding of the ways that women's responses to hegemonic masculinity are contoured by history, biography, and social structure. Some sobering findings may result, but these are worth the risk. The time has come to move beyond simplistic denigration of all acts of incorporation and accommodation and celebration of any kind of resistance. The situation is not so clear-cut. Many acts of resistance may in fact be racist, classist, and homophobic in their articulation. Romanticizing resistance does not make for good feminist cultural criticism.

Another avenue for inquiry is women's collegiate sport, specifically the social, political, and ideological contexts of the struggles over its definition and control prevalent in American sport and physical education since the 1920s. Questions about the nature of these struggles and their impact on the dominant, masculinist definitions of collegiate sport seem to be essential to understanding how hegemony is negotiated and secured in collegiate sport.

These struggles are interesting because they are not only complex but they also appear to be fraught with contradictions. By viewing them in their historical, political, and social contexts, perhaps we can better understand the accommodation, incorporation, and resistance to dominant male sporting organizations and practices that has occurred both individually and collectively in women's collegiate sport.

How might such an inquiry proceed? We could begin by examining the responses of women physical educators, coaches, and members of the Association for Intercollegiate Women's Athletics (AIWA) to the impact of Title IX (of the Educational Amendments Act of 1972). The developments around the enactment of Title IX allow us to look at the problems and promises associated with an attempt to achieve distributive justice through legislative process.

Title IX has had an enormous impact on sport. The nature of this impact and how it has been perceived and responded to by different groups is crucial to understanding the negotiation of power and prestige in sport. The struggles over this amendment, especially in the organizations representing women's sport (AIWA) and men's sport (National Collegiate Athletic Association, NCAA) provide a rich data source for understanding how hegemony is contested and won. For example, the NCAA was successful in defining the terrain of the struggle, and in so doing managed to develop alliances with women athletes, coaches, and administrators to secure control of the organization and structure of both women's and men's sport. The resulting processes of accommodation, resistance, and incorporation illustrate the complexities in challenging dominant social and cultural sporting practices.

We also should study the impact of powerful women physical educators and their organizations on the development of women's sport before Title IX. There is clear evidence that women can develop successful alternatives to male-defined sport, and the nature of these alternatives needs to be viewed in relation to the hegemonic practices they are opposing.

An initial exploration of these alternatives suggests that they are in fact politically conservative and represent a commitment to white, middle-class, heterosexual respectability and morality. The rejection of commercialized male sporting forms may be resistance, but this is not necessarily cause for celebration, especially when the alternative merely lauds a feminized version of the amateur sporting code. This is problematic because the history of the code is clearly middle-class, white, heterosexual, and androcentric. The articulation of a feminized code is not enough to challenge hegemonic masculinity. There appears to be no explicitly radical feminist opposition among women physical educators to male sporting practices. This needs to be explored, along with the impact of these alternatives on class, race, and gender relations. This resistance may ultimately have failed to challenge the dominant power relations in sport because it was framed in ways that simply reproduced the status quo in a different form.

My statements may anger some women physical educators who have been part of creating these alternatives. Although this is unfortunate, I believe I must risk their anger. It is important to closely examine how women have responded to and challenged sport's dominant power relations, in the hope that this work will illuminate how women's responses to hegemonic masculinity are contoured by their histories, biographies, and social structures, all of which can be both enabling and constraining. To get a view that is appropriately contextualized, we need more fully developed analyses of the dynamics of these processes and the subsequent actions and reactions of women working within them. This will help us avoid the traps of early cultural studies, which tended to celebrate any forms of resistance by subordinate groups to dominant (particularly class-based) social relations, even when this resistance was racist, sexist, or homophobic. Understanding the dangers of unquestioning acceptance of acts of resistance reminds us of the importance of continued critical reflection. This may, in turn, help us develop more inclusive theories and practices that do not perpetuate racist, ageist, classist, or other biases.

# Conclusion

In presenting this critical feminist analysis of sexual oppression in sport, my basic premise is that to understand the processes involved in creating and maintaining individual and systemic sexual oppression in sport, we must explore how different representations of gender relations help produce and reproduce male hegemony. One means of exploration is to examine how existing scholarship on gender issues in sport accommodates, becomes incorporated within, or resists dominant frameworks for defining sport. By defining the problem of sexual oppression in different ways this exploration would imply new strategies for dealing with the oppression.

A critique of categoric and distributive work on gender reveals the promises and pitfalls in analyzing "the facts" about women's performances or participation in sport. Understanding the assumptions underlying categoric and distributive analyses helps make explicit the political and ideological agendas associated with them. I want not to throw out the facts provided by categoric and distributive work but to subject them to a different, more critical analysis.

The analysis I am arguing for is relational feminist work on sport and leisure studies. Relational work links theory and practice in an attempt to understand the complex and often contradictory processes involved in the struggles over the maintenance of hegemony in sport. This understanding is an important step in providing the conditions that allow us to move from theorizing about oppression to taking action to challenge and change it. Bryson (1987) captures the difficulties feminists face in making choices about taking on male-defined sport:

> Over recent years much effort has gone into developing women's sport and reclaiming it. I have changed my position somewhat over that time from being unconvinced about the wisdom of becoming embroiled at all to being convinced that if we vacate the scene, we merely support masculine hegemony. (p. 359)

She goes on to suggest that we must act in a variety of ways to resist sexual oppression in sport and concludes that "what we must do is encourage the development of reflective and critical understanding and practice" (p. 359). This is, I believe, the essence of feminist critical cultural studies. If we accept this challenge we can develop our theories and practices in ways that will ultimately transform oppressive sporting structures and practices.

# Notes

1. See M.A. Hall (1978, 1981, 1988) for a comprehensive review and critique of research on women in sport and Birrell (1988) for an evaluation of the development and intellectual history of the research and scholarship on gender relations in sport.
2. See Del Ray (1978) for a discussion of apologists in sport.
3. See Birrell (1983), M.A. Hall (1981, 1988), and Theberge (1985) for a more thorough critique of this work.
4. Paul Willis (1982) provides an excellent detailed discussion of how sport is implicated in the production and maintenance of an ideology of male supremacy.

# References

Abbott, A., & Smith, D.R. (1984). Governmental constraints and labor market mobility: Turnover among college athletic personnel. *Social Work Occupation*, **11**, 29-53.

Acosta, R.V., & Carpenter, L.J. (1985). Women in sport. In D. Chu, J.O. Seagrave, & B.J. Becker (Eds.), *Sport and higher education*. Champaign, IL: Human Kinetics.

Allison, M.T., & Butler, B. (1984). Role conflict and the elite female athlete: Empirical findings and conceptual dilemmas. *International Review of Sport Sociology*, **19**, 57-68.

Anthrop, J., & Allison, M.T. (1983). Role conflict and the high school female athlete. *Research Quarterly for Exercise and Sport*, **54**, 104-111.

Baker, M.A. (Ed.). (1987). *Sex differences in human performance*. New York: Wiley.

Bell, M.M. (1980). Role conflict of women as athletes in the United States. *Arena Review*, **4**(2), 22-31.

Bem, S.L. (1984). Androgyny and gender schema theory: A conceptual and empirical integration. Paper presented at the Nebraska Symposium on Motivation.

Birrell, S. (1983). The psychological dimensions of female athletic participation. In M. Boutilier & L. San Giovanni (Eds.), *The sporting woman*. Champaign, IL: Human Kinetics.

Birrell, S. (1988). Discourses on the gender/sport relationship: From women in sport to gender relations. In K. Pandolf (Ed.), *Exercise and Sport Science Reviews* (Vol. 16). New York: MacMillan.

Birrell, S., & Richter, D. (1987). Is a diamond forever? Feminist transformations of sport. *Women's Studies International Forum*, **10**(4), 395-410.

Brake, M. (1985). *Comparative youth culture*. London: Routledge & Kegan Paul.

Bryant, J. (1980). A two year selective investigation of the female in sport as reported in the paper media. *Arena Review*, **4**(2), 23-30.

Bryson, L. (1987). Sport and the maintenance of masculine hegemony. *Women's Studies International Forum*, **10**(4), 349-360.

Carpenter, L., & Acosta, V. (1985). The status of women in intercollegiate athletics—A five year national study. In D. Chu, J. Seagrave, & B. Becker (Eds.), *Sport and Higher Education*. Champaign, IL: Human Kinetics.

Chu, D., Seagrave, J., & Becker, B. (1985). *Sport and higher education*. Champaign, IL: Human Kinetics.

Coakley, J.J., & Pacey, P.L. (1984). The distribution of athletic scholarships among women in intercollegiate sport. In N. Theberge & P. Donnelly (Eds.), *Sport and the sociological imagination*. Fort Worth, TX: Texas Christian University.

Cole, C. (1988). Softball as a feminist perspective. Paper presented at the Midwest Sociological Society Meetings, Minneapolis, MN.

Cole, C., & Birrell, S. (1986). Resisting the canon: Feminist cultural studies. Paper presented at the North American Society for the Sociology of Sport Annual Meetings, Las Vegas, Nevada.

Corrigan, P. (1979). *Schooling and the smash street kids*. London: MacMillan Press.

Critcher, C. (1986). Radical theorists of sport: The state of play. *Sociology of Sport Journal*, **3**, 333-343.

Deem, R. (1988). "Together we stand, divided we fall": Social criticism and the sociology of sport and leisure. *Sociology of Sport Journal*, **5**(4), 341-354.

Del Ray, P. (1978). The apologetic and women in sport. In C.A. Oglesby (Ed.), *Women and sport: From myth to reality*. Philadelphia: Lea & Febiger.

Duquin, M.E. (1978). The androgynous advantage. In C.A. Oglesby (Ed.), *Women and Sport: From myth to reality*. Philadelphia: Lea & Febiger.

Dyer, K.F. (1982). *Catching up the men: Women in sport*. London: Junction Books.

Fasting, K., & Sisjord, M.K. (1985). Gender roles and barriers to participation in sports. *Sociology of Sport Journal*, **2**(4), 345-351.

Fasting, K., & Tangen, J. (1983). Gender and sport in the Norwegian mass media. *International Review for Sport Sociology*, **20**(1/2), 95-108.

Greendorfer, S. (1978). Socialization into sport. In C.A. Oglesby (Ed.), *Women and sport: From myth to reality*. Philadelphia: Lea & Febiger.

Gruneau, R. (1975). Sport, social differentiation and social inequality. In D. Ball & J. Loy (Eds.), *Sport and social order: Contributions to the sociology of sport*. Reading, MA: Addison Wesley.

Hall, M.A. (1978). *Sport and gender: A feminist perspective in the sociology of sport*. CAHPER Sociology of Sport Monograph Series. Ottawa: Canadian Association for Health Physical Education and Recreation.

Hall, M.A. (1981). Sport, sex roles and sex identity. The CRIAW Papers/Les Documents de L'CRIAF. Ottawa: Canadian Institute for the Advancement of Women.

Hall, M.A. (1985). Knowledge and gender: Epistemological questions in the social analysis of sport. *Sociology of Sport Journal*, **2**, 25-42.

Hall, M.A. (1988). The discourse of gender and sport: From femininity to feminism. *Sociology of Sport Journal*, **5**(4), 330-340.

Hall, S. (1981). Cultural studies: Two paradigms. In T. Bennett, G. Martin, C. Mercer, & J. Woollacott (Eds.), *Culture, ideology and social process*. London: Batsford Academic & Educational.

Harris, D. (1980). Femininity and athleticism: Conflict or consonance. In D. Sabo & R. Runfola (Eds.), *Jock: Sports and male identity*. Englewood Cliffs, NJ: Prentice-Hall.

Hart, B., Hasbrook, C.A., & Mathes, S. (1986). An examination of the reduction in the number of female interscholastic coaches. *Research Quarterly for Exercise and Sport*, **57**(1), 68-77.

Hart, M.M. (Ed.). (1976). *Sport in the sociocultural process*. Dubuque, IA: Brown.

Hebdige, R. (1979). *Subcultures and the meaning of style*. London: Methuen.

Howell, F.M., & McKenzie, J.A. (1987). High school athletics and adult sport-leisure activity: Gender variations across the life cycle. *Sociology of Sport Journal*, **4**, 329-346.

Hult, J. (1976). Equal programs or carbon copies? *Journal of Physical Education and Recreation*, **47**, 24-25.

Inglis, S.E. (1988). The representation of women in university athletic programs. *Journal of Sport Management*, **2**(1), 14-25.

McLaren, P. (1989). *Life in schools: An introduction to critical pedagogy in the foundations of education*. New York: Longman.

McRobbie, A. (1978). Working class girls and the culture of femininity. In *Women Take Issue: Aspects of Women's Subordination*. London: Hutchinson.

Metheny, E. (1964). Sports and the feminine image. *Gymnasion*, **1**(4), 17-22.

Money, J., & Ehrhardt, A.A. (1972). *Man and woman boy and girl*. Baltimore: Johns Hopkins University Press.

Myes, A.M., & Lips, H. (1978). Participation in competitive amateur sports as a function of psychological androgyny. *Sex Roles*, **4**, 571-578.

Sparks, R. (1988). Ways of seeing differently: Complexity and contradiction in the critical project of sport and leisure studies. *Sociology of Sport Journal*, **5**(4), 355-368.

Theberge, N. (1984). Some evidence of the existence of a sexual double standard in mobility to leadership positions in sport. *International Review of Sport Sociology*, **19**(2), 185-195.

Theberge, N. (1985). Towards a feminist alternative to sport as a male preserve. *Quest*, **10**, 193-202.

Theberge, N., & Crank, A. (1986). Work routines in newspaper sports departments and the coverage of women's sports. *Sociology of Sport Journal*, **3**, 195-203.

Vickers, J.N., & Gosling, B.J. (1984). *The changing participation of men and women in the Canadian inter university athletic union (1978-1982)*. Ottawa: The Women's Representative Committee, C.I.A.U.

Wells, C.L. (1984). *Women and sport and performance: A physiological perspective*. Champaign, IL: Human Kinetics.

Wheatley, E. (1988). (Re)constructing sexualities in sport: Women speak "out" in rugby. Paper presented at the North American Society for the Sociology of Sport Annual Meetings, Cincinnati, OH.

White, C., & Brackenridge, C. (1985). Who rules sport? Gender divisions in the power structure of British sports organizations from 1960. *International Review of Sport Sociology*, **20**(1/2), 95-108.

Willis, P. (1977). *Learning to labour: How working class kids get working class jobs*. Sussex: Saxon House.

Willis, P. (1978). *Profane culture*. London: Routledge & Kegan Paul.

Willis, P. (1982). Women in sport in ideology. In J. Hargreaves (Ed.), *Sport, culture and ideology*. London: Routledge & Kegan Paul.

Wyrick, W. (1974). Biophysical perspectives. In E. Gerber, J. Felshin, P. Berlin, & W. Wyrick (Eds.), *The American woman in sport*. Reading, MA: Addison Wesley.

# CHAPTER 8

# Gender on the Sports Agenda

## Jennifer A. Hargreaves

## Introducing Gender

The concern to put gender on the sports agenda has been with us for some time. I am referring here to the theory and practice of Western sport and most particularly to sport in the UK. Gender issues in sport have been associated with sports feminism which emanated mainly from North America during the 70s in response to male dominance in sport and to sports sociologies which marginalize female sport and which reflect dominant gender relations in sport. The impetus has been widespread, but in the UK a solid feminist intervention in sport has occurred only in recent years, much of which has been part of a more general concern with women's leisure and with the relationships between class, patriarchy, and culture emanating from women's studies, cultural studies, and social history (Deem, 1986; Green, Hebron, & Woodward, 1987; Griffin, Hobson, Macintosh, & McCabe, 1982; Hargreaves, 1986, 1989a, 1990; Scraton, 1986; Talbot, 1988; Willis, 1982; Wimbush & Talbot, 1988).

However, in spite of the increasing level of theoretical sophistication of much of the writing, there is still a general tendency to focus on *differences* between men and women in sport, rather than on *relations* between them. This results in a general failure to incorporate, systematically, relations of power between the sexes, to relate them to other structures of power in society, and to deal with conflict and change. The specific ways in which sexism in sport is experienced and the different forms it takes for different groups of women at different times tend also to be inadequately theorized, and although increasing numbers of men as well as women are sensitive to the issue of gender in sport, there remains a glaring neglect in analyses of the

*Note.* This chapter was originally published in the *International Review for Sociology of Sport* (25)4, pp. 287-308, 1990. Reprinted here by permission.

effects of sexism in sport upon men. In addition, sport has important ethical and moral dimensions which are intrinsically related to gender, but the connections are either ignored or glossed over. For example, the "problems of drugs," the "problems of violence," and the "problems of commercialization" are topical issues in sports sociology which all have an important gender dimension but which are seldom related, systematically, to patriarchal relations as well as to capitalist relations.

This paper takes for granted the huge power that men still exert over women in sport whilst acknowledging that male power in sport is becoming less certain. It also recognizes the complexities and contradictions of gender relations in sports theory and practice. First of all, I discuss some of the major controversies in sports feminism and then suggest ways in which we might more profitably put gender on the sports agenda.

I am adopting here a controversial position when I characterize sports feminists as both *women and men* who share a desire for women to exercise more power and to achieve greater autonomy in sport. It is a desire for change. However, sports feminism is not a unified movement or idea. Some people, for example, argue that male domination should be reduced and that there should be more sports for women modelled on existing traditions, whereas others wish to subvert dominant ideas and to change people's attitudes and actions, and there are groups of women who believe passionately that female sports should be separate from, and qualitatively different from, traditional male sports. In order to understand present practices and to work for change, I think we should resist the idea that there is a possibility of theoretical absolutism in the sense that there exists somewhere, if only we can grasp it, a definitive theory of sport. But I am not arguing for a sort of eclecticism, or patching together of concepts from different and sometimes incompatible theories as if they were coherent. Theorizing, like sport, is to do with struggling over values which should be made explicit.

## Equality of Opportunity

The dominant pressure in sports feminism is the desire for equality of opportunity with men. It is based on the belief that, although male power in sport predominates, it is not inviolable. It represents a struggle by women, and by men on their behalf, to get more of what men have always had. The growing concern to provide equal opportunities by providing for females access to traditionally masculinized activities is a central feature of liberal democratic ideology, the intellectual and political framework of which is usually described as liberal-feminist. Liberal feminism has been defined as "an attempt to remove or compensate for the ascriptive and social impediments that prevent women from competing on equal terms with men, without otherwise challenging the hierarchical structures within which both sexes operate" (Miles & Middleton, 1989).

Liberal ideology embodies the notion that throughout the history of industrial society women have been approaching nearer to equality with men in all aspects of life and culture, a progressive process which in modern sport, it is argued, started during the late nineteenth and early twentieth centuries, continued during the inter-war and post-war periods and then accelerated in recent years. Liberalism is based upon the belief that our society upholds the principles of democracy, individual liberty, and freedom of choice by implementing social and legal reforms. Sports liberalism is associated with the roles of organizations which hold power and are implicated in the provision of sports resources—central government and other public bodies, such as local authorities, and sports organizations, such as the governing bodies of sport. For those who, like women, are characterized as deprived in sport, the practical implication of the philosophy of equality is to provide for them additional opportunities. In the UK, the 1975 Sex Discrimination Act, like Title IX in America, was intended to outlaw discrimination against women in the provision of (sports) goods, facilities, services, and premises (Pannick, 1983), and the "Sport for All" campaign, which is the official policy of the Sports Council, has identified women as a target group in the provision of sport (Sports Council, 1982, 1985, 1988). Such policies cohere with the policies of sports feminists who want easier access and better facilities, improved funding and rewards, equal rights with men under the law, top quality coaching on a par with men, and an equivalent voice with men in decision-making. Their demands are supported by empirical evidence—the facts that, for example, approximately twice as many men as women play sport in the UK and men participate in a greater number of activities and with greater frequency than do women (Sports Council, 1982, 1985, 1988).

Liberal feminism is essentially pragmatic. Women and men have been engaged in a process of struggle to relate the theory of equality of opportunity to practice and they have achieved notable successes, especially in the last decade. There is no doubt that, in advanced industrial countries like Britain, *more* sport is now *more* accessible to *more* women. Liberal feminism also implicitly embodies a rejection of biological explanations of women's subordination in sport: It assumes that there are no biological reasons for women's low participation rates, that biological differences between the sexes are less likely to affect participation in sport than differences within each sex, and that, given the opportunity, women can participate in the full range of sports that men enjoy (Dyer, 1982; Ferris, 1981). These implications are important because the most consistent justification for opposition to women's equality with men has been articulated in terms of the supposed limitations inherent in female biology. By taking action, liberal feminists have exposed myths about female biology and changed perceptions of the female body. There is an assumption that culture and not nature is the reason why so few women have been involved in sport and that any barriers that still prevent women from participating can be removed by rational intervention.

There are, however, contradictory implications in the liberal-feminist position. The conception of equal opportunities, symbolized in the phrase "catching up the men" (Dyer, 1982), is a limited one, concerned more with quantitative than qualitative change. The vision presented to us is an idealized one, as if the trend is inevitably an improving one and has few moral or ethical problems associated with it. Parkhouse and Lapin, referring to the USA, typify this position when they say, "Equality is a right, not a privilege. However, it has become apparent in this 'land of opportunity' that equal opportunity becomes a reality only if we act if that right is denied'' (1980, p. 31).

But such an articulation masks the weaknesses of the concept of equality. Gender inequalities are identified, but rarely are questions asked about where the values come from that perpetuate them and in whose particular interests they work. Questions such as, Equality for which particular women?, For what purpose?, and According to what criteria? are ignored.

Furthermore, equal rights for women embraces the idea that women are a homogeneous group and assumes that an increase in participation is an improvement for women *in general*. In reality, however, women from working-class backgrounds and from ethnic minorities are marginalized and the particularly difficult and sometimes unique problems faced by certain groups of women, such as single parents, the low paid, Asian women, lesbians, disabled women, and elderly women, are seldom addressed. Women from different backgrounds do not experience patriarchal culture in identical ways and they have different opportunities and expectations. Most advances for women in sport have occurred within the existing structures of sport, for white middle-class women, and for those already involved in competitive sport who have overcome the practical and ideological constraints that continue to inhibit vast numbers of other women from participating at all. It is also the case that statistics which show an overall increase in female participation, like those published in the *General Household Surveys, Social Trends*, and the *Sports Council Reports*, mask the smaller range of sports in which women participate in relation to men and their excessively low participation rates in minority sports. And elite sport, sports coaching, and sports administration are not egalitarian either, but based upon meritocracy and harsh competition. The most prestigious positions and well paid jobs in sport are held by men and the few women who hold powerful roles in sport are unrepresentative of women as a whole (White and Brackenridge, 1984). Equal opportunities in sport benefit in reality only a minority of women.

Liberal sports feminism also tends to overlook the limitations of legal reform and to underestimate the strength of entrenched resistance to changing attitudes and behavior. It is implausible to imagine that genuine equality will result from legal reforms when the power of men over women subtly permeates society or to think that sport could be changed fundamentally by legislation which embodies gender as an organizing principle (Hargreaves, 1990). Theoretically, liberal feminism fails to examine the extent and nature of male power in sport in the specific context of capitalism and fails to incorporate the ideological and symbolic dimensions of gender oppression. It takes for granted the distinctly masculine modes of thought and practice in sport as if they are inevitable, without considering that they are socially and historically constructed. The unconscious result is that it seems commonsense for women's sport to be modelled on men's sport. Such an implication embodies a failure, in theory and in practice, to recognize the complexities of gender relations in sport—in particular, those based on unequal divisions of power between different groups of men and different groups of women, as well as between men and women. The notion of equality for women fails to question which women want to be equal with which men. Far from challenging male sport, liberalism endorses it.

I am suggesting that there is a powerful tendency in this perspective to divert attention away from the gender-linked value system of established sport and to accept the dominant ideologies that support it. In essence, liberal feminists fail to question and examine the "moral and human consequences of the structures and procedures which have been created by a patriarchal society" (Talbot, 1988, p. 32). Margaret Talbot is alluding here to the endemic features of modern sport which render it harmful rather than enriching, such as aggressive competition, chauvinism, sexism, racism, xenophobia, physical and psychological abuse to athletes, violence, and the commodification of sport. Liberalism incorrectly embodies the popular idea that the allocation of increased resources for women's sport reflects a broad political and ideological consensus and in doing so fails to examine oppositional values and demands which are struggled over and which relate to broader structures of power and political considerations. Some sports feminists, for example, oppose the present structures of sport and of capitalist society and have actively reinterpreted sporting practice, constructing for themselves alternative models. Nonetheless, equal opportunities is by far the most popular approach and is accepted as commonsense by the majority of people pioneering for improvements for women. Of course, the incentives are always for women to get into traditional male sports—seldom is the movement in the opposite direction. Although the strategy of equal opportunities in sport has been the most influential and successful one, it fails to offer radical departures.

## Separatism

Separatism, in contrast, has several different orientations which have evolved since the formative years of female sport. The early forms of organized sport and physical education for females, which were established in the late nineteenth century, were not intended to question the values and practices of male sport. They were marked by their insular, separatist nature, developing mostly in separate spheres from men—in schools, colleges, and clubs—so that it was easy to define women's sport as qualitatively different from men's sport, in tune with conventional ideas about "femininity" and "masculinity." These early forms of female sport and physical education accommodated to traditional biological assumptions rather than challenging them (Hargreaves, 1979, 1987). Then, after the turn of the century, some sports feminists, in particular in North America, promoted a different philosophy by advocating separate sports for females on ethical and moral grounds. They were opposed to men's sport because they believed that it concentrated too much on aggressive competition and was over-specialized and corrupted by commercialization (Hargreaves, 1984; Theberge, 1985). Although for different reasons, both these models of separate sport for women provided the historical basis for the idea that there should be "feminine-appropriate" sports and "masculine-appropriate" sports, and an early pattern of sex-role stereotyping in sport was established. The long history of single-sex physical education in schools and separate sports for men and women has provided a practical and ideological foundation for separate sports to continue.

Better articulated and more forceful forms of separatism have developed in recent years, to a large extent as a reaction to the powerlessness, frustration and anger experienced by sportswomen who have suffered serious discrimination and experienced blatant male chauvinism. The fiercest struggles have tended to occur in traditional male sports and, not surprisingly, women who have experienced serious discrimination are often vehemently opposed to men in these settings. Their opposition to men's control of sport, rather than to the violent and aggressively competitive character of sport, is a popular contemporary separatist position. It espouses the belief that women should be able to participate in sports that are associated with conventional images of masculinity and fiercely controlled by men's organizations, such as boxing, golf, motor-racing, rowing, speed-skating, snooker, and weight-lifting. It is argued that to be separate is the first step towards wresting control from men and putting more sports for women "on the map." Such forms of separatism are not necessarily incompatible with the ideology of equal opportunity when they are seen as a way of balancing the advantages that men in sport have had for so long. They give women access to the most masculinized sports, create wider definitions of femininity and provide women with experiences to administer and control their own activities.

However, the argument also prevails among some feminist sports groups that the characteristics of male sport are reactionary and undesirable and they argue, like their predecessors, that women should not emulate men's sport, but should build, instead, alternative models of sport which are intrinsically more humane and liberating. The following quotation from Twin's (1979) book exemplifies this position: "Sports should not become for women what they have been for men: a display of aggression, a proof of toughness, and a kind of primitive communication that replaces emotional intimacy" (p. 164).

These expressions of separatism in sport focus on the male/female distinction and the assumption that conventional gender relations inhibit women's development. Those women who argue for separate sport for themselves do so because they feel their oppression *as women*. However, this invokes a rigid system of male domination, which is, invariably, an exaggeration. They believe that their common interests transcend differences and that independence from men is self-realization (Birrell & Richter, 1987; Theberge, 1985).

This philosophy of separate development in sport has characteristics in common with radical feminism which has been an important influence in theoretical debates about women's liberation. Radical feminists do not share a single doctrine, but they share in an opposition to patriarchy which, they argue, is the basis of other forms of oppression, rather than a by-product of them (Firestone, 1979; Millett, 1971). Patriarchy is defined as a system of power relations by which men dominate women. Radical feminists allege that the ability of men to dominate women is the most basic form of oppression because it is rooted in essential physical and psychological differences between the sexes. Characteristics normally ascribed to men, and associated with sport, such as strength, competitiveness, aggression, and assertiveness, are rejected, and characteristics popularly classified as female, such as co-operativeness, relative weakness, grace and tenderness, are celebrated. This is a distinctly "pro-woman" and "anti-male" stance which asserts not only women's difference from men, but their superiority over men (Weir & Wilson, 1984, p. 79).

The argument for separate development of sport for men and women which stems from this essentialist position is a problem when it is based on biologist assumptions. Ironically, women who argue in this way implicitly support the image of power invested in the male body by claiming that women have uniquely different characteristics from men. Male domination in sport is thus reducible to the distinctive biological natures of males and females which are treated as if they are culturally and historically universal. It is as if patriarchy is a biological system with an underlying uniformity. The idea of "feminine-appropriate" and "masculine appropriate" sports locks people into a fixed concept of the 'natural' which is blind to history and ignores changing feminine and masculine identities and different gender relations. It inaccurately presents all men and all men's sports as having similar characteristics.

## Positive Discrimination

But there is a strong cultural dimension which favors the argument for separate development. Because organized sport has been dominated by men and permeated by sexist attitudes and behavior for over a century, many women recognize the limitations of equal opportunity programs and there is growing evidence in North America and in the UK that in sports teaching, coaching, and administration, women have more scope and better prospects in single-sex organizations than when they have to compete with men in open competition in mixed organizations (White & Brackenridge, 1984). In common with women working in other fields, sports feminists have recognized that to create alternative models of sport where there is positive discrimination in favor of women is an expedient way forward at present. It is believed that to place women's experiences at the center of any analysis of sport is the only way to be sensitive to the specific needs of women. This is the reason why some women's sports groups have adopted an exclusionist policy and refused membership even to men who are sympathetic and supportive of women's needs in sport. It is argued that to exclude individual well-meaning men from women's sports organizations is to recognize the ways that men have structurally dominated women in such organizations and to admit them would be to deny the reality of women's socialized subjectivities. Increasing numbers of feminists wish to avoid the dangers of assimilating women's sport to male structures, and although their resistance to masculine hegemony in sport and active construction of alternative models of sport is marginal, it provides an important, organized challenge to dominant images (Birrell & Richter, 1987).

The provision of closed space for women in the form of women-only sports sessions is increasingly popular and provides new opportunities and benefits for women. The chance to be in an area with other members of their own sex is a "luxury" which many women rarely enjoy. It is the only condition under which some women will participate in physical activities, for religious or social reasons, and provides the only setting for them to gain confidence and enjoyment in their sporting bodies. Closed space for women removes fears of harassment, ridicule, and inhibition which they might experience in mixed groups and affords important opportunities for female bonding. It frees women from the day-to-day discrimination and sexism which they experience and provides them with a sense of control and autonomy which they otherwise lack (Clarke, 1988). When women take practical action for themselves, the relationship between theory and practice becomes clear and the feminist slogan "the personal is political" comes alive.

## Unnecessary Divisions

However, separate development for men and women embodies further complexities, contradictions, and serious problems. It recreates social divisions, specifically those between men and women, but also between different groups of women and different groups of men. The major division is between heterosexual males and females, which confirms dominant gender divisions in society. Pejorative attitudes to "deviant sexuality" have, however, resulted in further divisions in sport—there are, for example, specific sports situations which highlight sexual preferences because lesbians or gays bond together for understanding and companionship.

Although sport remains an area where women are constantly being exploited and unequal gender divisions are consistently being reaffirmed, nonetheless, the philosophy of separate development tends to exaggerate the overall extent of sexism in sport by ignoring non-sexist attitudes and non-sexist sports. As in other areas of life, in sport there are numerous, different male/female relationships and situations where sex and sexuality, as well as, for example, ethnicity, class, and age are unimportant. In some contexts women are unequivocally subordinated in their relationships with men, in other situations women collude in apparently subordinate roles, in some spheres women share power with men and have greater autonomy than in the past, and in a limited number of situations women wield power over men. Similarly, men's attitudes to women are numerous and varied—some men are reactionary and sexist in their dealings with women and resist women's claims for equality, but not all men oppress women. Some men actively seek equality with women and some seek forms of subordination, too. Although it is impossible to assess the extent to which changing gender relations may alter the "global pattern" of male domination in sport, radical feminist claims for separate development invariably ignore the ways in which gender relations have changed historically and are changing now. Separatist ideology carries the implication that only women can bring about changes in favor of women and that there are fixed limitations to the social changes which women might seek in sport. But, as Bell Hooks claims, "Since men are the primary agents maintaining and supporting sexism and sexist oppression, they can only be successfully eradicated if men are compelled to assume responsibility for transforming their consciousness and the consciousness of society as a whole" (Quoted in Hearn, 1984, p. 24).

If the opposite of domination is sharing, then it could be argued that a distinctly female culture is not progressive, but reactionary. Like John Clarke and Chas Critcher (1985), for example, who say that, "For all the signs of change, sport remains largely an area where existing gender roles are reestablished and confirmed. Segregation is its ultimate form" (p. 162).

Paul Willis (1982) suggests a radical alternative. His ideas coincide with those of feminists who want reciprocal relations between the sexes and who seek a qualitatively different model of sport for both *men and women*:

> Sport could be presented as a form of activity which emphasises human similarity and not dissimilarity, a form of activity which isn't competitive and measured, a form of activity which expresses values which are indeed unmeasurable, a form of activity which is concerned with individual well-being and satisfaction rather than with comparison. In such a view of sport, differences between the sexes would be unimportant, unnoticed. (p. 143)

Such a vision directs us to be less concerned about the biological gap between the sexes than about the meanings attached to it. The relationships between sex and gender, and nature and culture, raise theoretical questions about the ideological and symbolic means of perpetuating discrimination. Separatism is incompatible with the development of mixed sports and with the potential for direct power sharing between men and women or between individuals with different sexual identities. It is a particular problem because it tends to be advocated dogmatically and in a way which celebrates exclusionist policies and differences between people. Separatism excludes not only men, but many women as well and in its aggressive forms has failed to break down conventional and rigid sexual stereotypes which limit both sexes. It neglects, also, to look at ways in which women and men are exploited *together* in sport and how gender relations articulate with capitalist relations.

## Capitalist Relations and Gender Relations

Explanations of women's oppression in sport which emphasize biological differences make a number of theoretical omissions. Opposing men to women seriously underestimates, or even ignores, other dimensions of female oppression connected with such factors as class, economics, politics, and ideology. Such constructions tend to be resistant to the idea that men may also be oppressed and that gender relates in various ways to features of the social totality. It has been argued that macho models of sport which celebrate the male/female distinction are brutalizing and limiting, both for young males who are inducted into them and for females who copy them (Boslooper & Hayes, 1973; Brohm, 1978; Hoch, 1972; Sabo & Runfola, 1980; Vinnai, 1978). Most of these writers suggest that sport is one of the major contexts in which sexuality is mediated and assert that sexual repression is necessary for the survival of capitalism. They stress that modern sport is a repository for dominant ideology in its celebration of ruthless competition, aggression, and violence and in its embodiment of elitism, nationalism, racism, militarism, imperialism, and sexism, and maintain that the machismo ethos of sport, by bonding men together, becomes a fundamental expression of male power and domination over women. Their arguments are supported by psychological explanations derived from Freudian theory and notions of sexual sublimation. Brohm (1978), for example, claims that, "It is mainly through the sublimation of sexual drives that the practice of competitive sport contributes to the reproduction of the social relations of production" (p. 56).

The focus is upon males and the way that, through sport, their sexuality is sublimated to the needs of work discipline. In other words, sport is presented as a substitute—a way of regulating male sexuality and diverting young men from sexual problems. The celebration of sporting images of aggressive masculinity evokes contrasting images of less active, less athletic females.

Although in these formulations anything to do with sexuality is presented as secondary to the economic imperatives of capitalism, nonetheless, it is difficult to see how they can avoid being labelled as examples of biological reductionism: They implicitly reduce explanations to the level of some notion of "normal sexuality" and "normal" male and female behavior. They also share a tendency to assume that the relationship between gender relations and sport is a static one which fails to account for ways in which images of sexuality in sport have changed with the development of industrial capitalism or that different forms of femininity and different forms of masculinity co-exist. Individuals are presented as if they are passive recipients of sexist ideology which, in turn, is employed as if it is "total," containing no oppositional elements or variations of any sport. In this way sexism becomes a straightforward product of capitalist sport and there is a failure throughout this literature to explore in detail the ways in which gender relations have been undeniably and intimately bound up with economic and class determinants in *different* and *complex* ways, and how the interrelationships between these categories have varied historically (Hall, 1985).

## Class and Sexuality

More recently, the debate in feminist sports literature has taken up these points and become more sophisticated. It has certain characteristics in common with the general debate between radical feminists and Marxist feminists. The focus is on whether patriarchy or capitalism is the primary reason for women's oppression. In the case of radical feminism, it is argued that if it is patriarchal ideology that produces systems of cultural, social, economic, and political control, then a transformation of capitalism would not necessarily do anything to change such structures of power (Eisenstein, 1979, p. 28). Examples of women in Communist states who are said to be still subordinated to men are used to support this claim (Eisenstein). In contrast, Marxist feminism challenges essentialist notions of human nature, asserting that class is the root cause of women's oppression, and that problems of anything to do with sexuality are secondary (Hartmann, 1979). Whereas radical feminists claim that male domination and female subordination are universal because sexism has its roots in the prior facts of human biology and not in capitalism, Marxist feminists argue that ideas about gender and sexual difference are socially constructed, that the causes are effects of oppression are different in different societies, and that the character and extent of female oppression have changed historically. Marxist feminists claim that positing the major social division to be between men and women obscures the specific forms of exploitation of women in capitalist societies and, in particular, class differences between women. In their view, sexism in sport is perceived to be a component of bourgeois ideology which underpins the sexual division of labor, essential to the stability of capitalism. Traditional Marxists do not believe that equality between the sexes in sport could ever be achieved under capitalism.

An increasing volume of feminist research in Britain is showing how women's access to leisure, in general, and to sport, specifically, is mediated by social class (Deem, 1986; Green et al., 1987; Griffin et al., 1982; Hargreaves, 1989a; Talbot, 1988; Wimbush, 1986). Although more working-class females are participating in sport than ever before, it is still the case that active participation in sport plays no part whatsoever in the lives of the majority of working-class women. Most women who participate in sport are middle-class, most of those who actively campaign for the rights of women in sport are middle class, and, almost certainly, the majority of the few women who hold positions of responsibility and power in sport are middle class, as are those who theorize about it.

Research which focuses on working-class women is linked to the more general feminist critique of the family and to the domestic labor debate, which has identified the economic significance of housework and the way in which it reproduces labor-power. It shows how the oppressive characteristics of the private sphere of the home and the demands of domestic labour and mothering limit women's leisure, in general, but affect working-class women to a greater extent than their middle-class counterparts. But we need to know more about the specific ways in which class inequalities accentuate gender inequalities in sport. We also need a more complex theoretical analysis which can deal with the connections between class, gender, and power to control sports resources, than either radical feminism or orthodox Marxist feminism provides. This is an issue which socialist feminism has been concerned with. Socialist feminism developed out of a desire to reassess orthodox Marxist theory on the position of women in order to understand the complexities of the relationship between, and the relative independence of, capitalist relations and gender relations (Banks, 1981; Barrett, 1982; Weir & Wilson, 1984).

## Applying Hegemony to Sport

In common with socialist feminists, there are sports theorists who have tried to avoid the determinisms of economist Marxist analyses which stress the manipulative features of sport and fail to consider the extent to which individuals may be free to pursue activities that are creative and liberating. They have turned to the work of Antonio Gramsci, and specifically to the concept of *hegemony*, in an attempt to explain theoretically the complexities of the relationship between freedom and constraint in sport (Clarke & Critcher, 1985; Hargreaves, 1986). Gramsci resists the idea that people are merely "puppets of the system" and keeps intact what is arguably the inherent humanism of Marxism and the sense of culture as a way of life imbued with systems of meanings and values which are actively created by individuals and groups. The concept of hegemony has been used to explain continuities *and* discontinuities in sport: The ways in which dominant meanings and interests which are inherited from past tradition engender opposition and have to be defended, while new meanings and different interests are constantly being worked out and struggled for. Configurations of power are never static, but part of a continual process of change which incorporates negotiation and accommodation.

Hegemony describes a form of control which is *persuasive*, rather than coercive. It is not, however, straightforward indoctrination, but the result of people's positive reactions to values and beliefs which, in specific social and historical situations, support established social relations and structures of power. The concept of hegemony recognizes instabilities and complexities in the forms of domination produced in different social settings, such as families, schools, the media, leisure, and sport, and recognizes the ways in which sport is inextricably linked to other aspects of culture and to significant economic, political, and social arrangements. However, it does not assume that culture is the "whole of society," but, rather, that it is analytically distinct from political and economic processes and that, together with them, it makes up the totality of social relations. Economic and cultural forces are assigned mutually constitutive roles, rather than the former having a determining effect upon the latter. The concept of hegemony proposes a dialectical relationship between individuals and society, accounting for ways in which individuals are both determined *and* determining, and it proposes that cultural experiences such as sport can be both exploitative *and* worthwhile.

Ideology is a key concept for hegemony theorists. Rooted in human "praxis," it is described as an essentially social activity in which ideas and meanings cannot be separated from action. New ideas about sport cannot *change* sport, they can only, possibly, *lead* to change; to become real they have to be put into practice, and hence the key to change is the way people produce their lives in common. Ideas and meanings evolve, show continuity, and undergo change, not because of their internal content, but because people interrelate with one another in particular social situations, such as sport. Ideology is concerned with the creation, as well as the diffusion, of meaning. Dominant ideology produces cultural continuity, but dominant ideas are never the only ones, and there is always the potential for the development of oppositional ideas which can subvert the dominant ones and lead to cultural change.

By applying the concept of hegemony to an analysis of sport, its history can be read as a series of struggles for power between dominant and subordinate groups, and the concept of hegemony has been used to explain conflicts of interest over unequal sports resources in specific historical and social contexts. However, the theorists who have applied the concept of hegemony to their analyses of sport concentrate on antagonistic class relations. When reference is made to the relationship between class and gender, and even to the way that class and gender divisions are constructed together, there have been no attempts to explore this relationship rigorously or to look at the specific complexities of male hegemony in sport. Because of the relative silence about gender divisions in these accounts, there is an implication that class is the root cause of women's as well as men's oppression in sport, and that the problems of gender are secondary.

## Male Hegemony in Sport

I have suggested before that it is possible to apply the concept of hegemony specifically to male leadership and domination of sport (1986). Male interests predominate in most sports, and in many of them male hegemony has probably been more complete and more resistant to change than in other areas of culture. Nonetheless, male hegemony in sport has never been static and absolute, but is a constantly shifting process which incorporates both reactionary *and* liberating features of gender relations. The concept of male hegemony recognizes the advantages experienced by men, in general, in relation to women, but recognizes, also, the inability of men to gain total control. In sport, women are not totally manipulated, and it is misleading to treat either men or women as homogeneous groups. Some men and some women support, accommodate to, or collude in existing patterns of discrimination in sport that are specific to capitalism and to male domination, while other men and women oppose them and struggle for change. Male hegemony is not a simple male vs. female opposition, which is how it is often presented: To be opposed to male domination in sport is not the same thing as being opposed to men.

Sport is thus conceived as a constitutive process—part of life that is structured by society and history, but also the result of actions and changing relationships. In this formulation, consciousness is not passive, but incomplete, inconsistent and transitory. Neither is sport as an "all-or-nothing" phenomenon as determinist interpretations imply, but an area of life that contains numerous contradictions. Male hegemony is incomplete and the socialization of individuals into stereotypical gender roles is imperfect so that there is neither absolute incorporation into existing gender divisions in sport or total rejection of them.

The crux of feminist criticisms of orthodox Marxism is that sexual categories are not intrinsic to Marxist concepts, but have only been appended to them. It is argued, therefore, that orthodox Marxism fails to account for the complexities and contradictions in sport which embody specific economic and political arrangements and which intimately intersect with such factors as class, age, and ethnicity, as well as gender. Hegemony theory may provide a better framework for understanding how, in sport, as in other cultural activities, gender relations are part of a complex process specific to capitalist social relations. It can also deal with the complexities of the relationship between, and the relative independence of, capitalist relations and patriarchal relations.

## Making Women's Sport Political

Socialism and feminism are concerned with liberation. Class oppression and sexual oppression have been two major forms of oppression in human history; socialist feminists want to abolish both and are seeking a theory which does not subordinate one to the other. Michele Barrett (1982) explains:

> The contemporary Women's Liberation Movement has, by and large, rejected the possibility that our oppression is caused by either naturally given sex differences or economic factors alone. We have asserted the importance of consciousness, ideology, imagery and symbolism for our battles. Definitions of femininity and masculinity, as well as the social meaning of family life and sexual division of labour, are constructed on this ground. Feminism has

politicized everyday life—culture in the anthropological sense of the lived practices of a society—to an unparalleled degree. Feminism has also politicized the various forms of artistic and imaginative expression that are more popularly known as culture, reassessing and transforming film, art, the theatre and so on. (p. 41)

The concern with *meanings* which this quotation articulates is intrinsic to cultural politics, but has been almost entirely absent from feminist theories of sport. For example, very little is known about the specific configurations which maintain, or break down, male hegemony in sport, or the ways in which meanings in sport are produced, reproduced, resisted, and changed. Sportswomen as a whole have not been enthusiastic feminists, and feminist intervention in sport has lagged behind feminist attempts to "politicize" other areas of culture. However, this is changing, and sport is becoming part of a larger movement for female autonomy. The most dynamic feminism arises from personal experience and the most radical challenges for women's sport have been practical ones. Women are taking action and producing new versions of sport for themselves, which supports the view of sport as a constitutive, creative process, and presents an optimistic vision of the potential of women to transcend practical and symbolic forms of oppression in sport. But it is a struggle. Advances are not inevitable—there is incorporation, opposition, and failure. Sport is a site for freedom and constraint: It produces new opportunities and meanings for women and it reproduces prejudices and oppression.

Freedom for women in sport is visionary, and constraint looks back to the past. The history of women's sport can provide an understanding of the origins and causes of women's subordination in sport, and of the nature of resistance to change and struggle for change. A historical perspective is essential to understand how residual forms of sport for women co-exist with dominant and emergent ones. By looking at the experience of women historically, we can better understand male experience and the whole of the history of sport. Analyses of sport which can help to change it must incorporate experience, history, and social arrangements.

## Damaged Men

But freedom for women in sport is inextricably linked to freedom for men as well. Men have been described as "both guarantor and victim" of patriarchy (Reynaud, 1983, p. 114), and recent work on men and masculinities has been written by men who reject dominant ideas about their sex and are struggling to redefine them because, in their words, "Our power in society as men not only oppresses women but also imprisons us in a deadening masculinity which cripples our relationships— with each other, with women, with ourselves" (Segal, 1990, p. 287).

Men are seen as victims in the sense that our society forces them in a very brutal way to subjugate their sensitivities in favor of aggressive displays of masculinity and, as Messner (1987) argues, sport has become one of the most important channels for this process in a society where traditional male roles are in crisis. As he puts it, "Both on a personal/existential level for athletes and on a symbolic/ideological level for spectators and fans, sport has become one of the 'last bastions' of male power and superiority over—and separation from—the "feminization" of society (p. 54).

Some men who have sensed the brutalization of their own subjectivities have actively rejected aggressive competitive sports, but many others have been humiliated and suffered a sense of failure of manliness by being incapable of meeting the demands of traditional male sports and thus exclude themselves from sport altogether and miss out. Such experiences highlight the importance of this suggestion:

> . . . since the sports world is an important arena that serves partly to socialize boys and young men to hierarchical, competitive, and aggressive values, it is also an important context within which to confront the need for a humanization of men. (Messner 1987, p. 65-66)

Sex-role stereotyping in sport impoverishes both men and women: few of either sex have a wide and fulfilling range of movement experiences—those that are energetic, powerful, skillful, and exciting and those that are more expressive and sensuous, using the body with delicacy and flexibility. We need to examine more closely the lived complexities of men's as well as women's sporting experiences and the changing forms of masculinities and femininities in sport which are linked to changing values. Although many men in sport may be agents of oppression, men are not inherently oppressive and they have a primary role to play, with women, to eliminate in sport uneven gender divisions, the construction of chauvinist masculine identities, the treatment of women as sex objects, and the sexual harassment of women. Bell Hooks writes that, ''(Men) should share equally in resistance struggles. In particular men have a tremendous contribution to make to feminist struggle in the area of exposing, confronting, opposing, and transforming the sexism of their male peers'' (Quoted in Hearn, 1984, p. 24).

## Strategies for Change

The struggle against sexism and uneven gender divisions in sport should not suspend opposition to other differences and oppressions; we need to be clear and committed in our opposition and not apologetic and falsely tolerant about inhumane and unethical practices. We should work fiercely in sport for values that enrich not just the lives of individuals, but the fabric society. I would want to see more sports groups concerning themselves with, for example, environmental issues, aligning themselves with the German initiative ''Sportsmen and Women for Peace'' (Hargreaves, 1989b), speaking out openly against apartheid sport, and resisting government practices that are discriminatory, such as the British government's legislation to privatize leisure resources.

Chas Critcher (1986) has suggested that ''the only way to reform sport is to convert it into something else that ceases to be sport'' (p. 342). But, although there are numerous sportsmen and sportswomen who, in common with him, see little value in mainstream sport that has inhumane and destructive characteristics and who have a vision of how sport might change, the idea tends to remain at the level of theoretical discourse and is seldom put into practice. Not surprisingly, it is an idea which has never been treated seriously by those who are in entrenched positions of power in sport and resistant to fundamental change.

In the past, there has been a virtual absence of a unity between those who participate in sport and those who theorize about it, but now this link is being forged. From the 1950s, male standards in sports sociology became generalized standards, and women were evaluated by men, and evaluated themselves according to criteria created by men. Taking a critical stance now by placing women at the center is giving theory a new direction enabling men and women to deconstruct popular ideas and stereotypes which have been taken for granted and which have limited people for generations. Both theory and practice are contested spheres and are constantly changing and the unity between them is essential for the ''politicization'' of experience. This is different from liberal reformism. But gaining power is necessary for those who seek change and power comes from organization. For women to become a political force in sport, there must be an organization to attract them to the movement and to gain support to fight and win campaigns. The Women's Sports Foundation in the UK is a national association, inaugurated in 1985, which, in part, fulfills this role (Hargreaves, 1989a, p. 145). It works to politicize women's sport and to unite the theory and practice of women's sport in order to subvert male domination. It has made links with community and alternative sports ventures which are intended to be enjoyable, inexpensive, and non-elitist to a much greater extent than its American counterpart which is involved more in mainstream sport. But because the politics of sport is to do with struggles over resources, inextricably linked to political, economic, and ideological structures, the Women's Sports Foundation in the UK has only been able to acquire a shoe-string budget from the Sports Council and one commercial sponsor and its biggest resource is the creativity and energy of its members.

But although women share experiences and meanings which unite them as a group, there are also a great many differences between them. In addition to class, other factors, such as ethnicity, marital status, occupation, age, disability, and sexual orientation affect women's involvement in sport and point to ways in which women's sport derives meaning from the totality of social relations. All these categories are important to a proper analysis of women's sport which will enable change to occur. Although the sports feminist movement in the UK does not appear at present to represent authentically the needs of all women, there is growing concern to develop a broad base of women's sport which will incorporate the interests of those with diverse and special needs and varied backgrounds. Black sports feminists and lesbian sports feminists, for example, argue that power and oppression in sport derive from race and sexuality, as well as class and gender, and that their specific needs should be taken into account. Coordinating the efforts of feminist theorists and those involved in sports practice in such struggles provides the potential for understanding the limits and possibilities of female sport, based on actual social practices.

Sports feminists, in general, believe that women should be mobilized to change their life-styles and take part in sport because it provides unique opportunities for them to experience their bodies in an active, sensuous way, providing physical confidence, enjoyment, and fulfillment. However, there are differences about how such an idea might be implemented, related to ethical considerations and the larger structures of power.

Gender in sport is deeply contradictory and complex: Women are oppressed by men in sport, both women and men are oppressed in sport, and women and men experience freedom in sport. But definitions of oppression and freedom are not straightforward—they relate to the values which people hold and the context which they are in, which, in turn, affects what they do. The choices facing sports feminists are similar to those facing feminists involved in other aspects of culture:

1. Co-option into a male sphere of activity
2. A separatist all-female strategy
3. A co-operative venture with men for qualitative new models in which differences in the sexes are unimportant

I favor the third option—for resources to be concentrated on participatory, co-operative ventures to regulate and control sports competition in order to maximize its "valuable" elements and minimize its "destructive" ones. By stressing recreation, health, a full range of physical skills, and sensuous pleasure in movement, a practical and ideological shift away from an aggressive, male-dominated competitive model of sport would result. To some extent this is happening already, but the greatest power to control sport is still vested with men who hold traditional attitudes and who are involved in traditional sports; it is unrealistic to argue that entrenched practices which are underpinned by political and economic power can easily be changed. Since each of the strategies outlined above can help to break down male privilege in sport and open the way for greater autonomy for women, it may be more radical and expedient to encourage the development of women's sport in all these ways than to assert that only one approach is worthwhile. Such a philosophy embodies a creative tension. It recognizes the problems of change, but does not pretend to be neutral.

# References

*Arena Review*: Special Issue on Women's Sport (1984), Vol. 18, No. 2.

Banks, O. (1981). *Faces of feminism: A study of feminism as a social movement*. Oxford: Martin Robertson.

Barrett, M. (1982). Feminism and the definition of cultural politics. In R. Brunt (Ed.), *Feminism, culture and politics*. London: Lawrence and Wishart.

Bell Hooks (1987). Quoted in *The gender of oppression: Men, masculinity and the critique of Marxism* (p. 24) by J. Hearn, Brighton: Wheatscheaf.

Bennett, R.S., Whitaker, K.G., Woolley Smith, N.J., & Sablove, A. (1987). Changing the rules of the game: Reflections toward a feminist analysis of sport. *Women's Studies International Forum*, **10**(4).

Birrell, S., & Richter, D.M. (1987). Is a diamond forever?: Feminist transformations of sport. *Women's International Forum*, **10**(4).

Boslooper, T., & Hayes, M. (1973). *The femininity game*. New York: Stein and Day.

Boutilier, M.A., & San Giovanni, L. (1983). *The sporting woman*. Champaign, IL: Human Kinetics.

Brohm, J.M. (1978). *Sport: A prison of measured time.* London: Ink. Links.

Clarke, S. (1988). *Women and leisure.* Unpublished BSc dissertation, University of Surrey.

Clarke, J., & Critcher, C. (1985). *The devil makes work. Leisure in capitalist Britain.* London: Macmillan.

Coakley, J.J. (rep. 1989). *Sport in society: Issues and controversies.* St. Louis: C.V. Mosby.

Coakley, J.J., & Westkott, M. (1984). Opening doors for women in sport: An alternative to old strategies. In Eitzen, D.S., *Sport in contemporary society* (pp. 385-400). New York: St. Martin's Press.

Critcher, C. (1986). Radical theorists of sport: The state of play. *Sociology of Sport Journal,* **3**, 333-343.

Deem, R. (1986). *All work and no play?: The sociology of women and leisure.* Milton Keynes: Open University Press.

Dyer, K.F. (1982). *Catching up the men.* London: Junction Books.

Fasting, K. (1987). Sports and women's culture. *Women's Studies International Forum,* **10**(4).

Ferris, L. (1981). Attitudes to women in sport: prolegomena towards a sociological theory. *Equal Opportunities International* **1**(2), 32-39. London: Equal Opportunities Commission.

Firestone, S. (1979). *The dialectic of sex.* London: The Women's Press. *General Household Surveys,* London, H.M.S.O.

Gerber, E.R., Felshin, J., Berlin, P., & Wyrick, W. (1974). *The American woman in sport.* Reading, MA: Addison-Wesley.

Green, E., Hebron, S., & Woodward, D. (1987). *Leisure and gender: A study of Sheffield women's experiences.* (Final Report to the ESRC/Sports Council Joint Panel on Leisure Research). London: Sports Council.

Griffin, C., Hobson, D., Macintosh, S., & McCabe, T. (1982). Women and leisure. In Hargreaves, J.A. (Ed.), *Sport, culture and ideology.* London: Routledge and Kegan Paul.

Hall, M.A. (1985). How should we theorize sport in a capitalist patriarchy? *International Review for the Sociology of Sport,* **20**(1/2).

Hall, M.A. (1988). The discourse of gender and sport: From femininity to feminism. *Sociology of Sport Journal,* **5**, 330-340.

Hargreaves, J. (1979). *Playing like gentlemen while behaving like ladies: The social significance of physical activity for females in late nineteenth century and early twentieth century Britain.* Unpublished MA dissertation, University of London.

Hargreaves, J. (1984). Women and the Olympic phenomenon. In A. Tomlinson and G. Whannel (Eds.), *The five ring circus* (pp. 53-70). London: Pluto Press.

Hargreaves, J. (1985). Competition—A question of ethics. *Sportswoman,* **1**(1).

Hargreaves, J. (1986). Where's the virtue? Where's the grace? A discussion of the social reproduction of gender through sport. *Theory, Culture and Society,* **3**(1).

Hargreaves, J. (1987). Victorian familism and the formative years of female sport. In J.A. Mangan and R. Parkes, *From fair sex to feminism.* London: Frank Cass.

Hargreaves, J. (1989a). The promise and problems of women's leisure and sport. In C. Rojek (Ed.), *Leisure for leisure.* London: Macmillan.

Hargreaves, J. (1989b). Peace: A challenge for sport. *Sport and Leisure,* March-April.

Hargreaves, J. (1990). Sex, gender and the body in sport and leisure: Has there been a civilizing process? In E. Dunning and C. Rojeck (Eds.), *Sport and leisure in the civilizing process.* London: Macmillan.

Hartmann, H. (1979). The unhappy marriage of Marxism and feminism: Towards a more progressive union. *Capital and Class.* No. 8.

Hearn, J. (1984). *The gender of oppression: Men, masculinity and the critique of Marxism.* Brighton: Wheatsheaf.

Hoch, P. (1972). *Rip off the big game.* New York: Doubleday.

Kaplan, J. (1979). *Women and sports.* New York: Viking.

Kimmel, M. (1987). *Changing men: New directions in research on men and masculinity.* London: Sage.

Klafs, C.E., & Lyon, M.J. (1978). *The female athlete: Conditioning, competition and culture.* Saint Louis: V.V. Mosby.

Lenksky, H. (1986). *Out of bounds.* Toronto, Ontario: The Women's Press.

Messner, M. (1987). The life of a man's seasons: Male identity in the life course of the jock. In M. Kimmel. *Changing men: New directions in research on men and masculinity.* London: Sage.

Miles, S., & Middleton, C. (1989). Girls' education in the balance: The ERA and inequality. In M. Flude and M. Hammer, (Eds.), *The 1988 education reform act: Its origins and implications.* Lewis: Falmer.

Millett, K. (1971). *Sexual politics.* London: Sphere.

Oglesby, C.A. (1978). *Women and sport: From myth to reality.* Philadelphia: Lea and Febiger.

Pannick, D. (1983). *Sex discrimination in sport.* London: Equal Opportunity Commission.

Parkhouse, B.L., & Lapin, J. (1980). *Women who win.* Englewood Cliffs, NJ: Prentice Hall.

Reynaud, E. (1983). *Holy virility: The social construction of masculinity.* London: Pluto, quoted in Hearn, op cit.

Sabo, D.F., & Runfola, R. (1980). *Jock: Sports and male identity.* Englewood Cliffs, NJ: Prentice Hall.

Scraton, S. (1986). Images of femininity and the teaching of girls' physical education. In J. Evans, (Ed.). *Physical education, sport and schooling.* Brighton: Falmer Press.

Segal, L. (1990). *Slow motion: Changing masculinities, changing men.* London: Virago Press. *Social Trends.* London: H.M.S.O.

Sports Council (1982). *Sport in the community: The next ten years.* London: Sports Council.

Sports Council (1985). *Women and sport statement.* London: Sports Council.

Sports Council (1988). *Sport in the community: Into the nineties.* London: Sports Council.

Talbot, M. (1988). Understanding the relationships between women and sport: The contribution of British feminist approaches in leisure and cultural studies. *International Review for the Sociology of Sport,* **23**(1).

Theberge, N. (1985). Toward a feminist alternative to sport as a male preserve. *Quest,* **37**, 193-202.

Thompson, S.M. (1988). Challenging the hegemony: New Zealand women's opposition to rugby and the reproduction of a capitalist patriarchy. *International Review for the Sociology of Sport,* **23**(3).

Twin, S.L. (Ed.) (1979). *Out of the bleachers.* New York: The Feminist Press.

Vinnai, G. (1978). *Football mania.* London: Ocean Books.

Weir, A., & Wilson, E. (1984). The British women's movement. *New Left Review,* No. 148.

White, A., & Brackenridge, C. (1984). Who rules sport? Gender divisions in the power structure of British sports organisations from 1960. Paper presented at the *Olympic Scientific Conference,* University of Oregon.

Willis, P. (1982). Women in sport in ideology. In J.A. Hargreaves, (Ed.). *Sport, culture and ideology.* London: Routledge and Kegan Paul.

Wimbush, E. (1986). *Women, leisure and well-being.* Edinburgh: Centre for Leisure Research, Dunfermline College.

Wimbush, E., & Talbot, M. (Eds.) (1988). *Relative freedoms.* Milton Keynes: Open University Press.

# CHAPTER 9

# Labor Relations in Sport: Central Issues in Their Emergence and Structure in High-Performance Sport

*Rob Beamish*

Even before the 1988 Summer Olympic Games in Seoul, Canada's high-performance sport system had already attracted international attention, particularly among the Western bloc countries. In fact, long before Ben Johnson's positive test for stanozolol, Canada was frequently referred to as the East Germany of the West by athletes, coaches, and sport officials. The moniker was not due to drug use or Canada's athletic success; it was based on the fact that Canada's federal government had become extremely involved in its high-performance sport system.[1] Canada took steps in 1970 that led to the centralization, rationalization, and professionalization of its high-performance sport system to improve Canadian performances in international competition and to meet a number of federal government objectives related to national unity, international prestige, job creation, and the enhancement of the federal government's image among voters (see Cavanagh, 1985; Hallett, 1981; Macintosh, Bedecki, & Franks, 1987, pp. 42-55).

Although Canada's professionalized, high-performance sport bureaucracy can be examined from a variety of perspectives and with numerous questions in mind, the focus here is the changing character of the relationship between Canada's high-performance athletes on one side and the National Sport Organizations (NSOs) and Sport Canada on the other. Although the actual structure of Canada's high-performance sport system is complex, the major organizations are the following. First, the federal government (through the cabinet) allocates money to an arm's-length federal agency called Sport Canada. Sport Canada then uses some of this money to fund its own operations and distributes the remainder among more than

80 NSOs and a number of other organizations, such as the Coaching Association of Canada (CAC), the Canadian Sport and Fitness Administration Centre, and the Sport Medicine Council, to name only the most important (see Dubin, 1990, pp. 17-40 for a more detailed overview).

Although the Canadian situation serves as a case study regarding labor relations in high-performance sport, this chapter has relevance to more than a Canadian audience, because the trends and conditions described herein are now found in many Western bloc high-performance sport systems.

# The Emergence of the Athlete/Sport Administration Relationship in Canada

High-performance sport in the contemporary period has been constituted and is continually reconstituted by agents employing the same dominant hegemonic practices that pervade the industrialized, liberal democratic societies of today. That is, high-performance sport exists within and continually constitutes and reconstitutes a social environment that is dominated by an instrumentally rational approach to problem-solving (where science and technology are continually and creatively drawn upon to attain particular ends, and most social action takes place within large, bureaucratically organized institutions).[2] It is within this general environment that Canada's high-performance sport system was originally conceived and developed. It is also this worldview and its associated practices that NSO volunteers and professional administrators, government public servants, athletes, and coaches draw on in their sport-related activities.

## 1968-1973: Obligation-Free Scholarships

Prior to 1968, federal government involvement in high-performance sport in Canada was minimal. Leading up to 1968, however, Canadian success in international competition—particularly in hockey—had declined, and the federal Liberal party included in its 1968 election platform a promise to improve Canada's performances in international sport (see Macintosh et al., 1987, pp. 42-54). Promising to establish a national sports policy, Prime Minister Pierre Trudeau's Liberal government used the report of its 1968 Task Force on Sport (Task Force on Sport, 1969) to develop the *Proposed Sports Policy for Canadians* (Munro, 1970).

The policy established an arm's-length bureaucracy (Sport Canada) to coordinate Canada's high-performance sport system and a centralized Sport and Recreation Center that provided office space, printing facilities, and operating funds so NSOs could hire executive directors and develop more professional organizations. The policy also committed the government to the "Grants-in-Aid" program, which provided financial assistance to selected athletes in Canada. This new infrastructure and funding program unwittingly set in motion a chain of events and decisions that ultimately led to the emergence of a labor/management relationship between Canada's high-performance athletes and Sport Canada and the NSOs.

Through the Grants-in-Aid program initiated by the Proposed Sports Policy, the federal government agreed to allocate a maximum of $1,500 annually to selected athletes who were nominated for consideration by each NSO. Each grant, the *Proposed Sports Policy* noted, would "not be the usual athletic scholarship, the type that has so many conditions that it might as well be a business contract" (Munro, 1970, p. 14). However, Fitness and Amateur Sport (FAS)—the government department ultimately responsible for the distribution of funds to the sport system—became concerned, shortly after the introduction of the program, about Canada's potential medal performance in the 1972 Games. FAS then introduced its "Off the Top" program, which provided $2,000 for a very select group of athletes who, based on their performances, had demonstrated medal potential. This program was the first indication that the federal government could not afford the political costs of an athlete-funding program that was not performance-oriented. The magnanimity of the first program did not last long at all.

In addition to the fact that the Grants-in-Aid program was the first time that the federal government had provided funds to help athletes defray some of their training and competitive costs, there are two additional features of importance about the program. First, the Grants-in-Aid program only supported students; this decision would, by default more than anything else, have a dominant influence in the development and shaping of future federal government funding programs.

Second, by assuming that athletes were essentially students first and athletes second, FAS was implicitly drawing on what was by that time virtually a residual ethos of amateurism within the Olympic Movement; it assumed that international competition was a phase in athletes' lives through which they would pass as they moved on to their "real" careers. As a result, the ideology of amateurism lay at the foundation of Canada's first high-performance athlete funding programs, and this residual ideology continues to exert a strong influence.

Prior to 1973, although the federal government of Canada had introduced funding for high-performance athletes, the athletes themselves continued to compete mainly for rewards of social status in prestige and not remuneration. FAS linked its Grants-in-Aid funding to the athletes' positions in the formal education system by directing more money to university athletes than community college students, who in turn received more than high school students. FAS did not insist on a link between performance and the receipt of the grant once the NSOs had nominated athletes for funding (although some NSOs may have used performance criteria in choosing nominees). Finally, with the exception of the Off the Top program introduced in 1971, athletes had only to prove their educational status to receive Grants-in-Aid funding once they had been selected—the grants were essentially obligation-free scholarships.

## 1973-1976: The Athlete Hothouse

Between 1973 and 1976 Sport Canada and the Canadian Olympic Association (COA) undertook the first major actions that would lead, eventually, to the contracting of athletes' specialized skills and the linking of funding with performance. Part of the impetus for these new COA and Sport Canada programs lay in the internal dynamics of Canada's emerging high-performance system, but they were also shaped by important and long-standing forces for change within the international economy in general and their resultant impact on the international sport system as a whole.

During the post-war consolidation of monopoly capitalism, transnational firms reduced their economic competition with one another in the realm of prices and shifted their competition to the ''sales effort.'' That is, under conditions of monopoly or oligopoly, transnational firms did not try to increase their share of a particular market by price cutting; instead they engaged in an all-out effort to entice consumers to purchase their products irrespective of cost (see Baran & Sweezy, 1966; Mandel, 1975). Thus, throughout the 1950s and with escalating vigor in the 1960s, transnational firms attempted to expand their markets through a barrage of information, publicity, and propaganda designed to stimulate consumer demand. In short, advertising became a, if not the, central feature of the post-war economy during these two decades.

Television played a crucial role in the long-term development of post-war capitalism because it produced the large audiences that the transnationals required to spread their message. But television itself needed a product of sufficiently high caliber to attract the mass audiences that it would then sell to the transnationals as targets for their commercial sponsors. Sport—especially major championships like the Olympic Games—turned out to be an excellent vehicle for amassing a large audience of consumers with considerable spending power.

Within this context, professional and high-performance sport provided very different attractions for audiences. ''National'' professional sport businesses like the National Football League, the National Hockey League, or professional baseball drew large audiences through the drama of a season of performances that led into playoffs. This provided advertisers with a large audience of consumers over an extended season with the key attraction located in the unfolding of the standings and the emergent playoff action. There was a different elective affinity between television's need for audiences and the entertainment package provided by high-performance sport. The attraction in international sport, with its single-event format, was not the unfolding of a seasonal drama but the raw spectacle of peak human performance. This put very different demands on the high-performance sport system in general and the athletes in particular.

Television's ''demand'' for a continuous supply of record-breaking, world-class performances that would attract large audiences—particularly in the United States—meant that the entire system had to become more efficient (i.e., more professionalized).[3] To succeed as a viable entity in the post-war period of televised sport, high-performance sport needed athletes who could perform at the limits of human possibility. To meet this imperative, athletes required an increasingly wide array of professional support services—coaches, technical experts, and various administrative supports—and they had to train more extensively and intensively. To train on that scale required increasingly larger sums of money. This could be acquired in four ways: personal or family resources, a patron, the state, or the marketplace itself. The latter had an unavoidable performance imperative and state funding in most nations either always had or progressively began to acquire a performance imperative as well. The first two were options for a small handful of athletes, although the majority of high-performance athletes in the liberal democracies would draw heavily on family resources in the developmental stages of their careers and continue to use family funds as a vital supplement to other sources of remuneration.

While there was a performance imperative for the athletes in the emergent world of televised, commercialized, high-performance sport, there was also a performance imperative for the Olympic Movement as a whole. Without a world-class product, transnational corporations and thus television corporations would rapidly lose interest in high-performance sport as a spectacle. As a result, in the late 1960s a number of forces began to coalesce and reshape the international high-performance sport system. These forces included the following:

- The commercial imperatives of the transnationals outlined previously
- The need for superior human performances in the Games to ensure (and increase) the market value of the Olympic Games, which the International Olympic Committee (IOC) could then capitalize on in negotiations with the television networks
- The potential market value that a world championship held for an athlete through advertising contracts and commercial endorsements
- The ever-increasing standard of athletic performance needed to win championships as commercial endorsements became increasingly attractive to more and more athletes and as state sponsorship of athletes increased
- The willingness of governments to supply increasing amounts of resources to their international athletes to ensure success and international prestige
- The logic of an instrumentally rational, scientifically technological, bureaucratic society (see also Prokop, 1971)

In short, *Citius, Altius, Fortius* became, during the 1960s and early 1970s, a commercial and political imperative while its human-performance aspect placed even greater demands on the athletes themselves.

By the late 1960s, the trend toward the professionalization of all aspects of the high-performance sport system and its concomitant commercialization and politicization had created a crisis around the concept of "amateurism." This crisis, felt most acutely in downhill skiing in the late 1960s, resulted, in 1974, in the IOC's decision to drop the amateur clause from its *Charter* and leave all questions of eligibility to each International Sport Federation. The amateur clause was replaced by "Eligibility Rule 26" in 1971, but this rule was extremely restrictive and simply formalized Avery Brundage's desire to keep the Games amateur. The 1974 change in the Eligibility Rule led to the liberalization of who could take part in the Games. The new Eligibility Rule allowed athletes in many sports to receive payment for living and training expenses without losing eligibility for Olympic competition.

The change in the eligibility criteria obviously stands out as a watershed in the history of the Games in view of the impact it had on the subsequent escalation in the professionalization, commercialization, and politicization of high-performance sport. Less obviously, it helped create an environment in which labor relations would become an important feature in this sphere of "nonprofessional" sport.

While the dominant hegemonic forces and practices described here changed the world of high-performance sport in an irrevocable fashion, the residual ideology of the amateur athlete still remained. This legacy has proven to be one of the greatest moral and personal contradictions that modern high-performance athletes must address, and is one of the largest obstacles that prevents athletes from gaining their full, legitimate rights as employees of the countries for which they compete.

Against this background, athletes in Canada between 1973 and 1976 still sought positions on national teams for reasons of status, although other motivations were now possible. At the same time, leaders in Canada's high-performance sport system articulated a position that implied that Canada had to perform well in the 1976 Montreal Games. This need led Sport Canada and the COA to devise incentive-based programs to secure medals at the Games. As a result, Sport Canada and the COA added three new funding programs during the 1973 to 1976 period to complement the Grants-in-Aid program.

The first and most significant of the programs initiated in the early 1970s was introduced in 1972 by the COA and joined by the federal government a year later. Game Plan '76 was designed to improve Canadian performances at the 1976 Olympic Games; it was an explicitly performance-based athlete funding program. Athletes were ranked and funded on the basis of international performance. An "A Card" athlete had to rank among the top eight in the world and received $1,000 per year. "B Cards" went to athletes who ranked from 9th to 16th in the world and received $700 per year. Athletes with international potential received a "National Card" worth $300 a year. Game Plan required that athletes would complete a training program designed to yield medal-winning results. Finally, athletes signed statements of intent to complete the expected training program (Beamish & Borowy, 1987).

Second, in view of the international changes in high-performance sport described previously, a group of Canadian athletes lobbied the federal government in 1975 for additional funds to support Canada's high-performance athletes' training programs. Based on the results of two surveys conducted by athletes, it was apparent that Canadian athletes were struggling to train full-time while living well below the government's low-income cutoff line (popularly referred to as the poverty line) (Beamish & Borowy, 1987). These efforts resulted in two additional COA-sponsored programs from 1973 to 1976—the *Olympic Training Support Program* (OTS) and the *Lost Time Payments Program* (LTP).

The OTS program offered financial support in cases of demonstrated need to athletes preparing for the Olympic Games. In addition to need, the COA tied funds to the athletes' performances and to the athletes' commitments to an "acceptable" training program. The athletes completed an extensive needs survey and implicitly agreed to complete their training programs. OTS supplied athletes with, on average, $200 worth of support per month (Beamish & Borowy, 1987).

The LTP program reimbursed athletes whose training commitments forced them to take leaves of absence, without pay, from work. LTP provided athletes with up to $50 per day for a maximum of 75 days. Once again, the COA expected athletes to carry out a well-developed training program. The COA, NSO, and the athletes' employers signed contracts that approved the athletes' applications and established the conditions that would allow the athletes to train (Beamish & Borowy, 1987).

Sport Canada continued the Grants-in-Aid program from 1973 to 1976 but included a number of small yet significant changes. First, the grants were soon tied to athlete obligations with the NSOs and Sport Canada. Second, the NSOs were more selective in allocating grants to national and international level athletes. These trends led, in 1975, to the development of a more rationalized selection procedure, a slightly less open-ended statement of competitive obligations, and an explicit statement about the right of Sport Canada to withdraw funds from any athlete who failed to meet the conditions of the program by dropping out of school or failing to progress satisfactorily in his or her sport. As a result, the Grants-in-Aid program gradually shifted away from its original pre-1973 obligation-free status (Beamish & Borowy, 1987).

Overall, the 1973 to 1976 period involved a slow but certain movement toward contracting athletes' specialized capacities for athletic performance. Most significantly, the dominant practices in international high-performance sport placed continual pressure on Canadian athletes, Sport Canada, and the NSOs to provide greater resources and opportunities for athletes to train full-time. While this resulted in some increases in the funds available to athletes, it simultaneously created the conditions whereby administrators wanted increased control over them. In other words, as athletes enjoyed marginal gains in financial support, they paid for them through the growth of a sport bureaucracy that would monitor their performances and establish more and more formal regulations regarding their training and performances.

Thus, even though the number of funding programs increased from one in 1973 to four in 1976, there were ties between funding and international ranking (though it was more explicit in some programs than others) and more and more obligations tied to each program than existed prior to 1973. Accordingly, one of the most important outcomes of the 1973 to 1976 period was the significant increase in resources that sport administrators—especially Sport Canada's administrators—had to shape the entire development of the sport system. This model of a professional bureaucracy organizing and controlling the high-performance sport system was consistent with the dominant hegemonic practices within Canada during this period. Nevertheless, this fact should not prevent one from noting that this type of development was only *one possibility* and others, under different dominant, hegemonic practices could have been advanced.

Finally, the development of a professionalized sport bureaucracy established the objective conditions for the management/employee labor relations system that developed during the next ten years. Had the sport system developed differently—had there been a genuine coalition between the athletes, volunteer administrators, and government public servants, for example—then the labor relations situation that now exists would have been significantly different.

## 1977-1992: Wage Scales and Contracts

Between 1977 and 1992, athlete funding underwent three major changes. First, all funding programs were rationalized under the Athletes' Assistance Program (AAP) and controlled and directed exclusively by Sport Canada. Second, the criteria for AAP selection became more selective, and athletes' obligations were increased. Third, a contractually binding relationship between the athletes, the NSOs, and Sport Canada was created.

When Sport Canada consolidated all its funding programs under the AAP, it did not leave the AAP unchanged. On the contrary, once it had consolidated all athlete funding programs under the AAP by 1980, Sport Canada initiated a number of significant changes. First, Sport Canada began to slowly eliminate need as a criterion for funding, although it continued to fund athletes living at home at a lower level than athletes with comparable card status living away from home.

The second major change is the most significant with respect to labor relations in Canada's high-performance sport system. In 1980, Sport Canada indicated (in its *Guide to the Athletes' Assistance Program*) that it was developing a "National Sport Organization/Athlete Agreement" (Sport Canada, 1980, pp. 13-14). The major objective behind the 1980 rationalization of athlete funding was Sport Canada's desire to establish a more cost-effective funding system. Associated with this objective was the desire to ensure that athletes clearly understood the obligations and expectations that Sport Canada attached to AAP funding. This objective would be met by the NSO/Athlete Agreement.

In concert with the above changes in the funding system, Sport Canada introduced a High Performance Assistance Bonus in 1982 (See Beamish & Borowy, 1987, pp. 19-20). Through this bonus—a significant step toward a full, incentive-based funding system—Sport Canada furthered its argument that A- and B-Card athletes experience greater financial demands than lower ranked athletes. Even though athletes knew that training costs for international athletes were substantial and that a fall from eighth to tenth in the world was not associated with a reduction in training and competitive costs, the bonus allowed Sport Canada to introduce performance incentives into the system while maintaining that AAP was merely an assistance program.

The trend toward a performance-based funding system advanced further when Sport Canada totally removed the need component from AAP in 1983. Sport Canada (1983, pp. 2-5) argued that AAP was to supplement other forms of income. AAP funds were to help with living and training expenses and to relieve some of the pressures experienced while participating in international sport.

Sport Canada also expanded the statement of athlete obligations and included them within the 1983 AAP *Guide* (Sport Canada, 1983). The *Guide* noted that athletes had to follow a national team program, based on year-round principles and daily training, for a minimum of six months. Moreover, team athletes had to train in a centralized environment for at least three months. In addition, Sport Canada made the selection criteria for AAP more stringent and complex so that the number of countries competing, the representation of Eastern bloc countries, the frequency of international events, and the qualification system to enter world championships all became selection factors (Sport Canada, 1983). It was no longer enough to be among the top 8 or 16 in the world—all of the above criteria were designed to make selection more demanding.

The major move toward explicitly contracting athletes' skills came in 1984 when Sport Canada designed its first "generic" NSO/Athlete Agreement. The generic agreement included all the previous obligations and added several others, such as adherence to restrictive policies on doping and competition with athletes from South Africa, participation in commercial and promotional activities, and communication with NSOs on a monthly basis (Sport Canada, 1984a). Sport Canada also increased its control over Canadian athletes' training and competitive programs through the addition of small but significant clauses that stated that athletes' training programs must be clearly articulated by the NSO and supported and approved by Sport Canada. This particular change meant that athletes could no longer design and follow their own training programs unless Sport Canada approved them. The better an athlete produced, the higher his or her funding level. This meant that the funding structure in Canada's high-performance sport system was moving progressively toward an overt "piece-rate" system—that is, a system where athletes were paid in proportion to their output; the greater one's output, the greater one's income.

From 1984 to 1992, the most significant changes in the high-performance sport system related to the expansion of the carding system and the development of the NSO/Athlete Agreement. Thus, the 1984 AAP *Guide* explicitly informed athletes that failure to sign the NSO/Athlete Agreement meant disqualification from funding. The accreditation of an athlete by his or her NSO and the opportunity to compete internationally now rested on the acceptance of the NSO/Athlete Agreement (Sport Canada, 1984b). The central role that the Agreement was to play in the high-performance system was underscored further in 1986 when a copy of the Agreement was published inside the AAP *Policy and Guidelines* (Sport Canada, 1986).

Between 1984 and 1988, Sport Canada encouraged each NSO to amend the generic Agreement so it would fit the needs of each particular sport. At the same time, it noted that each NSO should establish a written appeals procedure for athletes who were sanctioned by their NSO for breaking any of the Agreement's clauses or stipulations. Athletes were also informed in the AAP *Policy and Guidelines* booklet that they could negotiate clauses in the Agreement.

From a labor relations perspective, these instructions from Sport Canada are significant more for what they did not cover than for what was actually undertaken. Thus, for example, with regard to the development and implementation of an appeals procedure, Sport Canada did not offer NSOs any funds or expertise to assist them with this exercise. Not only did this suggest a low priority to the NSOs; it left them with a very complex task to perform without any assistance. While the suspension of an athlete from his or her carding money does not involve a tremendously large sum of money—although to the athlete living below the poverty line it might appear large—the suspension of competitive privileges could put at risk thousands if not hundreds of thousands of dollars of existing or potential endorsement money for an athlete. The need for a fully legal appeal system is not something that any NSO or Sport Canada should have taken lightly (see Kidd & Eberts, 1982).

A second omission concerns the absence of any procedural guidelines that NSOs would have to follow concerning any and all NSO policies. In essence, by not requesting that NSOs establish procedural guidelines that would ensure that everyone who is a member of an NSO has some input into the development of NSO policies, Sport Canada and the NSOs were adopting, again by default (though possibly with full intent), a corporate-bureaucratic model for policy development and implementation.

According to the corporate-bureaucratic model, the professional administrators (management) within each NSO draft and propose policy. They then present this policy to the NSO's board of directors for approval and ratification. Once ratified, the policies apply to all members of the NSO even though not everyone has had an opportunity to influence the form and content of those policies.

In accepting this policy-making structure, the high-performance sport system was complying with the pressures of the dominant hegemonic practices that exist in Canada's instrumentally rational, market-based and bureaucratically structured society. Furthermore, by adopting this model, it ensured that athletes would not necessarily be included at the board level of the NSO. That decision established the conditions for the so-called adversarial labor/management model that characterizes the Canadian and American business sector as a whole. That is, by excluding labor (here athletes) from the corporation's (here the NSO's) major decision-making board, the two groups—labor and management—are seen to have *competing* interests, and thus bargaining is seen as a competition between adversaries.

Finally, Sport Canada's instructions to athletes concerning the negotiation of clauses in the NSO/Athlete Agreement also underscores a further significant decision by default. By presenting the opportunity to negotiate clauses in the singular, Sport Canada was reinforcing the individualist ethos that underlies so much of sport. Whereas sport is in reality a genuine social practice in which no athlete or coach or bureaucrat could exist as an isolated individual, Sport Canada's indication that athletes could negotiate their Agreements individually served to deflect attention from the social reality of high-performance sport. As a result, athletes believe that the only way they, as individuals, can enjoy any bargaining power is on the basis of their importance to the nation as international competitors. This ideology means that most athletes, no matter how successful they are, *never* enjoy any bargaining power. Thus, for example, men's and women's field-hockey players, archers, biathletes, and rhythmic gymnasts, because of the low profile of their sports, can be world champions and still have little bargaining power. Similarly, even relatively successful athletes in higher profile sports such as swimming, track and field, and gymnastics gain little leverage on the system as individuals. Collectively, athletes could have much more impact.

Individual bargaining also means that the only way athletes can hope to increase their bargaining power as individuals is to dedicate themselves even more to achieving world-class results. Finally, the instructions from Sport Canada also served to obscure a totally different way to amend the NSO/Athlete Agreement—through collective action. As the agency that is supposed to be looking after the interests of Canadian athletes, Sport Canada neglected to inform athletes that they as a group could bargain over and negotiate clauses within the NSO/Athlete Agreement. Such an "oversight" serves to reinforce once more the management/labor structure that came into being during the 1980s, with the NSOs and Sport Canada on the management side and the athletes supplying the labor needed to keep the system productive.

The only other changes of note in the sport system during the end of the 1980s was the expansion of the carding system. In 1986, Sport Canada introduced C1 and D Cards to extend the athlete ranking system downward and create a longer "career ladder" for high-performance sport athletes. This was followed in 1988 with the introduction of J and R cards, which related to early entry into the system for team sports. In all cases, these new entry-level cards offer minimal remuneration and serve to draw athletes into the high-performance system at very little cost to Sport Canada while extending its control deeper into the feeder system for high-performance sport.

# Working Conditions for Canada's High-Performance Athletes

The preceding historical overview of the relationship between Canada's high-performance athletes and Sport Canada sets the stage for a discussion of selected issues directly related to athletes' working conditions within Canada's high-performance sport system. To begin with, as athletes perform, they produce a commodity that has a number of uses. As noted earlier, the athletic spectacle is, first and foremost, a form of entertainment that consumers enjoy either directly or indirectly through one or more of the media. Second, this spectacle is the vehicle for advertisers to reach specific audiences to stimulate the consumption of their products. At the same time, national team athletes provide a number of important public services for their governments. In the case of Canada's high-performance athletes, they provide at least five such services.

1. Canadian athletes are a focal point for national unity; they can draw Canadians together in support of Canada's efforts in the international arena (see Munro, 1970).

2. Canada's national team athletes produce an important component of Canadian popular culture; they inform Canadians about what they are like and what makes them unique and interesting (see Kidd, 1982).

3. Canadian athletes, like those of the former German Democratic Republic, are a focal point for international prestige; the federal government hopes (partly on the basis of Canadian athletes' performances) that other governments will favorably weigh the strength of Canada in the world community.

4. Federal government officials believe that Canadian athletes draw other Canadians into sport, physical activity, and a healthy lifestyle (Munro, 1970).

5. Federal consulting firms have told the government that Canadian athletes are key agents in the sporting goods and entertainment industries. They provide lucrative entertainment for the media and are the backbone of the sporting goods industry in stimulating other Canadians to become active and purchase

the goods and services necessary for sport involvement. Of additional importance to the government, the growth of all these industries creates both more
jobs and greater tax revenues (Ross, 1969).

## Athletes' Remuneration

If athletes do provide so many public services for the federal government of Canada,
the question arises, How well are they remunerated for their efforts? Beamish and
Borowy (1988) argued that in both absolute and relative terms, the AAP provides
Canada's world-class athletes with a very low level of income. A-carded athletes
who rank among the top eight in the world currently receive only $7,800 per year,
and the majority of athletes earn less than $6,000. As a result, more than half (54%)
of Canada's world-class athletes are either barely balancing income and expenditures
or they are losing money—35% actually lose money each year (see Beamish &
Borowy, 1988, p. 4).

Since the institution of athlete funding, it was only in 1975 that Canada's world-
class athletes received remuneration that was above the federal government's low-
income cutoff lines. In every other year, athletes have earned less. In fact, over the
past seven years, funding for A, B, and C Cards has remained stagnant while the
poverty line has risen from $10,233 for a single individual living in a center of
more than 500,000 people to its current level of more than $12,000 (see National
Council of Welfare, 1989).

Table 9.1 compares the money that athletes make through the AAP compared to
other government workers—foreign service workers, clerks in the public service,
and armed service personnel. The table shows that the lowest-paid public servants
earn more than twice as much as Canada's best high-performance athletes. This
discrepancy is particularly hard to justify when one compares the skills each group
brings to the job and the importance of the service that each supplies to the government. If one believes in a scheme where there is equal pay for work of equal value,
then clearly Canada's national team athletes are not being paid their full value.

## Control Over Athletes

In 1984 Sport Canada formally implemented the NSO/Athlete Agreement. While
no one has yet tested the legal nature of the Agreement as a formal contract of
employment, there is little doubt that it formalizes considerable control over the
athlete. In fact, the Agreement exercises more control over the athlete than it would
if it were formally recognized as a contract of employment, because without a
formal employment contract athletes do not automatically have recourse to provincial
or national regulations regarding labor standards (Beamish & Borowy, 1988; Beamish, 1991).

An indication of how much control the Agreement exercises can be seen in the
following points. First, like all contracts of employment, the NSO/Athlete Agreement
formalizes an exchange relationship whereby the athlete will provide his or her

**Table 9.1    Comparative Incomes (1987)**

| Athletes | Artists | Foreign service officers | Public service clerks | Armed forces personnel |
|---|---|---|---|---|
| A Card $7,800 | A Award $32,000 | FS 2 $38,210- 55,242 | CR 3 $20,257- 22,137 | Officer $20,400- 25,200 |
| B Card $6,600 | B Award $14,000 | FS 1 $28,299- 39,025 | CR 2 $16,976- 18,423 | Private $11,000- 25,000 |

*Note.* From *Q: What Do You Do For a Living? A: I'm an Athlete* by R. Beamish and J. Borowy, 1988, Kingston, Ontario: The Sport Research Group. Copyright 1988 by Rob Beamish. Reprinted by permission.

specialized skills and services and agree to specific occupationally centered obligations in exchange for a specified level of remuneration and certain employer obligations. Second, the agreement will take force for a specified period of time (see Arthurs & Glasbeek, 1984).

The preamble to the Agreement indicates that only by signing the Agreement can an athlete remain an active competitor in NSO-sanctioned events, be certified as a member in good standing by the sport's international federation, and receive AAP funding. The section of the NSO/Athlete Agreement concerning athlete obligations readily indicates how much control the document exercises over the athlete. This section is the most extensive and detailed part of the document; few areas of an athlete's training and competitive duties are left out of consideration. The following indicates the extent of NSO control over the athlete that the Agreement permits.

According to the generic Agreement, athletes must follow an established training program, provide the NSO with "an annual training chart and monthly updates of changes to the chart or *any other appropriate information* that the NSO may request" (emphasis added), attend all mandatory training camps developed by each NSO, dress in the national team uniform while traveling or participating as part of the national team, "avoid alcoholic consumption to a level which would reasonably be expected to cause impairment in the Athlete's ability to speak, walk or drive, or cause the Athlete to behave in a disruptive manner," "avoid the use of banned drugs in contravention to the rules of the International Federation and Sport Canada policy," "submit at competitions and other reasonable times to *random* drug control testing upon request by the NSO, Sport Canada, the Sport Medicine Council of Canada or other authority designated to do so by the NSO," "participate, as requested, in any Doping Control/Education plan as formulated by the NSO in cooperation with Sport Canada and the Sport Medicine Council of Canada," and avoid participating in all competitions involving South Africans (Sport Canada, 1986, pp. 25-26).

Beyond these extensive training and competition obligations, the athlete must fulfill a set of broadly defined duties. These obligations cover a wide variety of lifestyle issues concerning the athlete's behavior, living conditions, and promotional activities for Sport Canada.

According to the NSO/Athlete Agreement, athletes "shall avoid living in an environment that is not conducive to high performance achievements or taking any deliberate action that involves significant risks for the Athlete's ability to perform or limits the Athlete's performance." He or she shall "avoid any action or conduct that would reasonably be expected to significantly disrupt or interfere with a competition or the preparation of any Athlete for a competition." Carded athletes shall "participate in reasonable non-commercial promotional activities as may be requested by Sport Canada on behalf of the Government of Canada." Finally, the athlete shall "participate in the Sport Medicine Council of Canada's Health Status Support Program if requested to do so by the (NSO)" (Sport Canada, 1986, pp. 26-27).

## Expanding Athletes' Obligations

The obligations indicated here represent only the minimal level of control that Sport Canada expects to see applied to carded athletes. Nevertheless, it is a degree of control that would be extremely unusual in most Canadian jobs. While the Agreement is restrictive in its generic form, when each NSO adapts it to meet its own particular circumstances the Agreement is almost always made more restrictive, and it is never made less restrictive. This is usually accomplished by expanding and refining the section on athlete obligations. These changes also tend to give the NSO greater control over the athlete's training and work process and, in many instances, actually reduce the NSO's obligations to the athlete.[4]

Several NSOs have tried to use the Agreement to ensure that athletes commit themselves to the program for specified periods of time without making a reciprocal guarantee to the athlete. Thus, for example, one specific NSO Agreement indicates that "three years involvement with the summer program is required before an athlete may be given permission to play semi-pro [name of sport] outside of Canada." In addition, the semi-pro teams signing these players may have to pay a release fee to the NSO in question and this fee may discourage semi-pro teams from picking up certain players. An Agreement from a different sport specifies that

a carded athlete agrees that acceptance of a place on the national team involves a commitment to the National team for at least two years and that his or her educational, employment and personal responsibilities will be arranged, as far as possible, to permit fulfilment of this commitment within this period.

In the following typical Agreement, training and competitive obligations are detailed.

A carded athlete covenants and agrees to participate fully in the Association's training program as determined from time to time by the officers of the Association and further undertakes and agrees to participate in, to the best of his or her ability, in all [name of sport] competitions within the national program as described in the attached annex.

While the expansion of NSO control over competitive and training obligations through the NSO/Athlete Agreement may not surprise many, there are also a variety of "lifestyle clauses" in the sport-specific Agreements. For the most part, such clauses allow for significant discretionary and interpretive latitude while the consequences of violation may be severe. Furthermore, the clauses extend NSO control into areas of the athlete's life that are beyond its jurisdiction as an employer. Many of these clauses allow the NSO to grant, as privileges, activities that are not the NSO's to dictate in the first place. As a result, athletes are routinely asked to give up such fundamental rights as the rights to privacy and freedom of speech.

Some of the restrictions placed on athletes by the sport-specific Agreements are demonstrated in the following sections selected from a variety of Agreements. In one sport, the Agreement notes that

no alcohol shall be consumed by the athletes except with the knowledge and *express approval* of the team leader. Permission of the team leader shall be granted for specific occasions only. The athletes, shall, when making use of this privilege, conduct themselves in a responsible way. [Emphasis added]

Sport-specific Agreements also commit an athlete to "conduct oneself as a representative of Canada and the [name of sport] team in a manner which is exemplary." In a similar vein, another Agreement insists that athletes "refrain from unacceptable behavior including, but not restricted to: breaking training or curfew at training camps or competitions, wilful damage to property." Finally, with regard to behavior, a different sport-specific Agreement is more precise. This Agreement notes that there will be "rules and regulations specific to the trip/event" and these "will govern the activities of the athletes on the trip. . . . [The rules and regulations] shall govern such matters as training, attendance at the [athletic venue], sightseeing, shopping, sunbathing, dating and setting of curfews."

Regarding the right to communicate with people outside of the national team, one sport-specific Agreement notes that "any athlete who is asked for an interview on radio, television or with the press shall obtain permission and guidance from the team manager. Whenever possible the team manager or coach should be present." A different NSO has specified that athletes "will not engage in casual and careless communication about the program's modus operandi which leads to misrepresentation of the High Performance Program."

# The Politics of Production in High-Performance Sport

High-performance athletes in Canada enter into a competitive environment at extremely early ages and their parents assume most if not all of the costs associated with their sport activity (Wiggins, 1988). It is important to emphasize that the age of entry into intensive competition and the long "apprenticeship" that athletes serve as they win their way through the feeder system is far more significant from a labor process and phenomenological viewpoint than most people realize.[5] The entire ideological system that athletes draw on and the practices that they accept as normal requirements of the job make sense, and can be fully grasped, only when one develops an understanding of athletes' objective conditions of training and competition from the athletes' perspective.

The product that athletes produce is, for them, directly related to the pursuit of the linear record so that they can win championships and progress toward the provincial, national, and finally international level. The ideological experience of this activity is overwhelmingly dominated by concerns related to the acquisition and refinement of the skills and strategies involved in the sporting activity and how science and technology can assist performance enhancement. The experience becomes overwhelmingly competitive and intense. Conflict, competition, and aggression are predominantly directed laterally—toward other competitors—or, in the overwhelming majority of instances, up the sport system only as far as the coach.

In terms of political relationships—the social relations in production—the athletic experience for many high-performance athletes involves some nationalist sentiments such as the importance of winning for their country or beating certain athletes/ countries, but it is predominantly local in focus. That is, the political dimension of high-performance sport at the site of production—training and competition—is narrowly focused on the production of superior performances and does not tend to extend to a complete understanding of the entire structure of the high-performance sport system and its global political significance.

Because winning is paramount, and the entire developmental process and experience of working one's way through the feeder system select only certain winners, the dominant ideology of scientific experts combines with the long-standing residual tradition of a coach's authority to create a set of political relationships in which the athlete is rendered substantially less powerful than his or her supervisors. This relationship is then reinforced continually through the routines of training, travel, team selection, carding selection, competition, and so forth.

Although there is no doubt that the products that athletes produce—the contest, the record, the spectacle—have uses that are exploited by the mass media, advertising firms, governments, and others, for the athlete the product has a very narrow meaning and significance. For the athlete the product is judged overwhelmingly, if not exclusively, by the "bottom line" of results. The imperative to win and the focused attention it receives has been most graphically substantiated in Canada's recent federal government commission into the use of banned substances by Canadian athletes.

## The Dubin Commission

Ben Johnson's positive test for a banned substance following his gold-medal and world-record performance in the 100 meters at the Seoul Olympic Games led to considerable embarrassment on the part of the Canadian federal government. The government's response was to impose an immediate lifetime ban on Johnson and to set up, through an Order-in-Council, the "Commission of Inquiry into the Use of Drugs and Banned Practices Intended to Increase Athletic Performance." Chief Justice Charles Dubin conducted the proceedings and held public hearings from January 11 to October 3 of 1989. During that time, 119 witnesses generated 14,817 pages of testimony, and Justice Dubin received an additional 295 exhibits (Dubin, 1990, p. xxi). Despite the alleged potential dangers associated with the extended use of anabolic steroids, several world-class athletes indicated to the commissioner that the goal of winning was of far greater significance than the perceived potential risks.

For example, sprinter Angella Issajenko noted that following a meet against the East Germans in 1979, she decided she wanted to be "just like them [the superstars].... I wanted to be just as fast as they were. . . . I thought if I went on an anabolics program, this would give me the extra edge I needed" ("Used Steroids," 1989, p. A1; see also Issajenko, 1990, pp. 71-90).

Weightlifter Jacques Demers indicated the same pressures to use steroids to attain his objectives—international-level performances. "To go to international competitions," Demers stated in an interview,

> you have to meet international standards and those are based on what the Russians and Bulgarians do. They are the best weightlifters in the world . . . and they take steroids. So if I am to go to the Olympics, I must take steroids. ("Demers," 1989, p. B5)

When Chief Justice Dubin noted that he could always quit, Demers countered,

> It's easy to say quit; I should quit after training three or four years? . . . I couldn't quit because I spent so much time training. After three years of training I wanted more and more. I wanted to go to the Olympic Games. ("Demers," 1989, p. B5)

In explaining what motivated him to begin using steroids, Demers said that he

> was training for 30 hours a week and making no progress. A Russian who was lifting the same as me in 1980 was much better three years later. Before I started my best lift was 140 to 142 kilos. After that I got up to 195. ("Demers," 1989, p. A15)

David Bolduc's testimony before the Dubin Commission indicated very clearly the overwhelming pressure that the bottom line of results ultimately holds for an athlete when she or he reaches the international level. "Today's society is much too demanding on its athletes, much too demanding," Bolduc emphasized to Justice Dubin. Caught in the catch-22 of taking steroids to reach the COA's Olympic standards and risking being caught, Bolduc opted to take steroids and risk the consequences. When the gamble failed, Bolduc commented on the overwhelming sense of depression that followed: "I felt that I had prepared for the Olympic Games

for 10 years. . . . It was too much for one person. I had taken a very serious decision
to devote myself to weightlifting and I had failed" ("Moral Bomb," 1989).

None of these experiences create an impetus that would lead the majority of
athletes to struggle for significantly different working conditions and a dramatically
altered high-performance sport sytem. For most athletes, better working conditions
really means *more demanding* training in the hope that it will lead to improved
performance. Most athletes tend to seek increased physical exploitation and stricter
authoritarian control. These sentiments make sense, of course, when viewed from
the perspective of the production process and the product that the athlete defines
as significant.

It is worth considering the impact that the residual notion of the amateur athlete
has on the current labor relations framework in high-performance sport. Although
virtually every high-performance athlete realizes that he or she trains long hours
and has made a significant commitment to sport, the tradition of the amateur athlete
seems to have kept the notion that they are really professionals, workers in an
enormous global entertainment industry, outside the considerations of most Canadian
athletes. Unlike professional football, hockey, or baseball players, who recognize
that what they do is a business and that they have a particular market value within
that business, few high-performance athletes make that connection or believe that
the same applies to them.

The legacy of the amateur athlete is used repeatedly by ex-athletes, coaches, sport
administrators, and the press to remind contemporary athletes of how well-off they
are. The term *amateur* has become a totalizing concept that appears to need no
explanation. The concept removes the athlete from the concrete, historical practices
of contemporary high-performance sport and establishes an antiquated, reactionary
definition. To break the hegemonic power of the residual and conservative meaning
of the term, athletes themselves have to situate their perceptions and definitions of
self within their own actual experiences in high-performance sport as the *ensemble*
of concrete practices that make up the system of high-performance sport. Once this
critical self-reflection is initiated, the hegemonic power of the practices that constitute
high-performance sport is opened to both theoretical and practical critique.

## Labor Relations in High-Performance Sport: The Future

From the athletes' perspective, the future prospects for improved remuneration,
working conditions, and control over the work process are quite bleak. There are
a number of powerful forces behind the status quo. The dominant hegemonic forces
that have constituted the current high-performance sport system remain largely
intact. The ideological dominance of bureaucratic and instrumental rationality have
not been challenged, despite the fact that Canadian performances have not improved
as much as many anticipated or desired. As more and more NSOs conform to the
corporate structure that Sport Canada is advocating so strongly, and as Sport Canada
moves to further develop and ultimately implement its own "objective" ranking
system for sport funding, then the working conditions for athletes will become more
controlled and supervised.

Another major force behind the status quo are the recommendations of Justice Dubin's "Commission of Inquiry into the Use of Drugs and Banned Practices Intended to Increase Athletic Performance." All 70 recommendations are based on premises that do not reflect the reality of contemporary high-performance sport. In his prefatory comments, Dubin (1990) noted:

> The use of banned performance-enhancing drugs is cheating, which is the antithesis of sport. The widespread use of such drugs has threatened the essential integrity of sport and is destructive of its very objectives. It also erodes the ethical and moral values of athletes who use them, endangering their mental and physical welfare while demoralizing the entire sport community. . . . I have endeavoured to define the true values of sport and to restore its integrity so that it can continue to be an important part of our culture, unifying and giving pleasure to Canadians while promoting their health and vitality. (p. xxii)

From this starting point, Justice Dubin (1990) recommended, laudably perhaps but unrealistically given the current political and economic realities, that Canada's sport system return to its original objectives of developing a broad base of participation and emphasized that fair play become its central motif. He recommended that the system ensure that there are high ethical standards practiced among all actors within the system and that funding be tied to the development of doping-control policies (Dubin, 1990). Finally, Dubin made a number of recommendations about how doping control inside Canada and internationally could be strengthened and should be more strongly enforced (Dubin, 1990).

In his recommendations directly affecting Canada's athletes Dubin virtually ignored all of the issues that I have outlined in this chapter regarding the emergent working conditions and labor relations faced by the nation's high-performance athletes, although he was not unaware of them (see Beamish & Kidd, 1990). He apparently refused to believe that the social practices that constitute high-performance sport are significantly different and more complex than his image of sport. By rooting all of his recommendations in a confused and contradictory moral system (see Overall, 1990), Dubin has provided guidance and advice that is both sociologically naive and potentially dangerous to contemporary high-performance athletes.

Following the Commission of Inquiry, the forces of reaction have gained a powerful set of government-sanctioned slogans to support their cause. Unfortunately, these slogans and the recommendations of the Dubin Commission of inquiry do little, if anything, to unravel the complex reality of high-performance sport in Canada and internationally, and it is athletes who will have to struggle alone in their attempts to excel within the system while continually fighting against it and all of its contradictions. An opportunity for open, frank, and constructive debate was lost, and the residual traditions of amateur, high-performance sport were strengthened in the process.

Despite the fact that a group of researchers and athlete advocates held workshops across Canada in the fall of 1987 and addressed many of the problems that confront athletes in the current structure, there is no mass movement to create change. Except for a large number of Francophone athletes, the majority of Canadian athletes had no interest in the political struggle to improve their working conditions. For most, sport was something they had chosen to undertake on their own, and the solutions to their problems were all seen in individualistic and voluntaristic terms. Of course, the overwhelming preoccupation with performing at an international standard to qualify for the next Olympic Games undercuts every athlete's enthusiasm about directing valuable time and energy away from performance enhancement toward the remote possibility of changing the athletes' position in the high-performance sport structure.

In the wake of the latest federal government task force report on high-performance sport in Canada (Task Force on National Sport Policy, 1988), it is clear that the current federal government would like to significantly reduce its role in the funding of high-performance sport. To achieve this objective, the government will require the NSOs to coordinate their efforts through the Sport Marketing Board to raise more and more of their funds through the private sector—at a time when the private sector is reconsidering the value it receives for the funds it directs to high-performance sport. The result of this new funding strategy and the current economic climate will inevitably lead to a reduction in funds available to athletes, an increasingly greater user fee component to sport, and greater control, obligations, and "accountability" placed on Canadian athletes.

These are the major forces supporting the status quo and the expansion of control over Canadian athletes. Are there any forces of progressive change? Thankfully for athletes, the answer is yes, but its significance and effectiveness may be quite limited *if* it actually works. Earlier in this chapter, it was noted that athletes receiving AAP funds do not enjoy the legal status of employee despite the fact that their working conditions, their NSO/Athlete Agreement, and their role in the sport structure make them de facto employees. Based on all of the available evidence, there is a strong argument that if an athlete receiving AAP funding challenged his or her status as an employee of either his or her NSO or the federal government through Sport Canada, that she or he would win the case. Once designated employees, the struggle for fair wages and better working conditions would not be won automatically, but the ground rules for those struggles would change dramatically.

Throughout the history of common-law decisions in the area of labor relations, the courts have recognized that employees are less powerful than employers. As a result, the common-law tradition and the governmental enactment of statutes have put into place such protections for workers as the legal right to form a collective bargaining unit, minimum wage, overtime pay when a workweek extends beyond a given limit, vacation pay, and, in several provinces, equal pay for work of equal value. Without formal recognition as employees, high-performance athletes would have to struggle to win every one of these rights. As employees, Canadian athletes receiving AAP funding would automatically receive that protection and could then form a certified bargaining unit and begin to negotiate a first contract of employment. These negotiations would not be easy, but even if the contract only contained small advances beyond the minimum standards required for all employees, Canadian athletes would have advanced their position enormously.

## Conclusion

High-performance sport has changed remarkably since the introduction of the modern Olympic Games. As marked as the changes have been, they have been equally uneven. Virtually every aspect of contemporary, international, high-performance sport is dominated by the ethos and practices of the bureaucratically controlled, instrumentally rational market society in which sport exists and thrives. The major exception is the relationship between high-performance athletes and sport administrators. Labor relations in high-performance sport are still dominated by the residual notion of the amateur athlete and the continued refusal of both groups to recognize that high-performance sport has become an overt employee/employer relationship. Once that emergent reality is recognized and accorded legal status, labor relations in high-performance sport will undergo revolutionary change as they are brought into the reality of the late 20th century.

## Acknowledgment

The material presented in this chapter was gathered in research projects funded by the Max Bell Foundation and the Social Sciences and Humanities Research Council. I would like to acknowledge the generous support of both these agencies.

## Notes

1. Canada was not the first country in the Western bloc to establish a centralized, bureaucratically rational system that was designed to enhance international performance. The Federal Republic of Germany began a somewhat similar program in 1967 in preparation for the 1972 Summer Olympic Games it hosted in Munich (see Bette, 1984, pp. 25-28). Australia began, in 1984, its own federally controlled, rationalized high-performance sport system (Australia, 1984; Macintosh, Bedecki, & Franks, 1987, p. 185).

2. While this assessment of contemporary industrial, capitalist society is consistent with most sociological accounts, the themes were first seriously and systematically introduced by Max Weber (1956) and became a central motif in the work of the Frankfurt School (see Habermas, 1968; Jay, 1973). In sport study, the Germans have developed an extensive literature on the domination of instrumental rationality and bureaucratic structure through debates and explorations around *Das Leistungsprinzip* (the achievement/ performance principle) and the relationship between work and free time (see, in particular, Eichberg, 1979; Grupe, 1982; and Heinemann, 1975 concerning the former and Güldenpfenning, 1980; Habermas, 1958; Lenk, 1972; and Rigauer, 1969 regarding the latter). The problems have also been addressed

in English sport sociology, though not as extensively (see Beamish, 1982a, 1982b, 1990; Ingham, 1975).

3. Although the economic dimension was extremely important here, one should not overlook the political issues that coalesced with the commercial imperatives of televised sport. Throughout the post-war period, governments in both the Eastern and Western blocs have used the Games to publicize particular political ideologies. This too meant that performances had to be of a world-class order.

4. In the following material, there are several direct citations from sport-specific NSO/Athlete Agreements. Due to a commitment to confidentiality, the NSO in each particular example has not been identified.

5. During the 1970s and early 1980s there was a renewed interest among sociologists in the labor process itself. Thompson (1983) provides a good overview of this literature. The key contributions were made by Braverman (1974a, 1974b) and Burawoy (1979, 1985). My interest here is primarily in the process Burawoy (1985, p. 49) termed the "production of consent" within the labor process.

# References

Arthurs, H.W., & Glasbeek, H.J. (1984). *The individual employment relationship. Labor law and industrial relations in Canada* (2nd ed.). Toronto: Butterworths.

Australia. (1984, September). Joint statement by Prime Minister P. Hawke and Hon. J.J. Brown, Minister of Sport, Recreation and Tourism, Canberra.

Baran, P., & Sweezy, P. (1966). *Monopoly capital*. New York: Monthly Review Press.

Beamish, R. (1982a). Sport and the logic of capitalism. In H. Cantelon and R. Gruneau (Eds.), *Sport, culture and the modern state* (pp. 141-198). Toronto: University of Toronto Press.

Beamish, R. (1982b). Sport, value, and the fetishism of commodities: Central issues in alienated sport. In A. Ingham & E. Broom (Eds.), *Proceedings from the first regional symposium for the International Committee for the Sociology of Sport* (pp. 82-101). Vancouver.

Beamish, R. (1990). Alienation in sport: The situation in Canada's high performance sport system. In T. Saeki (Ed.), *Sport and Humanism* (pp. 125-134, 403-411). Kobe, Japan: Rokko.

Beamish, R. (1991). Zur Professionalisierung des Hochleistungssports in Kanada: Eine Untersuchung zum Arbeitnehmerstatus der kanadischen Hochleistungssportler(innen) [On the professionalization of high performance sport in Canada: An investigation into the employee status of Canadian high performance athletes]. *Sportwissenschaft, 21*, 70-78.

Beamish, R., & Borowy, J. (1987). High performance athletes in Canada: From status to contract. In T. Slack and C.R. Hinings (Eds.), *The organization and administration of sport* (pp. 1-35). London: Sport Dynamics.

Beamish, R., & Borowy, J. (1988). *Q: What do you do for a living? A: I'm an athlete.* Kingston: The Sport Research Group.

Beamish, R., & Kidd, B. (1990). A brief to Justice Charles Dubin, commissioner for the inquiry into the use of drugs and banned practices intended to increase athletic performance.

Bette, K.-H. (1984). *Strukturelle Aspekte des Hochleistungssports in der Bundesrepublik* [Structural aspects of higher performance sport in the Federal Republic of Germany]. Sankt Augustin: Verlag Hans Richarz.

Braverman, H. (1974a). Labor and monopoly capital. *Monthly Review, 26*, 1-133.

Braverman, H. (1974b). *Labor and monopoly capital*. New York: Monthly Review Press.

Burawoy, M. (1979). *Manufacturing consent*. Chicago: University of Chicago Press.

Burawoy, M. (1985). *The politics of production*. London: Verso Books.

Cavanagh, R. (1985). *High performance sport in Canada: A study in state hegemony*. Unpublished Master's thesis, Queen's University, Kingston.

Demers puts scandal, weightlifting aside. (1989, February 3). *The Globe and Mail*, p. A15.

Dubin, C. (1990). *Commission of inquiry into the use of drugs and banned practices intended to increase athletic performance*. Ottawa: Minister of Supply and Services.

Eichberg, H. (1979). *Der Weg des Sports in die industrielle Zivilisation* [The road to sport in industrial society] (2nd ed.). Baden-Baden: Nomos Verlagsgesellschaft.

Grupe, Ommo. (1982). *Bewegung, Spiel und Leistung im Sport* [Movement, play and performance in sport]. Schorndorf: Verlag Karl Hoffmann.

Güldenpfenning, S. (1980). Entwicklung und Bedeutung der Diskussion über "Sport and Arbeit" [The development and significance of the discussion about "sport and work"]. In *Texte zur Sporttheorie und Sportpolitik* (pp. 10-57). Köln: Pahl-Rugenstein.

Habermas, J. (1958). Soziologische Notizen zum Verhältnis von Arbeit und Freizeit [Sociological notes on the relation between work and free time]. In *Konkrete Vernunft: Festschrift für E. Rothacker* (pp. 219-231). Bonn: Bouvier Verlag.

Habermas, J. (1968). *Technik und Wissenschaft als "Ideologie"* [Technique and science as "ideology"]. Frankfurt/M.: Shurkamp Verlag.

Hallett, W. (1981). *A history of federal government involvement in the development of sport in Canada: 1943-1979*. Unpublished doctoral dissertation, University of Alberta.

Heinemann, K. (1975). Leistung, Leistungsprinzip, Leistungsgesellschaft [Achievement, the achievement principle, the achieving society]. *Sportwissenschaft, 5*, 119-146.

Ingham, A. (1975). Occupational subcultures in the work world of sport. In D. Ball and J. Loy (Eds.), *Sport and the Social Order* (pp. 333-390). Don Mills: Addison Wesley.

Issajenko, A. (1990). *Running Risks*. Toronto: Macmillan of Canada.

Jay, M. (1973). *The dialectical imagination*. London: Heinemann Educational Books.

Kidd, B. (1982). Sport, dependency, and the Canadian State. In H. Cantelon and R. Gruneau (Eds.), *Sport, culture, and the modern state* (pp. 281-303). Toronto: University of Toronto Press.

Kidd, B., & Eberts, M. (1982). *Athletes' rights in Canada*. Toronto: The Queen's Printer.

Lenk, H. (1972). Leistungssport und Leistungskritik heute [Performance sport and the critique of performance today]. *Universitas, 27*, 827-840.

Macintosh, D., Bedecki, T., & Franks, C.E.S. (1987). *Sport and politics in Canada*. Montreal: McGill-Queen's Press.

Mandel, E. (1975). *Late capitalism* (J. De Bres, Trans.). London: New Left Books. (Original work published 1972)

"Moral bomb" awakens athletes. (1989, February 4). *The Toronto Star*, p. B5.

Munro, J. (1970). *A proposed sports policy for Canadians*. Ottawa: Department of Health and Welfare.

National Council of Welfare. (1989). *1989 poverty lines*. Ottawa: Minister of Supply and Services.

Overall, C. (1990). Ethics and high performance sport. Presented at *After the Dubin Inquiry: Implications for Canada's high-performance sport system*, September 27-29. Queen's University, Kingston, Canada.

Prokop, U. (1971). *Soziologie der Olympischen Spiele: Sport und Kapitalismus* [The sociology of the Olympic Games: Sport and capitalism]. Regensburg: Carl Hanser Verlag.

Rigauer, B. (1969). *Sport und Arbeit* [Sport and work]. Frankfurt/M.: Suhrkamp Verlag.

Ross, P.S. (1969). A report on physical recreation, fitness, and amateur sport in Canada (Parts I and II). Submitted to the Government of Canada through the Department of Fitness and Amateur Sport.

Sport Canada. (1980). *Guide to the athletes' assistance program*. Ottawa: Ministry of Supplies and Services.

Sport Canada. (1983). *AAP guide*. Ottawa: Ministry of Supplies and Services.

Sport Canada. (1984a). NSO/Athlete agreement. Mimeographed document distributed to all NSOs by Sport Canada in 1984.

Sport Canada. (1984b). *AAP Guide*. Ottawa: Ministry of Supplies and Services.

Sport Canada. (1986). *AAP policy and guidelines*. Ottawa: Ministry of Supplies and Services.

Task Force on National Sport Policy. (1988). *Toward 2000: Building Canada's sport system*. Ottawa: Ministry of Supplies and Services.

Task Force on Sport (1969). *Report of the task force on sports for Canadians*. Ottawa: Department of National Health and Welfare.

Thompson, P. (1983). *The nature of work*. London: Macmillan Press.

Used steroids for years star sprinter tells probe. (1989, March 14). *The Globe and Mail*, pp. A1/A2.

Weber, M. (1956). *Wirschaft und Gesellschaft* [Economy and society] (2 Vols.). Tübingen: Mohr Verlag.

Wiggins, C. (1988). *A profile of Canada's high performance athletes*. Unpublished Master's thesis, Queen's University, Kingston, Ontario.

# CHAPTER 10

# Professional Team Sport and the American City: Urban Politics and Franchise Relocations

*Kimberly S. Schimmel*
*Alan G. Ingham*
*Jeremy W. Howell*

Throughout this essay, we shall assert that any analysis of the professional sport and community relation that avoids considering the logic of capital accumulation will fall short of completing its intellectual journey. Implicit in our review is the assumption that it is not reductionist to trace the development of professional sports' internal economy from its period of trial and error to its current cartelized and concentrated form. Nor is it reductionist to relate franchise relocations and stadium construction to the broader forces of capital disinvestment and reinvestment and to the impact of disinvestment and reinvestment decisions on cities and communities. An adequate theorization of the professional sport and community relation requires (a) concern for the logic of capitalist relations as an ever-present constraint or enablement or both, and (b) concern for the ways in which the logic is experienced, understood, and acted upon by individuals and collectivities in the historical periods in which they have their being. This is to say that the logic of capital accumulation can never fully determine social, political, and cultural relations. Relations in the

*Note.* Portions of this chapter are reprinted and adapted from "Professional Sports and Community: A Review and Exegesis" by A. Ingham, J. Howell, and T. Schilperoort. In *Exercise and Sport Sciences Reviews* by K.B. Pandolf (Ed.), 1987. Copyright 1987 by Macmillan Publishing Company. Reprinted and adapted by permission.

social, political, and cultural realms are determined in part by the economic forces and relations of production, but they have their own active, constitutive moments.

Sport historians have mostly focused on urbanization and industrialization as determinants in the growth of "spectatoritis." Sport economists generally have neglected to analyze historical and environmental determinations and have focused on the prevailing economic arrangements *in* professional sport and how they impact direct and indirect consumption. That is, the analysis of franchise relocations has been dominated by a microeconomic perspective that focuses on profitability vis-à-vis win/loss records, metropolitan sizes, the size and "influence" of television markets, and demographic considerations such as the racial and income composition of inner cities. While these analyses are invaluable to understanding franchise relocation, they are insufficient, for they do not always address the *political* economy of investment, disinvestment, and reinvestment. In short, microeconomic analysis often provides a text that lacks a context. Subdisciplinary fragmentation thus has created an intellectual lacuna—we have not probed the relationship between a transformed environment and a transformed internal economy of professional sport.

We will attempt to situate the franchise relocation problem not only within the microeconomy of the professional sport industry, but also within the broader context of urban politics. In addressing the professional sport industry as a capitalist enterprise that operates under the logic of capital accumulation, we assert that profit-seeking alone does not adequately explain the location decisions of franchise owners. The forces that contour these decisions are not exclusively economic; they are also political. Thus an adequate examination must attempt to integrate historical, social, economic, and political forces that define the conditions in which professional sport is immersed.

We shall first focus on the development of modern sports economic calculus—a calculus that was not present in the early trial-and-error days of professional sport but emerged as professional leagues embraced a more instrumentally rational approach to capital accumulation and to survival in the marketplace. Such strategies eventually would produce a condition of artificial scarcity—more cities and communities wanting franchises than there were franchises available. The cases of professional football in two Ohio cities are highlighted to illustrate the transition period when incorporation into the emerging cartel offered city officials greater assurance that their communities could retain their teams.

Next we draw on the works of Howell (1984) and Schimmel (1987), who focus on relocation decisions made by owners Carroll Rosenbloom, Al Davis, and Robert Irsay in Anaheim, Los Angeles, and Baltimore. The decisions of these franchise owners paint in broad relief the contradiction between the profit motive and the norms of reciprocity that are presumed to exist between a "community" and its professional sports franchise. Norms of reciprocity are, in fact, ideologically constructed and mobilized to generalize and naturalize the private interest of capital to appear in the public good. We raise issues concerning the articulation of capital investment/disinvestment decisions, the policies of substate (county and city) officials, and the dominant practices of modern professional sport franchise owners.

We then attempt to situate the political economy of modern professional sport within the broad context of urban politics—politics that are contoured by the intercity competition for capital investment and that articulate the "needs" of both private and public sectors in a strategy of pro-growth. Specifically, we focus on Indianapolis, Indiana, which like many other older American cities has faced urban crises of great proportions. Its responses illustrate the conflicts that arise when massive redevelopment policies are implemented to attract capital investment.

Finally, we refer to the strategies of civic boosterism and image-making that seek to legitimize political solutions to urban crisis by symbolically constructing the consensus. We suggest that sport, as civic ritual, may articulate with these broader strategies better than other forms of consumerist collective consumption.

# Residuals and Transitions:
# Sport From Social to Abstract Space

According to Vincent (1981), there were 850 clubs launched between 1869 and 1900, of which 650 went out of business in two years or less. Only 50 lasted 6 years or more. As Vincent (1981) states: "Teams came and went with such frequency that to this day there is no comprehensive list of nineteenth-century professional teams even though baseball is a sport with a record and statistic for just about everything" (p. 97). With such a record of failure, why would anybody invest?

The emergence of crowds at patrician, occupational, and local club games is one reason. Also, according to Vincent, anybody seeking to affirm their "leading citizen" status, seeking political office, seeking patronage at their shops, restaurants, and saloons, or seeking to increase beer and whisky sales would give baseball a try. However, this "twilight" period of commercialism and semiprofessionalism, as Voigt (1966) aptly names it, did not last. Many communities could not insure gate receipts. Many teams, for financial reasons, could not complete their schedules. Many players would not insure their loyalties and, in what was called "revolving," jumped from team to team at will. To use modern terminology, as free agents, players sold their services to the highest bidder. Moreover, club owners placed more economic interest on their own clubs (utility maximization) than they did on the welfare of a league (joint profit maximization).

These problems made it difficult for baseball firms to find security in the marketplace. Supply obviously exceeded demand and demand, in many cities, was inadequate for owners to meet operating expenses, given the free-agency status of players. Both the market and the labor force "needed" to be disciplined. Cartelization (in the form of collusive competition between league-member firms) and monopsony (the exclusive right to enter into a contract with a player and to reserve the player's services through the use of a perpetually renewable contract) seemed to be the answer.

Enter William Hulbert, who radically reorganized the baseball industry in 1875 and 1876. An organizational meeting was held in Louisville in December 1875 that involved C.C. Chase, W.N. Haldeman, and J.J. Joyces of Louisville and G.A. Fowle,

A.G. Spaulding, and W.A. Hulbert of Chicago (Tarvin, 1940, p. 10). On February 2, 1876, a selected group of owners met behind locked doors in a room at the New York Grand Central Hotel; although the meeting was known to the press, it was passed off as a rules committee meeting (Seymour, 1960; Vincent, 1981; Voigt, 1966, 1971). William A. Hulbert, owner of the Chicago club, had a different agenda: He wanted a new league, the National League. The new league would bring order out of chaos, but it would stratify the game. There would be *one* major league; it would be the prestige league. Hulbert's meeting would eventually force a decision: Which firms would be included in the prestige set and which excluded? The meeting would set the stage for the emergence of monopolistic practices in the marketplace and monopsonistic practices concerning the interfirm competition for athletic labor— the reserve clause.

Although the initiation of a new major league would be fraught with difficulties (acquiring players from excluded hometown clubs, generating a schedule, choosing between teams in the same city for league membership, combating rival, player-organized leagues, etc.), the National League would survive and set a precedent for business practices in American professional sport. Although Hulbert could not have envisioned it at the time, his experiment would eventually make cartelization, monopoly, and monopsony taken-for-granted features of the American sport industry regardless of whether or not the league was exempted from the antitrust act. In the long run it would turn ownership of professional sport firms over to those of affluence, substituting the rational calculus of business and accelerating a process already underway—the attenuation of the organic ties between ball club and community. Functional rationality in the organization of the sport enterprise would begin to contour substantial rationality in the sphere of collective consumption. It is important to note that Hulbert and his colleagues set a precedent that other professional sports would ignore in their own periods of trial and error, but which they would eventually embrace for exactly the same reasons in the later stages of their economic development. The production of artificial scarcity in the consumer marketplace increased consumer demand. For the favored few, membership in the prestige set meant increased profits. For the excluded, termination of production or merger with the favored became the norm. Thus, the decision of baseball's National League to return to an eight-club format resulted in the cities of Louisville, Baltimore, Cleveland, and Washington joining the ranks of the dispossessed (Tarvin, 1940, p. 24).

This economic concentration and cartelization scenario has been played out not only in baseball, but also in basketball, football, hockey, and soccer. Professional football, for example, had 58 teams in two leagues in the 1920s, 30 teams in the 1930s, and 32 teams in three leagues in the 1940s. By the 1950s, mergers, failures, and exclusions reduced the number of teams to fourteen, and one league (The National Football League) had control over the U.S. market.

During the formative years, football followed a pattern much like the one we have described for baseball. To show how complicated things were in the precartelization period, take the case of the Dayton Triangles, one of the founding members of the NFL in the 1920s.

The 1929 Dayton Triangles became the 1930 Brooklyn Dodgers who became the 1940 Brooklyn Tigers, who merged with the 1945 Boston Yanks, who became the 1949 New York Bulldogs, who became the 1950 New York Yanks (and were joined by many key players from the floundering Baltimore Colts in 1951), who became the 1952 Dallas Texans, who eventually became the reborn [Baltimore] Colts in 1953 [and who relocated to become the Indianapolis Colts in 1984]. (The National Football League, 1982, p. 111)

Players moved around, too:

This movement, as well as the use of college players playing under assumed names, was summed up best by Hall of Fame coach Earle (Greasy) Neale. Neale, himself an early nomad, said, "I recall playing end across from Knute Rockne [Notre Dame's famed coach] on six different Sundays, with six different teams, with Rock using six different names." (The National Football League, 1982, p. 111)

The emergence of the NFL as *the* league would provide some stability for a time. However, in the 1960s, the American Football League was reborn and, thanks to television revenues, was able to mount a successful challenge to the NFL in the marketplace. Challenges of rival leagues must be dealt with, because a rival league is not bound by the monopoly and monopsony agreements of the extant league. Thus, a merger produced the current NFL.

The expansion, contraction, merger scenario and its impact on affected cities and communities has not attracted much interest in the sport-studies academic community, perhaps because the community-studies orientation to analysis has been sporadic in recent years. With a few notable exceptions (Hardy, 1981, 1982; Katznelson, 1979, 1981) we seem to have lost an anthropological perspective in the history and sociology of sport. What can we do to assist the revival of the community studies approach in sport studies and, at the same time, adequately address the transformation of the producer-consumer relationship in professional sport?

Up to this point, we have adumbrated what is generally known; namely, that the entrepreneurial history of professional sport is replete with examples of firm terminations, league expansions and contractions, and mergers between leagues and teams. At this point (and in response to the aforementioned question) we shall assert that each instance of termination, relocation, league contraction and expansion, and of mergers between leagues and clubs represents moments of continuity and discontinuity that are themselves manifestations of broader forces linked to community formation, deformation, and reformation (Howell, 1984; Howell & Ingham, 1984; Johnson, 1978; Staudohar, 1985; Weistart, 1984).

## Ironton

Ironton, Ohio, had a population of 14,007 in 1920. It was an iron-producing city. The Ironton Tanks were founded in 1919 and were built on a tradition of semiprofessional football that began in 1893. At the time of their founding, "professional" football was in a chaotic state. Crowds were small; club rosters combined college players under assumed names, ex-college players, and local boys (some of whom received game fees). Teams developed their own schedules (fixture lists), and games took place between league teams and "sandlot" teams (Barnett & Terhune, 1979, pp. 14-15). Teams shifted in and out of leagues; sport entrepreneurs applied for franchises but failed to field teams.

The Ironton team started with a roster of World War I veterans. They had backers, and the community took an active interest in the team, pushing for a new stadium and an upgraded schedule. In 1926, a group called Beechwood Stadium Corp. held a meeting and initiated a fund-raising campaign. Stadium Corp. raised $33,500 for the stadium and provided money to recruit players from other regions. Such players were lured by contracts and by offers of teaching positions in Lawrence County high schools (Barnett & Terhune, 1979, pp. 17-18).

In twelve seasons, the Tanks accrued a record of 85 wins, 14 ties, and 19 losses. The wins included victories over such NFL teams as the Chicago Bears, the Portsmouth Spartans, and the New York Giants (Barnett & Terhune, 1979, pp. 14-15). Yet the Tanks folded at the end of the 1930 season. In their twelve seasons, the Tanks provided the people of Ironton with a sense of civic worth. As Harold Rolph (Barnett & Terhune, 1979) expressed it:

> The athletes were not tramps. Well maybe one or two, but I think five or six of them married Ironton girls lived here year round. They really added to the community. If you were a Tank, you were invited to the finest homes in town and the townspeople like to associate with the players. (p. 18)

But Ironton was not big enough or prosperous enough to support professional football, and the Depression did not help. Slow population growth and the shift of the iron and steel industry to Pittsburgh, Youngstown, and Cleveland assisted in the material deformation of the Ironton community. In addition, Ironton seemed to have lost a local area "boosterism" race to the cities of Huntington, Portsmouth, and Ashland (Barnett & Terhune, 1979, p. 17). Presumably, had Ironton's economy remained strong, the club would not have folded. Yet, the capital disinvestment/ investment decisions within the iron and steel industry may be only a partial explanation for the Tanks' elimination. We can find no evidence in Barnett and Terhune's article or in the *Official NFL Encyclopedia* that the Tanks were affiliated with either the NFL or the AFL. Could the lack of affiliation with these two leagues also have been a factor? Ironton in the 1920s lacked a diversified, economic infrastructure; the Tanks were not "protected" by whatever security league affiliation might provide. Whatever the combination of causes, we sympathize with Barnett and Terhune's (1979) summary:

> It is ironic that just as the Tanks reached their time of greatest glory they were forced to disband. Pushed by the Depression, professional football became a "big city-money game." No longer would small towns, with a lot of pride

and heart, be able to challenge the big cities. . . . A golden era for football and Ironton died together. (p. 20)

The socially embedded would succumb to more abstract economic calculus.

## Portsmouth

Portsmouth, Ohio, a winner in the "boosterism" war against Ironton, provides a relatively similar story, a story that reminds us that short-term victors can be long-term losers in the capital accumulation/capital mobility "game." "The citizens of Portsmouth viewed their hometown as a city on the move in the 1920s" (Barnett, 1980, p. 7). It had a slightly more diversified economy than Ironton: Steel, shoes, bricks, railheads, and riverheads provided the infrastructure. Moreover, Portsmouth's population was growing at a faster rate than Ironton's. There probably was optimism in Portsmouth: "The citizens of Portsmouth must have ignored the Oct. 24, 1929, 'Black Thursday' stock market crash when they decided to push for an NFL franchise. The Portsmouth National League Football Corporation was capitalized at $25,000 on June 12, 1930" (Barnett, 1980, p. 8). Prior to this time, the Portsmouth Spartans must have been an unaffiliated club—they had competed against Ironton in the 1920s in semiprofessional games. In the 1930s Portsmouth played a now-familiar tune: "Growth and prosperity—and winning football teams—seemed automatic" (Barnett, 1980, p. 7). Portsmouth joined the National Football League.

The Portsmouth Spartans were competitive on the field, but not economically. The auditor's report in 1931 indicated that the Spartans lost more than $16,000 on the season and were $27,000 in debt (Barnett, 1980, p. 9). Despite economic difficulties, the Spartans played well. However, the larger markets of the big cities were beginning to contour the development of the professional football industry. The Depression also was exerting its own determinations—people could not afford the price of admission. Perhaps because they were a league-affiliated team, the directors of the Portsmouth Spartans had an option that Ironton did not. They could look for greener pastures and relocate the franchise. The Spartans became the Detroit Lions and were reaccepted into the NFL in the summer of 1934. Barnett (1980, p. 10) states that this relocation was a bittersweet experience for football fans in Southern Ohio. The original Spartans won the NFL championship in the colors of the Detroit Lions.

## Linking Material Capital to Cultural Capital

What these two examples suggest is that in America, as elsewhere in the late capitalist nations, the logic of capital accumulation and the mobility of capital vis-à-vis cities and communities have created disproportions between regions and cities in their capacities to underwrite the profit margins of capitalists and, consequently, in their capacities to provide the infrastructure for collective consumption. This point has been neglected by the majority of scholars in sport studies—we have not consulted the works of urban geographers and urban political scientists (Castells, 1978; N.I. Fainstein & S.S. Fainstein, 1982a, 1982b; S.S. Fainstein, N.I. Fainstein, Hill, Judd, & Smith, 1983; Gregory & Urry, 1985; Harloe & Lebas, 1981; Harvey,

1973, 1978, 1985a, 1985b; Rosenthal, 1980; Smith, 1979). Thus, we are currently unable to link the internal reorganization of the economy of sport leagues and the termination or relocation of professional sport franchises to the broader forces that contour capital's investment/disinvestment decisions. Are the two even related? We think so.

How the investment/disinvestment decisions (including those of sport firms) influence a city's or community's symbolic sense of itself also requires further research. Immediately, a "chicken and egg" problem arises. Did some cities or communities materially and symbolically deform (e.g., plant closures due to declining demand, high levels of unemployment, urban blight, crime, etc.) before franchises moved, or did franchise relocation occur and add to community deformation (loss of identity, loss of "trickle-down" economic benefits)? Did cities and communities deform and seek to reform (central business district renewal projects, for example) by including stadium construction in their renewal schemes? Does stadium construction imply to capital's investors that, where there is boosterism, a good business climate prevails? No thorough analysis exists of the articulation between material capital (e.g., industry, services, finance) and cultural capital (i.e., the resources and capacities to influence what the culture should be and, in terms of the culture industry, the control over the means of its commodified production and distribution).

A response to these questions minimally requires what we phrase a problematic that does the following:

- Takes into account the trial and error period of entrepreneurial sport.
- Looks at the early franchise termination/relocation process involving smaller cities whose economic prosperity was linked to a major capital investor and, hence, was subject to the market demand/price fluctuations for the product of that industry—an issue of economic diversification and city size.
- Looks at recent relocations that have occurred within the league-defined monopoly boundaries, that is, cities or counties that have lost their franchises to other cities or counties in the same (league-defined) market territory (e.g., the Rams from L.A. County to Orange County; the Giants from New York City to the Meadowlands, New Jersey). Here, the social-symbolic community is technically defined (market radius) by the league. From the league's perspective, fans are simply required to travel elsewhere to see their "local" team play. From the city or county perspective, however, the trickle-down benefits and boosterism benefits have been transplanted, and civic identity has been questioned.
- Looks at recent relocations from one (league-defined) market to another—the latter being geographically distanced from the extant consumers (e.g., Dodgers from Brooklyn to Los Angeles; Raiders from Oakland to Los Angeles; Colts from Baltimore to Indianapolis). Here, the franchise violates the norms of reciprocity between itself and the community by denying the community access to its product, the trickle-down economic benefits, and the symbolic source of community sentiment.

We await such a systematic investigation, but even brief excursions into these problematics can be revealing. We have made a brief excursion into the first two.

At this point, we will provide an overview of the prevailing economic arrangements of professional sport leagues.

# Dominant Practices: Professional Team Sports, Economic Calculus, and Recent Relocations

## The Economic Calculus

To explore the modern problematic involving franchise relocations, it is necessary to relate the decisions of teams (firms) and the decisions of leagues to the prevailing logic of capital accumulation in the professional sports industry. Many scholars have addressed the structure of the professional sport industry and evaluated how it transacts its business (Davenport, 1969; Noll, 1974; Quirk, 1973; Quirk & El Hodiri, 1974; Staudohar, 1985; Weistart, 1984). The professional sport industry, like other capitalist enterprises, has an economic rationale anchored in the logic of capital accumulation. In its current commodity form, sport involves both collusion and competition—collusion in the form of common trade practices and competition on the field to produce an event that has both dramatic and exchange value. Individual sport leagues (e.g., the National Football League, the National Basketball Association, the National Hockey League, and Major League Baseball) control the production and marketing of the sport event. In other words, the league is an institutional structure that formalizes rules governing the players (their eligibility, allocation, and contracts), the event (official rules of the game), the season (number of games played and the determination of a league champion), and the franchises (number and location). For the league to function as a viable economic institution, it has been claimed, uncertainty in the outcome of league contests must be assured (Davenport, 1969; Quirk, 1973).

Continued domination by one team in the league would, according to the theorists, lessen the dramatic value of the contest in the long run. More to the point, such a scenario would ultimately lead to lack of interest in league games, lessening the league's ability to command high prices. Thus, to promote joint profit maximization, the league operates to disperse playing talent and instill public confidence in the honesty of the game. As Davenport (1969) points out:

> A sports firm requires worthy partners to produce a game that is to be sold. . . . In short, we find in this industry a demand which depends on the relative strength of different participants. Any one club cannot produce alone the utility streams provided by games and a championship race. (p. 6)

Essentially, the professional sport league is a cartel. Noll (1974) argues that it is a cartel with a remarkably complex set of rules and practices designed to restrict business competition (for athletes) among its members and divide markets among firms in the industry.

For example, each league operates as a cartel by imposing three major types of restrictions concerning interteam competition for player services, sale of broadcasting rights, and location and relocation of franchises (Noll, 1974). The first restriction, monopsony, is designed to control the costs of acquiring players by restricting interteam bidding. League rules once specified procedures for drafting new talent whereby top free agents are awarded to teams based on reverse order of finish in league standings. Rules pertaining to the specifics of player contracts vary between leagues. However, their aggregate effect does more than discourage competitive bidding: Provisions also exist that constitute a mechanism for circulating marginal players among teams. Such provisions are designed to reduce disparity in quality between the best and the worst teams in the league (Noll, 1974). Although monopsony, and the players' responses to it (e.g., unionization, collective bargaining, and strike) have been explored by a number of scholars (see especially Rivkin, 1974; Scoville, 1974; and Staudohar, 1986), they are not directly relevant to the analysis of franchise relocation. Rather, it is the restrictions placed on the consumer market that command greater attention.

The second way a league acts as a cartel is by manipulating the sale of the product of the industry. Both broadcasts of games and admission to games are subject to league regulations. The league exercises control over national broadcasts of games and imposes rules enabling individual teams to control broadcasts within their local territories. Here, leagues negotiate national television and radio contracts and determine how revenue is dispersed among the teams in the league. Local television and radio contracts are negotiated by individual teams; however, the league assures that each is guaranteed exclusive rights to broadcast its home games to the local market and that these broadcasts are not interfered with by other teams in the league. Additionally, teams exercise control over the sale of their own admission tickets. Although ticket prices may vary from team to team, revenue sharing of gate receipts is mandated by most leagues. For example, in basketball (NBA), the home team receives 100% of the money earned by fan attendance at games. Home football teams (NFL), on the other hand, may only retain 60% of the gate with 40% being collected by the visiting team (Quirk, 1973). As Quirk (1973) emphasizes,

> gate-sharing is not argued on the basis of some notion of ''fairness'' but rather because, by acting to equalize revenue potential, its effect is to enhance the competitive aspects of the sport and thus improve the economic viability of the league. (p. 195)

A third illustration of league cartelization is its control of franchise location, relocation, and number. Each team is granted a market area and the right to behave monopolistically within that league-defined geographical location, selling its own tickets, broadcasting its own games, and vending its own concessions (depending on stadium ownership or terms of lease). These are a franchise's traditional sources of income. Generally, no team may move into another team's market area without consent of the existing team. Further, existing teams may not relocate without permission from the majority of the cartel members.

The market area that a single team controls (or wishes to control) is of primary import to an analysis of franchise relocation. As Quirk (1973) has shown, teams located in the largest market areas (defined by population) have tended to dominate league standings. Here, there seems to be a relationship between revenue potential and playing strength. Small-city franchises and second franchises in a city seem to experience competitive difficulties both on the field and in the ledger. As Ingham and Hardy (1984) have expressed the case, the sport industry's economic calculus equates low profits or capital loss with game won-loss percentage. In the long run, such a correspondence produces a spiraling effect. Simply put, teams experiencing economic woes cannot offer commanding prices for player services; teams lacking top playing talent are usually near the bottom in league standing and draw less revenue from consumers.

## The Impact of Television

A calculus based on population size of market areas holds generally, but television has its own determinations. Cities can be ranked on the strength of viewing habits. As Michener (1976) poses the issue: Why would the NFL grant a football franchise to Tampa, Florida? The answer:

> At present two major measurements are used to determine the television potential of a city. Area of Dominant Influence (ADI) allocates every county in the United States to that metropolitan area which dominates its viewing habits. Designated Market Area (DMA) assigns districts according to their viewing habits during prime time and is therefore a more sophisticated measure of advertising potential than the cruder geographic allocations of ADI . . . Tampa may rate only twenty-seventh in population, but rates in television potential ahead of such established markets as Cincinnati, Buffalo, Denver, New Orleans, and San Diego. (pp. 305-307)

Because franchises are granted the right to negotiate local television contracts for games that are not included in the national broadcast contracts, local viewing habits are crucial when considering the revenue potential of market areas. As Ingham, Howell, and Schilperoort (1987) expressed the point, "professional football's economic calculus takes into account the *over-the-air* television market—its media value based upon how much an advertiser should pay relative to pure media efficiency" (p. 437). Media markets, and more recently cable television and luxury box rentals, are additional sources of income for professional sport franchise owners.

## Relocation

Operating under the logic of capital accumulation, sport firms jockey to monopolize the largest revenue-producing areas. An owner of a marginal low-profit franchise may envision higher profit potential in another area and request permission of the league (cartel) to relocate when his or her present lease expires. Bearing in mind that the financial strength of the cartel depends in large part on the relative profits of each member firm, there exist many strong incentives for such a request to be approved: Because of gate-sharing rules, all owners reap financial benefit from a team that procures larger game attendance; other owners of low profit franchises may wish to set precedents in the event that they may someday seek greener pastures; for wealthier clubs, moves delay the day when substantive changes have to be made in league rules to distribute revenue more evenly; and a proposal that is rejected is almost certain to leak to the press. Such an event may result in a decline in fan support and loss of revenue for the franchise that had desired to relocate. Given these incentives, the relocation of a franchise to an area of larger profit potential is economically beneficial for the entire league (cartel) and is usually not opposed (see Quirk, 1973).

If an existing team does not move in, a city that wants to obtain a professional sport franchise may be granted an expansion team (disregarding the possibility of rival league formation). Here again, the size of the league is determined by its existing members. When a league decides to expand, its members determine the location of expansion and the price the new team must pay to be included in the league (Noll, 1974). Expansions are rarely granted, however, because increasing the number of franchises in the league dilutes both the capital gain of existing franchises and the player talent pool.

By restricting the supply of its product, the members of the sport cartel create conditions of scarcity. Scarcity, it would appear, is a double-edged sword. As indicated earlier, Quirk (1973) suggests that restricting the number of franchises in the league and generally permitting free movement to areas of greater profit potential results in higher revenue for the cartel. A product high in demand and low in supply can command a high price. However, as Noll (1974) observes: "Regardless of the legal standing of the rules, they are effective as long as all concerned agree that the number of franchises should be limited and that teams should not compete for the same fans" (p. 9). In other words, the cartel's strength is vested in all the members acting as a group. Ingham et al. (1987, p. 436) argue that league-defined conditions of scarcity may weaken the strength of the cartel. Because such a high demand exists for the product in low supply, incentives exist for individual teams to act in violation of league rules. This seems especially pertinent in the case of franchise relocation. In the event that a relocation request is denied by the cartel (e.g., Al Davis's request to relocate his Raiders from Oakland to Los Angeles in 1983), the incentives are so powerful that owners may be willing to pursue litigation aimed to restore their right to search out entrepreneurial advantage.

## Intracity and Intercity Relocations: An Economic Scenario

It is commonly believed that hosting a professional sport franchise enhances a community's prestige. As Okner (1974) stated, many people believe that "no place really can be considered to be a 'big town' if it doesn't have a professional baseball or football team" (p. 327). However, obtaining or retaining a professional sport franchise entails a number of public policy issues. These public policy concerns have been explored by Johnson (1978, 1982, 1983, 1985, 1986). Johnson (1986) notes that currently there are nearly 50 American cities hosting professional sport franchises. Most if not all franchises receive public subsidies, commonly in the form of below-market rents for their use of publicly owned stadia or tax abatements for privately owned sports facilities. Since 1980, in nearly half of these cities, professional sport franchise owners have demanded an increase in public subsidies. As Johnson (1982) states: "Almost without exception, removal of the franchise from the host community was an implied, it not explicit, threat underlying negotiations" (p. 210).

Johnson, along with Quirk and El Hodiri (1974), points out that franchise relocation has been the rule rather than the exception. According to Johnson's (1982) data, since 1950 a total of 78 franchise relocations have occurred in leagues that existed two or more years. Further, the appearance of franchise stability in a particular league may be deceiving. For example, according to Johnson (1982) the National Football League recognized only one approved franchise shift (Chicago to St. Louis) in the period between 1962 and 1982. However, 19 of 28 National Football League clubs changed stadia. Since these changes occurred within the league-defined geographic area of "home territory" (a 75-mile radius), they were not considered to be actual relocations. The Rams' move from Los Angeles County to Orange County, California, and the Giants' move from New York City to the Meadowlands, New Jersey, are recent examples of moves that have occurred within league-defined monopoly boundaries. These moves, however, were accompanied by loss of economic benefits and loss of a tenant from a sport facility that has few alternative uses. As well, a nationally visible source of civic pride is lost by the old host community.

## Watts Vs. Anaheim: The Case of the Rams

On February 15, 1978, a full-page advertisement appeared in the *Los Angeles Times* (p. III-6) encouraging Carroll Rosenbloom, the owner of the L.A. Rams, to move his NFL franchise from Los Angeles County to the city of Anaheim, Orange County. The advertisement was paid for by the Committee to Relocate the Rams to Orange County. Speaking as "concerned community leaders and dedicated Ram football fans" the Committee sought to extoll the demographic virtues of Orange County vis-à-vis Watts as a venue for professional football: 1.7 million people, the ninth largest county in the U.S.A., and 10 million people living within a 40-mile radius of Anaheim stadium. Moreover, in comparison to Watts (the site of the L.A. Coliseum), Anaheim offered comfort, safety, and convenience. These proclaimed attributes would promote fan enjoyment of home games and would be factors in the betterment of professional football.

The timing of the advertisement was well-conceived. Rosenbloom had had difficulties with the L.A. Memorial Coliseum directors over stadium improvements. Rosenbloom wanted the Coliseum to be a more profitable football stadium. This required a lowering of the field to allow more seats closer to the sidelines and the construction of luxury boxes. Obstructing such renovation was the fact that the City of Los Angeles had applied for the 1984 Summer Olympics and would need the track around the playing field to be left in place at least through the summer of 1984. Rosenbloom downplayed these issues. Instead, he alluded to the fact that the

Rams did not want to be a burden to the taxpayers by incurring a public subsidy for stadium renovation. If the Rams moved "across town" the taxpayers would be relieved and the fans could continue to support the team (*L.A. Times*, July 26, 1978, p.I-1).

It is evident that both the Committee to Relocate the Rams and Rosenbloom invoked fan interests (fan protection, fan convenience, fan enjoyment) and taxpayer interest (it will cost you less if we move and will cost you more to renovate) as reasons for relocation. Yet, we note that (a) Ram attendances had been declining from a high point of 73,000 in 1973 to a low point of 59,000 in 1977 (*L.A. Times*, March 25, 1979, p. I-1); (b) Anaheim had agreed to provide executive offices and a practice field adjoining the stadium; (c) Anaheim had agreed to expand the Anaheim facility from a capacity of 43,250 to 70,000; and (d) Anaheim would install 108 luxury boxes in the renovated stadium. Furthermore, Rosenbloom and the "City" of Anaheim were involved in a $125 million commercial development project (shopping/hotel/office) to be constructed on an area adjacent to the stadium—it was expected to be completed over a 10- to 15-year period. For Rosenbloom, Anaheim offered incentives that Watts could not. As an L.A. citizen noted:

> Even if the [L.A.] Coliseum Commission had lowered and enclosed the stadium and provided soft seating, air-conditioning, closed circuit T.V. and indoor parking it would have made no difference because they could not offer a deal for a shopping center/hotel complex in a prosperous white neighborhood. (*L.A. Times*, August 4, 1978, p. II-1)

Some interesting sport/community problematics are suggested here. First, in terms of capital investment/disinvestment decisions, was the relocation another example of not only intercity competition but of intracity (central city-satellite city) competition? It would appear so. When compared to the already deteriorating Watts area of South-central Los Angeles—a poor area with high unemployment and minority group habitation—Orange County would appear as a better investment risk. Second, what role do so-called "entrepreneurs in the public interest"—in this case the Committee to Relocate the Rams—play in contouring the decisions of franchise owners? Which ideologies of progrowth, trickle-down benefits and scenarios of good business climate do franchise owners listen to, and why?

In the contest of "communities"/counties, Anaheim emerged victorious. But what of the loser? The capital logic that, at one time, had brought investment and growth to inner-city Los Angeles now threatened it with disinvestment, decline, and decay. In the realm of professional sport, the L.A. Coliseum had lost its principal tenant and stood to lose $750,000 a year in rents, not to mention Watts's loss of derived income and whatever civic pride the Rams brought to the local environs. Could the disinvestment decisions of Rosenbloom be reversed? Could a $750,000 deficit that would have required a resubsidization by the City of Los Angeles and Los Angeles County to keep the Coliseum alive be met? Apparently not, for in a perverse move, given past experiences, the Coliseum Commission sought another NFL franchise. There was a major obstacle in this. The relocation of the Rams had occurred *within* the 75-mile territorial limits. Therefore, the relocation, despite the fact that it crossed county lines, was not treated as a relocation per se—it was simply a switch of stadiums within the existing boundaries of a declared market area. Bearing this in mind, Pete Rozelle (the NFL Commissioner) noted that Los Angeles County (and Watts) could not be guaranteed a new (relocation or expansion) franchise. A relocation would violate Rule 4.3 of the League constitution, which prevented any relocation into fixed market boundaries without the consent of a majority (three-fourths) of the NFL owners. Disappointed by this proclamation, the Los Angeles Coliseum Commission, on September 13, 1978, filed an antitrust lawsuit that charged the NFL with conspiracy to restrain trade in violation of the Sherman Act. It is hard to gauge the relative weight that the Coliseum Commission placed on the economic survival of the Coliseum, the economic survival of Watts, the symbolic, civic pride of Los Angeles, the blow to "boosterism" strategies, and proclamations of progrowth. As assemblywoman Teresa Hughes expressed the situation:

> We are overlooking a big damage that can be done to inner-city, the psychological damage of a big ball team moving out of that which is now a very, very poor community, which was an affluent community back in the 1920s and 30s when this was a choice area. We had palatial homes. Some of those homes are still standing and decaying just as the coliseum is standing and decaying.
>
> The (Rams) probably have a very nice place down there in Anaheim, but the unemployment is not as high as it is in south-central L.A. By allowing the Coliseum to decay, by providing a situation that would motivate the Rams to abandon our community, you're going to add fuel to the fire of unemployment.
>
> It's not just the Rams I am pleading for. It's not just the Coliseum. It's the entire repercussion . . . of what we can do to bring life back into the community. (*L.A. Times*, August 9, 1978, p. I-1)

In short, the relocation would materially and symbolically exacerbate the community deformation process. Abstract, cartelized agreements concerning territoriality ignored the social, segmental interests of Watts. But L.A. County would fight back in an attempt to reform the deformed. The Coliseum Commission not only filed an antitrust suit but also "advertised" its facilities to any NFL franchise willing to relocate. Given the Los Angeles market size, this was a strategic maneuver, even if it involved the sequestering of public monies for eventual stadium refurbishment.

## Oakland Vs. Los Angeles: The Case of the Raiders

The tactics of the L.A. Coliseum Commission bring us to the issue of between-market-area relocations—the case of the Raiders. As the relocation debate continued in California, Al Davis, managing general partner of the Oakland Raiders football franchise, began to show an interest in the Los Angeles market. Davis was experiencing difficulties with the Oakland Coliseum Commission concerning his demands for stadium improvement, which would total $15 million. In addition, Davis wanted the Commission to build luxury boxes (*L.A. Times*, July 8, 1982, p. III-1).

Although the Oakland Raiders had been a successful and profitable franchise (every home game sold out since 1968), it was evident that substate and city subsidies to professional football franchises elsewhere were increasing at a rate greater than in Oakland. The stadium was losing ground to others in seating capacity and other teams were now benefiting from luxury box income. Davis sought greener pastures.

Meanwhile, the L.A. Coliseum Commission, still in search of a tenant, began to entice the restless Davis and his Raiders. In order to ''get'' Davis, the L.A. Coliseum needed to be refurbished. ''Get the Raiders'' became a civic mandate, and L.A. County and city officials and boosters greased their machines. By January 1980, a package deal of approximately $17 million had been offered to the Raiders. It included the construction of 99 luxury boxes, three practice fields, improved dressing rooms, and relocation expenses. The funds for renovations included $5.5 million from the L.A. City Council, $5 million from the L.A. County Board of Supervisors, and $5 million from the L.A. Olympic Organization Committee.

Davis's continued negotiations with the Oakland Coliseum Commission failed to match the incentives provided by Los Angeles—stadium size and improvements, broadcast revenues, and the potential pay television (cable) opportunities. Davis would follow the yellow-brick road; both economics and fate dictated it. Said Davis,

> The environment forces people to act. I always believed I could beat it, I could make the environment work for me. But this time it's making me act in a way I never thought I would. . . . I will take into account loyalty to the community and the fans but I will also give myself an opportunity I never thought I would. I'm going to weigh the opportunity. I would hope you wouldn't treat this as an indictment of anybody, but this is where we ended up. (*Oakland Tribune*, June 14, 1980, p. D-1)

Davis also noted, ''I have a lot of love for the fans in Oakland. . . . The people are excellent. . . . They [Oakland Coliseum Commission] ruined it, destroyed it'' (*Oakland Tribune*, May 8, 1982, p. D-1). The Raiders relocation required, according to the NFL constitution, the approval of other NFL franchise owners. The approval never came. In reply, Davis publicly committed himself to relocation and, in March 1980, joined the L.A. Coliseum Commission in its antitrust litigation against the NFL—a suit that the NFL was to lose in the courts.

NFL Commissioner Pete Rozelle rendered an opinion to which he seemed steadfastly committed:

> What public consumer, or fan interests are served by an antitrust principle that compels a sports league, under threat of treble-damage liability, to permit its most successful and best supported teams to put themselves up for public auction whenever the current [franchise-stadium] leases expire?
>
> When Congress approved the AFL/NFL merger in 1966, the Congressmen wanted assurances from the clubs that there would be no franchise shifts so long as the clubs were being well supported. The League gave its word to Congress that no franchise would relocate without demonstrating that either the fans in the present location were not supporting the club or that it had an

untenable stadium situation. Neither of these conditions were present when the Raiders proposed their move to Los Angeles.

If—as the Los Angeles Coliseum and the Raiders claimed—Oakland community interests and other values at stake in the Raiders' case cannot be respected under the anti-trust laws, then I believe something is wrong with the existing antitrust principle. (From a release supplied by Leonard Koppett, Editor, *The Peninsula Times Tribune*)

## Baltimore and the NFL's Colts: A Political Economy Scenario

Baltimore is a city whose postwar urban crisis left it with the same kinds of problems experienced by other old American cities. Like them, Baltimore responded with an ambitious progrowth campaign that equated private capital investment/accumulation with the public interest. This growth initiative resulted in an ambitious redevelopment strategy that sought to reestablish business and upper-class control of urban space. Unlike some cities, however, Baltimore's class struggles and social conflicts resulted in a serious legitimation crisis for the local regime's progrowth ideology, and lower- and middle-class resistance to the local state's growth strategies peaked in the late 1960s.

The postwar shift in the nation's economy left Baltimore's aging downtown core with many structures that were rapidly becoming obsolete. The economic trend away from centrally located manufacturing (Baltimore's mainstay) threatened the economic viability of Baltimore's central business district. With this shift came a concomitant loss of jobs and population from the city's core.

The availability of FHA mortgages and the construction of Baltimore's 695 Beltway accelerated the flight of thousands of middle-income whites from the inner city. The relocation of these residents to the suburbs depressed the downtown retail market to the point of near failure. At the same time, the predominantly black, low-income population in the inner city increased and was entrapped. The city's business and government leaders of the late 1950s and early 1960s faced the prospects of growing social stress in a downtown that was increasingly shunned by its former users (Lieberman, 1982). In a comprehensive study of Baltimore, Sherry Olson (1976) wrote:

> By 1960, the whole downtown was ready for retirement. It was physically obsolete, financially stagnant, and psychologically demoralized. Baltimore began to feel the economic competition with other cities changing their skylines and a fiscal competition with its own ring of suburbs. This produced a do-or-die sense of crisis among certain financial interests. (p. 50)

It was against this backdrop that the city's business and government leaders embarked on a series of ambitious revitalization projects in the 1960s.

In 1960, Baltimore's mayor set forth a revitalization agenda designed to attract capital to the downtown. The policies formed by Baltimore's public entrepreneurs were tailored to the interests of private capitalists. A wide array of federal aid and local incentives were combined to virtually eliminate economic risk to private developers. According to Lieberman (1982), the local state played four key roles in the attempt to revitalize Baltimore's central business district. First, it built a physical infrastructure that would entice and support private development. Infrastructure changes included new streets and expressways, a public transit line, a pedestrian walkway, and the creation of attractive public open spaces. Second, it strengthened its investment in public institutions that it hoped would improve the environment for downtown activities. These public institutions included the University of Maryland, the State Office Complex, the University of Baltimore, City Hall Municipal Center, and the Community College of Baltimore. Third, local government representatives offered broad administrative assistance (e.g., assembling target sites for redevelopment, providing low-cost development loans and loan guarantees) to private capital. Finally, the local government involved the citizenry by conducting electoral campaigns and sponsoring festivals in downtown renewal areas. Eventually private capital and government leaders joined forces in a concerted effort to revitalize downtown Baltimore.

Reshaping Baltimore was not quite as socially benign as Lieberman alludes. Enticing private capital by "improving the environment for downtown development" (Lieberman, 1982, p. 37) entailed displacing large populations of low-income blacks. Publicly supported urban renewal strategies and government-sponsored displacement of selected populations coincided. The rate of displacement accelerated from 600 households in 1950 to 8,000 households in 1970. In the period between 1951 and 1970, 75,000 people had been displaced—80% to 90% of which were black (Olson, 1976). The intensity of this displacement created housing gaps and accentuated social stress in the mid-1960s. As Olson (1976) states:

> The public housing waiting lists were filled with hard to relocate people. It became obvious to everyone (it had always been obvious to the black community) that urban renewal meant black removal. The implications were laid bare and there was a crystallization of resistance—black resistance to removal, resistance of adjoining communities to a relocation spillover threat, and resistance of neighborhoods to construction of new projects. (p. 54)

The public uproar over such massive and rapid governmental actions greatly hampered the effectiveness of Baltimore's political machine in the late 1960s. The public that supported expenditures of $38.8 million (including $10.5 million of city bond funds) in 1959 to build the downtown Charles Center defeated a $3 million redevelopment bond issue in 1968. Finally, the city's political machine and its growth strategy was supplanted. In 1971, Baltimore elected a new mayor, William Donald Schaeffer, on a platform that included a firm commitment to housing programs and residential neighborhood interests (Berkowitz, 1984). Learning from the mistakes of the 1960s, Mayor Schaeffer set forth a new agenda. In the 1970s, municipal agencies were reorganized, rehabilitation (rather than clearance) of low-income neighborhoods was stressed, and fuller citizen participation was sought.

In 1970, half of Baltimore City's workforce consisted of blue-collar laborers (Baltimore Chamber of Commerce, 1986). Major Schaeffer's platform in 1971 included the funding of an economic development program with the purpose of strengthening industrial retention and attraction. The bond issue that had been defeated in 1968 was approved in 1971 and led to the creation of Baltimore Economic Development Corporations (BEDCO). From 1976 to 1984 BEDCO was responsible for creating or maintaining approximately 24,000 jobs and increasing revenue from real estate taxes by over $3 million per year (Berkowitz, 1984). The success of the BEDCO project helped to increase public trust and confidence in Schaeffer's future projects.

In addition to his attempt to strengthen Baltimore's industrial capacity, Schaeffer also attempted to increase the city's ability to capture tourist dollars. The focal point of this attempt was the massive Inner Harbor Project. Public funding for the project totaled approximately $100 million. Of this total, $75 million was provided by federal grants and $17 million in city bond funds, block grant funds, and state grants—Baltimore did not have the power to abate real property taxes and does not offer local grants (Berkowitz, 1984). Baltimore's limited powers necessitated creative financial backing for many projects that were often underwritten by the State of Maryland.

Although Schaeffer received solid public support, some skepticism caused by the political mistakes of the 1960s still existed. Many individuals simply did not view Baltimore as a tourist mecca, but rather as an old, traditional blue-collar town. In a poignant essay titled "The Image: Does it Matter?" Sherry Olson (1976) wrote:

> The mayor and his business leaders are concerned about the city's image among port users, in international trade, and in national tourism. . . . Baltimore was known for the Preakness and for its sports teams—the Colts, the Orioles, the Bullets, and the Clippers. Does it matter whether the teams are sold to some other town? Which of dozens of promotional schemes . . . will put across a Baltimore image? Will a $100 million stadium make Baltimore more visible? Or will it make it look more like Dallas? (p. 87)

Baltimore did not choose to build a new stadium but did continue its efforts to attract tourists' dollars. In 1976, the Baltimore Office of Promotion and Tourism (BOPT) was created to market Baltimore externally and design activities for attracting area residents to the Inner Harbor ("Harborplace"). By 1984, buildings representing approximately $1.5 billion in new private, public, and institutional investment were completed, under construction, or committed in the Inner Harbor (Berkowitz, 1984).

Baltimore of the early 1980s was economically and socially healthier than it was two decades prior. It enjoyed an increased tax base downtown and more public housing in residential areas. Berkowitz (1984) refers to Baltimore as an economic development success story. From 1970 to 1983, household income rose by 7.8% annually (to $27,000), which spurred an annual 8% gain in total retail sales (Urban Land Institute, 1986). Baltimore's commitment to the tourist industries produced an 8% increase in service occupation jobs between 1970 and 1984 (Baltimore Chamber of Commerce, 1986).

What Baltimore did not enjoy, however, was its relationship with Colts owner Robert Irsay. Whether one took an optimistic or pessimistic view of Baltimore's economic health, the loyal football community looked for some stability, some continuity in the guise of the NFL's Colts. However, the long and tumultuous lease negotiations between Irsay and the Baltimore Stadium Authority in 1984 called into question the "norms of reciprocity" that exist between franchise and community. Irsay's list of displeasures concerning Memorial Stadium included problems with parking, conflicts with surrounding residents, and structural problems with the 30-year-old stadium itself. Irsay openly shopped the Colts around to all parts of the country to spur Baltimore into meeting his demands for change. Irsay's threats of relocation perpetuated the animosity toward him from fans and the local press. With growing cynicism, the press accused the franchise owner of alienating the city from the team. On February 27, 1984, fears that Irsay would put the team up on the auctioning block were confirmed as the front page of the *Baltimore Sun* read: "Indianapolis Makes Offer to Irsay for Colts."

Eventually Baltimore, Phoenix, and Indianapolis would be in direct competition for the Colts. As the bidding war dragged on, uncertainty regarding the high costs of competition grew in Baltimore. The press increasingly showed a bias toward pulling out of the Colts war and a few Baltimore residents, although endeared to the Colts, expressed concerns over the costs of retaining them. For example, one Baltimore resident wrote:

> To my way of thinking, it is almost obscene that our leadership should be so sedulously engaged in the effort to find Irsay most favorable interest terms for his business operations while foreclosures and harsh bankruptcies apace in Maryland.
>
> Irsay and his business interests will be served, whether here in Baltimore or wherever he chooses to relocate. The plight of the little person, the home-owner or small business owner, brought to the brink of ruin in the wake of disastrous federal fiscal policy will not be attended to unless the people force the issue. (*Baltimore Sun*, March 25, 1984, p. K6)

Likewise, referring to the increasingly expensive inducements being offered to Irsay vis-à-vis the capital being supplied for social services, another citizen wrote:

> Somewhere along the line, we have lost our sense of values and proportion. At the same time, roads and streets need fixing, education is short-changed, people cannot buy homes because of high interest rates and the bay needs cleaning up—just to mention a few problems we are facing in this time of fiscal stress.
>
> I would tell Robert Irsay to take his team and go, but don't forget to pay local governments for past rents, taxes, etc., that we have coming to us. (*Baltimore Sun*, March 27, 1984, p. K6)

By the time the above letters to the editor were written, the end to the intercity competition for the Colts was near. On March 27 Phoenix retracted its bid, saying it could no longer match the inducements offered by Baltimore and Indianapolis. Although Irsay made no verbal indication that he had reached a decision, on March 28 a fleet of moving vans arrived at the Colts training complex in Owings Mills. The vans remained at the complex all day as rumors of an impending move spread throughout the Baltimore area. Carloads of fans, reporters, and photographers drove to the complex. Police were dispatched to the area to keep ''order'' and to keep traffic from blocking the streets. Around midnight, March 29, Irsay ordered, probably because of an eminent domain initiative, the packed vans to Indianapolis. The Baltimore Sun's morning headline read, ''Baltimore's Colts Are Gone: Irsay Ends the 31-Year Marriage.''

> Under the cover of darkness and downpour, the Baltimore Colts galloped to Indianapolis early yesterday in a caravan of Mayflower trucks to end the city's 31-year era in the National Football League.
> Reneging on a promise, the team's controversial owner, Robert Irsay, did not even call the mayor to say good-bye. (*Baltimore Sun*, March 30, 1984, p. 1)

Johnson (1984, pp. 210-218) asserts that the acquisition or retention of a sports franchise is a project that city officials find hard to resist. Their victory in the franchise hopscotch game not only promotes community consensus but also provides the opportunity for civic officials to demonstrate leadership skills. Given this scenario, we can perhaps understand Mayor Schaeffer's chagrin: ''I'm trying to retain what little dignity I have left in this matter. If the Colts had to sneak out of town at night, it degrades a great city. . . . I hate to see a man cry'' (*Baltimore Sun*, March 30, 1984, p. 1). Baltimore's mayor had lost the hopscotch game, and Baltimore faced more than just a financial loss.

Although these accounts of the Tanks, Spartans, Rams, Raiders, and Colts are only illustrative, they do raise some interesting issues concerning the articulation of capital investment/disinvestment decisions, the practices of substate (county and city officials) and the policies of franchise owners. Our illustrations do suggest that the producer-consumer relationship has been transformed (see Clarke & Critcher, 1985, pp. 95-97). They suggest that the policies of sport-firm owners now articulate more with the capital investment/disinvestment decisions of the hegemonic fractions of the dominant class and with the tax abatement/public subsidy decisions of substate (city and county) officials, and less with the aspirations of the localized consumer. Cities suffer economically and consumers psychologically when franchises abandon them. Policy issues, therefore, confront city officials every time lease negotiations take place. Important political decisions must be made by officials who wish to retain or obtain a professional sport franchise in their communities.

It is easy to see why city officials and their constituents wish to host the sport event; that is, why people ''choose sport.'' But why does sport (its entrepreneurs) ''choose'' certain peoples (cities)? Are symbolic explanations alone sufficient? Or must we assume from intercity bidding wars that owners whose teams are on the auctioning block will award the team's services to the most lucrative bid? Does the logic of capital accumulation alone explain the investment decisions of the sport entrepreneur? Finally, what constitutes a good business climate for sport?

# The Emergent as Merely Novel: Redefining the City and the Relationship Between Pro Sport and Progrowth

The logic of capital accumulation and the mobility of capital vis-à-vis cities and communities creates disproportionate economic growth between cities and regions. The dramatics of uneven growth patterns are exemplified in the changing conditions of our urban areas. Here, a brief explanation of the economic trends that have affected American cities is necessary. We argue that the ways cities have responded to these trends lies at the heart of the professional sport franchise relocation problematic.

Changing patterns of production continually affect the economic and social character of American cities. In the postwar period, the condition of older central cities changed sharply. A national trend toward decentralization resulted in a nationwide shift in both population and industry from the central cities to the suburbs (Smith, 1979). By the 1970s, whole metropolitan regions began contracting as the population shifted from the industrial north to the southern "sun belt." Because of what has been termed "white flight," the central-city zones became poorer and inhabited by minority ethnic groups. Middle- and working-class whites moved out. By 1980, 55% of blacks and only 24% of whites lived in central-city zones (N.I. Fainstein & S.S. Fainstein, 1983). On the whole, central-city zones had become places where minority groups and low-income whites were encapsulated in "obsolete sectors of the economy and deteriorating physical environments" (S.S. Fainstein & N.I. Fainstein, 1983, p. 4).

Manufacturing continues to decline. The growth sector of the U.S. economy since the 1960s has been in the service industries. According to N.I. Fainstein and S.S. Fainstein (1983), in fourteen cities that showed an increase in total private employment between the years 1969 and 1978, services were the most rapidly expanding industry. Even in cities where private employment contracted, service employment expanded. Contracting cities lost an average of 404,000 jobs in manufacturing, retail, and wholesale trade while gaining 47,000 service jobs.

By the mid-1970s, capital accumulation priorities included expansion of white-collar industries, high-technology manufacturing, and consumption services. An integrated vision of the new city emerged as being a corporate headquarters center, with a central business district of office buildings, specialized shops, restaurants, hotels, and luxury apartments. The expanding service industry has been targeted by many cities in their attempt to redevelop their cores. Although cities have used various incentives and have experienced varying amounts of success in their capital accumulation objectives, there has been remarkable consistency in the sociospatial aim of redevelopment policies: to reestablish business and middle-class control of urban territory (N.I. Fainstein & S.S. Fainstein, 1983).

Here, two important points must be made. First, U.S. cities raise the majority of their revenue locally (mostly in property taxes). This system of finance compels the local government to maintain its revenue base by enticing investment that increases the market value of real property. Since lower-income populations contribute much less to revenues than they draw from social expenditures, a city acts in its financial best interest by excluding (or relocating) such households and attracting upper-income residents. Second, it is the substate (i.e., the city government) that takes responsibility for the functioning and outcome of the urban economy, even though capital effectively controls production of most goods and services. To reiterate an earlier point, capital's domination establishes a social dependency on private investment and accumulation (i.e., profit) for the provisions of employment and the built environment. To advance the material interests of its citizens, the substate is placed in the position of having to facilitate capital accumulation (N.I. Fainstein & S.S. Fainstein, 1983). Therefore, it acts to aid local firms to remain and expand, encourage other firms to relocate or open branch facilities, and create a sociospatial urban environment that stimulates the formation of new businesses. It is the growth model (i.e., its trickle-down effects) that underlies public and private support for urban redevelopment.

The politics of redevelopment are not without conflicts. Indeed, the substantive character of redevelopment policy creates a relatively constant set of fault lines—unchanged since the 1950s—by which conflicts can be defined. These conflicts become the "urban trenches" (Katznelson, 1981) in which redevelopment skirmishes are fought. N.I. Fainstein and S.S. Fainstein (1983, pp. 255-256) provide a detailed list of these fault lines. The critical point here is to realize that the city is not a unitary political entity. Physical and economic development policy decisions embody class and racial interests. As S.S. Fainstein and N.I. Fainstein (1983) note: "There are always distinct social groups who win and lose, regardless of whether political conflict becomes overt" (p. 2).

The point is that how a professional sport firm (operating under league-defined conditions of artificial scarcity) makes its decisions to stay or relocate may be contoured by the ways entrepreneurs in the public interest and entrepreneurs in the private interest combine to address these fault lines in their political solution to the urban question. The urban question, as Castells (1978) defines it,

> expresses the fundamental contradiction between, on the one hand the increasing socialization of consumption (as a result of the concentration of capital and the means of production), and on the other hand, the capitalist logic of the production and distribution of consumption. . . . In an attempt to resolve these conflicts, the state increasingly intervenes in the city; but, as an expression of a class society, the state in practice acts according to the relations of force between classes and social groups, generally in favor of the hegemonic fraction of the dominant classes. (p. 3)

What this might mean is that franchises make decisions to relocate not only on the basis of sport's economic calculus, but also on the degree to which entrepreneurs in the public interest make decisions conducive to capital accumulation within the hegemonic fraction of the dominant classes.

In many cities, the building of new sport facilities and the attempt to lure professional franchises has articulated with the broader strategies of progrowth and urban redevelopment. With the shift toward a service-oriented economy many cities have attempted to revitalize their cores through the development of an amenity infrastructure. The most ambitious of these cities have included in their redevelopment schemes the building of sports stadia as a foundation for capturing tourist dollars. Public and private entrepreneurs hope that urban amenities (including convention centers, shopping malls, luxury hotels) will attract private investment and re-create lifeless downtown areas into activity centers. The manner in which the progrowth/community-as-a-whole ideology is advanced and the extent to which taxpayers (literally) buy into it makes for interesting study.

# The Politically Redefined City: Indianapolis and the Progrowth Ideology

The city of Indianapolis is the site of one of the most intensive and successful progrowth coalitions in the country. Public and private entrepreneurs have collaborated to advance a revitalization campaign with the stated objective to turn Indianapolis into a mecca for tourists and conventioneers—despite its central location, this posed a formidable challenge for a city that has no mountains, seashores, or major rivers. Perhaps realizing the city's aesthetic limitations, these entrepreneurs mobilized public consensus by using sport as a foundation on which to build an amenity infrastructure.

Prior to its new growth strategy, the backbone of Indianapolis' economy was heavy manufacturing. Especially prominent were plants related to the automobile industry. This made Indianapolis vulnerable to the capital disinvestment spurred by national economic downturns and foreign competition in the auto industry.

## Flight from Indianapolis

In the 1960s and 1970s downtown Indianapolis was dying. The core of the city was dirty and filled with vacant, dilapidated buildings. As in many other old, industrial cities, businesses and residents were fleeing from the central business district, leaving behind a core with a weak tax base from which to draw revenues. A 1976 city planning study (see Bamberger & Parham, 1984, p. 13) concluded that if Indianapolis's strategy was to encourage residents to move away, it had achieved its objective very successfully. At one point, the central business district lost 20 residents per day; from 1970 to 1979, 45,000 citizens fled the city. When city officials reviewed Indianapolis's development patterns they discovered an almost total mismatch between where projections indicated development was supposed to occur and where development was in fact occurring. At the same time, the national economic recession of 1974 and 1975 forced many Marion County residents out of their jobs. From 1978 to 1982, an additional 35,000 private sector jobs were lost in Marion County (Bamberger & Parham, 1984). Indianapolis was facing an urban crisis of great proportions. Its response to this crisis illustrates the conflicts that arise when massive redevelopment policies to attract capital investment are implemented.

## Political Restructuring

The biggest step toward successful and rapid redevelopment occurred in 1970. That year the city's government was completely restructured to form its current city-county system, referred to as Unigov. Unigov combined the city and county governments into one body and made the mayor of Indianapolis the undisputed chief political executive of the entire area. In addition to expanding the Mayor's powers, Unigov circumvented the flight of jobs, middle-class citizens, and tax dollars to the suburbs. No longer would the city have to compete with its own suburbs for capital investment. The social expenditures required by the high-risk, low-income population in the city's core would become the partial financial responsibility of the more affluent suburban residents. This was not unique to Indianapolis: Other cities have adopted this approach to the urban crisis. What was unique, however, is the fact that the formation of Unigov could occur without voter approval.

The Unigov system, created by a single act of the Indiana legislature, increased Indianapolis's population by approx. 250,000 persons and its geographical area by some 275 square miles. It also diluted the city's black population from 30% of the total to 15% of the total. Leaders in Indianapolis's black community who opposed the Unigov legislation argued that this decrease drastically reduced the effectiveness of black participation in the political process (Owen & Willbern, 1985).

Since its adoption, Unigov has secured a solid line of Republican mayors who have loyally courted corporate business cooperation in designing the city's economic and sociospatial future. The public-private partnership ethic has been a driving force behind Indianapolis's growth plan. After the adoption of the Unigov system a number of business-based committees were organized. The most significant of these committees was the Corporate Community Council, which is composed of the "chief decision-makers" of the largest firms in Indianapolis and was founded to place corporate resources behind "selected" projects (*Wall Street Journal*, July 14, 1982, p. 32). Thus, the power of the local state and the influence of private capital merged to form political solutions to Indianapolis's urban question. The Unigov system greatly reduced the bureaucracy involved in implementing these solutions by combining 46 former city and county agencies into six departments with one chief executive (the Mayor). Building permits, zoning and housing codes, regional planning, and other governmental mechanisms were vastly streamlined. Publicly provided financial support can in some cases be leveraged without voter approval. In reference to Indianapolis's partnership ethic, the chairman of the city's largest bank told the *Wall Street Journal* (July 14, 1982, p. 1): "Some people say an elite runs this town. I don't like that word. I prefer leadership."

## The Indianapolis Image

In 1975, William H. Hudnut was elected to his first of three terms as Indianapolis's mayor. Hudnut's election is second only to the adoption of Unigov in importance to Indianapolis's revitalization history. His skill at advancing the progrowth ideology was manifested in a dramatic change in the city's built environment. In 1976, Hudnut argued, it would be necessary to build and promote an Indianapolis image (a point to which we will return). The image he chose to build was Amateur Sports Capital of the United States. Thus, entrepreneurs in the public interest planned their entire growth strategy using sport to build an amenity infrastructure.

In 1980, the pace of Indianapolis's downtown development exploded. That year the Greater Indianapolis Progress Committee published "The Regional Center General Plan," which outlined to the year 2000 the city's revitalization objectives (*The Christian Science Monitor*, October 4, 1985, p. 1). During the next 4 years over $126 million in public and private resources was invested in downtown, state-of-the-art sports facilities. Among the highlights were a $21-million swimming and diving complex, a $7-million tennis complex, a $6-million track and field stadium, and a $2.5-million velodrome. Funding was provided by public and private sources. The local state provided grants, tax abatements, and industrial revenue bonds. The Lilly Endowment contributed philanthropic resources to these facilities.

In February 1981, Mayor Hudnut announced plans to begin construction on the proud centerpiece of Indianapolis's growth plan—the Hoosier Dome. At a projected cost of $61 million, the Hoosier Dome was to be built in conjunction with the expansion and renovation of the Indianapolis convention center. The Capital Improvements Board (the Dome's authorities) proposed that 50% of the construction be funded by the corporate and philanthropic communities and 50% by a revenue bond issue.

In the downtown area, the Hudnut growth scheme branched out to include other types of development to attract middle- and upper-class populations. The city's Department of Metropolitan Development assembled enough financial incentives to convince developers to break ground on a $180-million Circle Center Retail Mall. A consortium of three Indianapolis banks provided $32 million to developers to renovate Union Station—that is, to turn an underused structure into a hotel/retail project adjacent to the Hoosier Dome. Moreover, a host of large luxury hotels, including a $40-million Convention Center hotel, were either planned or constructed. From 1980 to 1984, 16 new restaurants were added to the downtown area (Bamberger & Parham, 1984), and a total of $1.5 billion was invested in inner-city construction between 1974 and 1984 (Indianapolis Project, Inc., 1986).

Providing inner-city housing was another major focus of the Hudnut growth initiative. The vacant structures that were left in the wake of centrifugal migration produced an abundant inventory of buildings suitable for conversion into condominiums and luxury apartments. From 1980 to 1984, nearly 40 buildings were purchased for such conversion (Bamberger & Parham, 1984). Public and private entrepreneurs assisted the implementation of luxury apartment, townhouse, and condominium construction projects that proliferated throughout the city. Interestingly, while upper-class housing was supported, a program to assist lower-class home buyers was denied, and public housing was suffering from neglect.

In May of 1984, the *Indianapolis Star* revealed that the city was in danger of losing millions of dollars in federal mortgage money because no local bank could be found to loan the public housing mortgages. Local bankers gave various reasons for not participating (*Indianapolis Star*, May 6, 1984, p. 11). However, the important point here is: The same financial community that was willing to "shave their profits"

(Bamberger & Parham, 1984, p. 16) to help fund capital investment projects in the downtown was unwilling to participate in a noncompetitive program to assist low-income residents.

In June of 1984, a federal official for the Department of Housing and Urban Development (HUD) sharply criticized Indianapolis's housing policy, calling their efforts to provide low-income residents with adequate housing "atrocious." HUD's censure of Indianapolis's public housing efforts unveiled the stark realities of the class-biased attempts at urban rehabilitation.

The *Star*'s article underscored one of the main criticisms of the growth strategy voiced by community leaders—that city officials were so consumed with efforts to revitalize the downtown that the needs of the residential sectors (particularly those composed of minorities) had been neglected. Indianapolis's Urban League President expressed the point to the *Baltimore Sun*:

> I'm not knocking the growth, I can show you relative progress here for blacks. But we have not really been financial recipients from the massive development that has occurred, and the feeling in the black community is while we're building a city with bricks and mortar, the inclination is to forget the human side. (*Baltimore Sun*, 1985, February 18, p. 3B)

These sentiments were supported by an Indianapolis-district state legislative representative who told the *Wall Street Journal*:

> I have difficulty supporting a stadium [the Hoosier Dome] when our schools are woefully underfinanced and other city services are inadequate. The Mayor and the Lilly Foundation wanted the stadium, so it was built. That's the way things get done here. (July 14, 1982, p. 1)

The senator's concerns are typical of many critics of stadium projects who argue that money approved (by voters) to subsidize sport stadiums and arenas should have been spent to improve social services. But, as Johnson (1982) and Lipsitz (1984) have pointed out, this argument is misdirected. Funding used for franchise subsidy usually originates from a city's capital budget, whereas public service funding originates from a city's operational budget. The operational budget is much less flexible and city officials are unwilling to increase operational expenditures by millions of dollars to attack social problems. In the words of Lipsitz (1984): "It is not that the voters make an incorrect choice; it is that the nature of our system gives them no meaningful choice in the first place" (p. 14). This was especially true in the case of Indianapolis; voters had no choice at all. Funding for the Hoosier Dome did not require voter approval.

But perhaps none of these social problems were as glaringly eye-catching as the empty Hoosier Dome. When the roof was inflated in 1984, neither Indianapolis nor any other city had made great strides toward being awarded a new franchise, and the NFL had made no indication that it planned to expand. Indianapolis thus was forced to lure an existing team. It looked to Baltimore; it was successful.

## The Colts Franchise

Luring the Colts franchise from Baltimore provided tremendous support for Indianapolis's progrowth campaign both within and outside the Indianapolis community. Robert Irsay's capital investment decision helped to legitimate the local state's growth strategy. Further, local boosters publicized the strategy's success, thereby attracting the attention of future capital investors. Irsay moved his team to Indianapolis despite the fact that both Baltimore and Phoenix offered him more lucrative contracts. A comparison of the bids (*Indianapolis Star*, April 1, 1984, p. 21A) is provided in Table 10.1. Paying less in relation to the other cities' offers helped Indianapolis growth advocates to argue that the team's financial impact on the community would be as "noticeable as the domed stadium" (*Indianapolis Star*, March 30, 1984, p. 31). To reiterate an earlier point, the logic of the progrowth model equates business interests with the interests of the community as a whole. In Indianapolis, progrowth advocates wasted no time before leveraging the Colts arrival to refine the ideology that contends private capital accumulation trickles down to benefit the entire city.

Likewise, civic boosters scurried to use the publicity surrounding the Colts move to advertise Indianapolis's climate to other capital investors. The Indianapolis Project, Inc. sent letters to 33 publications explaining that the Colts move should be included in financial sections and general news stories concerning Indianapolis's growth (*Indianapolis Star*, June 23, 1985, p. 10). In 1984, four major firms (Purolator Courier, the Hudson Institute, Overland Express, and the Dana Corporation) moved their national headquarters to Indianapolis. According to Bamberger and Parham (1984), Dana was attracted to the city by its central location, "by Indiana's generally good business climate, and by Indianapolis' image as progressive, affordable, and free of many typical urban problems" (p. 17). It is to the problematic of "image" that we now turn.

# Promoting Civic Identity Through Boosterism and Civic Ritual

To maintain or recapture physical, social, and economic health, cities (substate governments) must compete against one another for capital investment. There is an intangible in all of this: "boosterism." Boosterism is a managed activity. Dennis Judd (1983) expresses the case with reference to Denver: "It is important to understand that Denver's post-World War I growth was carefully sought by business and government leaders. Like every other city in America, 'boosterism' has been a central feature of local politics. Growth has never been left to the vagaries of chance" (p. 171). The medium of boosterism's expression is both institutionalized (Chambers of Commerce, Boards of Trade) and ad hoc (e.g., the Committee to Relocate the Rams to Orange County).

In the case of the Committee to Relocate the Rams, its composition included developers, airport representatives, mayors, members of various Chambers of Commerce, insurance executives, corporate executives, businessmen, existing (in Orange

**Table 10.1  Bids to Host the Colts Franchise**

| Inducement | Indianapolis | Baltimore | Phoenix |
|---|---|---|---|
| Length of lease | 20 years | 6 years | 12 years |
| Terms of loan | $12.5 million at 8% interest for 10 years. Capital Improvement Board to pay the difference to a prime rate of 14%. | $15 million at 6.5% interest for 10 years. Local business to apply $500,000 toward repayment. | $15 million at 8% interest. No payment due on principle for years. |
| Training facility | City would build a $4 million facility giving Irsay the option to buy or pay $15,000 per year in rent. | City would buy current facility for $4.4 million then charge Irsay $1 per year in rent. | None offered |
| Guaranteed revenues | $7 million annually from ticket and luxury suite rental | 43,000 tickets per game | $7 million annually |
| Stadium rental | Hoosier Dome: $25,000 annually for 8 games | Baltimore Memorial Stadium: commensurate with gate revenues | Sun Devil Stadium: free for 20 years. |
| Other | $25,000 for moving expenses. Portion of game-day expenses paid. Capital Imp. Board would receive right to match any offer to buy the Colts during Irsay's lifetime. | $7.5 million in improvements to stadium. Luxury suites added to stadium. | Build a new stadium downtown. |

County) sport firm executives, food chain/concession executives, and local state assemblymen. In short, a powerful coalition decided to boost Anaheim vis-à-vis Watts and to provide the late Carroll Rosenbloom, the owner of the Rams, with the incentives to relocate his franchise.

Boosterism—which seeks to equate the interests of business, the ideology of progrowth, with the interests of the "city as a whole" (see Smith & Keller, 1983, p. 160)—now appears as a campaign that not only promotes the material interests of the hegemonic fractions of the dominant classes but also seeks to legitimize "political" solutions to the urban crisis by symbolically reconstructing the consensus (e.g., by blurring the fault lines to which we have alluded).

One manner in which the consensus may be symbolically constructed is by using the vehicle of sport. It may well be that the presence of a professional sport team in a city enhances the prestige of the community as a whole. It may well be that trickle-down benefits of growth do marginally offset public subsidies in the form of rental agreements that favor franchise owners and the loss of income from property taxes that could have been paid by others who may have occupied the same site (Okner, 1974). It may be that professional sport is more capable of naturalizing public/private, abstract/social relations and of translating state/civic/civil differences of interest into the "good of the whole" than other forms of consumerist collective consumption. It is possible that the social construction of the progrowth ideology is facilitated when it articulates with acquiring or retaining a professional sport franchise.

It is here that we arrive at our final problematic. Does professional sport transcend the contradictions and conflicts of everyday life? Does it temporarily suspend our consciousness of contradictions and conflicts? Or does it reproduce such contradictions and conflicts in its economic arrangements, staging processes, capital-labor relations, and so forth? We might answer "yes" to all of these questions.

We turn to the concept of civic ritual. The symbolism associated with rituals (in the form of festivals, "mass" spectacles, and other cultural performances) has been of interest to anthropologists, sociologists, folklorists, and historians. A common theme has been the relation of ritual to identity, be it personal or social, and the ways in which ritual establishes links between individuals and their subcommunity, between subcommunities and the community as a whole, be it a substate formation (e.g., a city) or the nation.

That the symbolism of a ritual can induce communal bonding has been noted by Turner (1974): Symbols per se can promote the imagination of community (Cohen, 1985). Victor Turner (1974) introduced the concept of "communitas"—a special experience during which individuals are able to rise above those structures that materially and normatively regulate their daily lives. Communitas is a manifestation of feelings of collectivity that unite people across the boundaries of structure, rank, and socioeconomic status (see Harding, 1983, p. 851). He distinguishes three forms of communitas: the spontaneous and short lived; the ideological representation of spontaneous communitas; and the normative, subcultural attempt to maintain the relationships of spontaneous communitas on a more permanent basis.

For Turner, communitas has been eroded by the forces of modernity. Where it remains is in the fragmented, segmental, categoric levels of solidarity (Turner, 1974, pp. 84-86). This concept is intriguing. If, as Turner asserts, it is present only at the subcommunity level, then civic rituals as vehicles for the holistic regeneration of community would have no meaning or "function"—a civic ritual would be a waste of time, money, and effort in the affirmation or assertion of collective identity. We can agree with Turner that *spontaneous* communitas is difficult to achieve in a rationalized, differentiated, stratified, individualized society. Yet this does not mean that there is an absence of effort to regenerate it under a changed (structural and cultural) set of circumstances. The state, the substates, and the hegemonic fractions of the dominant class do seem willing to use resources in an attempt to ideologically reunite the structurally disassociated. These attempts at recovering the community as a whole necessitate a better understanding of the power of ideology and the ideology of power (Therborn, 1980). Here, we are recognizing the articulation of public symbolism with politics per se (Cohen, 1974). Rituals indeed have a political character—to construct the illusion of consensus.

We are suggesting that a *civic* ritual not only is designed to blur the distinctions between state and civil society, but also requires the combined resources of both. A civic ritual thus combines the dominant and the situated, subordinate cultures in a framework of unequal complementarity and involves state or substate agencies in the provision of the infrastructural means for the ritual's consumption (e.g., transport, facilities, and policing). In short, an inaugural ceremony for a President is a state ritual; a "street fair" is a civil ritual in ideal-typical terms. Professional sport events cut across ideal-typical distinctions. Perhaps this is why entrepreneurs in the public interest and entrepreneurs in the private interest are able to initiate urban development schemes by soliciting support for stadium construction and by engaging in an inducement war with other cities for the acquisition of an expansion or relocation franchise.

Yet a civic ritual that seeks to blur the state/civil society distinction and to mask the contradictions and conflicts in civil society per se can also reproduce distinctions, contradictions, and conflicts. In any parade, there are those who ride in the floats, the "official" cars, and on the horses. There are those who watch from the sidelines. In any sport arena, there are those who observe from luxury boxes and those who observe from the general admission bleachers. In the United Kingdom, there has been a tradition of distinction—the "cloth caps" who have *stood* in the terraces and the "trilbies" who have *sat* in the covered portion of the ground. In the United States, there is more to the reproduction thesis. Capital investment/disinvestment decisions determine who (i.e., which collectivities) will be privileged to partake in sport as civic ritual. Collectivities thus are ranked!

## Acknowledgment

We would like to acknowledge the assistance of Jim Duthie, Elliott Gorn, Steve Hardy, John Loy, and Dick Martin for their comments on earlier drafts of this paper. We also acknowledge the contributions of the anonymous reviewers.

# References

Baltimore Chamber of Commerce. (1986). *Discover a new Baltimore*. Baltimore, MD: Author.

Bamberger, R.J., & Parham, D.W. (1984, November). Indianapolis's economic development strategy. *Urban Land*, pp. 12-18.

Barnett, C.R. (1980, September). The Spartans live on (in Detroit). *River Cities Monthly*, **6**, 7-10.

Barnett, C.R., & Terhune, L. (1979, September). When the Tanks were tops. *River Cities Monthly*, **1**, 14-20.

Berkowitz, B.L. (1984). Economic development really works: Baltimore, Maryland. *Urban Affairs Annual Reviews*, **27**, 201-222.

Castells, M. (1978). *The urban question*. London: MacMillan.

Clarke, J., & Critcher, C. (1985). *The devil makes work: Leisure in capitalist Britain*. Houndsmills: MacMillan.

Cohen, A. (1974). *Two-dimensional man: An essay on the anthropology of power and symbolism in complex society*. Berkeley, CA: University of California Press.

Cohen, A.P. (1985). *The symbolic construction of community*. London: Ellis Horwood and Travistock.

Davenport, D. (1969). Collusive competition in major league baseball: Its theory and institutional development. *American Economist*, **14**(2), 6-30.

Fainstein, N.I., & Fainstein, S.S. (1982a). Restoration and struggle: Urban policy and social forces. *Urban Affairs Annual Reviews*, **22**, 9-22.

Fainstein, N.I., & Fainstein, S.S. (Eds.) (1982b). *Urban policy under capitalism*. Beverly Hills, CA: Sage.

Fainstein, N.I., & Fainstein, S.S. (1983). Regime strategies, communal resistance, and economic forces. In S.S. Fainstein, N.I. Fainstein, R.C. Hill, D.R. Judd, & M.P. Smith (Eds.), *Restructuring the city: The political economy of urban development* (pp. 245-281). New York: Longman.

Fainstein, S.S., & Fainstein, N.I. (1983). Economic change, national policy, and the system of cities. In S.S. Fainstein, N.I. Fainstein, R.C. Hill, D.R. Judd, & M.P. Smith (Eds.), *Restructuring the city: The political economy of urban development* (pp. 1-26). New York: Longman.

Fainstein, S.S., Fainstein, N.I., Hill, R.C., Judd, D.R., & Smith, M.P. (Eds.) (1983). *Restructuring the city: The political economy of urban redevelopment*. New York: Longman.

Gregory, D., & Urry, J. (Eds.) (1985). *Social relations and spatial structures*. Houndsmills: MacMillan.

Harding, R.F. (1983). Ritual in recent criticism: The elusive sense of community. *Publications Modern Language Association*, **98**, 846-862.

Hardy, S. (1981). The city and the rise of American sport: 1820-1920. *Exercise and Sport Sciences Reviews*, **9**, 183-219.

Hardy, S. (1982). *How Boston played: Sport, recreation and community, 1865-1915*. Boston: Northeastern University.

Hardy, S. (1985, May). *Entrepreneurs, organizations, and the sport marketplace: Subjects in search of historians*. Paper presented at the meeting of the North American Society for Sport History, Vancouver, British Columbia.

Harloe, M., & Lebas, E. (Eds.) (1981). *City, class and capital: New developments in the political economy of cities and regions*. London: Edward Arnold.

Harvey, D. (1973). *Social justice and the city*. Berkeley, CA: University of California.

Harvey, D. (1978). The urban process under capitalism. *Urban Regional Research*, **2**, 101-131.

Harvey, D. (1985a). *Consciousness and the urban experience*. Baltimore: Johns Hopkins.

Harvey, D. (1985b). *The urbanization of capital*. Baltimore: Johns Hopkins.

Howell, J.W. (1984). *A tale of three cities: The relocation of professional football franchises and the dialectics of profit and community.* Unpublished master's thesis, University of Washington.

Howell, J.W., & Ingham, A.G. (1984, July). *Sport as serialized civic ritual: The dialectics of profit and community formation/deformation.* Paper presented at the Olympic Scientific Congress, Eugene, Oregon.

Indianapolis Project, Inc. (1986). *Highlights of the Indianapolis Story.* Indianapolis, IN: Author.

Ingham, A.G., & Hardy, S. (1984). Sport, structuration, subjugation, and hegemony. *Theory, Culture, & Society,* **2**, 85-103.

Ingham, A.G., Howell, J.W., & Schilperoort, T.S. (1987). Professional sport and community: A review and exegesis. In K.B. Pandolf (Ed.), *Exercise and Sport Sciences Review,* **15**, pp. 427-465. New York: MacMillan.

Johnson, A. (1978). Public sports policy: An introduction. *American Behavioral Scientist,* **21**(3), 319-344.

Johnson, A. (1982). The uneasy partnership of cities and professional sport: Public policy considerations. In N. Theberge & P. Donnelly (Eds.), *Sport and the sociological imagination.* Fort Worth, TX: Texas Christian.

Johnson, A. (1983). Municipal administration and the sport franchise relocation issue. *Public Administration Review,* **43**, 519-528.

Johnson, A. (1985). The professional sport franchise relocation issue. In J. Frey & A. Johnson (Eds.), *Government and sports: Public policy issues.* Totowa, NJ: Rowman & Allanheld.

Johnson, A. (1986). Economic and policy implications of hosting sport franchises: Lessons from Baltimore. *Urban Affairs Quarterly,* **2**, 411-433.

Johnson, A.T. (1984). The uneasy partnership of cities and professional sport: Public policy considerations. In N. Theberge & P. Donnelly (Eds.), *Sport and the sociological imagination* (pp. 210-227). Fort Worth, TX: Texas Christian University.

Judd, D.R. (1983). From cowtown to sunbelt city: Boosterism and economic growth in Denver. In S.S. Fainstein, N.I. Fainstein, R.C. Hill, D.R. Judd, & M.P. Smith (Eds.), *Restructuring the city: The political economy of urban redevelopment* (pp. 167-201). New York: Longman.

Katznelson, I. (1979). Community, capitalist development and the emergence of class. *Politics and Society,* **9**, 203-237.

Katznelson, I. (1981). *City trenches: Urban politics and the patterning of class in the United States.* New York: Pantheon Books.

Lieberman, E. (1982). A changing downtown. In L.H. Nast, L.N. Krause, & R.C. Monk (Eds.), *Baltimore: A living renaissance* (pp. 36-42). Baltimore: Waverly.

Lipsitz, G. (1984). Sports stadia and urban development: A tale of three cities. *Journal of Sport and Social Issues,* **8**(2), 1-18.

Michener, J. (1976). *Sports in America.* New York: Random House.

National Football League, The. (1982). *The official NFL encyclopedia of pro football.* New York: New American Library.

Noll, R.G. (1974). The U.S. team sports industry: An introduction. In R.G. Noll (Ed.), *Government and the sports business* (pp. 1-32). Washington, DC: The Brookings Institute.

Okner, B. (1974). Subsidies of stadia and arenas. In R.G. Noll (Ed.), *Government and the sports business* (pp. 325-347). Washington, DC: The Brookings Institute.

Olson, S.H. (1976). *Baltimore.* Cambridge, MA: Ballinger.

Quirk, J. (1973). An economic analysis of team movements in professional sports. *Law and Contemporary Problems,* U38P, 42-66.

Quirk, J., & El Hodiri, M. (1974). The economic theory of a professional sports league. In R.G. Noll (Ed.), *Government and the sports business* (pp. 33-80). Washington, DC: The Brookings Institute.

Owen, C.J., & Willbern, Y. (1985). *Governing metropolitan Indianapolis: The politics of Unigov.* Berkeley, CA: University of California.

Rivkin, S. (1974). Sports leagues and the federal anti-trust laws. In R.G. Noll (Ed.), *Government and the sports business* (pp. 387-410). Washington, DC: The Brookings Institute.

Rosenthal, D.B. (Ed.) (1980). *Urban revitalization*. Beverly Hills, CA: Sage.

Schimmel, K.S. (1987). *Professional sport franchise relocation within the context of urban politics: A case study*. Unpublished master's thesis, Miami University, Oxford, Ohio.

Scoville, J. (1974). Labor relations in sports. In R.G. Noll (Ed.), *Government and the sports business* (pp. 185-220). Washington, DC: The Brookings Institute.

Seymour, H. (1960). *Baseball: The early years*. New York: Oxford.

Smith, M.P. (1979). *The city and social theory*. New York: St. Martin's.

Smith, M.P., & Keller, M. (1983). Managed growth and the politics of uneven development in New Orleans. In S.S. Fainstein, N.I. Fainstein, R.C. Hill, D.R. Judd, & M.P. Smith (Eds.), *Restructuring the city* (pp. 126-166). New York: Longman.

Staudohar, P.D. (1985). Team relocation in professional sports. *Labor Law Review, 36*(9), 728-733.

Staudohar, P.D. (1986). *The sports industry and collective bargaining*. Ithaca, NY: Industrial and Labor Relations Press.

Tarvin, A.H. (1940). *Seventy-five years on Louisville diamonds*. Louisville, KY: Schuhmann.

Therborn, G. (1980). *The ideology of power and the power of ideology*. London: New Left Books.

Turner, V. (1974). *Dramas, fields, and metaphors: Symbolic action in human society*. Ithaca, NY: Cornell University.

Urban Land Institute. (1986). *ULI market profiles: 1986*. Washington, DC: Author.

Vincent, T. (1981). *Mudville's revenge: The rise and fall of American sport*. New York: Seaview.

Voigt, D.Q. (1966). *American baseball: From gentleman's sport to commissioner system*. Norman, OK: University of Oklahoma.

Voigt, D.Q. (1971). *America's leisure revolution*. Reading, PA: Albright College Bookstore.

Weber, M. (1958). *The protestant ethic and the spirit of capitalism*. New York: Scribner's.

Weistart, J.C. (1984). League control of market opportunities: A perspective on competition and cooperation in the sports industry. *Duke Law Journal, 1984*(6), 1013-1070.

# CHAPTER 11

# Civic Ideology in the Public Domain: Victorian Ideology in the "Lifestyle Crisis" of the 1990s

*Alan Clarke*

McIntosh (1963) argued that the Olympic games transport us back to 776 B.C. There is certainly great strength in the Olympian tradition. Other sports also carry traditions with them, creating Halls of Fame and icons of memorable moments. The events, the leagues, and the personalities become fixed in history. Successes and failures are analyzed and discussed over and over. Sports should not be dismissed even by those who have no interest in them, because they are integral to social formation and important to many cultures.

I propose to do two things that are often greeted with skepticism. First, I shall argue that sports are an important cultural form and should be treated with the degree of serious interest that other cultural forms receive. Sport is not only a popular culture, it is a participative culture that involves more people in its active production than any other. It should not be relegated to the ghettos of the sports pages and the specialist press but recognized as an integral element of society. I will attempt to produce a comprehensive political economy of sport that holds the production and consumption elements within sports in balance.

Second, during the 1980s in the United Kingdom we saw a great deal being written about the development of sport, particularly the attempt to "target" groups for a significant increase in their participation (with a concern to develop the theoretical initiatives taken up by sport studies in the 1960s). We have certainly witnessed something of a sport explosion. Targeting an active producer/consumer group may create different agendas depending on who is doing the targeting—the state or the private (civil) sectors or "voluntary," self-determined interest groups. The questions of who gets what, why, and how are thus considered.

# Theoretical Overview: Articulating Mills With Williams

What constituted the motivation for the increase in sport and the driving force behind the expansion? As C. Wright Mills (1959) so vividly demonstrated, the answer demands the application of the sociological imagination. This requires a combination of three elements: Mills argued that an appreciation of history, social structure, and biography are necessary for an account to be comprehensive. This account of the development of sport has a broad historical sweep, from the social origins of sport in preindustrial societies to the concerns of the postindustrial period. I will also analyze the formal and informal patterns of sport, the professional and the amateur, and the active and passive opportunities for participation.

Similarly, social structure is an elusive object of study, giving observers problems of monitoring the continuity and changes that make social structures seem so important within an analysis of social behavior. This becomes particularly difficult if all the dimensions mentioned above are to be retained within the analysis.

For sport, the element of biography or personal life-history may appear the easiest facet to hold on to, yet it is difficult to grasp the salient dimensions of a biography without understanding the context within which that biography is taking place. The selection of relevant examples from a life can only be made when the criteria of relevance have been established. The work on sports literacy (Rogers, 1977) that has been undertaken as a means of understanding the different participation patterns within diverse social groups demonstrated this quite dramatically. Rogers's report revealed that those sports that had not been experienced during childhood were unlikely to be taken up in later life; this "sports literacy" was at least as important as what had been practiced for understanding and predicting future levels of participation.

Most biographies do not dwell on what the subject did not do; they are records of what the subject accomplished. For a sport historian, it is vital to rectify this tendency, and this may be accomplished if everyday life is established as the central focus for the documentary. All too often, the everyday and the commonplace were omitted in the "Great Man" thesis of social development. Only recently has the routine and the ordinary been taken into account (Bailey, 1989). The grandiose histories of our societies have focused not on the people but on the famous, the economic process, and perhaps the cultural fads and fancies of the time. But "ordinary" people contribute to the reproduction and transformation of the social milieu.

Systematic attention to what ordinary people really did with their working lives and their free time has begun to emerge from the reconstructions that have been undertaken by social or cultural historians (Yeo & Yeo, 1981). However, there is a limitation to many of these histories. While they focus on the institutionalized provision of sport, they may miss some of the informal and "unorganized" forms of sport that are so important within self-generative communities. This has an especially important impact on the accounts presented by women's sport activities because they have been largely excluded form the official provision of sport (Deem, 1988).

In arguing for retaining a historical context in the study of sport, I make no attempt to present this as a simple model of the historical process. Even using the broad terminology that has sometimes been used to construct the history of social formations, there can be problems in constructing an approach that is too simple to account for the changes that have taken place. For instance, using the rural versus urban environment in this analysis is problematic, because the process of transition has been more complicated than such a dichotomy would suggest. Cities existed before the industrial revolution and village life continues still, but the patterns of life that were and are encountered are historically specific to the period and have been influenced by many changes. There is now sufficient evidence both in the United Kingdom and the United States that the experience of sport is clearly different from the prevailing conditions prior to the industrial revolution (Butsch, 1990; Ingham, 1978).

If we can accept the classic labels that have been pinned on previous periods—such as rural, traditional, preindustrial—we can see that developments have shaped society in definite ways. Looking at the past, it is possible to see a self-regulating and self-initiating pattern around sport that seeks to elide many of the rigid distinctions now in operation. Clarke and Critcher (1985) state: "It is simply inadequate to argue that industrialization created leisure, which has subsequently grown to today's level. In fact, industrialization in Britain began by *destroying* leisure" (pp. 48-49, original emphasis). The rigors of the assembly line were an unknown challenge to the self-determined pacing of the working life of the working classes. Factory hours, mechanized production, and long working hours, often including multiple shifts, imposed a new discipline on many people. In short, it is easy to pose the processes involved in the development of sport into the rationalized patterns found in the 1990s as encapsulating or reflecting technology's and bureaucracy's cognitive styles (Berger, Berger, & Kellner, 1973) without catching the complex and sometimes contradictory social processes that were involved in these developments.

It is here that Williams (1977) provides a helpful framework for the analysis of sports. In his review of the working of cultural processes he identifies (within the dominant form of culture) patterns of behavior that are explicable in terms of cultural forms experienced in earlier forms of society. These residual forms are at some distance from the effective dominant culture but can be incorporated into it. Williams's focus is on cultural patterns, but I will identify how forms of sport and sporting organization also demonstrate these residual forms. These forms of experience coexist with new patterns of behavior, referred to by Williams as "emergent" forms, which represent the new elements within social formations. They can also be located within the development of sport, in the arrival of new modes of participation, competition, and spectating and in the way sport has been restructured to combine established elements with new elements of the contemporary dominant culture.

My analysis of emergent and residual forms of sport explores emergent forms of sporting culture as *commodified, commercialized, constrained, cash rich,* and *controlled.* Residual forms are *creative, commercially supported, constructive, cash poor*, and *controlled*. However, it is worth noting that there is a division between market-sensitive emergent forms (which may indeed be market led) and residual forms that rely on the action of individuals and groups to construct their own opportunities within the existing levels and types of sport provision.

# Sport in the Victorian Era

The origins of sport lie in public expressions and patterns of life that emphasize the communal. When we look back to the Victorian era we are looking at a blueprint for the processes involved in the making of contemporary sport. Industrial processes introduced sport as something segmented from the rest of society, so that it had to be catered to by specialized provision. Provision could itself become institutionalized in both the public and commercial sectors. Prior to the Victorian period, sport had been first and foremost "open" both in its organization and in the locations where it took place.

This was most noticeable in the one tangible legacy we have from that period—the public house. It is possible to see the publicans as the main sporting entrepreneurs in the 1880s, with animal and human sports falling under their remit. These sports included football, cricket, pugilism, wrestling, footraces, cudgeling, bellringing, horse racing, and various forms of animal baiting (bull, cock, dog, bear, and badger were all fair game). Violence was inherent in many of these forms but was normally contained within the levels of tolerance of the time—which admitted a far higher level of personal, social, and political violence than would be acceptable today (Elias & Dunning, 1986). Yet in the 1880s, the popular forms of sport were not only condoned but supported by the aristocracy. This could have been because the sport of the laboring masses was, at least at holiday time, the sport of the ruling oligarchy. Thus custom, self-interest, and inclination led to patronage (Bailey, 1978).

## The Impact of Industrialization

In the 1880s British society was in transition, on the brink of capitalist industrialization, and this brought a major transformation to the routines and rhythms of people's lives. Capitalist business and their sports were transformed as new moral and legal controls appeared over their behavior and attitudes. This was by no means a unique experience; other industrializing countries (e.g., the United States) demonstrated similar patterns.

Sporting activities cannot be separated from the legal framework that exists in the society at large and the changes in that framework that accompanied the industrialization process. They supported and sharpened some of the social trends that directly affected sport. Legislation, including the Enclosure Movement and changes in the Poor Law, demonstrated a general trend toward legal and moral suppression of the emergent working classes (Haywood, Kew, & Bramham, 1989). Confinement, containment, constraint, and restraint would affect both labor and leisure. Articulating with this was a separation of the customary economic and cultural rights as the cultural processes became subject to further legislation, with many rights of the preindustrial period being removed. Game laws and laws concerning theft from work went alongside legislation affecting the rights of people to gather in public places. The tone of this period is neatly captured in the mission of a small group known as the Society for the Suppression of Vice, which was designed to protect the Sabbath and undertook this task by ensuring that prohibitive legislation was enforced.

## Hegemony or Social Control?

Historically, all forms of sport have become subject to much greater levels of control than in earlier social formations. The form and extent varies, but the trend is always toward greater control. The ruling classes have long recognized that control is easier if it follows normally from expectations and habit rather than from coercion and constant policing. The routinization of sport and the founding of safe patterns of sport follow from this basic principle. Holidays were a particular problem. They tempted workers into profligacy, but cutting the number of holidays did not prevent the old habits; it forced the pastimes underground. By the 1850s the trend of reducing bank holidays had been reversed, with holidays recognized as being identifiable and containable. Such containment was made easier by the emergence of regular police forces to keep a sense of "order" on the streets. Programming for bank holidays also became possible when it was recognized that the "masses" would be available on set days—racing meetings, football and boxing matches, and fairs were reorganized to coincide with the new patterns. There is also evidence that sport programs changed with the introduction of Saturday afternoon as a general half-holiday in 1873, which resulted in the mass availability of people to become sporting players and punters.

The ruling classes had established certain forms of sport, and these dominant forms had a powerful influence on the rest of society. Their enjoyment of horse racing (with the current British racing classics being established in the late 1770s), shooting, hunting, and fishing provided a series of pastimes that were in one sense exclusive—almost by invitation only—and also trend-setting for the lower classes. The trend toward legitimate activities was reinforced by the attempt to proscribe some of the older pastimes. However, a ban is no simple thing to enforce, and many sports simply went underground when declared illegal. Others survived in milder form; pugilism emerged in the more controlled and commodified form of boxing. Some forced their way into the space provided by the demise of the "blood sport" competitions. Cricket appeared as an emergent form and had the benefit that there were few objections to women watching such a genteel game.

Beyond the confines of sport, there were many innovations during the period with popular theater, pantomime, and circuses providing new forms of urban entertainments. After the Beer Act of 1830, publicans sought to extend the range of services they provided to compete with the rivals in the gin houses and the theaters. The "free and easies" and the saloons date from this period. The saloons were to be an important staging post for the development of the music hall and so have a vital role in the history of popular cultural forms. The theoretical debates that have taken place in the sport studies journals about the definition of sport were given life during this bourgeoisification period, when the definitions of "man's work" and "woman's work" became operative and were a part of the everyday experience (Deem, 1988).

By the middle of the 1880s there were three factors to be considered in the development of sport. There was (1) a reorientation of middle-class patterns with increased regulation of sport, which sometimes accidentally and sometimes deliberately influenced and were passed on to the working classes; (2) the expansion of local government in the rapidly growing urban areas into the municipal provision of sport; (3) the introduction of a heavy capitalization of sport with the introduction of licensing and the major involvement of private companies in sport provision.

## Organized Sport

The roots of organized sport have been well-documented as a means of redirecting the public school ethos toward what would later be referred to as "muscular Christianity" and at the same time controlling the natural exuberance of public schoolboys (Dunning & Sheard, 1979). The rational recreation movement, a forceful extension of the Sunday School movement, emerged as a powerful lobby, with their message of sobriety, thrift, and individual responsibility leaving little room for many of the traditional pastimes. Clarke and Critcher (1985) draw the title of their book from the extension of the Protestant work ethic, which was encapsulated in this movement: "The Devil makes work for idle hands." Recreation had to be designed to fill the emptiness of time away from work so that this time could be used profitably in building character, discipline, and responsibility, rather than encouraging irresponsibility, delinquency, and moral degeneracy.

Examples of codification (such as football and rugby union) follow this period and have led to some simplistic interpretations, with sport being presented as somehow bestowed on the masses by the good grace of the bourgeoisie and aristocracy. Although this may have been the case, as always with the growth of sport the process is not so simple. Some newly codified (e.g., soccer/football) sports were taken up by largely working-class groupings; others were reserved for the middle classes (e.g., rugby union, rowing) and here the codification was used precisely to exclude the working classes. To add a final twist to the picture, some working-class sports were appropriated by the middle classes. In cricket, it is particularly clear that there was a relationship of patronage between the gentlemen and the professional players, but this was reinforced by a form of patronism, which emphasized that making a living through playing sport was in itself demeaning. There are, even now, some who would argue that the amateur, relatively less rationalized approach to sport is still haunting the performances of British sports players at the highest levels of competition.

The class alliances and the power relations surrounding organized sport were rarely ones of equivalence; rather than removing class differences, they served to reinforce them. The upper and middle classes brought time, capital, and some organizational skills to the sports; the working classes brought energy and a paying audience. The history of sports is largely the story of how these two clashing contributions have been resolved and how professionalism was introduced into and negotiated within each sport (Dunning & Sheard, 1979).

## Municipal Provision

The local authorities were largely dependent on two factors before they could become involved in sport provision. The populations they were designed to cover had to be sufficiently large and densely grouped to make provision sensible. They were also dependent on the enabling legislation of the 1840s to allow them to raise money and spend capital and revenue resources on sport. Initially, much of this development, especially the provision of parks, was to be found in the donations of land and buildings from newly successful local businesses, but by the 1870s the authorities were purchasing land with the sole purpose of using it as public park land. Libraries and swimming pools stem from this same period and both demonstrate the moral character of much of the provision. Libraries had their stock regularly checked and censored by the Committee to ensure that the books were of the right character for the readers. Swimming pools served a similar dual function by allowing exercise in the standard 20 or 25 feet straight tanks while providing public slipper baths for washing. Some authorities combined this double function with a third by building a civic laundry in the same complex. This demonstrates the public welfare basis still apparent in the rhetoric surrounding public sector initiatives and the politics of what Coalter (1989) called ''recreational welfare.''

Local authorities also controlled sport developments through their widening powers for local planning. This, with the growth of the police forces and the local magistrate's rights to grant licenses for drinks and entertainments, saw the increased policing of public festivals of all kinds—the music halls, the racecourses, the public houses and the streets were all subject to greater regulation. Streets were redefined as thoroughfares rather than public spaces, denying their established role as meeting places, and people were kept moving to enable shopkeepers to pursue their trade effectively.

The range of public provision for sport was extended during this period, and some of the forms of sport were redefined. Publicly supported and publicly provided forms represented an emergent form of sports behavior that combined elements of previous forms with the new cultural pattern of recreational welfare provision. The impact of this change was so great that it effectively became the dominant culture for sports provision in England until the 1980s. It is an important example of how the patterns we study change over time, appearing in dominant and challenging positions at different periods.

## Capitalization

There has always been a commercial relationship between the providers of entertainments and of alcohol and their customers—the publicans might be viewed as sport's first entrepreneurs. However, the period we are now considering was marked noticeably by a change in that relationship, with the basis of provision requiring a heavier capitalization than had previously been seen. Companies and chains of providers came into the sport markets. Publicans faced competition from the music halls, with the 1850s and 1860s seeing large-scale growth in the music halls. By taking the music from the public house and putting it within the "theater," the halls were able to charge fees for what had previously been freely available. The halls required heavy investment; a London music hall (by 1866 there were 33) was funded with an average of £10,000.

The Music Hall Proprietors Association was formed to negotiate license agreements and served to change the nature of the music hall from a bawdy, drunken, and ribald form of entertainment into a form of theater with little, if any, of the old associations with drink, food, and prostitution. The tables and chairs of the original design, which were styled to re-create the atmosphere of public houses, were replaced with neat rows of seats, effectively controlling the audience. Interestingly, this anticipated the 1980s "modernizing" initiatives to curb violence at soccer grounds by creating the all-seat stadium and, thereby, pacifying the rough, "cheek and jowl," ribald terraces that were and are the targets of policing in a carceral space. The material presented was controlled by tight contracts with the artists that obliged them to remove any "offensive" material from their acts. Magistrates, police, and proprietors worked out a compromise that left the performers with little bargaining power to reject the contract offered by the proprietors. The public had even less influence.

Sports witnessed a similar shift, with the matches being removed from open spaces and re-presented within the confines of the new sports stadia. This shift began the transformation of the relationship between the participant and the spectator, producing the divide we currently see in the professional sports. The sports became a package that can be sold back to the people who "support" the sport and the team. To sustain the infrastructure of the new sports meetings you are obliged to purchase tickets to your own home ground, subverting the tradition of local support into a cash relationship. Again, the formulation of a new cultural pattern is shaped directly by changes in the social structure and the local conditions surrounding particular sports and geographical locations.

## Commercialization

For the analysts of sport, commercialization has become a key component. Far more than the amount of investment is involved with the process of commercialization as it relates to the relationships among the providers, the provision, and the audience. It is possible to see three kinds of relationship within the provision of sport: self-determination, citizenship provision, and free market supply. These three models structure the delivery of the services and facilities in different ways.

Sport is far more complex than most products. It regularly involves a combination of factors that occur only occasionally in the usual marketplace relationships of provision and purchasing. Imposing a market strategy on sport industries has long been seen as difficult, and this has resulted in parts of the sport market being separated from the mainstream of sport studies as they become more market-organized. Sport scholars have seen hotels, catering, accommodation, and most recently tourism established as subjects in their own right. These subjects deal with the managerial implications of the markets rather than the hedonistic free-choice models of sporting pluralism. However, it is difficult to think of sport as a market if all the most obvious examples of the market forces are moved to other disciplines. For the purposes of this analysis, and for the development of a political economy of sport, it is necessary to regain a holistic concept of sport that includes the moments of production and consumption, choice and purchase, assembly and distribution, advertising and decision making.

An interesting aspect of the commercialization of sport has been the structuring of the public/civil and civic market through a commodification of sport. This introduces a pattern that is well-established in other sectors of the market and lies at the heart of the capitalist production system (Featherstone, 1990). The production process results in a plethora of products that have to be differentiated. Products are made identifiable by the ascription of unique properties and recognizable brands. The sport market is now patterned in the same way. We are able to purchase branded sports goods, buying an image of ourselves as well as a pair of running shoes. Our teams offer us "official" souvenirs, replica kits, and team jackets. The look can cost more than attending the games. This contribution to the finances of the players, clubs, and leagues should not be overlooked (Clarke & Madden, 1988). In the United States, the National Basketball Association is a prime example of this commodity franchising strategy.

Alongside this identification, commodification also does two things to the way sport is practiced and constituted. Commodification is based on a system of exchange, a cash nexus that positions sport as a produced and purchasable item. This replaces the image of popular sport as a spontaneous and self-generated set of activities with a system of sport constructed and offered within the marketplace. It also extends the notion of consumption into sport in a way that was difficult to argue prior to industrialization (Bailey, 1989). This differentiates not only between the products but also between the purchasers and consumers of those commodities. One of the consequences of this differentiation is that sport becomes a less-public form and constitutes a way of dividing, segmenting in marketing terms, the population. Much of the communal focus and community base is threatened by this appeal to a series of segmented markets.

Alan Warde (1990) has pointed to the need to clarify the cycle of production and consumption and identify more carefully the distinct stages of that cycle before we can produce an analysis of the final benefit or enjoyment that arises from the event. Sequential analysis highlights four elements: the process of production, the conditions of access, the manner of delivery, and the environment of enjoyment. While I have not used Warde's categories as part of the conceptual scheme, they are particularly helpful in looking at the way people come into contact with sport, and the processes that lie behind even the simplest act. If we map his sequential analysis onto the notion of biography with which Mills left us, we can begin to see how a more sophisticated analysis becomes possible. If we take sports participation, a biographical approach leads to looking at the patterns of participation in various sports by the individuals taking part. However, if we adopt the biographical approach to the conditions of access, a number of interesting questions emerge. We must ask whether the conditions of access to sports are or have ever been equally distributed throughout the range of sports that are or have ever been available within a society. We can then explore the constraints on the individual when they consider taking up tennis, soccer, wind surfing, or hang gliding.

There are constraints on all sports, but they operate at different levels. For instance, it is arguable that all sports require special equipment, but even here there is a sharp difference between the availability of the equipment and the price of the necessary gear. In England, it is possible to go to public parks and hire tennis courts, racquets, and balls, which removes the need to own your own equipment. However, as one progresses within the sport it may be desirable to obtain your own set of equipment; this is espeically the case where you are intent on joining a tennis club where everyone has their own equipment. At this level, the question becomes more complex.

The marketing of sports equipment and the image it creates can cause additional barriers to entry; you may have a tennis racket, but it may not be a Boris Becker special. With tennis you require only one partner; with wind surfing and hang gliding none is strictly necessary, but the cost of the equipment is higher. For soccer larger numbers of people are necessary. The entry barrier may not be the cost of equipment but the rigors of finding a set of players to make up a regular team, even for five-a-side games in a gym.

A further problem emerges when the conditions for participation are examined in terms of the facilities needed. The more sophisticated the participation, the greater the level of facility needed. Moreover, with the closing down (officially or informally) of public space the acquisition of such facilities becomes more problematic. Games that used to be played in the street are now policed and moved on, but even if they were not the increase in car ownership and speed of travel would make such activities much more difficult—and dangerous—to undertake. Sports are therefore moved into the specialized areas of provision and participation concentrated into spatially constructed marketplaces.

Contemporary texts suggest that in the commercialized world of sport there are at least three major types of sport providers in operation, all occupying sectors of the same market but all operating with a distinct set of motives that establish different patterns of behavior (Gratton & Taylor, 1985). We can identify them as occupying the private, the public, and the voluntary sectors of the market and begin to use these terms to unpack some of the elements of their operations that distinguish them from one another.

## The Public Sector

In some aspects the public sector is the easiest to begin with, as I have already considered the growth of local authority in an earlier section. I have shown how the Victorian period was characterized by the emergence of the local authorities and their assumption of some responsibility for the provision of public sport facilities. It is important to remember the centrality of recreational welfare and the dual function of many of these facilities, with public health being as important as public enjoyment. Although the interpretation of the actual level of public well-being that can be produced from the provision of sport remains an open question, this public welfare role continues to guide many local authorities' policies toward sport. A consideration of the British Sports Council Campaign, "Ever Thought of Sport," to maximize participation by the young, reveals that those public welfare intentions were written explicitly into the terms of reference for the project. The value of the facilities provided by the public sector has tended to be measured in terms of usage, throughput, and other participation rates. Schemes are often appraised on a quota method of standards set per 1,000 of population and special needs are rarely, if ever, taken seriously into account. There are honorable exceptions to this generalization but most local authority sport staff would accept the overall sentiment being expressed.

The Victorian origins established a regime of targeting in which the functional and the utilitarian were the norm. Currently, facility planning is undertaken to ensure maximum usage, and special efforts are made to encourage the participation of certain sections of society. Having demonstrated the health-promoting and character-building qualities of sport, the reformation of this Victorian tradition in the 1980s saw the unemployed as a natural focus, and, hence, they have become a major target for public sector sport facilities, particularly during the "off peak" time (Glyptis, 1988). Essentially, "targeting" is a dual-edged sword. On the one hand, it suggests a "welfare for all" ideology. On the other hand, it, in practice, suggests a program for the already state socialized, self-stigmatized groups in our societies. In both cases, the self-responsibility and the "Pull yourself up by your bootstraps" pragmatism is evident—the liberal, but not the social *democratic* ideology becomes the defining fantasy that defines reality. It is a Billy Graham utopia that only appeals to the already converted.

Several authorities have experimented with a "passport," entitling local residents or certain categories of user to free or discounted services for all or part of the week. Although this passport included notions of payment, it still gave a tangible representation to the idea that the local people had the right to use the sport facilities and that the local authority *had the duty* to ensure an adequate level of service. In effect, these passport-to-sport schemes gave direct expression to the arguments about citizenship rights in a modern society. As citizens, the passport holders of the sport kingdom were legitimately entitled to participate in sports. They were entitled to demand of the local authorities that they provide a level and range of services to meet their legitimate demands and expect those demands to be met.

Coalter (1989) has suggested that there is an unresolvable dualism if freedom and constraint are used as polarities. The arguments also revolve around the exploration of rights in civil society and the extension of those rights. There is, however, a more fundamental question that relates to the nature of freedom within society. The debate hinges on a definition of freedom as a negative freedom, expressed as a freedom from interference in choosing sport forms. However, there is a broader freedom that speaks to a positive sense of freedom, the *freedom to do* rather than the freedom from interference.

This allows an extra dimension to the legitimate demands made by sport users and the extent of provision offered to them. It is particularly important in exploring the notion of citizenship rights that follow from this. Coalter's (1989) dualism becomes a simplification when this ideological dimension is retained, for it is no longer a simple opposition between freedom and constraint but a politically determined definition of what sort of freedom and what types of constraints are being debated. These debates happen far from the marketplace, but they determine the terrain on which sport developments take place.

Attempts to extend a positive definition of freedom can be interpreted as a further attempt to extend the realms of control. Wilson (1988) argued that there is a danger that the expansion of the state role has blurred the line between the state and civil society. The extra layers of public-sector provision also extends the areas subject to the regulation and jurisdiction of the state. Those who argue for the role of sport as a controlling force within society use this to support their view that the private is increasingly overseen by the guardians of society. However, the extension of regulation is also accompanied by an extension of citizenship, as Wilson (1988) states:

> There gradually emerges the idea that, in addition to civil and political rights, a modicum of economic security and in T.H. Marshall's words (1950, p. 8) "the right to share to the full in the social heritage and life of a civilised being according to the standards prevailing in the society." These social rights are distributed according to non-market criteria. The right to sport is included among those expanded entitlements. (p. 10)

This leaves the local authorities with a difficult problem of meeting needs and educating the public as to what their best interests are within a framework of what is available and the budgetary constraints under which they have to operate. This is particularly important for a nonstatutory service, as the bulk of public-sector sport is in England and Wales. Only libraries enjoy a statutory position within legislation governing local government. The local authorities are in essence providing a service for their public on an "open-ended" basis. Facilities will be available on a first come first served basis, with priority given at certain times and certain facilities for educational bookings. This is both because schools are a good source of revenue in the era of cross-charging within a local authority and because the school children are one of the target groups defined within the social welfare role of the authority's provision. Of course, all of the contradictions of "unrespectable" and "respectable" welfare articulate here.

## The Private Sector

There are important changes in progress in the local authority sector at present with the introduction of compulsory competitive tendering (CCT) for sport services. What this "privatization" means in practice is that outside firms, private enterprises, can bid to provide services currently provided by the local authority, and if their tender undercuts the one put in by the local authority the facility and service is handed over to the private company. There have been many bitter arguments within authorities about the change of ethos this might entail within the provision. For instance, the practice of offering free or reduced-price sessions for disadvantaged groups could well be discontinued as the authorities' policy objectives are replaced by those of the tendering company, which may well not include the obligation of the "social conscience" demonstrated by the authority to its citizens.

We can see a clearer example of the implications of this logic if we look at the private sector's role in providing sport facilities at present. Again, it is possible to criticize this model for being simplistic, but it will serve as a general descriptor of how the market appears to work. At the heart of private investment in leisure sport is a desire to see a return on the investment (or, in other words, a profit) (Gratton & Taylor, 1988). This is inherent in the nature of capitalist investment. Sport facilities and services tend to be highly cost intensive, and the profit margins appear quite small when compared to other forms of investment. If we look at hotels we can see that there is a far greater margin on the customers' expenditure in the bars and the restaurants than on the hire of the actual hotel rooms. This is acceptable to hoteliers because the profit stays within the same center, but if we extend the analogy to the provision of sports facilities we can see why there is an emphasis in private provision on supplying all aspects of leisure-sport-fitness needs—the fitness center will have bar and cafe, the snooker clubs a bar and restaurant. The margins are the key to a successful investment (Roberts, York, & Brodie, 1988).

The private sector is also characterized by a form of provision that is relatively specialized, concentrating on demonstrating an expertise in a particular field, and therefore exclusive. Whereas in the public sector any provision has to be geared to the maximum number of people, in the private sector the niche in the market may be defined very narrowly and still allow a return on the investment. This exclusivity has its price, and the private sector covers much of its overhead by the levy of membership fees for the use of its facilities. These will either replace or supplement charges for use of the facilities themselves, but will normally be at a considerably higher rate than those charged in the public-sector facilities. As a consequence, the attitude toward the customer is somewhat different from that experienced in the public sector. It is recognized that the customer has alternatives and that they will have to be satisfied with the facility and the provision before they will return. In the private sector competition is recognized as a tangible operational force.

Within the private sector there is still a hint of the mentality that argues that the people who use the public facilities do so because they have nowhere else to go. The atmosphere created in private facilities is one of a comfortable, warm, and welcoming environment where people of your sport—and the art of niche-marketing strategy is to be able to create the right kind of atmosphere for any sort of person—can gather, relax, and enjoy themselves. Exclusivity[1] in commercial terms means exclusive to you and your kind of person. Mixing means meeting with people who are not like you but are sufficiently similar not to be threatening. Pricing plays an important part in the selection process, producing a barrier effect, but there are some facilities that require references and sponsors before you can be admitted to the sanctity of membership.

## The Voluntary Sector

To see Williams's notion of residual cultures in sport we have to address the third sector involved in leisure provision. The voluntary sector operates on the borders of both styles of provision, achieving a combination of both ways of working and yet establishing their own distinct patterns. The rationale most often expressed for participation in voluntary organizations is to further a particular interest that is not adequately provided for by either the public or private sectors. It is identifiable by the way that amateur enthusiasts give their time and effort to promoting their chosen pastimes. They are "voluntary" insofar as their participation involves them in the mutual production and mutual consumption of their chosen forms of sport (Hoggett & Bishop, 1985). Volunteers are now big business, and some of the operations that are officially classified as voluntary can outperform some of the private-sector organizations, but this should not eclipse the significance of the patterns of behavior that allow this sector to flourish.

The voluntary sector is particularly important for sport as it allows for a great diversity of interests to be provided for without the investment of large resources from either of the other two sectors. There is a significant amount of cross subsidy between the public sector and the voluntary (such as the use of public facilities by voluntary organizations). This creates a strong sense of interdependence between the sectors. In many areas voluntary organizations draw on the expertise of public-sector staff to help them with their bookkeeping and management problems. The links to the private sector again often arise in kind, although the granting of money through gifts or sponsorship is increasingly common (Bishop, 1987). However, it is important to recognize that this is not a challenge to the residual culture; sponsorship from local publicans was an important element in the origins of many local voluntary organizations, and this tradition continues. The continuity is, of course, not a direct parallel with regional, national, and international concerns now involved in the sponsorship of events and activities within the sports world. For certain events, the sponsorship business becomes more important than the sport itself, and this presents a challenge to the traditional model.

It is within the voluntary sector that it is possible to see the true spirit of sport as free time coming alive, with the motivation of the organization being self-generating and self-directing. If the sport pluralists are correct, then this is where their findings come closest to realization. It is not as spontaneous as with the preindustrial forms of sport, but it does share with those times the reliance on individual effort to sustain initiative and keep the particular sport form moving on. Raymond Williams has pointed to the importance of identifying the traces of past practices within our social and cultural formations. Here we see those residual practices well-expressed, with many of the traditional roles still well-represented. There is a notional parity within voluntary organizations that reaches back beyond the industrialization process, although those who have worked with and within voluntary groups know only too well that honorary and temporary positions can ossify with alarming alacrity. It is, often, where the spirit of voluntarism meets the outside world (in the form of leagues, bookings, committees, etc.) that this transformation of informal participatory democracy becomes a more formalized and coded system. At this stage it becomes possible to speak of "members" of a voluntary organization when really the term should have more of the flavor of partners in action. If voluntary organizations continue to grow and to develop bureaucratic systems they will soon be in a position of having customers in the strict analytical sense, and that will transform the nature of their operation dramatically.

What we can see in the voluntary sector is a model of provision that does not easily divide producers and consumers. The act of production is at one and the same time the act of consumption or is at least facilitative of the consumption by the same person who was responsible for the production. Here again we can see the residual patterns of the preindustrial mode with production and consumption linked in the same act and the same person. Small-scale local clubs and organizations are still bridging the gap that industrial society has produced in the dominant patterns of sport. Within the voluntary sector many of these distinctions can be elided within the social system of the group.

The problem may well be one of the image we hold of sport as being idle and individual free time (Clarke & Critcher, 1985). The more sport becomes organized and institutionalized, the more the amount of support the institutions provide grows, and the more the sport industries become an area of production as well as of consumption. It may not be necessary to go as far as Saunders (1986), who suggested the replacement of urban sociology with a new sociology of consumption, building on Castell's notion of collective consumption. Castells (1978) suggests that the fundamental urban question refers to the organization of the means of collective consumption at the basis of the daily life of all social groups. Typically it involves questions of provision in areas such as housing, education, health, commerce, transport, etc., but there are cultural issues involved as well. Increasingly, to resolve the popular demands for increased provision, the State intervenes in the political economy of the city and in a city's cultural politics—generally on behalf of dominant rather than subordinate group interests. Saunders's idea follows from this. Specifically, what now seems to be happening is that the traditional social and class cleavages are becoming re-presented as cultural cleavages and consumption cleavages, and it is at this point contradictions emerge between the increasingly collective and interdependent character of the process of consumption and its domination by the interests of private capital (Castells). To resolve the contradictions and to reduce the potential and extant conflicts therein, state intervention becomes necessary not only to take charge of the less profitable sectors and services listed above, but also, as a form of appeasement, to fill pronounced cultural consumption voids in areas of leisure. In a sociology of consumption, state, private, public, and voluntary provisions need to be addressed both in terms of collaboration and of segmentation— hegemony and "coercion" concerning "targeted" populations. The public sector targets on political, moral-juridical grounds. The private sector—more specialized in their agendas—targets the we-ness consumer. But whether one views the problematic in dichotomous terms (state vs. civil) or trichotomous terms (state vs. civil vs. voluntary), one thing is clear: It is necessary to look at patterns of consumption within sport as a way of understanding the developments of the 1990s.

These patterns of consumption were at the heart of Rojek's (1985) attempt to analyze the dynamics of sport when he proposed an analysis of the "deep rooted historical tendencies which give contemporary leisure relations their specific organizational forms" (p. 19). Following Ingham's (1978) critique, Rojek (1989) identified four patterns as being particularly salient to both representational and recreational sport: individuation, commercialization, pacification, and privatization. In discussing individuation, Rojek was concerned to highlight those processes that allow the demarcation of the individual as a specific person who is publicly recognized as separate and distinct from others. This is in part a process that creates likeness as well as distinction as fashions define people in and out of an emergent grouping. Some of the strongest individual styles of the sport boom involve a process that looks very similar to cloning. However, what is at the heart of the process identified by Rojek is the demarcation of the individual as a focus for sport consumption and demonstration. As we have seen with the entry barriers to sport, the individual is both the participant *and* the market for the providers of sport. This allows for the commercial exploitation of a situation that has new layers of complexity being introduced into a highly structured marketplace.

We have already seen how commercialization has effected the patterns of sport provision, and this is clearly linked to Rojek's use of the term *privatization*. What Rojek is referring to is not the process of compulsory competitive tendering, but the trend to see the home and the family as the major site of sport experience in contemporary society. The domestic consumption of sport is apparent not only in the passive forms of sport, such as watching television and the rapid growth in the videotape market, but also in active forms as evidenced by the sales of exercise videos and home gymnasiums. The tendency towards the pacification of sport extends the debate around the control of sport (A. Clarke, 1992). However, it also speaks to the trend identified in the civilizing process to pacify sports in civilized societies by removing and reducing the amount and type of violence found in and around the sports (Elias & Dunning, 1986).

I recognize the historical contradictions in both Elias and Dunning. Dunning is an acolyte of Elias, but Dunning has to turn to Max Weber to try to distinguish between affectual versus instrumental violence. Pacification is not a subcultural "accommodation" to the modernity/civility process of social development. Incivility is a dialectic of continuity and discontinuity and a product of the kind of dislocations in history, structure, and biography that occurred when centrist, coalition politics failed and thereby allowed "re-formist" politics (e.g., Thatcher and Reagan) to seize the strategic space left by a misdirected and confused electorate (J. Clarke, 1991). The civilization thesis proposed by Elias and his acolytes cannot deal with the evolutionary and diachronic *if* it cannot handle the conjunctural and synchronic. I think we need a debate which counterposes the idea of civilization with Marcuse's notion of surplus repression (Marcuse, 1966).

A similar argument is presented in McConachie's account of the pacifying of American theatrical audiences (McConachie, 1990). What is being proposed here, by analogy, is an analysis grounded in a structural analysis of the power relations involved around sport. This analysis is based on a concern to identify how access to the sporting and sport markets is structured in class terms and how that structuring is presented and re-presented through the ideological struggles around sport. We have already seen how this occurred historically, but it is also necessary to follow this through in the accounts of the present day. Class analyses have been heavily criticized for being reductionist, but when the structuring of the sport market through the structuring of the housing market, the transport market, and the labor market is considered, then explanations in class terms still seem to offer a way of approaching the patterns of sport. However, class must be seen within the context of the power relations in society and not in isolation.

# Conclusion

This chapter has attempted to put forward an analysis of sport that reflects the artificial division of the object of analysis into fragmented specialism. Sport studies has benefited from an interdisciplinary approach, and this analysis has drawn on that approach. Locating recreational-leisure sport within historic and cultural contexts allows the development of a grounded political economy. However, this is a political economy that accepts the remit of the traditions of political economy but not the value system normally associated with it. Lord Robbins (1976) identified the way that political economists, from Adam Smith onwards,

> not only described how the economic system actually worked, or could work, but also how, according to the assumptions of the author, it ought to be made, or allowed, to work. This usage was followed in general by the majority of classical economists. Thus description and prescription enjoyed a common title.
> (p. 1)

With the changing nature of recreational-leisure sport and the volatility of the sport markets, this ability to speak to how the world ought to be becomes increasingly important.

The consideration of the modes of consumption of sport presented earlier is informed by a value system that does not rely on an atomistic but a holistic approach that puts the people first. Adopting a socialist position allows the development of a critical perspective that looks to the unpacking of the hegemonic relationships. By locating these relationships within the historical analysis, it becomes possible to trace through the significance of the changes in the market. Williams's concern for and appreciation of residual and emergent forms is a clear reminder that the dominant forms of current practice are not the only important forms. Some of the trends toward more public enjoyment of leisure time—civic festivals, communal bonfires, and street fetes as well as the more clearly oppositional forms of sport—demonstrate a major challenge to the incipient individualism of the private market.

The values of public consumption rather than private, of inclusive rather than exclusive sport, and the reemergence of joint sport forms reveal that the current set of dominant forms have not eclipsed all other forms.

Who gets what, why, and how? The provision may be personal (as in the health and fitness boom) or corporate (in the development of facilities and services to produce a healthy, happy, and incorporated worker), but the change in operational logistics has consequences whether or not the people responsible have changed. The private sector logics determine the day-to-day adjustment of the services just as certainly as the development of the music halls into national theater chains changed the nature of the music hall in the *fin de siecle*.

The impact of emergent forms has been to prioritize the commodification and individuation of the sporting culture. The market has a new role to play, not just in provision of facilities but through the developing infrastructure that now supports and sustains sport (e.g., the increasing influence of technology and the advertising industry). The residual forms survive within this framework through the activities of their members rather than because of the benefits of the system. The interconnections between the roles should not blind us to the possibilities constructed in and through these residual forms. They are a strong expression of deeply held cultural traditions and can have an ideological significance that moves far beyond the confines of the sporting culture. It is the articulation of private lives, corporate agendas, the state and the tort liability, and the insurance industry that may be the *ultimate* articulation. In this "civic"[2] articulation, the social-exchange cost-benefit ratio as negotiated in the realm of "public" representation may have little bearing upon the biographies of citizens in whatever "republic" you care to name. What is leisure without health, housing, and food? Is leisure provision a palliative to uncomfortable political decisions? We face the legacy of possessive individualism (the original liberalism); but we also face "positive liberty" (Macpherson, 1973, p. 117). "Thus in the capitalist market society the arrangements made to promote the maximizing of utilities necessarily prevent an effective right of individuals to exert, enjoy, and develop their powers" (Macpherson, 1973, p. 35). Capital is mobile; cities and citizens are not. This is the human cost of "social" neglect in the "new" capitalist structure.

There is also the problem of gender relations within the new historical conjuncture and the deeper organic movements of the social psychology of everyday life (see Sennett, 1974), and the rates of crime (contributing to brutalization) that in focusing upon "street" crime neglect "suite" crime and become the key factors of discontent (real and perceived) that seem to lack political solutions vis-a-vis the urban condition. The contradiction between "law and order" strategies, "community" versus "martial" policing, and self-determined "voluntary" interventions (see Lea & Young, 1984) could form a humanistic coalition, albeit contoured by the extant symmetries of power. Our triadic coalition for the sport, leisure, and wellness agenda that embraces the traditional social cleavages of class, race, and gender as if they could be utopian irrelevancies cannot be realized in our post-industrial age.

None of these ideological challenges nor the changes in form and participation need be considered irreversible. There remains in the United Kingdom a strong attachment to recreational welfare and rational sport, and this will affect private as well as public sector providers. The universality of sport rights is not being directly challenged, and the citizens will certainly protest if those rights are eroded surreptitiously through "changes of management." Local communities still retain the capacity to contribute to and control their own sport—not as consumers or passive players in the market, but as active agents, commissioning their own performances. The image of preindustrial sport may have been embellished, but the potential for sport to be active, self-directed, and self-developing does not have to remain mythical. It can be achieved in and around the market as it now exists but only if the power to shape the programs is returned to the people who are the actual or vicarious participants. They are the true proprietors of our sporting traditions and our sporting futures. It is for them that the sporting culture speaks the loudest. It is the anomaly, resistant yet incorporative, that preserves marginal freedom.

Clarke and Critcher (1985) ask, like the cult television show, "Are we being served?" How far can we as consumers insert our leisure wants into a state or a "centrist" urban politics whose proponents articulate provision with electoral votes, or into a sense of cultural power derived from those who lack the "official" access to the politics of cultural power and the power of subcultural diversity? The targeting of "groups" is the ultimate failure of a political economy and a true destruction of the essentialist component of consumer choice. As Clarke and Critcher (1985) state: "Choice is restricted to how we dispose of our *personal* resources. But we exercise little control over the social allocation of those resources" (p. 203). The negotiated triad is with us. Socialization, subcultural fantasy, and sport cannot transcend structural allocation. A triadic coalition of the public, the private, and the voluntary could be a workable solution; but maybe we, even with our "special interests," cannot escape the Victorian legacy of civic ideology.

## Notes

1. Exclusivity means "shutting out"—a form of social closure. It means "chariness of admitting members." Usurpation means the biting into resources of the exclusive and privileged. Many of the underprivileged have no political power to usurp. They are forced to take it or leave it. Most leave it! (Parkin, 1979).
2. *Civic* seems to be the best way to describe the triad coalition (however hegemonically contoured) between the state (or sub-state), private (civil), and public (however hetero- or homogeneous) "general" interest.

## References

Bailey, P. (1978). *Leisure and class in Victorian England: Rational recreation and the contest for control 1830-1885*. London: Routledge.

Bailey, P. (1989). Leisure, culture and the historian: Reviewing the first generation of leisure historiography in Britain. *Leisure Studies*, 8(2), 107-127.

Berger, P., Berger, B., & Kellner, H. (1973). *The homeless mind: Modernization and consciousness.* New York: Vintage Books.

Bishop, J. (1987). The voluntary sector in leisure. *Leisure Studies Association Newsletter,* Brighton, U.K.

Butsch, R. (Ed.) (1990). *For fun and profit: The transformation of leisure into consumption.* Philadelphia: Temple University Press.

Castells, M. (1978). *City, class and power.* Houndsmills: Macmillan.

Clarke, A., & Madden, L. (1988). The limitations of economic analysis: The case of professional football. *Leisure Studies,* 7(1), 59-74.

Clarke, A. (1992). Figuring a brighter future: An answer to the new formations of football hooligans. In E. Dunning & C. Rojek (Eds.), *Figurational accounts: the civilising process and leisure* (pp. 201-220). London: Macmillan.

Clarke, J. (1991). *New Times and old enemies: Essays on cultural studies and America.* London: Harper Collins.

Clarke, J., & Critcher, C. (1985). *The devil makes work: Leisure in capitalist Britain.* London: Macmillan.

Coalter, F. (1989). Leisure policy: An unresolvable dualism. In C. Rojek (Ed.), *Leisure for leisure: Critical essays* (pp. 5-17) London: Macmillan.

Deem, R. (1988). Feminism and leisure studies: Opening up new directions. In E. Wimbush & M. Talbot (Eds.), *Relative freedoms: Women and leisure* (pp. 5-17). Milton Keynes: Open University Press.

Dunning, E., & Sheard, K. (1979). *Barbarians, gentlemen and players.* London: Martin Robertson.

Dunning, E., & Rojek, C. (Eds.) (1992). *Figurational accounts.* London: Macmillan.

Elias, N., & Dunning, E. (1986). *Quest for excitement.* Oxford, UK: Basil Blackwell.

Featherstone, M. (1990). Perspectives on consumer culture. *Sociology,* 24(1), 5-22.

Glyptis, S. (1988). *Leisure and the unemployed.* Milton Keynes: Open University Press.

Gratton, C., & Taylor, P. (1985). *Sport and recreation: An economic analysis.* London: Spon.

Gratton, C., & Taylor, P. (1988). *The sport industries: An overview.* London: Comedia.

Haywood, L., Kew, F., & Bramham, P. (1989). *Understanding leisure.* London: Hutchinson.

Hoggett, P., & Bishop, J. (1985). *Organising around enthusiasms.* London: Comedia.

Ingham, A. (1978). *American sport in transition: The maturation of industrial capitalism and its impact upon sport.* Unpublished Ph.D. dissertation, Amherst: University of Massachusetts.

Lea, J., & Young, J. (1984). *What is to be done about law and order?* New York: Penguin.

Macpherson, C. (1973). *Democratic theory: Essays in retrieval.* Oxford: Oxford University Press.

Marcuse, H. (1966). *Eros and civilization.* Boston: Beacon Press.

Marshall, T.H. (1950). *Citizenship and social class.* Oxford: Oxford University Press.

McConachie, B.A. (1990). Pacifying American theatrical audiences 1820-1900. In R. Butsch (Ed.), *For fun and profit: The transformation of leisure into consumption* (pp. 47-70). Philadelphia: Temple University Press.

McIntosh, S. (1963). *Sport in society.* Oxford: Oxford University Press.

Mills, C.W. (1959). *The sociological imagination.* New York: Oxford University Press.

Parkin, F. (1979). *Marxism and class theory: A bourgeois critique.* New York: Columbia University Press.

Roberts, K. (1981). *Leisure.* London: Longman.

Roberts, K., York, C.S., & Brodie, D.A. (1988). Participant sport in the commercial sector. *Leisure Studies,* 7(2), 145-157.

Robbins, L. (1976). *Political economy: Past and present.* London: Macmillan.

Rogers, B. (1977). *Rationalising sport policies.* Strasbourg: Council of Europe.

Rojek, C. (1985). *Capitalism and leisure theory.* London: Tavistock.

Rojek, C. (1989). Leisure and the ruins of the bourgeois world. In C. Rojek (Ed.), *Leisure for leisure: Critical essays* (pp. 92-114). London: Macmillan.

Saunders, P. (1986). *Social theory and the urban question.* London: Hutchinson.

Sennett, R. (1974). *The fall of public man: On the social psychology of capitalism.* New York: Vintage Books.

Warde, A. (1990). Introduction to the sociology of consumptions. *Sociology,* **24**(1), 1-4.

Williams, R. (1977). *Marxism and literature.* Oxford: Oxford University Press.

Wilson, J. (1988). *Politics and leisure.* London: Unwin Hyman.

Yeo, E., & Yeo, S. (Eds.) (1981). *Popular culture and class conflict.* Brighton: Harvester.

# Index